Beethoven

Symphony No. 3 in E-Flat Major
Op. 55
Sinfonia Eroica

Creation, Origins and Reception History
Incorporating
Contextual Accounts of Beethoven and His Contemporaries

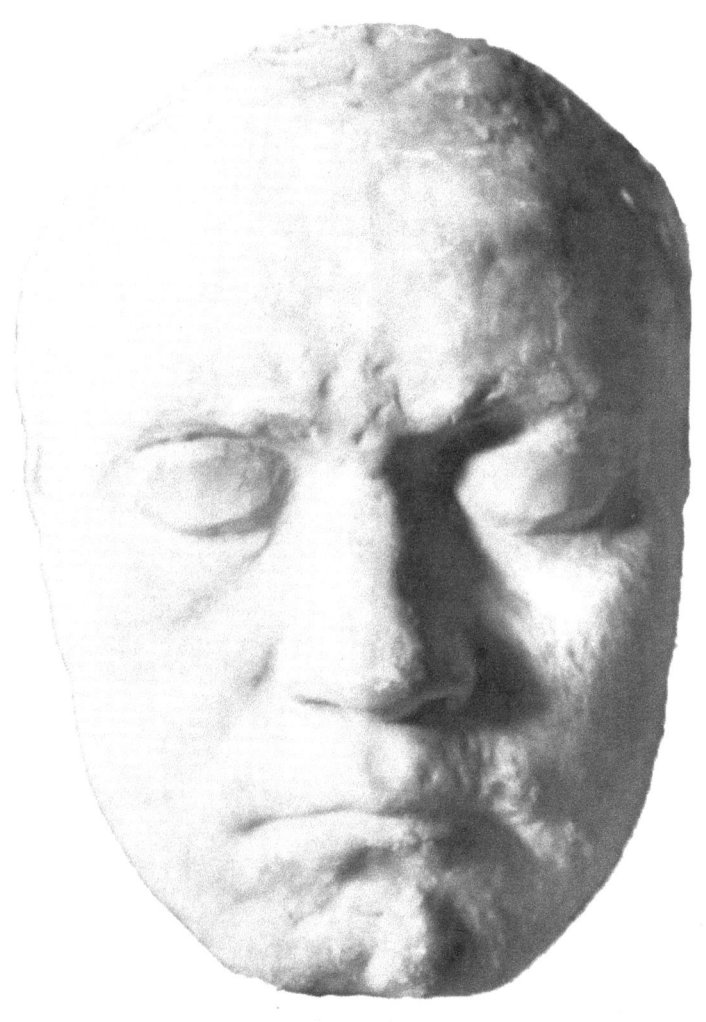

BEETHOVEN

As depicted by the life mask taken by Franz Klein in 1812
(derived from a copy in the author's possession)

BEETHOVEN
SYMPHONY NO. 3
IN E-FLAT MAJOR
OP. 55
SINFONIA EROICA

CREATION ORIGINS
AND
RECEPTION HISTORY

Incorporating contextual accounts of
Beethoven and his contemporaries

Terence M. Russell

Jelly Bean Books

The right of Terence Russell to be identified as the
Author of the Work has been asserted by him in accordance
with the Copyright, Designs and Patents Act 1988.

Copyright © Terence M. Russell 2024

Published by
Jelly Bean Books
136 Newport Road
Cardiff
CF24 1DJ

ISBN: 978-1-917022-75-0

www.candyjarbooks.co.uk

All rights reserved.
No part of this publication may be reproduced, stored in a
retrieval system, or transmitted at any time or by any means,
electronic, mechanical, photocopying, recording or otherwise
without the prior permission of the copyright holder. This book is
sold subject to the condition that it shall not by way of trade or
otherwise be circulated without the publisher's prior consent in any
form of binding or cover other than that in which it is published.

CONTENTS

AUTHOR'S NOTE	I
INTRODUCTION	IX
EDITORIAL PRINCIPLES	XIV
BEETHOVEN'S FINANCIAL TRANSACTIONS	XVI
HISTORICAL PERSPECTIVE: AN ANTHOLOGY	1
Allgemeine musikalische Zeitung	2
Sir John Barbirolli	12
Daniel Barenboim	12
Terry Barfoot	14
Paul Bekker	16
Luciano Berio	18
Hector Berlioz	19
Leonard Bernstein	22
Ernst Bloch	24
Alexander Brott	25

Alfred Peter Brown	26
Michael Broyles	28
Hans von Bülow	30
Pablo Casals	32
Barry Cooper / William Drabkin	34
Louise Elvira Cuyler	38
Samuel Basil Deane	40
Philip G. Downs	40
George Dyson	43
Alfred Einstein	45
Hans Conrad Fischer and Erich Kock	47
Hans Gal	48
Donald J. Grout and Claude V. Palisca	50
George Grove	52
Nikolaus Harnoncourt	54
Christopher Headington	56
Gordon Jacob	58
David Wyn Jones	59
H. C. Robbins Landon	61
Ernst Markham Lee	64
Lewis H. Lockwood	65
Nicholas Marston	66
Bohuslav Martinů	69
Adolf Bernhard Marx	70
Dennis Matthews	70
Wilfrid Mellers	72
Yehudi Menuhin	73
Paul Mies	75
Anton Neumayr	76
Ernest Newman	78
Margaret Notley	80
Richard Osborne	81
Hubert Parry	83
Leon B. Plantinga	85

Romain Rolland	86
Charles Rosen	87
Gioachino Rossini	89
Stephen Rumph	90
Camille Saint-Saëns	92
Clara Schuman	93
Marion Scott	95
George Bernard Shaw	97
Robert Simpson	103
Thomas Sipe	104
Maynard Solomon	105
William Preston Stedman	108
Michael Steinberg	109
Richard Strauss	110
Peter Tchaikovsky	112
Donald Francis Tovey	113
Richard Wagner	118
Anton Webern	123
Conrad Wilson	124
BEETHOVEN AND VIENNA: GESTATION OF THE *EROICA* SYMPHONY	126
Beethoven's growing fame	127
Portraits	129
Anecdotes: descriptions of Beethoven	131
Deafness – Heiligenstadt	135
Residences: Beethoven and Vienna	142
Music-making in Vienna: concert venues	144
Beethoven's orchestra	173
Beethoven as conductor	156
Beethoven and heroism	159
Beethoven and Napoleon Bonaparte	168

CREATION ORIGINS — 180
- Beethoven's compositional process — 181
- The *Eroica* sketches — 184
- Autograph score — 189
- Beethoven's negotiations with publishers — 192
- Dedicatee — 207
- Title Page — 208
- Beethoven's tempo indications — 209
- Publication — 214

RECEPTION HISTORY — 220
- First performances — 221
- Subsequent performances — 231
- Transcriptions — 249
- Early reception in France — 253
- Early reception in England — 260

LATER RECEPTION: MUSICOLOGY — 269
- Theodor W. Adorno — 270
- Terry Barfoot — 272
- Paul Bekker — 273
- Luciano Berio — 276
- Hector Berlioz — 278
- Joseph Braunstein — 281
- Alfred Peter Brown — 282
- Michael Broyles — 285
- Neville Cardus — 288
- Eliot Carter — 290
- Anne-Louise Coldicott — 291
- Barry Cooper — 292
- Louise Elvira Cuyler — 293
- Samuel Basil Deane — 296
- Anatal Doráti — 299
- Philip G. Downs — 300

Romain Rolland	86
Charles Rosen	87
Gioachino Rossini	89
Stephen Rumph	90
Camille Saint-Saëns	92
Clara Schuman	93
Marion Scott	95
George Bernard Shaw	97
Robert Simpson	103
Thomas Sipe	104
Maynard Solomon	105
William Preston Stedman	108
Michael Steinberg	109
Richard Strauss	110
Peter Tchaikovsky	112
Donald Francis Tovey	113
Richard Wagner	118
Anton Webern	123
Conrad Wilson	124
BEETHOVEN AND VIENNA: GESTATION OF THE *EROICA* SYMPHONY	126
Beethoven's growing fame	127
Portraits	129
Anecdotes: descriptions of Beethoven	131
Deafness – Heiligenstadt	135
Residences: Beethoven and Vienna	142
Music-making in Vienna: concert venues	144
Beethoven's orchestra	173
Beethoven as conductor	156
Beethoven and heroism	159
Beethoven and Napoleon Bonaparte	168

CREATION ORIGINS 180
- Beethoven's compositional process 181
- The *Eroica* sketches 184
- Autograph score 189
- Beethoven's negotiations with publishers 192
- Dedicatee 207
- Title Page 208
- Beethoven's tempo indications 209
- Publication 214

RECEPTION HISTORY 220
- First performances 221
- Subsequent performances 231
- Transcriptions 249
- Early reception in France 253
- Early reception in England 260

LATER RECEPTION: MUSICOLOGY 269
- Theodor W. Adorno 270
- Terry Barfoot 272
- Paul Bekker 273
- Luciano Berio 276
- Hector Berlioz 278
- Joseph Braunstein 281
- Alfred Peter Brown 282
- Michael Broyles 285
- Neville Cardus 288
- Eliot Carter 290
- Anne-Louise Coldicott 291
- Barry Cooper 292
- Louise Elvira Cuyler 293
- Samuel Basil Deane 296
- Anatal Doráti 299
- Philip G. Downs 300

AUTHOR'S NOTE

I have cherished the idea of making a study of the life and work of Beethoven for many years. This statement requires a few words of personal reflection. I first encountered Beethoven in my early piano lessons — Minuet in G major, WoO 10, No. 2. At the same time I became acquainted with his piano pupil Carl Czerny — *Book One, Piano Studies*. My heart sank when I discovered the rear cover advertised a further *99* books in the same series — scales, arpeggios studies for the left hand, studies for the right hand — all the way to his Op. 824! By coincidence, my *Czerny Book One* was edited by Alec Rowley — who had the same surname as my music teacher. In my childish innocence, I often wondered why *he himself* never appeared to give me a lesson!

In my teenage years I found myself drawn ever closer

to Beethoven's music in the manner that ferromagnetic materials are ineluctably held captive in the sway of a magnetic field. The impulse to which I yielded is well described in words the conductor Bruno Walter gave in one of his rare public addresses:

> 'It is my belief that young people at that age are more easily impressed by what is heroic and grandiose; that they more easily understand works of art in which passionate feelings are violently uttered in raised accents, and that the lighter sounds of cheerfulness are less impressive to them.'

I do indeed recall the stirring effect made on me on first hearing the Overture *Egmont*, the unfolding drama of the Fifth Symphony and the declamatory opening chords of the *Emperor* Piano Concerto.

I resolved to read everything I could about Beethoven, starting with Marion Scott's pioneering English-language study of the composer in *The Master Musicians series*. My father took out a subscription for me for *The Gramophone* magazine, enabling me to read reviews of the new 'LP' recordings — none of which though I could afford! The LP was then — 1950s — beginning to supplant the 78 rpm shellac records, stacks of which could be purchased for as little as six pence each in 'old' money. I listed to the radio to hear Anthony Hopkins 'Talking about music' and to other musicological luminaries including Howard Fergusson, Hans Keller, Paul Hamburger, Denis Matthews, and Peter Stadlen.

At this same time, I had the privilege of hearing Beethoven's music performed by the *Hallé Orchestra* under the baton of Sir John Barbirolli, and experienced the *Carl*

Rosa Opera Company perform the composer's only opera *Fidelio*, I borrowed the piano-reduction score from the City Library to become better acquainted with this moving work — only to find the score's fists full of notes were well beyond my capabilities. Nonetheless, since then *Fidelio's* every note has been woven into my DNA. I also recall the period when the *London Promenade Concerts* were designated 'Friday night is Beethoven night'.

Through these influences I resolved to visit Vienna to see where Beethoven had lived and worked. But how? The support for such travel was beyond the means of my family. Fortunately, in my final year at school (1959), an opportunity presented itself. I saw a poster that stated *WUS — World University Service* — required volunteers to work in the Austrian town of Linz to help relocate refugees who were living there in improvised wooden shacks — displaced and dispossessed victims of the Second World War. To those participating all expenses would be paid together with free accommodation — in one of the crumbling wooden shacks! From Linz, I planned to make my way to Vienna.

I applied to *WUS* and, despite being a mere school-leaver, I was accepted. The *WUS* authorities doubtless reasoned the building-trade skills I had acquired during my secondary education in the building department of a technical school would be useful. This proved to be the case. At the refugee camp I dug trenches and was allowed to assist as a bricklayer. All about me were wide-eyed children eager to help but mostly getting in the way. I recall one afternoon when a reporter from *The Observer* newspaper paid a visit to our construction site to gather material for an article he was writing on European post-war recovery — he generously admired my trenches and brickwork!

Of lasting significance was another visit, this time from a Belgian priest. He took a group of us to the nearby

Mauthausen Concentration Camp, recently opened as a silent and solemn memorial to those who had perished there. It was a deeply moving experience. Years later I learned of the views of the ardent Beethovenian Sir Michael Tippet. After the horrors of the *Holocaust*, he posed the question for mankind: 'What price Beethoven now?' He posited: 'Could we any longer find solace in Beethoven's setting of Schiller's *Ode to Joy* and its utopian vision — "Be embraced you Millions"?'

My refugee contribution duly came to end and Vienna beckoned. On arrival there I found scenes reminiscent of *The Third Man* and *Harry Lime*. I recall, for example, encountering cobblestones piled high in the streets waiting to be replaced after having been disturbed by the heavy armoured vehicles that had so recently passed over them. But Vienna was welcoming. I visited the houses where Beethoven had lived and worked and paused outside others associated with him that were identified by a commemorative plaque and the Austrian flag. A particularly memorable occasion was attending a recital in the great salon within the palace of Beethoven's noble patron Prince Lobkowitz — the very one where the *Eroica* Symphony had been premiered. Ultimately, my steps led me to the composer's first resting place in the *Währinger Ortsfriedhof*. I paid silent homage to the great man and, as I did so, discovered nearby the resting place of Franz Schubert to whom Beethoven was an endless source of admiration and inspiration.

I felt a youthful impulse to discover yet more about Beethoven and his music. But absorption in musicology would have to take second place. My chosen career beckoned in the guise of architecture — 'the mother of the arts' and 'the handmaid of society'. There was room though for Beethoven's music and from that time on it has been my constant companion through attendance at recitals, in concerts and music-making in the home. And at home a reproduction of Franz Kline's 1812 study of the composer has greeted me each day for more than half a century.

On my retirement from a career in architectural practice, research and university teaching, the opportunity finally presented itself for me to devote time to researching Beethoven musicology. Having attained my eightieth year also emboldened me to make progress with my good intentions!

With these autobiographical remarks outlined I will say a few remarks about my working method— see also the comments made in *Editorial Principles*.

As a member of staff of The University of Edinburgh, I had the good fortune to have access to the *Reid Music Library*, formed from a nucleus of books bequeathed by General John Reid and augmented over the years by such custodians as Sir Donald Francis Tovey, sometime *Reid Professor of Music* and renowned Beethoven scholar. Over a period of three years, I made a survey of the many works in the Reid collection. I consulted each item in turn making records on paper slips — many hundreds — that I deemed to be relevant for my researches. I confined my searches to book-publications, as reflected in my accompanying bibliography. All of this was quite some years ago, the cut-off date for my researches being 2007. Beyond this date I have not surveyed any further works. I am mindful though that Beethoven musicology and related publication continue to be a major field of endeavour in the manner of the proverbial 'ever rolling stream'.

In the intervening years since completing my archival researches, personal tribulations associated with family illness and bereavement slowed my progress in giving expression to my projected intentions. Latterly, however, with renewed energy, and more time at my disposal, I have been able to make progress. My studies take the form of a set of monographs. The first set of these, trace the creation origins and reception history of each of Beethoven's piano sonatas and string quartets. The resulting texts also incorporate contextual accounts of Beethoven and his contemporaries. Also included in my musicological surveys are two related Beethoven anthologies. The set of monographs in question, identified by short title, are:

Beethoven: An anthology of selected writings.
Beethoven: The piano sonatas: An anthology of selected writings.

The Piano Sonatas:
Op. 2–Op. 28
Op. 31–Op. 81a
Op. 90–Op. 111

The String Quartets:
Op. 18, Nos. 1–6
Op. 59, Nos. 1–3 (Razumovsky); Op. 74 (The Harp); Op. 95 (Quartetto serioso)
Op. 127, Op. 132 and Op. 130 (Galitzin)
Op. 131, Op. 135; Grosse Fuge, Op. 133 and Op. 134 (Fugue transcription)

I provide further information about these studies in the introduction to each individual monograph. Suffice it for me to state here the basic premise upon which my work is founded. I believe it is rewarding, concerning the life of a great artist, to find connections between who he *was* and what he *did*; in Martin Cooper's words 'between his personality, as expressed on the one hand in human relationships, and on the other in artistic creation'. (*Beethoven, The Last*

Decade) That is not to say I consider it essential to the enjoyment of Beethoven's music to know this or that fact about it. His music can be enjoyed, as millions do, with — in Robert Simpson's apt phrase —'an innocent ear', for what it is and how it reaches out to us in purely musical terms without any prejudging of its merits based upon extra-musicological facts. Maynard Solomon expresses similar thoughts:

> 'It is doubtless true that we need have no knowledge whatever of a composer's biography, or knowledge of any other motivating factor of any kind, to appreciate the artwork on some fundamental level.' (*Beethoven Essays*, 1988, p. 116)

I must make a further point. I am mindful that a scholar who ventures into a field of study that is not rightly his may be regarded with some suspicion. In this regard I can but ask the reader to place his or her trust in me in the following way. I have attempted to bring to my work the care which publishers and their desk editors have required of me in my book writings relating to architecture — listed elsewhere.

As inferred, it is now more than sixty years since I paid homage to Beethoven in Vienna's *Währinger Ortsfriedhof* and my warmth of feeling towards the composer and his music have grown with the passing of the years. My studies are not intended to be propaedeutic — that would be pretentious. However, if in sharing with others what I have to say contributes to their knowledge and understanding of the composer, and thereby increases their own feelings towards him and his works, my own pleasure in bringing my work to completion will be all the more enhanced.

When Beethoven arrived in Vienna, he was unknown. He was armed though with a note of encouragement from his youthful friend and benefactor Count Ferdinand Waldstein. It contained the often-quoted words: 'Receive Mozart's spirit from Haydn's hands.' Some forty years later Beethoven passed away in the House of the black-robed Spaniards at 200 *Alservorstädter*, the *Glacis* where he had lived since the autumn of 1825. Soldiers had to be called to secure the doors to the inner courtyard of the house from the pressure of onlookers. His body was blessed in the *Alservorsttädt Parish Church*, schools were closed and perhaps as many as 10,000 people formed a funeral procession — an honour ordinarily reserved for monarchs. The *Marcia Funebre* from the composer's Op. 26 Piano Sonata was performed at the funeral ceremony. Franz Grillparzer read the funeral oration. Franz Schubert, who, as remarked in life so admired Beethoven, was one of the pallbearers. The composer's mortal remains were lowered into a simple vault. Beethoven now belonged to history.

Dr Terence M. Russell
Edinburgh 2020

To the foregoing I am pleased to add the following works:

The Piano Concertos
The Symphonies: An Anthology of Selected Writings
Symphony No. 1 In C Major, Op. 21
Symphony No. 2 in D Major, Op. 36
Symphony No. 3 in E-flat Major, Op. 55
Symphony No. 4 in B-flat Major, Op. 60

TMR
2024

INTRODUCTION

In the evolution of culture – taken in its widest meaning to signify attainment in the arts and other manifestations of human intellectual achievement – a work comes along, but only occasionally, that transforms the very landscape of the field of endeavour to which it belongs. At its noblest, such a work is recognised for being epochal, transformative, even life-enhancing. Such epithets have been bestowed upon Beethoven's *Eroica* Symphony in recognition of its originality and the manner in which it elevated the genre of symphonic composition to a new and unprecedented level. This being the case, it is not surprising that, in the words of the ardent Beethovenian Leonard Bernstein: 'There have been more words written about the *Eroica* Symphony than there are notes in it; in fact, I should imagine that the proportion of words to notes, if anyone could get an accurate count, would be flabbergasting.' Notwithstanding, he postulates: 'And yet, has anyone ever successfully "explained" the *Eroica*? Can anyone explain in mere prose the wonder of one note following another or coinciding with another so that we feel that it's exactly how these notes *had* to be?' (*The Joy of Music*. 1959). This book, drawing extensively on the writings of respected authors, attempts to address these questions.

We open our account of the *Eroica* Symphony with an assessment of its place in the history of the evolution of orchestral music — more particularly that of symphonic music — to provide the reader with what we describe as *A Historical Perspective*. This part of our text takes the form of an anthology, derived from the writings of musicologists and others who have reflected on the significance of Beethoven's Third Symphony, Op. 55.

Many influences had a bearing on the creation-origins of the *Eroica* Symphony. With these in mind, we consider Beethoven in Vienna, at the period of gestation of the *Eroica* Symphony, and his growing fame both at home and abroad. On a more personal level, we record how he appeared to his contemporaries, in the formal portraits taken of him and through the anecdotes and descriptions left by those who met and worked alongside him. Central to this part of our narrative, is Beethoven's awareness of his deteriorating hearing and of the torment he endured at Heiligenstadt when endeavouring to come to terms with his misfortune. We discuss his new-found resolve to find 'a new way' and his triumph over what we describe as his 'dark night of the soul'.

We trace the composer's footsteps back to Vienna and identify the various locations where he lived and worked. We broaden the scope of our discussion to consider music-making in Vienna and the concert venues available to Beethoven. In this context, we reflect on Beethoven the conductor, perhaps more correctly, Beethoven the *would-be* conductor. We consider the importance to Beethoven of the concepts of self-sacrifice and heroism that found expression in his music to the Ballet *Die Geschöpfe des Prometheus* ('The Creatures of Prometheus') and make reference to other of his compositions charged with inner-meaning. We draw this part of our discussion to a close with remarks bearing on Beethoven's complex relationship with the ideals of Napoleon Bonaparte and his association with the *Eroica* Symphony.

The period between Beethoven turning his mind to the composition of the *Eroica* Symphony and its eventual publication was protracted and took many twists and turns. We trace the events and circumstances in question as manifest through his private communings, with his sketchbooks, and his prolonged negotiations with publishers. As we reveal, Beethoven vacillated over the title of his Third Symphony and its eventual dedicatee. With performance and interpretation in mind, we give consideration to Beethoven's thoughts about tempo indications and their implications for contemporary performance.

The *Eroica* Symphony was first heard in a number of private performances under the auspices of Beethoven's patron Joseph Franz Maximilian, the seventh Prince of Lobkowitz. These first performances were, in effect, trial rehearsals that enabled Beethoven to give further consideration to the scoring of his new and monumental composition. The first public performance took place in the Theater an der Wien on Sunday evening, 7 April 1805. We trace these events and those others bearing on the early reception of the *Eroica* Symphony. Noteworthy are: Beethoven's first public appearance as a composer of large-scale orchestral compositions; the progressive reception of the *Eroica* Symphony in the first two decades of the nineteenth century;

the extent to which this pioneering creation divided opinion, amongst even the enlightened musical cognoscenti of the day; the better-understanding of the music made possible through the genre of piano transcriptions of the score and adaptations of it for various instrumental ensembles; and the reception of the *Eroica* Symphony in France and England.

We close our account of the *Eroica* Symphony by tracing its reception through the nineteenth and twentieth centuries. Our text here is presented in the form of a further anthology of writings derived from the works of musicologists and others who have reflected on the musicological significance of Beethoven's Third Symphony. Musicologist Richard Osborne writes:

> 'In formulating the *Eroica* Symphony, Beethoven contemplated the heroism of the young Napoleon and the heroism of the fire-stealing and god-defying Prometheus; and to those contemporary and Classical precedents he added his own heroic defiance of deafness and incipient despair.' (Richard Osborne in *A Guide to the Symphony*,1995)

Beethoven authority Berry Cooper writes:

> 'In musical substance, emotional power and narrative content, the *Eroica* marks a true watershed in the history of the symphony.' (Introduction to: Study Score, *Eroica* Symphony, 1999)

We learn of Beethoven's own estimation of the *Eroica* Symphony from the poet-musician Christoph Kuffner; known to Beethovenians for providing the composer with the lyrics for his *Choral Fantasy*, Op. 80. Kuffner became acquainted with Beethoven in the summer of 1817 when the two were living in Heiligenstadt. One day, finding Beethoven in good humour, he ventured to ask him 'which of his symphonies was his favourite?'

> "The *Eroica*", replied Beethoven. 'I should have guessed the C minor?', Kuffner responded. Beethoven was unequivocal: "No, the *Eroica*." (Alexander Wheelock Thayer, *Life of Beethoven*, 1967)

TMR

EDITORIAL PRINCIPLES

By its very nature a study of this kind draws extensively on the work of others. Every effort has been made to acknowledge this in the text by indicating words directly quoted or adapted with single quotation marks. Wherever possible, for the sake of consistency, I have retained the orthography of quoted texts making only occasional silent changes of spelling and capitalization. Deleted words are identified by means of three ellipsis points ... and interpolations are encompassed within square brackets [ ]. Quoted words, phrases and longer cited passages of text remain the intellectual property of their copyright holders.

I address the reader in the second person, notwithstanding that the work is my own — produced without the benefit of a desk editor. It follows that I must bear the responsibility for any errors of misunderstanding or misinterpretation for which I ask the reader's forbearance. A collaboration I must acknowledge is the help I received from the librarians of the *Reid Music Library* at the University of Edinburgh. Over the three-year period it took me to compile my reference sources, they served me with unfailing courtesy, often supplying me with twenty or more books at a time. In converting my manuscript into book-format, I wish to thank my editorial coordinator, William Rees, for his support and painstaking care. I would also like to thank Shaun Russell (no relation) for his work designing the covers for each of the volumes.

My admiration for Beethoven provided the initial impulse to commence this undertaking and has sustained me over the several years it has taken to bring my enterprise to completion. That said, I am no Beethoven idolater. I am mindful of the danger that awaits one who ventures to chronicle the work of a great artist. I believe it was Sigmund Freud who suggested that biographers may become so disposed to their subject, and their emotional involvement with their hero, that their work becomes an exercise in idealisation. In response to such a charge let me say. First, I am no biographer. I do however make reference to Beethoven's personal life and his relationships with his contemporaries, consistent with my sub-title. Second, I acknowledge Beethoven has his detractors. Accordingly, I have not shrunk from allowing dissentient voices, critical of Beethoven and his work, to be heard. These, however, are few and are silenced amidst the adulation that awaits the reader in support of the endeavours of one of humanity's great creators and one who courageously showed the way in overcoming personal adversity.

TMR

BEETHOVEN'S FINANCIAL TRANSACTIONS

Beethoven's negotiations with his music publishers make many references to his compositions. Today they are recognised for what they are — enduring works of art — but referred to in his business correspondence they appear almost as though they were mere everyday commodities — for which he required an appropriate remuneration. Beethoven resented the time he had to devote to the business-side of his affairs. He believed an agency should exist, for fellow artists such as himself, from which a reasonable sum could be paid for the work (composition) submitted, leaving more time for creative enterprises. In the event Beethoven, like Mozart before him, had to deal with publishers largely on his own. Beethoven, though, did benefit in his business dealings from the help he received from his younger brother Kasper Karl (Caspar Carl). From 1800, Carl worked as a clerk in Vienna's Department of Finance in which capacity he found time to correspond with publishers to offer his brother's works for sale and – importantly – to secure the best prices he could. In April 1802 Beethoven wrote to the Leipzig publishers Breitkopf & Härtel: '[You] can rely entirely on my brother who, in general, attends to my affairs.' Whilst Carl promoted Beethoven's interests with determination, he appears to have lacked tact and made enemies. For example, Beethoven's piano pupil Ferdinand Ries – who for a while also helped the composer with his business negotiations – is on record as describing Carl as being 'the biggest skinflint in the world'.

The currencies most referred to in Beethoven's correspondence are as follows:

> Silver gulden and florin: these were interchangeable and had a value of about two English shillings.
> Ducat: 4 1/2 gulden / florins: valued at about nine shillings.
> Louis d'or: This gold coin was adopted during the Napoleonic wars and the French occupation of Vienna and Austria more widely. It had a value of about two ducats or approximately twenty shillings or one-pound sterling.

Beethoven was never poor – in the romantic sense of 'an artist starving in a garret'. On arriving in Vienna in 1792, he was fortunate to receive financial support from his patron Prince Karl Lichnowsky who conferred on him an annuity of 600 florins – that he maintained for several years. Between the months of February and July of 1796, Beethoven undertook a concert tour taking in Prague, Dresden, Leipzig and Berlin. He was well-received and wrote to his other younger brother Nikolaus Johann: 'My art is winning me friends and what more do I want? ... I shall make a good deal of money.' Later on, in 1809, Napoleon Bonaparte's youngest brother Jérôme Bonaparte offered Beethoven an appointment at his Court with the promise of an income of 4,000 florins. Alarmed at the prospect of losing Beethoven – now the most celebrated composer in Europe – three of Vienna's most notable citizens, namely, the Archduke Rudolph (Beethoven's only composition pupil), Prince Kinsky and Prince Lobkowitz settled on the composer the same sum of 4,000 florins. Inflation, however, brought about by the Napoleonic wars, soon eroded its value; personal misfortune to Lobkowitz and Kinsky also took its toll.

Beethoven undoubtedly had to work hard to secure a reasonable standard of living. Notwithstanding, despite his occasional straitened circumstances, he contributed generously to the needs of others. For example, he allowed his works to be performed at charitable concerts without seeking any benefit to himself; in 1815 his philanthropy earned for him the honour of Bürgerrecht – 'freedom of the City'.

Beethoven earned a great deal of money when his music was performed, to considerable acclaim, at several concerts held in association with the Congress of Vienna (1814–15). He did not, though, benefit from it personally; he invested it on behalf of his nephew Karl. It is one of the misfortunes of Beethoven's life that in money-matters he was in somewhat culpably improvident. This is poignantly evident in a letter he wrote on 18 March 1827 to the Philharmonic Society of London – just one week before his death; the Society had made him a gift of £100. He sent the Society 'his most heartfelt thanks for their particular sympathy and support'.

TMR

'To great lives there comes in their June prime an hour of plenitude, ardent and spring-like, when the spirit of the sap splits the bark, and from dawn to evening, the whole tree is at once flower and fruit, wing and song. The imprisoned forces, the genii of joy and those of sorrow, the demon of the species, the frenzied thrust of the creative need, break through the narrow let of the flood-gates of the days, and, out of the furnace of B without seeking any benefit to himself eing, project the flood of God, the unknown Self. In moments such as these, trials, sickness, and the most grievous wounds all serve to liberate the stream; the pick of suffering pierces the soul and makes an issue for fire. And the soul's laceration is the spirit's intoxication. Who can say that the one negates or is inconsistent with the other? They are one; they are the rhythm-beat of genius. As long as his strength keeps growing, the harnessed joy and sorrow bear him along; he makes of them his team, which he drives where he will. He it is who wills the route. His energies rise up in legions. But he holds them bound; he assembles them and launches them to conquest the world.

'I am not playing with words! These images are only reflections, shadows of fire that dance across the roadway. Let us into the forge! Let us see if ever a Napoleonic will has more v ictoriously manipulated an incandescent mountain of matter! Even in the life of Beethoven, itself exceptional, this period of three years is unique. It rightly bears the title of Eroica. It is an Etna; and within, the Cyclopes are forging the shield of Achilles.

'The Eroica is a miracle even among Beethoven's works. If later he went further, never did he take so big a single stride. It is one of the Great Days of music. It inaugurated an era.'

Romain Rolland, *Beethoven the Creator*. Garden City, New York: Garden City Publications, 1937, pp. 61–62 and p. 101.

HISTORICAL PERSPECTIVE: AN ANTHOLOGY

We open our account of the *Eroica* Symphony with an assessment of its place in the history of the evolution of orchestral music – more particularly that of symphonic music. Out text takes the form of an anthology derived from the writings of musicologists and others who have reflected on the significance of Beethoven's Third Symphony. The texts selected are from various periods and reflect the differing styles of expression and register of language characteristic of their time. Thereby, they convey the evolving estimation felt for this work from the period of its first appearance to closer to the present day.

Our selection of writings embrace Beethoven's resolve to find a 'new way' in his compositional style; the manner in which he transformed symphonic form – enlarging his previous symphonic orchestration to such an extent that changed the history of the symphony (its huge size being twice the length of a Haydn or Mozart symphony); the manner in which Beethoven embodied his temperament in music — a lesson on the conquering of self and triumph over adversity; the concept of the hero as enshrined in musical form — a hero of revolution and the guardian of liberty; and the *Eroica* Symphony as no less than a precursor to the Romantic era in music.

ALLGEMEINE MUSIKALISCHE ZEITUNG (AMZ)

The *Allgemeine musikalische Zeitung* (*General Music Newspaper*) was a German- language periodical that commenced publication in 1798 under the direction of its owner and founder Gottfried Christoph Härtel. Its publisher was Breitkopf & Härtel of Leipzig with whom Beethoven had many negotiations. The periodical reviewed musical events taking place in the German-speaking nations and in other countries. As such, it was among the first to bring to the attention of the musically-minded public an awareness of Beethoven's compositions and of their originality — that the periodical's contributors frequently found to be disturbing. In 1800, the *AmZ* published a review ostensibly in celebration of Joseph Haydn, to whom it accorded 'the first place' with regard to his symphonies and quartets, stating, 'wherein no one has yet surpassed him'. Beethoven, a still relatively unknown composer, was not, however, overlooked; the reviewer commented how he may even usurp the venerable master 'if he calms his wild imaginings'. In due course the *Allgemeine musikalische Zeitung* received news of Beethoven's compositions with increasing respect. In view of the significance of these writings about Beethoven's *Eroica* Symphony, we take a close look at them as they appeared in their chronological sequence during the composer's lifetime.

The *Eroica* Symphony received its first public performance on 7 April 1805 at the Theater an der Wien; the work had already been performed at private concerts in the Vienna Palace of Beethoven's patron Prince Lobkowitz. The *AmZ* reviewed the Symphony in its issue of 17 April 1805, stating Beethoven's 'very special friends' and 'music connoisseurs alike' were divided in their opinions. One group, the composer's 'very special friends', maintained the Symphony to be 'a masterpiece' and that it bore 'the true style for more elevated music'. They believed if the music did not please at present — tacit awareness of the dissentient views of others — that was because 'the public is not sufficiently educated in art to be able to grasp all of [the work's] elevated beauties'. With a note of qualified optimism, doubtless of little comfort to Beethoven, the reviewer added: 'After a thousand years ... they will not fail to have their effect.' As we shall see, the merits of the *Eroica* Symphony were realised much sooner!

As for Beethoven's detractors, they considered his newest Symphony 'manifest a completely unbounded striving for distinction and oddity'. They maintained genius did not proclaim itself by simply 'bringing forth the unusual and the fantastic, but rather by creating the beautiful and sublime'.

The *AmZ*'s contributor identified a third group who were 'undecided'. They acknowledged the *Eroica* Symphony contained 'many beautiful qualities' but found them 'completely disjointed'. The duration of the Symphony — by far the longest to date — also disturbed them; they regarded it as 'becoming unbearable to the mere amateur'. They looked back to the composer's first two Symphonies in C, Op. 21 and in D, Op. 36 that they believed would secure a place for Beethoven 'in the ranks of the foremost instrumental composers'. With regard to his Op. 55, however, this group feared, 'if Beethoven continues on this path, both he and the public will come off badly'.

In the 1 October 1806 issue of the *AmZ*, its music correspondent wrote once more about the *Eroica* Symphony. The article in question was ostensibly concerned with Beethoven's recently published (1805) arrangement of his Second Symphony – described as 'rightly celebrated' – for piano, violin and cello. Concerning the *Eroica* Symphony, music critics were clearly coming to terms with its challenges as is evident from the tone of this particular article. The correspondent wrote of the work as being 'rich in ideas and artistic development' and acknowledged its format was 'broader, deeper, and more drawn out'; moreover, they acknowledged – that is, they were reconciled to the fact – that it took an hour to perform in a spacious interpretation that included the composer's first-movement repeats. This was, however, too much for the critic in question who considered 'true, great genius must respect the capacity of his audience to comprehend and enjoy'. Setting aside this particular misgiving, the critic acknowledged: '[The Symphony] is certainly one of the most original, sublime, and deepest products that this entire genre of music has to show.'

The following year, the 27 February 1807 issue of the *AmZ* drew its readers' attention to forthcoming performances of what was now styled 'Beethoven's Grand Symphony in E flat'. These were to take place before 'a vary select society' of devotees of Beethoven's music. The *AmZ's* music correspondent is assumed to be referring to the so-called *Liebhaber Konzerte* – 'Music Lover's Concert' – that had been recently established in Vienna. Admission to the concerts was strictly controlled and tickets were not on sale to the general public. Beethoven subsequently conducted performances of the *Eroica* Symphony at the *Liebhaber Konzerte* on 6 December 1807 and on 2 February 1808.

In the issues of the *AmZ* for 1807, the contributors cited performances of the *Eroica* Symphony outside of Vienna. On 29 April, the journal carried an article titled 'News from Leipzig'. The centre-piece of the text was a description of performances of the *Eroica* Symphony that the critic likened, in its majestic scale, to 'a whole repository of new opera overtures'. The Leipzig audience had been prepared for the occasion with programme notes specially written for the occasion. We learn:

> 'The most educated friends of art in the city were assembled in great numbers [and during the performance] a truly solemn attentiveness and deathlike silence reigned and was sustained ... throughout the whole.'

Such, apparently, was the enthusiasm for the composition that it had to be given twice-more in the following weeks. The members of the orchestra were given additional rehearsals for which a full score was made available, 'so that even the slightest triviality would not escape observation'. The use of a full score was something of an innovation at the time, since orchestral music was usually performed with recourse to orchestral parts only. The *AmZ* correspondent recorded how the close of each performance ended 'with loud demonstrations of applause [that] gave vent to well-founded enthusiasm'.

On 17 June 1807, the *AmZ* correspondent carried a further report of a performance of the *Eroica* Symphony, outside of Vienna, under the heading 'News from Prague'.

It appears this was the first rendering of the work in that city since the correspondent remarked, 'finally *we* heard this colossal work'. The event had been anticipated with some excitement with the composer being compared with the widely read German Romantic writer Jean Paul. Beethoven is described as 'scorning all fetters, he expresses himself with all the depth and genius of his soul'. The music made a deep impression upon 'a not uneducated circle of listeners'. The musicians clearly played their parts (no pun intended) in a performance described as 'exemplary' with the tempos, in particular, 'being well chosen'.

A measure of the widening acceptance of the *Eroica* Symphony is conveyed in an announcement published in 1807 in the *AmZ's* sister music journal, the Leipzig-based *Zeitung für die elegante Welt* – 'Newspaper for the elegant World'. The correspondent first recalled the 'extraordinary effect' the Symphony had made on the Leipzig audiences (see above) and how it had 'already aroused astonishment in other great cities'. The writer further enthused:

> 'It belongs among a few symphonies that, with their spirited energy, set the listeners' imagination into sublime flight and sweep his heart away to powerful emotions.'

The second part of the article is of particular interest. The author acknowledged 'there are so few orchestras complete and accomplished enough to perform such a difficult work suitably'. With this in mind, the writer of the article drew attention to the endeavours of the Leipzig composer and Director of Music August Eberhard Müller; he had recently prepared a four-hand piano-transcription of the score. This, the correspondent averred, would enable the music enthusiast 'to repeat this music to oneself'. This transcription for piano of the *Eroica* Symphony was one of the earliest of its kind. As a genre it would, in due course, attain almost mythic status under the hands of Franz Liszt.

In the 6 January 1808 edition of the *AmZ*, the music critic reflected on the performance of the *Eroica* Symphony given the previous December (see above). He still had to be fully convinced though of the merits of the work. He acknowledged the composition contained 'much that was sublime and also beautiful' but for him the music was 'mixed with much that is harsh'. Furthermore, he had the temerity to propose the Symphony 'would only obtain the pure form of a finished work of art through a *rearrangement*' [italics added]. Later in the year, on 10 February, the *AmZ* reported a further transcription of the *Eroica* Symphony, this time for Piano Quartet. Notwithstanding being in such a reduced form, the correspondent considered 'it has as much and as good an effect as is possible for pieces that depend so much on the effect of the wind instruments in opposition to the strings'. The writer, however, added the proviso: 'All four players must be rather accomplished in order to perform the Quartet properly.'

Two years elapsed before the *Eroica* Symphony received further notice in the pages of the *AmZ*. It did so in the issue for 7 February 1810 in a review of a performance that took place in the Thaeter an der Wien; this was a *benefit* concert held in support of the Theatre's poor fund. Beethoven was a staunch supporter of such philanthropic enterprises and, over time, made several of his compositions available without thought of profit to himself; years later he received the freedom of the city of Vienna in recognition of his generous actions. By now, Beethoven's Op. 55 was so well-established in the symphonic repertoire that the *AmZ's* correspondent confessed: 'It would be superfluous here to say anything about the value of this artistically rich and colossal work.' Instead he reflected on the performance itself. Despite the length of the work, that he considered was such as to fatigue both artists and listeners, the piece 'came across so well that it was possible to obtain great enjoyment from it'.

On 23 January 1811, the *AmZ* reported on a performance of the *Eroica* Symphony that filled the second half of the first concert of the year in Leipzig – 'to the lively satisfaction of the extremely numerous listeners'. Evidently, they listened 'with heightened attention until the final chord'. The orchestra shared in the critic's praise for the occasion. He observed how its members had played the work 'with unmistakable enjoyment and love' and also 'with as much precision and fire' and yet 'with also as much delicacy as it demands'. Three years later, the *AmZ* music critic reported on a further rendering of the *Eroica* Symphony that had taken place in Leipzig. The Funeral March had clearly made such a moving impression that the music critic prefaced his piece with words from Johann von Sala-Seewis's *Das Grab* – 'The Grave': "The grave is deep and still / and horrible its brink!" (This text so entranced the young Franz Schubert that he set the lyrics no fewer than five times.) The critic in question suggested Beethoven's funeral march should be listened to with the thought in mind of 'a magnificent person ... being led to the grave'. He personified the music, suggesting it conveyed: 'All the pain and all the joys of this earthly life.'

On 25 January 1815, the *AmZ* reported on the first concert of the season from Munich. The *Eroica* Symphony made such a 'grand, sublime effect', that it reduced the music critic to remarking: 'We are ever more amazed by the creative power of this great composer.' In the same year, the *AmZ* carried an article by the respected philosopher and music theorist Johann Amadeus Wendt titled,

'Thoughts about the New Art of Composition and about van Beethoven's Music'. Wendt hypothesised:

> 'No one else is likely to display [Beethoven's] boldness of imagination, the flights of which carry us (as in the *Sinfonia Eroica*) on the field of battle where the golden hopes and glorious heroic era of one nation are defeated while another nation celebrates its day of resurrection, or again into the gay embrace of nature to join the jovial peasants, as in the *Pastoral* Symphony.
>
> 'We do not by any means intend an apology for descriptive music or for "musical painting", for Beethoven, like his teacher Haydn, seems to have a propensity; no, except for a few instances of playfulness, Beethoven remains what a musician can be: a painter of passions.'

Wendt was one of the earliest writers to compare Beethoven with Shakespeare:

> 'Could we then call him the Shakespeare of music? For he is as capable of portraying and expressing in tones the innermost depths of the struggling heart as the sweet magic of innocent love; the bitterest, deepest pain as delight rejoicing aloud to the skies; the most grandiose as the most graceful; yet his spirit inclines most devotedly towards statements of deep grandeur, and sets the highest emotions in harmonious accord.'

The following year, the *Eroica* Symphony was performed in Kassel but only elicited a restrained response from the *AmZ's* music critic. Writing in the issue for 30 October

1816, he described the work as 'ingenious' but considered it to be 'too long'. This was despite the fact that, in order to offer the audience some respite, the last movement was performed separately from the first three movements with an interval in between.

Seven years elapsed before the *AmZ* made further reference to the *Eroica* Symphony. By 1823 it had been supplanted in the journal's pages by reviews of Beethoven's other symphonies, notably the Fifth, Sixth, and Seventh. The *AmZ* issue for 18 June 1823 was, however, noteworthy. It announced the publication, for the first time on the Continent, of the composer's First, Second, and Third Symphonies *in full score*. The edition was brought out by Nikolaus Simrock in Bonn and Cologne. A measure of the grandeur of the *Eroica* Symphony is conveyed by a comparison of its score's pagination with that of its predecessor the Second Symphony in D major – at the time of its composition it was believed to be the longest symphony yet written. The D major occupied 162 score pages compared with the *Eroica's* 231 pages!

In 1824, the *Berliner Allgemeine musikalische Zeitung* – one of the *AmZ's* companion music journals – made reference to the *Eroica* Symphony. A short article appeared in its issue of 4 February 1824 – probably written by Beethoven's biographer Adolph Bernhard Marx (*Ludwig van Beethoven: Leben und Schaffen*. Berlin, 1859). The Symphony was played before a small audience but was rewarded with a performance that was rendered 'with the utmost precision'. At its close, the audience displayed 'the greatest thanks' and 'with the loudest possible applause to the creator of these harmonies'. Later in the year, on 5 May, the *Berliner Allgemeine musikalische Zeitung* reported once more on a 'most brilliant' performance of the *Eroica* Symphony. The occasion was significant for having been directed by the German composer and violinist Karl (Carl) Möser. He was a leading figure in Berlin's musical life and had the distinction of directing the first performance in Berlin, in 1826, of Beethoven's Ninth Symphony. Such was the audience's appreciation of the *Eroica*, and of Möser's direction of the players, that each movement of the work 'was acknowledged by the most-lively applause'.

We close our selection of citations referring to the *Eroica* Symphony, derived from the *Allgemeine musikalische Zeitung*, with reference to a short article that appeared in its issue of 7 December 1825. The author first bestowed fulsome praise on Beethoven proclaiming: 'His works are so rich so new, and so imaginative that it is almost unbelievable that the art of instrumental composition can be advanced any further.' The writer could not, though, resist making a pejorative aside:

> 'However, it is often the case with him that in his intention to create something even more original he becomes incomprehensible to the listener and degenerates into bizarrerie.'

He acknowledged, though, that the *Eroica* Symphony, the *Pastoral* Symphony, and the Opera *Fidelio* 'belong to the most exquisite things we have in music'.

Wayne M. Senner, Robin Wallace and William Meredith, editors, *The Critical Reception of Beethoven's Compositions by his German Contemporaries*, Lincoln: University of Nebraska Press, in association with the American Beethoven Society and the Ira F. Brilliant Center for Beethoven Studies, San José State University, 1999, Vol. 1, pp. 15–16, p. 86, pp. 32–40 and Vol. 2, pp. 169–70, pp. 201–04. Many other reviews from the *AmZ* are cited in

Anton Felix Schindler, *Beethoven as I Knew Him*, edited by Donald W. MacArdle and translated by Constance S. Jolly from the German edition of 1860. London: Faber and Faber, 1966, pp. 182–3 and pp. 518–21.

SIR JOHN BARBIROLLI

In 1960 the British conductor and cellist Sir John Barbirolli accepted an invitation to succeed Leopold Stokowski as Chief Conductor of the Houston Symphony Orchestra. In so doing he alternated his schedule with his beloved Hallé Orchestra back home in Manchester, also making regular visits to the present-writer's home town Sheffield. On 10 March he wrote from Huston to his violinist friend Audrey Napier Smith of the progress he was making with his concerts:

> 'Splendid opening concerts (*Eroica* strangely enough) but I had to work very hard getting the orchestra back to its real shape. Strange how the *Eroica* exhausts me these days. It may well be because I am really beginning to plumb its depths. It really is a tremendous piece, isn't it?'

Michael Kennedy, *Barbirolli, Conductor Laureate: The Authorised Biography*. London: Hart-Davis, MacGibbon, 1973.

DANIEL BARENBOIM

In his autobiography *A Life in Music*, the Argentine-Israeli born pianist and conductor Daniel Barenboim outlined his views on the manner in which Beethoven brought order to his creations though the apparent disorder of his preliminary thoughts – reference to his numerous musical sketches:

'Complexity – until methodically analysed – is chaos. After analysis, it is revealed as an accumulation of orderly details. Beethoven's sketchbooks show that his method of composing went from the complex to the simple. The final version, as we know it, is often considerably simpler than his first version. A composer's initial inspiration, like the initial reaction of an interpreter, is often disorderly and therefore unnecessarily complex. If one wanted to oversimplify it, one could say that the distinction between a great composition and a lesser one is that the great compositions have all been worked out from the complex to the simple – not in a primitive sense, but from the point of view of greater clarity.'

Turning to a consideration of the nature of music, more generally — and eventually leading to the *Eroica* Symphony — Barenboim states:

'Every work of art has "two faces", one directed towards eternity and the other towards its own time. There are conventions or fashions of a certain epoch, and some compositions express an epoch. This aspect of a composition may be of little interest to future generations. The part that remains is the spirit of the work, its essence ... A musical composition should be seen as existing by itself, and not as having been created for a purpose, however positive or beneficial ... A certain musical atmosphere may remind us of a love scene, another of a majestic procession, but these evocations are representative of us and not of the music. I often experience totally different feelings about the same piece of music at different times. It may be an oversimplification to say that if one feels sad, a piece of music may enhance this feeling, and if one is happy, one may find the same piece of music joyful. There has, of course, never been an occasion to think of the funeral march of the *Eroica* Symphony as happy music, but this is the exception rather than the rule.'

Daniel Barenboim, *A Life in Music,* London: Weidenfeld & Nicolson, 1991, p.55 and pp. 215–16.

TERRY BARFOOT

Terry Barfoot was a music educator and founder of *Arts in Residence* that provided music appreciation courses at country-house venues in rural England. He also contributed to summer schools at The Royal Opera House and Oxford. In June 2005 the BBC devoted a whole week to performances of Beethoven's music. Each broadcast was accompanied with specially commissioned programme notes for which Barfoot contributed on 6 and 10 June when the *Eroica* Symphony was broadcast. He introduced these programmes by first remarking:

'Although in his Second Symphony Beethoven had begun to move beyond the traditional concept of the classical symphony, his *Eroica* remains a staggering achievement taking the genre into hitherto uncharted regions. Here, in 1803, we have a symphony which in performance lasts nearly a full hour, a symphony whose first movement alone is as long as many symphonies in their entirety. Yet nothing about the *Eroica* is inflated or grandiose; on the contrary, the work is a model of economy and precision.'

Barfoot next considered the work's construction:

> 'Beethoven enlarged his previous symphonic orchestration only by the addition of an extra horn; it is therefore the size and scale of the symphonic concept which are expanded, but in purely musical terms. The logical and emotional power of the music carries the listener along and to achieve his aim Beethoven employs numerous characteristic devices ... off-beat accents ... dissonant harmonies ... the most tremendous symphonic tension ... [a] great sense of emotional strength ... .'

Barfoot connects the creation of the *Eroica* Symphony with the composer's personal circumstances, stating:

> 'Such a composition could have been created only by a truly great figure, and the struggle confronting Beethoven with his increasing deafness had already been made apparent in the moving *Heiligenstadt Testament*, which he had written in 1802. He had realised that only through creating his music could he sustain the will to live. And it is the strength of his will that we encounter in the first two movements of this remarkable symphony.'

Terry Barfoot, *Symphony No. 3, Op. 55 (Eroica): Notes to*

the BBC Radio Three Beethoven Experience, Monday 6 and Friday 10 June 2005, www.bbc.co.uk/radio3/Beethoven

PAUL BEKKER

The music critic and musicologist Paul Bekker considered the advance Beethoven made, musically speaking, with the *Eroica* Symphony:

> 'The great advance from the Second to the Third Symphony is commonly regarded as a kind of miracle, and the distance between the two works, the importance of the change represented, is unmistakable. It is not, however, incomprehensible. It arose necessarily in Beethoven's dawning consciousness of his great destiny as a composer. Certain musical forces were liberated in him; they had existed previously, but the round of more-or-less commonplace activity had prevented them from unfolding. The more Beethoven developed as man and artist, the more they struggled for liberty of expression; and at last the "poetic idea" broke upon the world with an appearance of catastrophic suddenness.'

Bekker believed the transformation in Beethoven's art was inevitable:

> 'The process was not incomprehensible, but was logically necessary in the Beethoven we know. He could no longer compose symphonies of the old type. He longed for a subject into which he could put his very soul, and being an artist highly sympathetic to the intellectual tendencies of his

time, he fell upon that of heroism. His pulse kept time to that of the age ... .'

Of Beethoven's subsequent disaffection with Bonaparte, and his mission to embody the concept of heroism in music, Bekker remarks:

'Beethoven might tear up the dedication, but the work itself was complete. The touches which make it so lively a picture of a great heroic figure of history remain. The general idea of heroism had been conceived in terms of the individual. Beethoven does not portray philosophical or religious heroism. His hero is a man full of limitless energy, combative, restless, active, employing his powers to the full without hesitancy of afterthought. To present this heroism of deed in the symphonic form, to derive four different statements of the heroic-will in action, from the single underlying concept, was the task which Beethoven set himself.'

Bekker reflects:

'Beethoven employed three models for his *Eroica* — Napoleon, [General Ralph] Abercromby, and Prometheus; but he was interested in them not as persons but as types of the strength of man's will, of death's majesty, of creative power; on these great abstractions of all humanity can be and do, he built his tone poem.

'In the *Eroica*, Beethoven taxed his powers to the uttermost, and even his genius could not readily regain the heights there attained ... He turned for the moment to lighter matter, but with

> the knowledge that he could impress whatever he touched with his marvellous command of his material.'

Paul Bekker, *Beethoven*. London: J. M. Dent & Sons, 1925, pp. 153–55, and p. 166.

LUCIANO BERIO

The musicologist Rossana Dalmonte interviewed the Italian composer Luciano Berio and asked him if he considered Beethoven would have conducted his symphonies more authentically than Herbert von Karajan? This prompted Berio to respond: '[Conditions] were so different then [in Beethoven's time], from every point of view, that comparisons are impossible.' He elaborated:

> 'Just think that Beethoven conducted the Third and Fourth Symphonies with an orchestra of about thirty musicians! ... The performances of a modern orchestra with ninety players are almost transcriptions when compared with the conditions that prevailed then: not that there's anything wrong with that — on the contrary.'

Berio exemplified his personal experience of the virtues of Beethoven-performance using limited orchestral resources:

> 'Several years ago [sometime in the 1970s], when I was working on the television programme *C'è Musica e Musica*, I allowed myself the satisfaction of recording part of the Third Symphony with the same number of players that Beethoven used (twenty-nine).'

Berio confessed to being anxious:

> 'I was afraid that the different quality and power of the sound from woodwind and brass would alter the orchestral equilibrium, especially in the *fortissimo*. But it didn't.'

Berio concluded:

> 'It was an unforgettable experience to hear an *Eroica* as transparent and as well-defined as chamber music ... Extremely dilated and explosive chamber music!'

David Osmond-Smith editor and translator, *Luciano Berio: Two Interviews with Rossana Dalmonte and Bálint András Varga*. New York; London: Boyars, 1985, p. 132.

HECTOR BERLIOZ
Hector Berlioz's enthusiasm for the music of Beethoven is well documented. He himself gave expression to it in his *A Travers Chants, Etudes Musicales, Adorations, Boutades et Crtiques*, an English edition of which was translated and edited by Edwin Evans and was published in 1911 under the title *A Critical Study of Beethoven's Nine Symphonies, With a few words on his Trios and Sonatas, a Criticism of Fidelio and an Introductory Essay on Music*, London, W. Reeves, 1911. More than thirty years after Beethoven's death his works were little known in France. Those that were performed, in particular the orchestral works, were usually premiered in severely edited and truncated form and were typically received with hostility. The symphonies were con-

demned for being 'bizarre, incoherent, diffuse, bristling with harsh modulations and wild harmonies, bereft of melody, over the top, too noisy, and horribly difficult to play'. Amidst such clamour, the views of Hector Berlioz were an oasis of calm and reason, albeit with more than a touch Gallic passion.

In 1828, Berlioz heard Beethoven's Third and Fifth Symphonies for the first time when they were performed at the Paris Conservatoire — an experience he found overwhelming. Of the Third Symphony he later enthused:

> 'Unquestionably, the most famous of his symphonies is also the first in which Beethoven gave free scope to his vast imagination without taking as a guide or support an extraneous idea. In the First, Second, and Fourth Symphonies, he gave more-or-less extended forms previously known; invested them with all the poetry that his vigorous youth could bestow — brilliant, passionate, and inspired. In the Third one (the *Eroica*) the form tends toward greater breadth, it is true, and the idea also reaches a greater height. But we cannot fail to recognize in it the influence of one or other of those divine poets to whom from early days, the great artist had created a temple in his heart.' [Berlioz is alluding here to such authors as Homer and Horace with whose works Beethoven was familiar and which he often quoted, aphoristically and in contrived puns, in his many letters to friends and publishers.]

A Travers Chant, 1862; translated by Jacques Barzun and quoted in: Jack Sullivan editor, *Words on Music: from Addison to Barzun*. Athens: Ohio University Press, 1990, p. 114.

Berlioz urged a deeper understanding of Beethoven's title to the *Eroica* Symphony:

> 'It is a serious mistake to truncate the title which the composer provided for the Symphony. It reads: *Heroic Symphony to Commemorate the Memory of a Great Man*. As will be seen, the subject here is not battles or triumphal marches, as many, misled by the abbreviated title, might expect, but rather deep and serious thoughts, melancholy memories of imposing grandeur and sadness, in short, a *funeral creation* for a hero. I know few examples in music of a style where sorrow has been so unfailingly conveyed in forms of such purity and such nobility of expression.'

It is apparent from what Berlioz next has to say that French audiences, in the early-mid nineteenth century, regarded the *Eroica* Symphony as being less appealing than other of the composer's works:

> 'Beethoven may have written more striking works than this Symphony, and several of his other compositions make a greater impact on the public. But it has to be admitted that the *Eroica Symphony* is so powerful in its musical thought and execution, its style so energetic and so constantly elevated, and its form so poetic, that it is the equal of the composer's very greatest works. Whenever this Symphony is performed, I am overcome with feelings of deep and, as it were, antique sadness, yet the public seems hardly moved. One must feel sorry for the predicament of the artist: though fired

with such enthusiasm he has not managed to make himself intelligible even to an elite audience and make it rise to the level of his own inspiration. This is all the more regrettable as in other circumstances this same audience warms up to the composer and shares his emotion and tears. It is fired with an ardent and genuine passion for some of his compositions, which may be equally worthy of admiration but are nevertheless no more beautiful than this work.'

A Critical Study of the Symphonies of Beethoven, derived from *A Travers Chant.* The Hector Berlioz website, translation by Michel Austin.

LEONARD BERNSTEIN

The American composer, conductor, pianist, educator and humanitarian Leonard Bernstein was described by the music critic Donal Henaham as 'one of the most prodigiously talented and successful musicians in American history'. Bernstein's admiration for Beethoven approached reverence. This is evident in the many recordings he made of the composer's music alongside his equally numerous performances of the five piano concertos. Moreover, he expressed his thoughts about Beethoven's music in lectures, not least when he held the tenure of the Charles Eliot Norton Professorship of Poetry at Harvard University (1973–74). His lectures on Beethoven's symphonies, originally destined for television, are today available on *You Tube*. In the December 1957 issue of *The Atlantic Monthly*, Bernstein contributed an article titled *Speaking of Music*. Of the challenges posed by attempting to talk about the phenomenon of the human response to organized sound, he stated:

> 'Ultimately one must accept that people enjoy listening to organized sound (*certained* organized sounds anyway); that this enjoyment can take the form of all kinds of responses ... and that people who can organize sounds so as to evoke the most exalted responses are commonly called geniuses.'

Bernstein gave fuller expression to this belief in a manner that is fitting to our account of Beethoven's Third Symphony, Op. 55:

> 'There have been more words written about the *Eroica* Symphony than there are notes in it; in fact, I should imagine that the proportion of words to notes, if anyone could get an accurate count, would be flabbergasting. And yet, has anyone ever successfully "explained" the *Eroica*? Can anyone explain in mere prose the wonder of one note following another or coinciding with another so that we feel that it's exactly how these notes *had* to be? Of course not.'

Discussing *form* in Beethoven's music Bernstein generalized:

> 'Many, many composers have been able to write heavenly tunes and respectable fugues. Some composers can orchestrate the C major scale so that it sounds like a masterpiece, or fool with notes so that harmonic novelty is achieved. But all this is mere dust — nothing compared to the magic sought by them all: *the inexplicability ability to know what the next note has to be.* [Bernstein's emphasis] Beethoven had this gift in

a degree that leaves them all panting in the rear guard. When he really *did it* – as in the Funeral March of the *Eroica* – he produced an entity that always seems to me to have been previously written in Heaven, and then merely dictated to him. Not that the dictation was easily achieved ... There is a special place carved out in the cosmos into which this movement just fits, predetermined and perfect.'

Leonard Bernstein, *The Joy of Music*. New York: Simon and Schuster, 1959, pp. 11–12 and pp. 28–29.

ERNST BLOCH

The philosopher Ernst Bloch is known for his Marxist views and outlook for a humanistic world free from oppression and exploitation. Alongside his major intellectual interests, he also had close friendships with musicians, including Berthold Brecht and Kurt Weill, and writers on music including Theodor Adorno. With the foregoing in mind, he offers the following generalization about the music of Beethoven:

'[In] Beethoven's music the detail is nothing and vitality in the broad context is everything – energy, directness, conflict-torn departure and resolution which is not re-possession but entirely gain. Thus, in his developments, so thoroughly torn apart, Beethoven never acknowledges the theme's opportunity for delicate, calm, solitary self-enrichment. He recognises only the emotive quality of its exploration as the boldness, the *élan* of an adventure stated in the intrinsic harmonic-

> rhythmic substance. With Beethoven we enter the room and breathe the relationship. We have the most vivid feeling that here, everything is compressing itself by turns, and thus, through the changing atmospheric pressure, so to speak, we ascertain the height and depth of the terrain — more than that, we acquire a true sailor's instinct and even genetic instinct for the atmosphere and its laws.'

Turning to a consideration of the *Eroica* Symphony, Bloch writes in characteristic fashion:

> 'In the *Eroica*, "the two principles" in the thematic material are put fully to work; the antagonism derived from society is the at the same time that of the explosion which led to it in the first place — the French Revolution. It was for the same reason that the *Eroica* became the first conscious and the most consummate sonata-symphony. Its first movement in particular represents the Luciferan world of the Beethoven sonata. Thus, it is not the will of the entrepreneur that lets loose its socially-waring subject here, but something which supremely exceeds that and comes from a far more ancient level — the will of Prometheus.'

Ernst Bloch, *Essays on the Philosophy of Music*, Cambridge: Cambridge University Press, 1985, p. 32 and p. 233.

ALEXANDER BROTT
In his Memoirs, co-written with Betty Nygaard King (Editor,

Encyclopedia of Music in Canada), the Canadian conductor Alexander Brott writes of his pioneering of the *Eroica* Symphony:

> 'In January 1959, I guest-conducted the Edmonton Symphony Orchestra in a programme that included their first performance of Beethoven's *Eroica*. It was a privilege to introduce this magnificent music to an orchestra and its community. The fact they had never played so important a work gives you an indication of the development of orchestras in Canada compared to Europe and the United States.'

Alexander Brott and Betty Nygaard King, *Alexander Brott: My Lives in Music*. Oakville, Ontario; Niagara Falls, New York: Mosaic Press, 2005.

ALFRED PETER BROWN

The American musicologist Alfred Peter Brown remarks on the advance the *Eroica* Symphony represents in relation to its immediate predecessor the Second Symphony Op. 36:

> 'Although Opus 36 remains a powerful utterance, it only partially prepares one for Symphony No. 3 in E-flat major, Op. 55, the *Eroica* ('Heroic'). Symphonies No. 1 and No. 2 were compositions in which unity of response was discernable from their recurring themes and other motifs. In the *Eroica*, the coherence of the idea is multifaceted; It occurs on the purely musical as well as on the characteristic/programmatic levels. The extended

structure — more than twice the size of the normal eighteenth-century symphony — wells up from a common unifying concept of the heroic being — Prometheus transformed first into Bonaparte and then into a more abstract hero. The Third Symphony is but one indicator of Beethoven's intense interest in the heroic.'

Elaborating on the connection between the Prometheus legend and the *Eroica* Symphony, Brown elucidates:

> '[The Symphony's] heroic content ... derives from Beethoven's Ballet *The Creatures of Prometheus*. As the [Greek-German musicologist] Constantin Floros has argued, the second act of *Prometheus* contains four numbers that are analogous to the four movements of Opus 55:
>
> Una danza eroica military scene, No. 8 first movement
> Una tragica scena death of Prometheus, No. 9 second movement
> Una giuocosa scena resurrection of Prometheus third movement
> Danze festive *Prometheus* Finale fourth movement'

Brown proposes:

> 'None of these allusions would have been arcane to a turn-of-the-century audience: they must have been readily apparent to those who heard the early renditions of this new Beethoven symphony at the Lobkowitz residence in Vienna in 1804.'

Brown summates:

> 'The unity of the *Eroica* Symphony goes far beyond its topic and principal melodic material. The openings of each movement unfold in an extraordinary manner. The primary, secondary, and tertiary keys of each movement are manipulated to fit into a large cyclic complex. Previous to the *Eroica*, unity of key was a given; it now becomes an organic concept. The individual movements are stretched over wider expanses by avoiding complex closure and by delaying the realization of earlier implications. It is this inevitability of Beethoven's ideas in the *Eroica* and their expression that set a new concept for symphonic composition. It also set a standard that Beethoven himself may never have exceeded or duplicated; in his own view the *Eroica* was his finest symphony.'

Alfred Peter Brown, *The Symphonic Repertoire. Vol. 2, The First Golden Age of the Viennese Symphony: Haydn, Mozart, Beethoven, and Schubert.* Bloomington, Indiana: Indiana University Press, 2002, p. 460 and p. 475.

MICHAEL BROYLES

The American musicologist Michael Broyles identifies two significant influences that contributed to shaping the development of Beethoven's pioneering orchestral music. First, he argues 'the orchestral sonority becomes the dominant sonority for the next ten years' and likewise the sound of the orchestra itself 'becomes an essential element in

Beethoven's symphonic style'. Second, he makes reference to 'the sheer magnitude of Beethoven's artistic growth in the symphonic medium from Symphony One to Three'. This, Broyles describes as 'unprecedented for such a time-span'. It disposes him to further remark:

> 'When one considers that prior to 1800 Beethoven had never written a symphony, and that by 1804 the *Eroica* was complete, the rapidity with which he conquered this genre must be considered one of his outstanding accomplishments.'

Of the *Eroica* Symphony itself Broyles writes:

> '[The] pivotal nature of the *Eroica* is in itself eloquent testimony to the centrality of the symphonic medium to Beethoven at this time. Regardless of the reasons or motivation, the historical fact remains, it is the *Eroica* that demarcates a break with the past and delineates many of the themes that give the heroic decade its name [1800–10].'

Broyles elaborates:

> 'There is considerable irony in this, the conventional historical interpretation of the *Eroica* (with which I do not disagree), for in spite of all that is new and innovative, the *Eroica* remains firmly within the framework of the symphony style of Classicism. Its artistic success is due precisely to Beethoven's ability to understand the essence of that style and then to exploit it to its limits. The

Eroica is pivotal partly because it exhausted the Classical symphony style. None of the remaining symphonies surpass the *Eroica* as a quintessential essay upon what that style was about. And even within the *Eroica*, especially in Beethoven's handling of the last movement, there is a hint that Beethoven was aware of the bridge that he was burning.

'The *Eroica* then is the culmination of a brief but highly important stylistic cycle in Beethoven's compositional development.'

Michael Broyles, *Beethoven: The Emergence and Evolution of Beethoven's Heroic Style*. New York: Excelsior Music Publishing Co., 1987, p. 63.

HANS VON BÜLOW

Although today remembered as one of the most famous conductors of the 19th century, and for his aphorism 'Bach is the Old Testament and Beethoven the New Testament of music', recollections from his early days remind us of his formidable powers as a virtuoso pianist. He pioneered the innovation of performing the complete series of Beethoven piano sonatas and was known for the challenging nature of some of his recitals — challenging both to himself and his audience. On one occasion von Bülow played the last five Beethoven piano sonatas in a single evening and on another occasion he opened his recital with a performance of the *Hammerklavier* Piano Sonata and concluded the evening with the *Diabelli* Variations.

As recalled in: Peter Yates, *Twentieth Century Music: Its Evolution from the end of the Harmonic Era into the*

Present Era of Sound, London: Allen & Unwin Ltd., 1968.

The Czech composer and music critic Joseph Foerster has left recollections of Hamburg's musical scene in the late nineteenth century. In particular, he recalls the exacting demands von Bülow imposed upon himself. Foerster writes: 'His effervescent spirit could bear no easy-going manner approach, his pure artistry no half measures.' Foerster remembers the occasion when von Bülow was performing the F-sharp major Piano Sonata in Hamburg's Konviksaal. Although he was well into his performance he stopped because one string of the piano was out of tune, only resuming when the problem was rectified. In his role as orchestral conductor, von Bülow could be no less demanding of his audience. There was the occasion, for example, when, following a performance of Beethoven's Ninth symphony, he thanked the audience for their applause, apologised that Beethoven, who should receive it, could not attend but as a mark of respect proceeded to have the whole of the finale repeated!'

As recalled in: Kurt Blaukopf and Herta Blaukopf, *Mahler: His life, Work and World*, London: Thames and Hudson, 1991, p. 92.

The American music critic and author Harold C. Schonberg includes Hans von Bülow in his survey of *The Great Conductors*. He relates how von Bülow invariably conducted from memory — unheard of at the time — and when performing the Funeral March from the *Eroica* Symphony would replace his usual white gloves with a black pair!

During the concert season 1891—92, von Bülow conducted the Berlin Symphony Orchestra in what was his fiftieth appearance before the players. The programme included a performance of the *Eroica* Symphony that he preceded with an address to the audience in which he made provocative references to Napoleon. He derided the words *liberté, egalité, fraternité*, and, with Teutonic music in mind, suggested they should be replaced with 'cavalry', 'infantry', and 'artillery'. Accordingly, he dedicated the evening's performance 'to the brilliant star of Germany', further intimating the Symphony should have been dedicated to Bismarck not Napoleon! The speech divided the audience and was received with a mixture of hisses and cheers.

During von Bülow's tenure as resident conductor at Meiningen, he adopted as his assistant the twenty-one-year old Richard Strauss. From him we learn of von Bülow's temper, autocracy, of his exhorting the players to perform from memory — some could and others couldn't — and of his exhortation: 'Learn to read the score of a Beethoven symphony accurately ... and you will have found its interpretation.'

Harold C. Schonberg, *The Great Conductors*, Simon & Schuster, 1967, pp.171–72.

See also: Bruno Walter, *Theme and Variations: An Autobiography.* London: H. Hamilton, 1948, p. 50.

Strauss followed Bülow's advice and, in his capacity as orchestral conductor (he was given to describing himself as 'Kapellmeister', rather than as 'composer') he marked the scores of Beethoven's symphonies with von Bülow's own directions. On one occasion Strauss was so moved by Bülow's interpretation of the *Eroica* Symphony that afterwards, backstage, he burst into tears — disposing Bülow, of similar emotional temperament, to place a consoling arm about his protégé.

Wilhelm Kurt, *Richard Strauss: An Intimate Portrait.* London: Thames and Hudson, 1999, p. 33.

PABLO CASALS

The author Ma J. Corredor interviewed the celebrated

Spanish cellist, composer, conductor, and humanist Pablo Casals, offering him propositions to which he was invited to respond. In the course of the interview Casals first offered some generalizations about the greatness of Beethoven:

> '[The] greatness of Beethoven does not lie in the amount of discoveries he made but in the significance of his message. In my opinion, anything that has been said — truly or falsely — about him will not diminish the radiance of the light such a mind has brought us, and it will always be looked upon as one of the most glorious gifts humanity has received.'

When invited to agree with the suggestion Beethoven's later compositions are 'deeper' and 'musically superior' to his earlier ones, Casals responded with measured caution:

> 'The Beethoven of the later years seems to hover in a mysterious and sublime sphere. In any case, I would not dare to say that, purely as "works of art", the later are superior to the early ones ... Of course ... deafness naturally affected Beethoven's character. However, I would say that the great strength of his mind already protected him from the usual banalities of life which surrounded him just as they do each of us.'

Ma invited Casals to consider remarks made by the conductor Wilhelm Furtwängler: "With Beethoven great discoveries, especially the invention of themes and details, are numerous. But that is not what his genius is made of ... his intuition goes much further ...". Casals responded:

'As for the themes, it is true that we can find in his notebooks all the transformations they underwent, which show the difficulties he encountered before these themes finally took shape. If we take the slow movement of the *Eroica* Symphony, we shall see how many phases it went through before its completion. Nothing of the kind happened with Mozart or Schubert, whose themes emerged entire and complete in themselves, at least, so it seems to me.

'Beethoven, I feel sure, had to fight with his material, and his works did not reach perfection until they had undergone many transformations.'

Ma J. Corredor, *Conversations with Casals*. London: Hutchinson, 1956, pp. 139–43.

BARRY COOPER / WILLIAM DRABKIN
(See also, Nicholas Marston)

The British musicologist Barry Cooper is internationally recognised for his scholarly studies of the life and work of Beethoven. In addition, Beethovenians have him to thank for his reconstruction of a performing edition of the composer's Tenth Symphony – from the many surviving sketches that were left incomplete at the time of his death. Pianists are no less in debt to Cooper for his edition of the Piano Sonatas for The Associated Board of the Royal Schools of Music (ABRSM). This incorporates Beethoven's three youthful *Kurfürstensonaten* (WoO 47) – dedicated to the Elector (Kurfürst) Maximillian Fredrick – that Cooper is known to consider are unjustly neglected. In addition to numerous scholarly articles relating to Beethoven and his work, Cooper has authored and co-authored three book-length studies of the composer (1990, 1991, and 2000) from which we cite the writings that follow.

In July 1823, Beethoven wrote a letter to his former piano pupil Ferdinand Ries in which he remarked: 'Between ourselves the best thing of all is a combination of the surprising and the beautiful.' Remarking on this, Cooper (1990) observes:

> 'There are countless examples of this ability [to surprise] throughout [Beethoven's] entire output, and they pervade his minor works almost as much as his major ones. Sometimes the surprise comes from an unexpected chord, a well-known case being the opening of the First Symphony with its out-of-key dominant seventh. On other occasions there is an unexpected melodic turn, such as the C sharp in the opening theme of the *Eroica* Symphony.'

Cooper considers how Beethoven's temperament is reflected in his music:

> '[It] is difficult to be certain, but some connections seem to be clear. He was generally regarded as an irascible person and he clearly had sudden bursts of anger more often than most people. His music in places reflects this trait: it probably contains a higher proportion of *sforzandos* than that of any other major composer; it also contains some ferocious discords virtually unmatched by any of his contemporaries, such as a passage in the *Eroica* Symphony [first movement, illustration 4.2] ...'.

*

Cooper discusses how extra-musical ideas, such as suffering often associated with death, influenced a number of Beethoven's orchestral compositions; he cites, by way of illustration, *Christus am Ölberge* and the incidental music to Goethe's play *Egmont*. He continues:

> 'Another work concerned with the death of a hero in the *Eroica* Symphony (1803–04), with its funeral second movement and its statement, on the title-page of the first edition, that it was written "to celebrate the memory of a great man". [There] are strong political overtones for, as is well known, it was originally to have been dedicated to Napoleon as a champion of freedom, but Beethoven tore up the title-page of the manuscript when he heard that Napoleon had proclaimed himself Emperor. The work then became regarded as an expression of heroism in general, of any and every hero, including, no doubt, Beethoven himself as the better side of Napoleon.'

Barry Cooper, *Beethoven and the Creative Process.* Oxford: Clarendon Press, 1990, p. 22, pp. 46–47 and p. 52.

In Cooper's following study of Beethoven (1991), his co-author and musicologist William Drabkin discusses Beethoven's expansion of form — placing that to be found in the *Eroica* Symphony within the context of other of the composer's large-scale compositions:

> 'It is difficult to determine what motivated Beethoven to begin writing sonata movements on a vast scale: the longest 18th-century, first-move-

ment forms are found in the late piano concertos of Mozart, and also in some of his string quartets. Possibly Beethoven learnt something from both repertories: the quartets (especially K. 515 in C major) for their breadth of phrasing, the concertos for their profusion of themes. The increased size of the exposition led to a proportional lengthening of the development section. Here, Beethoven seems to have found his own solution: to write not one but two developments, which could then be joined by further transitional material. A glimpse of this process is provided by the first of the quartets in F Op. 59, No.1, where there is a clear indication of an imminent return to the tonic at bar 152, barely forty bars after the exposition. But now harmony veers away from the home key and eventually leads to a fugato, extending the development section by a further ninety bars. Similar composite development sections are found in the *Eroica* Symphony and the *Waldstein*, *Appassionata* and *Hammerklavier* Sonatas.'

William Drabkin, *Musical Form Innovations* in: Barry Cooper, editor, *The Beethoven Compendium: A Guide to Beethoven's Life and Music.* London: Thames and Hudson, 1991, p. 205.

Cooper has contributed to *The Master Musicians* series of publications (2000), following on from the earlier studies of Beethoven in this series by Denis Matthews (1985) and Marion Scott (1940). Writing of the significance of Beethoven's compositions following his stay at Heiligenstadt, when he endeavoured to come to terms with his loss of hearing, Cooper remarks:

> 'The first works conceived after Heiligenstadt are extremely important in this respect: the Oratorio *Christus am Oelberge* (Christ on the Mount of Olives) and the *Eroica* Symphony, both of which has deep personal significance ...'.

Of the *Eroica* Symphony he adds

> 'Although clearly in the symphonic tradition of Haydn and Mozart, it far exceeds any previous symphony in length, complexity, and grandeur of conception, while its originality and its intriguing extra-musical associations provide endless scope for reflection. The true hero of the work is Beethoven himself.'

Barry Coper, *Beethoven: The Master Musicians Series*. Oxford: Oxford University Press, 2000, pp. 122–23 and p. 133.

LOUISE ELVIRA CUYLER

Writing of the *Eroica* Symphony, the American musicologist Louise Elvira Cuyler recalls how the work initially divided public opinion:

> 'Beethoven's *Eroica* Symphony, his first composition in the grand and spacious style we now associate with him, had a mixed reception at its first [public] performance. One critic thought it a "tremendously expanded, daring and wild fantasia"; but [Carl] Czerny, a major pianist of the day [and Beethoven's pupil], recalled that at the first

> performance an auditor from the gallery called, "I'll give another *kreutzer* [a German coin of small denomination] if the thing will stop". Another faction, which included Beethoven's special coterie of friends and many cognoscenti of the day, held that this was "the true style of high-class music" — and their opinion has, of course, turned out to be the prophetic one. The *Eroica* announced in vehement tones, that the day of music as an exalted art that approached a religion had come. Music has never been the same since then.'

Cuyler concludes by relating the *Eroica* Symphony to Beethoven's following three symphonies:

> 'Beethoven's *Eroica* Symphony was an important landmark in the evolution of musical style as well as in the composer's own artistic growth. But Beethoven's later works did not necessarily bear the mark of this masterpiece. Certain of its techniques, notably that of extended development, became Beethoven's for life, but he never recaptured the exalted mood that produced the *Eroica*. The next three symphonies must be regarded as a group, for Beethoven apparently turned from one to the other in writing them; their numbers represent the probable order of composition ... Of the three that followed the *Eroica*, the Fourth is retrospective in many qualities; the Fifth might be viewed as the "logical" successor to the *Eroica*; and the Sixth is unique: in it, Beethoven shows a strain of gentleness and tenderness that he rarely disclosed.'

Louise Elvira Cuyler, *The Symphony*. New York: Harcourt Brace Jovanovich, 1973, pp. 59–65.

SAMUEL BASIL DEANE

The Irish musicologist and academic Samuel Basil Deane, known as Basil Deane, introduced his study of the *Eroica* Symphony stating:

> 'The Third Symphony, the *Eroica* (E-flat major, Op. 55, 1803–04), marks an expression of musical scale which is without precedent in instrumental composition. How far this expansion is directly due to the non-musical associations of the work is impossible to decide. It is most improbable that Beethoven thought of the symphony as a connected series of tableau, each related in its programmatic content to some aspect of heroic endeavour. On the other hand, two of the movements have programmatic associations, one explicit, the other implicit. So, it may be that Beethoven's natural tendency at this stage, to expand his musical forms, was supported by his reflection upon his original subjects. At all event he displays a breadth of vision and a mastery of design which are altogether Napoleonic.'

Samuel Basil Deane, *The Symphonies and Overtures* in: Denis Arnold and Nigel Fortune editors, *The Beethoven Companion*. London: Faber and Faber, 1973, pp. 288–89.

PHILIP G. DOWNS

The American musicologist Philip G. Downs contributed a

chapter to Paul Henry Lang's treatise *Classical Music* that he titled 'Beethoven's "New Way" and the *Eroica* Symphony'. The origin of the words in parenthesis is as follows. Sometime during 1800–01, following the composition of the Piano Sonata, Op. 28 (*The Pastoral*), Beethoven expressed dissatisfaction with his music to his intimate friend the mandolinist Wenzel Krumpholz: 'I am far from satisfied with my past works; from today on I shall take a *new way*.' [italics added] Downs responds:

> 'The *Eroica* Symphony shows signs arising from Beethoven's "new way" in that it succeeds in accomplishing a thing that Beethoven only once again succeeded in doing on such a wide scale. The first movement succeeds in reconciling the formal, spatial requirements of the traditionally conceived sonata form with a discursive, narrative, temporal drama. The sonata is almost invariably described as a dramatic form in music. Beethoven's achievement in the *Eroica* is to create in music something analogous to theatrical drama.'

Downs considers the spacious grandeur of the *Eroica* Symphony:

> 'The tendency towards the grandiose was always a pronounced feature of the Beethoven style. In the earliest published works there is an obvious enlargement of the scale of operations of Haydn and Mozart which undoubtedly is prompted by the fashion of the times, but which one cannot help suspecting is also partly a conscious assertion of Beethoven's independence, if not superiority. The length of the first movement of the *Eroica* Sym-

phony need not be dwelt upon, except to say that its proportions came into being not simply as the search for impressiveness through size, but largely because of the conscious juxtaposition of the new and the organic with the traditional and the formal.'

Downs draws his evaluation of the *Eroica* Symphony to a close with summative words:

'[The] dramatic purpose of the *Eroica* Symphony is to provide a lesson on the conquering of self. It is fruitless to talk about the hero of the Symphony being Napoleon or General Abercrombie or even Beethoven himself. [see *Creation Origins*] The work of art is not the author of it, although it certainly is a projection of part of the author. The forces which so nearly overwhelmed Beethoven, and which ultimately resulted in the Heiligenstadt Testament and the rejection of suicide as a way out of difficulty, certainly appear in the musical parable.'

Philip G. Downs, *Beethoven's "New Way" and the Eroica* in: Paul Henry Lang, *The Creative World of Beethoven*. New York: W. W. Norton 1971, pp. 83–102.

Elsewhere Downs reflects:

'[What] is completely new is the way Beethoven manages the dimensions and the way he makes disparate materials relate together to communicate a spiritual attitude ... Beethoven had been accustomed to painting on a large canvas on an additive principle, i.e. by the cumulative application of different melodic material to a widely used form ... [He] certainly follows the additive principle ... and the *Eroica* contains a sequence of varied melodies that is only paralleled by the corresponding section of his Ninth Symphony.'

Philip G. Downs, *Classical Music: The Era of Haydn, Mozart, and Beethoven.* New York: W.W. Norton, 1992, pp. 597–98.

GEORGE DYSON

The English musician and composer Sir George Dyson was invited to contribute to Beethoven's Death Centenary (1927) in a special edition of *The Musical Times*. By way of introducing what he has to say about the *Eroica* Symphony, we first cite the following extract from his essay, concerning questions of expression and interpretation in Beethoven's music, that he couched in suitably laudatory terms:

> 'The outstanding pianist will always demand problems of interpretation on which to feed the zeal of his evangel. For him, Beethoven is food indeed. And there has been no player of high rank who has not counted it a triumph to present to the world, at whatever expense of labour and thought, the truth of a message so exacting. In the pursuit of expression Beethoven was merciless. Pianoforte, quartet, orchestra and chorus, all alike he stretched to the utmost. He forgets that there are limits to the powers of an instrument, limits to the capacity of a human interpreter. Above all, he forgets himself. He would crouch under the desk to suggest a pianissimo. He would gesticulate

wildly and ludicrously to emphasize a fortissimo. He would caress the piano into quiet ecstasies which his friends never forgot. He would thrash it into turmoil that made them almost afraid. Moods so intense are not for every man, though there can be no supreme artists without them. When the heat of his passion demands the impossible, it is because his vision is of things beyond man's power to describe. In pursuit of that transcendence Beethoven spent himself. And if his fire sometimes scorches us it consumed his own ardent soul no less.'

George Dyson, in: *Music & Letters: Beethoven: Special Number*, London: Music & Letters, 1927. p. 210.

In his survey of classical music, Dyson positioned the *Eroica* Symphony in the context of Beethoven's intended gesture of celebration of Napoleon Bonaparte and the wider context of the aristocratic patronage that prevailed at the period of the work's composition:

'The story of Beethoven's *Eroica* Symphony is well known. He planned it as a tribute to Napoleon, the hero of revolution and the guardian of liberty. When Napoleon accepted the status of Emperor, Beethoven was so enraged he tore the Title Page and stamped in fury. This act of homage, and its subsequent revocation, was a symptom of the attitude adopted by all those who had democratic sympathies. In Beethoven's case it meant this and more. His family's livelihood, his traditions, and the whole environment in which his art had hitherto been practised, had owed their very existence to a system of patronage inseparably bound to the old order to the resources and privileges of an aristocracy still almost feudal in its assumptions. The enlightened patron could no doubt be marvellously instrumental for good. He could encourage a fine taste with all the force of an autocrat. But he was still an autocrat, he held the fate of his servants at his will, his pleasure was their law, and however generously and humanely he might use these powers, the world was beginning to feel the system was inherently intolerable.'

George Dyson, *The Progress of Music*. London: Oxford University Press, Humphrey Milford, 1932, pp. 184–85.

ALFRED EINSTEIN

The German-American musicologist Alfred Einstein is perhaps best known — certainly to Mozartians — for having revised and enlarged the so-called Köchel Catalogue of his works (1936), and to Schubertians for his study of the composer, *Schubert* (English transaltion,1951). During his lifetime, Einstein was known to a wide readership through his many articles on classical music. On 23 June 1934, he wrote an article in the London *Daily Telegraph* titled, 'Rest and Unrest: Music's Changing Function in a Changing World'. He took as his subject the *Eroica* Symphony:

'Beethoven expressed a strange wish when he gave his *Eroica* to the world, or rather, one that has come to appear strange to us. He wished the work to be placed at the beginning and not at the end of the concert programme. He considered his Symphony too long, too difficult and exhausting to be performed at the end of the evening when the audience might not be alert, attentive and understanding.

'Nowhere today is there a conductor who respects Beethoven's wish. No-doubt the present-day conductor would plead that the *Eroica* long ago ceased to be a difficult work, and that in dimensions and pretentions it has been outdone by dozens of other symphonies.'

Einstein adds — provocatively: 'And he would be right; modern conductors are always right! There is no contradicting them.' He then asks: '[Why] is it that modern conductors always put the *Eroica* at the end of their programmes?' He offers the following suggestion:

'The reason is that, in spite of its one-hundred-and-thirty years of age, the *Eroica*, though it may have been surpassed in dimensions and pretentions, has never been surpassed in effect. The conductor wants his audience to disperse with minds freshly stamped with the most powerful impression of the whole concert. And no matter how jaded and drooping the audience, it cannot help responding to the *Eroica's* whip and spur — most certainly not when the theme of the finale is shouted out by eight horns — as I can remember having heard it once.' [Beethoven's authentic score requires just three horns]

Catherine Dower, *Alfred Einstein on Music: Selected Music Criticisms*. New York: Greenwood Press, 1991, pp. 168–69.

Writing about form and content in music of the Romantic era, Einstein asserts:

> 'Beethoven — not in all of his works, but in all of his important works — "tamed the forces of chaos," found complete formal expression for his thoughts, and filled outlines of the broader dimensions with the most energetic expression. The first movement of the *Eroica* is, today just as on the day it was written, one of the wonders of music, supremely alive in every detail yet completely unified, supremely clear yet most powerfully impulsive. And what applies to this movement applies to the whole Symphony.'

Alfred Einstein, *Music in the Romantic Era*. London: J.M. Dent Ltd., 1947, p. 66.

HANS CONRAD FISCHER AND ERICH KOCK

In their study of Beethoven, Hans Conrad Fischer and Erich Kock position the *Eroica* Symphony in the context of those of Haydn and Mozart:

> 'We have 107 of Haydn's symphonies and 48 of Mozart's. Measured against such standards, Beethoven's Nine symphonies seem few indeed. Yet it was Beethoven who originated the concept of a unity between separate movements, originating in a basic theme, which has practically no equivalent in earlier works. With the *Eroica*, Op. 55, for example, the symphony has completely moved away from its original functions as an operatic introduction or background music for

the Court. "The central poetic concept of human grandeur, which is the basic theme", of a symphony, is derived from a "definite and real example". The new dimensions of expression achieved by the [*Eroica*] Symphony are also responsible for its extraordinary length — it lasts for a good fifty minutes. "Beethoven realised this and so he wanted it to open the concert in order that the special effect he intended it to produce would not be lost". [Claus Canisius] Even though there are several debts to Haydn and Mozart in the first two symphonies, the melodic richness and the artistry of melodic development in the Third Symphony reach a unique grandeur that can hardly ever be surpassed.'

Hans Conrad Fischer and Erich Kock, *Ludwig van Beethoven: A Study in Text and Pictures.* London: Macmillan; New York, St. Martin's Press, 1972, p. 88.

HANS GAL
In his survey of *The Golden Age of Vienna*, the Austrian-British composer and author Hans Gal reserves a special position for Beethoven whom he describes as *The Master Builder*. He elaborates:

'Beethoven is the first representative of the modern intellectual type, whose range of interests is not confined to his art. Wherever one looks into his letters, subjects of general interest are touched ... a great mind, a wide, comprehensive conception assert themselves everywhere ... Beethoven — like Michelangelo, who offers the most obvious parallel among the great artists — is the prototype of such a living volcano. Like Michelangelo, he had the titanic power of moulding the eruptive material, of imposing on it his creative will. It is the most demoniac of all elements: Chaos, both the eternal source and eternal contradiction of Cosmos, the ordered world.'

Writing of the *Eroica* Symphony, Gal contends

'The first work in which [Beethoven] realised his own vision of a monumental conception, the *Sinfonia Eroica*, was probably the most staggering novelty in the history of music. There is not only a new style, a new sound, a new greatness of form and design, but a completely new attitude to the world of the artistic personality. No obedient servant of his liege-lord had ever been so able to conceive such music. Here the artist feels himself equal to the greatest of this world. It is not unlikely that the title of the Symphony, still more its dedication to the Consul Bonaparte, was an afterthought. It would have been an odd compliment, anyway, to glorify a living hero with his own funeral celebration. When, shortly after the completion of the score, the hero proclaimed himself Emperor of France and thus made a parody of himself to the idealistic republican, Beethoven, in a fit of rage, tore the idol down from the pedestal he had erected for him. The story is well known and borne out by the crumpled and torn Title-Page of a manuscript copy of the Symphony, on which the half-erased traces of Beethoven's hand-written dedication are still visible. His ferocious outburst betrays his self-reproach: he could not forgive himself for having debased his ideal by linking it to an individual, though the greatest of his time, and his human weakness. In its impersonal grandeur, *Sinfonia Eroica* stands out as the noblest monument of heroism as a pure idea, higher and loftier than its realisation by any mortal hero.'

Hans Gal, *The Golden Age of Vienna*, London: Max Parrish & Co. Limited, 1948, pp. 44—46 and pp. 51—52.

DONALD J. GROUT AND CLAUDE V. PALISCA

The American-born Donald J. Grout and the Italian-born Claudia V. Palisca — both musicologists — consider the fascination that music held for the emerging Romantic generation bearing upon its 'revolutionary element, the free, impulsive, mysterious, demonic spirit, the underlying conception of *music as a mode of self-expression*' [their words and italics]. As evidence, they cite the pioneering essay (1813) by the German writer and composer E. T. A. Hoffman who remarks:

> 'Beethoven's music sets in motion the lever of fear, of horror, of suffering, and awakens just that infinite longing which is the essence of romanticism ... He is accordingly a completely romantic composer.'

Grout and Palisca comment:

> 'Hoffman was not unaware nor unappreciative

of the importance of structure and control in Beethoven's music, nor in that of Haydn and Mozart, whom he also called "Romantic" ... Romantic or not, Beethoven was one of the great disruptive forces in the history of music. After him, nothing could ever be the same again; he had opened the gateway to a new world.'

Of the *Eroica* Symphony they remark on the origins of the work's title:

'The Third Symphony in E flat, composed in 1803, is one of the most important works of Beethoven's second period. The Symphony bears the title *Eroica*, the "heroic Symphony". There is evidence that Beethoven intended to dedicate the Symphony to Napoleon, whom he admired as the hero who was to lead humanity into the new age of liberty, equality, and fraternity. The conductor [and pianist-composer] Ferdinand Ries, however, told the story that when he heard that Napoleon had himself proclaimed Emperor (in May 1804), Beethoven, in his disappointment at finding that his idol was only another ambitious ruler on the way to becoming a tyrant, angrily tore up the Title Page containing the dedication. This is probably an exaggeration, but the Title Page of Beethoven's own score, which survives, originally read *Sinfonia grande intitolata Bonaparte* ('Grand Symphony entitled Bonaparte') and he corrected it to *Geschrieben auf Bonaparte* ('Composed on Bonaparte').'

When the Symphony was eventually published in Vienna in 1806 it bore the title:

Sinfonia Eroica ... composta per festeggiare il sovvenire di un grand Uomo – 'Heroic Symphony ... composed to celebrate the memory of a great man'.

Grout and Palisca conclude their introductory remarks to the composition stating:

> 'Indeed, the Third Symphony stands as an immortal expression in music of the ideal of heroic greatness. It was a revolutionary work of such unprecedented length and complexity that audiences at first found it difficult to grasp.'

Donald Jay Grout and Claude V. Palisca editors, *A History of Western Music*, London: J. M. Dent, 1988, pp. 636–37.

GEORGE GROVE

The name Grove is familiar to generations of music lovers through association with *Grove's Dictionary of Music and Musicians* of which Grove was the inspiration and source. Sir George Grove, however, did not receive a formal education in music and trained as a structural engineer, being admitted as a graduate of the Institution of Civil Engineers. He worked in this capacity for the first thirty years of his life and it was while he was engaged on the Britannia Bridge that he became known to such luminaries of the age as Robert Stephenson, Isambard Kingdom Brunel and Sir Charles Barry. Grove later made a change of career and was appointed in 1849 to the secretaryship of the Society of Arts – at the period of gestation of the Great Exhibition of 1851. When the exhibition relocated to Sydenham, in the guise of The Crystal Palace, it was as a result of the actions of

Grove that the German-born August Manns was appointed, first as bandmaster and later as the conductor of a full-size orchestra. Manns presided over regular concerts for more than forty years, Grove providing numerous programme notes that later formed the basis for his *Dictionary*.

Many of Beethoven's works were performed at The Crystal Palace under the direction of August Manns including overtures, concertos, symphonies and choral works. *Fidelio* received a concert performance in 1859 and in 1866 the resident orchestra had to be augmented for a rendering of the *Eroica* Symphony that was billed as 'a special event'. A detailed inventory of the works of Beethoven performed at The Crystal Palace, and the role played by Sir George Grove, will be found in: Michael Musgrave, *The Musical Life of the Crystal Palace*, Cambridge: Cambridge University Press, 1995.

Writing of the *Eroica* Symphony, Grove commences:

> 'A special interest will always attach to the *Eroica* apart from its own merits, in the fact that it is Beethoven's first symphony on the "new road" which he announced to [his friend Wenzel] Krumpholz in 1802: "I am not satisfied ... with my works up to the present time. From today I mean to take a *new road*." This was after the completion of the Piano Sonata, Op. 28 [*Pastoral*], in 1801. Great as is the advance in the three Piano Sonatas of Op. 31, especially that in D minor [*The Tempest*], and the three Violin Sonatas of Op. 30, especially that in C minor, over their predecessors, it must be confessed that the leap from Symphony No. 2 to the *Eroica* is still greater. The Symphonies in C and D, with

all their breadth and spirit, belong to the school of Haydn.

'The *Eroica* first shows us the methods which were so completely to revolutionise that department of music — the continuous and organic mode of connecting the second subject to the first, the introduction of episodes into the working-out, the extraordinary importance of the Coda. These in the first movement. In the second there is the title of "March", a distinct innovation on previous custom. In the third there is the title of "Scherzo", here used in the symphonies for the first time, and also there are the breadth and proportions of the piece, hitherto the smallest of the four, but now raised to a level with the others; and in the finale, the daring and romance which pervades the movement under so much strictness of form. All these are steps in Beethoven's advance of the symphony; and, as the earliest example of these things, the *Eroica* will always have a great historical claim to distinction, entirely apart from the nobility and beauty of its strains.'

George Grove, *Beethoven and his Nine Symphonies*. London: Novello, Ewer, 1896, pp. 49—50.

NIKOLAUS HARNONCOURT

Between June and July 1990, Nikolaus Harnoncourt recorded a number of Beethoven's symphonies. Mindful of Harnoncourt's reputation for 'historic performance practice', Professor Hartmut Krones — Head of the Department of Musical Studies and Performing Practice at the Vienna College of Fine Arts — asked Harnoncourt about his approach to the interpretation of the composer's orchestral music. Krones asked Harnoncourt if he ever did any 'retouching' of Beethoven's scores? Harnoncourt responded:

> 'I ... do not do any retouching whatsoever as a matter of principle, neither octaving nor reallocation of certain notes/passages to other instruments. If Beethoven had not possessed instruments that were capable of more, or of playing differently, then he surely would not just have distributed certain notes differently – this would have changed the whole instrumentation significantly. And that's why I think it is always a mistake to change individual notes or registers. I believe in the correctness of the composer's instrumentation and the correctness of the overall linguistic character, both with regard to individual notes, and as regards the overall sound. A particularly good example of this is the point where the trumpet takes up the main subject of the *Eroica* – it breaks off at 'G'. Many recordings assume that the old trumpet was not capable of playing B flat and get the modern instrument to play this note after all. But I am convinced that Beethoven did not leave out the B flat on the trumpet because the instrument could not play it, but because he wanted to show how the hero had failed. If the 'victory note' is not heard radiantly, but instead is taken up quietly by the flute and then by the strings, then this I see as an important statement about the content of the music, and not as something that can be eliminated by retouching.'

Nikolaus Harnoncourt, *Introductory notes to the the Chamber Orchestra of Europe*, conducted by Nikolaus Harnoncourt, June–July, 1990.

CHRISTOPHER HEADINGTON

The English composer, pianist, and musicologist Christopher Headington published extensively on classical music. Writing of Beethoven, the musician, he observes:

> 'No history of music can offer a simple answer. But it can draw attention to Beethoven, a composer whose work attracts experts and public alike. In this, his art resembles that of Shakespeare. Beethoven believed in the message of the choral Finale of his last symphony, "Be embraced, ye millions!" For him, all men were brothers under God.'

Of the grandeur of, and mythology implicit in, Beethoven's Third Symphony Headington remarks:

> 'The *Eroica* Symphony itself presents us with a mystery unless we admit the existence of some spiritual level onto which the drama of the music moves. Why should the slow movement, a mighty funeral march, be followed by an exhilarating scherzo? Berlioz suggested funeral games around the hero's grave such as are described in Homer's *Iliad*, and since Beethoven knew Homer's work the idea is at least plausible. But then how do we explain the triumphant finale? The best clue comes from Beethoven himself. For this finale he used an

important theme from *Prometheus*; so perhaps his hero has been translated to a higher, godlike sphere. We remember that Beethoven copied into his diary Kant's phrase, "The moral law in us and the starry sky above us". As for the question whether such a literary programme as this is likely, we have the composer's own note for a projected later work: "In the adagio the text of a Greek myth — or *Cantique ecclésiastique* — in the allegro a Bacchic festival". Not many people would think of mixing a Christian hymn with a pagan festival in the same work. Nor would they equate a Greek myth with a hymn as alternatives for the slow movement; but for Beethoven, on whose shelves the Bible (in two languages) and the Christian mystic Thomas à Kempis stood beside the writers of the ancient world, both were valid attempts made by Man to commune with the Creator.

'The most striking novelty about the music of the *Eroica* Symphony is its sheer size. Lasting about three-quarters of an hour, it is roughly double the length of a symphony by Haydn or Mozart. Indeed, the first movement, except for the Fifth Piano Concerto, which shares the same key of E flat, is the longest he ever wrote ... Naturally, length alone does not ensure grandeur. But Beethoven's whole design is grand; we are never reminded, as we sometimes are by ambitious works of lesser men, that the great prehistoric dinosaurs were sluggish creatures with tiny brains. As a matter of fact, in many ways the *Eroica* offers examples of economy. Was there ever a shorter introduction to a symphony than these two chords, compared by Lenard Bernstein to two mighty pillars: [illustrated in the original text].'

Christopher Headington, *Beethoven* in: *The Bodley Head History of Western Music*, London: The Bodley Head, 1974, pp. 155–6 and p. 167.

GORDON JACOB

The English composer and educator Gordon Jacob contributed introductions to the Penguin Books series of pocketbook miniature scores. Writing of the advances Beethoven made in the *Eroica* Symphony he states:

'The *Eroica* is a tremendous step forward from the style of the first two symphonies. These, though we can see plenty of hints in them of Beethoven's mature style, are in the Haydn tradition and follow to a great extent the formalistic conventions of the late eighteenth century. With the *Eroica*, Beethoven shed all obvious influences and became completely individual. In a letter written in 1802, he states his dissatisfaction with his music up to that time. [The origin of this anecdote derives from the recollections of Beethoven's piano pupil Carl Czerny. Beethoven confided his feelings about his compositions to his close friend Wenzel Krumpholz, as recorded in: Oscar George Theodore Sonneck, *Beethoven: Impressions of Contemporaries*: Oxford University Press 1927, p. 31]

'The immense length of the work compared with any previous symphony, particularly the length of the first movement and the use of variation-form in the finale, show that even in its broad outlines this symphony was an innovation, an impression which is still further reinforced by the highly personal way in which its ideas are presented and developed.'

Gordon Jacob, Introduction to: *Beethoven, Symphony No. 3 in E flat, Op. 55*, London, Penguin Books, 1954, pp. 12–13.

DAVID WYN JONES
David Wyn Jones was professor of music at the University of Cardiff with a particular interest in the music of Haydn and Beethoven and their relationship with the musical life of the City of Vienna. In his *Life of Beethoven*, Jones identifies the *Eroica* Symphony with the genre of the variation-form that Beethoven exploited, to a considerable, extent during his early years in Vienna:

> 'Apart from the scale of the [*Eroica* Symphony], which builds on the experience of the Second Symphony as well as the A major Violin Sonata [Op. 47, *The Kreutzer*], this Symphony reflects two other recent preoccupations. First, the finale was to use the same compositional approach found in the Piano Variations [Op. 35] being prepared for publication by Breitkopf & Härtel: essentially a set of variations on a theme taken from the *Prometheus* Ballet ... The Symphony expands further on the standard approach to the writing of variations, allowing them to overspill the structural boundaries of their original theme,

with the result that the [final] movement has an unprecedented sense of expansive discovery.'

Jones poses the question:

'Whether the entire Symphony was conceived in order to accommodate the possibilities that Beethoven glimpsed when writing the Piano Variations, or whether the idea of using the same material arose after he had conceived the earlier movements cannot be answered.'

David Wyn Jones, *The Life of Beethoven*. Cambridge: Cambridge University Press, 1998, pp. 74–75.

In his later study *The Symphony in Beethoven's Vienna*, Jones discusses a further innovation of the composer to which he refers as 'The Programme Symphony':

'Beethoven's three programme symphonies are spread evenly across his symphonic output from 1799 to 1813; the *Eroica* in 1803, the *Pastoral Symphony* five years later in 1808, and *Wellington's Victory* a further five years later in 1813. Their subject matter, individual and universal heroism, followed by the escapist, partly secular sacred-world of the pastoral and, finally, the graphic evocation of battle and victory, were familiar ones to Beethoven's audiences and, as Richard Will has demonstrated [*The Characteristic Symphony in the Age of Haydn and Beethoven*, 2002] constitute a continuation of practices in the classical symphony that go back decades.'

Jones closes this part of his study with the summation:

> 'Between them, the *Eroica* Symphony and *Wellington's Victory* denote the range of musical experience covered by the term programme symphony, from the work that takes the extra-musical as a point of departure in order to explore it in heightened abstraction to a work in which the extra-musical controls rather than liberates the composition.'

David Wyn Jones, *The Symphony in Beethoven's Vienna*. Cambridge: Cambridge University Press, 2006, pp. 174–76.

H. C. ROBBINS LANDON

The American musicologist and historian H. C. Robbins Landon is perhaps best known for his championing of the music of Haydn and for his account of the last years of the life of Mozart. His scholarship also embraced the life and work of Beethoven. The present writer memorably recalls attending a lecture of Landon's when he spoke for a full hour, without notes, without faltering and with considerable passion, on the subject of Beethoven's Opera *Leonora* – the first version of the later, and much revised, *Fidelio*.

With regard to Beethoven's teacher Haydn, he had composed his so-called *London* Symphonies between 1791–95, thereby drawing to a close his remarkable sequence of 104 numbered symphonies. Beethoven had taken his aging mentor's mantle with his First Symphony, Op. 21 (1801) and his Second Symphony, Op. 36 (1804) Haydn did not return to the symphonic genre ever again. When the German composer and music critic Johann Friedrich Reichardt visited Haydn in 1807, he found the infirm composer seated very stiff and almost rigid – not unlike a living wax-figure. Haydn exclaimed to his visitor: 'Ah, I have strained my spirit too much; I'm already just a child.'

With these words as context, Landon contends:

> 'Beethoven had hardly composed a single work which, as it were, obliterated Haydn's (or Mozart's) fame; but in 1804 we have a work of Michelangelo-like proportions, the *Sinfonia Eroica,* which in power, size and concept was as towering, and as final (in the sense of overall stylistic-considerations) as the ceiling of the Sistine Chapel – both creations written, it would seem, by the hands of "a giant on the walls of some primitive temple". With the *Eroica*, Beethoven began a new era which would lead to the *Missa Solemnis*, the Ninth Symphony and the late quartets: and he could not, it seems, begin on this long road until his only serious rival and former teacher was out of the way.'

H. C. Robbins Landon, *Haydn: The Years of 'The creation'*, 1796–800. London: Thames and Hudson, 1977, p. 282.

Elsewhere, Landon writes in similar vein, placing the *Eroica* Symphony in its Haydn-Mozart context:

> 'It is obvious that it never occurred to Haydn (or Mozart) to enlarge the size and scope of the symphony as Beethoven was to do with the *Eroica*: but by applying symphonic principles to the mass form, Haydn was able to create a new

> kind of symphony written for the glory of God (and the name-day of Princess Esterházy) and greatly increasing the "orchestra" of the work by having a choir as well. In a way, Haydn's problem was Beethoven's (and everyone's, moreover, after 1805): what could a symphonist do after having composed a *Prague* or E flat (K. 543), *Jupiter* or G minor (K. 503)? A symphony in B flat (No. 102) or a *Drum Roll*, a *Clock* or *London*? Or, indeed, a First or Second Symphony by Beethoven? Beethoven wrote the *Eroica*, Haydn wrote the *Nelson* Mass; and both wielded musical power in an unprecedented fashion.'

H. C. Robbins Landon, *Haydn: Chronicle and Works: Haydn, the Late Years, 1801–1809*. Bloomington: Indiana University Press, 1977, p. 134.

Writing of the *Eroica* Symphony more generally, Landon elaborates:

> '1804 was the year of the *Eroica*, the work which more than any other except Beethoven's own Ninth, changed the history of the symphony. Its huge size – twice the length of any Haydn or Mozart symphony – and vast complexity, made it more than problematical for many of Beethoven's contemporaries. Up to now, with very few exceptions, Beethoven's compositions had been almost unmitigatedly successful; with the *Eroica*, Beethoven began to move forward faster than many of his contemporaries could comprehend. Yet even the most difficult of

Beethoven's compositions, such as the last string quartets, always had their staunch admirers.'

H. C. Robbins Landon, *Beethoven: His Life, Work and World.* London: Thames and Hudson, 1992, p. 108.

ERNEST MARKHAM LEE

Ernest Markham Lee was an English composer, author, lecturer, pianist and organist whose engagingly readable *The Story of the Symphony* (1916) endeared itself to many music lovers and helped them to become acquainted with the symphonic repertoire of the period. Lee introduces his discussion of the *Eroica* Symphony by stating:

'Beethoven was not a composer who made much use of titles for his music ... But for his Third Symphony, which stands in E flat (Op. 55), he used the title *Eroica*, Although its date of composition does not stand very far away from that of the Second Symphony, it marks an enormous step forward, not only by reason of its length but by virtue of its glorious themes and the superb beauty of its musical thought, which allow it to remain, more than a hundred years after its composition, as one of the masterpieces of musical creativeness.

'The *Eroica* will always stand out amongst symphonies by reason of its mighty strength, its marked individuality and beauty, and its historical significance. Beethoven took for the theme of his tone-painting a subject of no mean order — the grandeur of Napoleon, the soldier and emancipator of his century. It is well known how angry

> the composer was when he heard later that Napoleon had assumed the title of Emperor, and how hastily he tore off the title page of his manuscript in disgust. The music, however, remains to us as an imperishable monument to Beethoven's genius. The heroic mould is preserved throughout, and the subsequent dedication "to the memory of great man" is pathetic, and at the same time appropriate.'

Ernest Markham Lee, *The Story of the Symphony*. London: Scott Publishing Co., 1916, pp. 50–51.

LEWIS H. LOCKWOOD

Lewis H. Lockwood is an American musicologist recognised for being one of the foremost authorities on Beethoven. His studies of the composer include: *The Creative Process* (1992), *Music and Life* (2003), *The String Quartets* (2008), *The Eroica Sketchbook* (2013), *The Symphonies* (2015), and studies of Beethoven's contemporaries – *Beethoven's Lives* (2020). It is a measure of Lockwood's standing that he was invited to contribute a chapter to Alan Tyson's *Beethoven Studies* series. In this he opens his account stating:

> 'Surely no other Beethoven symphony – not even the Fifth or Ninth – has evoked a wider flood of commentary, whether in the vein of biography historical, analytical, or broadly interpretive. In the vein of biography, one could fill an anthology with variants on the thesis, by now the most obvious of common-places that this Symphony marks a decisive turning point in Beethoven's development. Wagner, whose published remarks

on the *Eroica* are only outnumbered by his writings on the Ninth, regarded the *Eroica* as the first work which Beethoven thrust forward in what was to be his own fully individual direction. [Richard Wagner, *Beethoven, Programme Notes for the Eroica* Symphony, Vol. 9, Leipzig, 1914] Equally canonic by now is the famous episode in which Beethoven abandoned the dedication of the Symphony on receiving news of Napoleon's imperial ascendency ... [Alan] Tyson suggests that the work forms part of a crucially important output, and definable segment of Beethoven's creative growth, from about 1801 (and his first accommodation to his growing deafness) to the completion of the first *Leonora* in 1805. In this "heroic" phase, as Tyson calls it, Beethoven finds his way to the realisation of heroic themes on oratorio and opera, with the *Eroica* as a monumental mid-point in this tremendous development. *Prometheus* and *Christus am Ölberge* lie before it; the explicit affirmation of personal redemption and political freedom in *Leonora* comes directly after.' [The reference to Alan Tyson is: 'Beethoven's Heroic Phase', *Musical Times*, cx, 1969, pp. 139–41]

Lewis Lockwood, *'Eroica', Perspectives and Design* in: Alan Tyson editor, *Beethoven Studies 3*. Cambridge: Cambridge University Press, 1982, pp. 85–86.

NICHOLAS MARSTON
Nicholas Marston is Professor of Music Theory and Analysis in the Faculty of Music, King's College, Cam-

bridge. He includes the study of Beethoven manuscripts amongst his research interests. He wrote the notes to accompany John Eliot Gardner's recording of the *Eroica* Symphony, remarking:

> 'While the first edition, published in 1806, declared this to be a "Heroic Symphony composed to celebrate the memory of a great man", the *Eroica* was entitled *Bonaparte* before Napoleon declared himself emperor and thereby famously incurred Beethoven's pro-republican wrath. Yet many listeners will deem the "great man" to be Beethoven himself: for the *Eroica* is one of the most astonishing pieces ever written, and one which profoundly affected the subsequent history of music.
>
> 'The main compositional work took place in 1803, but it now seems that the earliest sketches were made around autumn 1802, after Beethoven had finished sketching the Piano Variations Op. 35. The connection is highly significant, for the *Eroica* finale is based on a theme used in Op. 35: a theme, moreover, whose ancestry recedes further, through the Contradanse WoO 14, No. 7, and the ballet music *Die Geschöpfe des Prometheus.*'

Marston remarks on the contemporary music that may have been a source of influence on Beethoven when he composed the *Eroica* Symphony which, however, he asserts 'does not prejudice its overwhelming novelty':

> 'For example, the influence of French revolutionary hymns and band music stands behind much of its rhetoric. This influence is especially relevant

to the funeral march which forms the slow movement. Beethoven had in fact written a "Funeral march on the death of a Hero" in his Piano Sonata Op. 26 of 1800–01, but the gestures of that movement seem wholly conventional compared to the *Eroica* march, with its concluding and highly suggestive fragmentation of the main theme.'

He summates:

'Each movement of the *Eroica* holds some special feature of interest – from a purely sonorous point of view, the writing for three horns in the third-movement Trio represents a departure from the first two symphonies – but it is the first which most immediately signals Beethoven's unilateral declaration of a new mode of symphonic thought.'

Nicholas Marston, Liner notes accompanying the recording of the *Eroica* Symphony by the *Orchestre Révolutionnaire et Romantique* conducted by John Eliot Gardner, 1994.

Elsewhere Marston writes:

'It was with the *Eroica* ... that Beethoven changed the nature of the symphony once and for all. One of the first and most characteristic products of what has been termed Beethoven's "heroic phase" (Tyson, 1969) – a phase notable for the composition of uncompromising works on the largest scale, often bound up with extra-musical ideas – the *Eroica* was far larger and more complex than any symphony previously written. All this is certainly true of the huge first movement with its wealth of thematic material and remarkable tonal breadth (a theme which may be derived from the opening subject, but which is to all intents and purposes new, appears in the remote key of E minor in the development).'

Nicholas Marston, [The] *Symphonies* in: Barry Cooper, *The Beethoven Compendium: A Guide to Beethoven's Life and Music.* London: Thames and Hudson, 1991, p. 214.

BOHUSLAV MARTINU

In the summer of 1944 the Czech composer Bohuslav Martinů was exiled in America and was longing for, and concerned over, his native homeland. He sought refuge and solace by Lake Winneepesukee in New Hampshire where he leaned of the landing of the Allied troops in Normandy. Already at work on his Third Symphony, this news filled him with spirit and fulfilment and emboldened him to complete the work. Writing of the Symphony he remarks:

> 'The Third Symphony is my pride ... It is tragic in tone and I was sick for home when I wrote it. It consists of three movements and has a very real symphonic pattern ... The pattern I had in mind was Beethoven's *Eroica.* I look upon it as my first real symphony. It is the only one that was written to order. I wrote it from the heart, as an offering to the Boston Symphony Orchestra.'

Milos Safránek, *Bohuslav Martinů, His Life and Works.* London: Allan Wingate, 1962, pp. 236–37.

ADOLF BERNHARD MARX

Adolf Bernhard Marx made significant contributions to music criticism in his role as editor of the influential periodical *Allgemeine musikalische Zeitung*. He was an admirer of Beethoven's music and paid homage to him in his *Ludwig van Beethoven: Leben und Schaffen*, (Berlin, 1859). In this he devoted no fewer than 33 pages to an account of the *Eroica* Symphony. He opens his discourse with rhetorical questions and enlarges on what Beethoven and his music meant to him:

> 'What did Beethoven want? What could he give? Simply a composition of great and noble design? So, our aestheticians would advise him — those aestheticians, old and new, who see music only as a play of forms, who expect only the most generalized evocation of unspecified feelings, since it is incapable of "expressing the concrete". Beethoven had a different point of view. As an artist, he could do nothing with lifeless abstractions; to create life, life from out of his own life, was his calling, as it is for all artists. The artist knows what his art is capable of; he before all others; he alone.'

As quoted in: Robin Wallace, *Beethoven's Critics: Aesthetic Dilemmas and Resolutions during the Composer's Lifetime*. Cambridge; New York: Cambridge University Press, 1986, p. 47.

DENNIS MATTHEWS

Denis Matthews is remembered by many primarily for being a concert pianist with a particular liking for the music of the first Viennese school, notably that of Haydn, Beethoven and Schubert. However, in his role as professor of music at the University of Newcastle (1971—81), he wrote extensively about Beethoven, inspiring a younger generation thereby. Writing of the greatness of Beethoven he remarks:

> 'Beethoven sought, above all, independence: his greatest teacher was to be his own experience. It taught him early on that enduring art must satisfy in opposite, complementary ways. There is the emotional impact of music — "from the heart to the heart" [Beethoven's words]— but there is also the desire to satisfy the mind and to arrange ideas in their most potent form. Call it, if you like, the architectural quality of music. Even the unskilled listener senses when a piece is well made, because the composer's struggle with form forces him to channel and to crystallize his thoughts.'

Denis Matthews, *Beethoven, Piano Sonatas*, London: British Broadcasting Corporation, 1967, p. 11.

Writing of the influence of French revolutionary-style music on Beethoven's own compositional outlook, Matthews remarks:

> 'The new French "revolutionary" style, touched on with reference to *Leonore*, did not only leave its mark on opera: its influence can be felt on a good deal of Beethoven's instrumental music, even the three Marches for piano duet, Op. 45 that he wrote in 1802 and 1803. It showed expectedly in a work originally intended for Bonaparte: in the

rousing martial tuttis of the *Eroica*, in the fanfare of horns in the Trio and the Scherzo, and the apotheosis of the opening theme itself, far transcending its amusing kinship with the Overture to Mozart's *Bastien et Bastienne*.'

Denis Matthews, *Beethoven, Master Musicians*. London: J. M. Dent, 1985, pp. 37–38.

WILFRID MELLERS

The English musicologist and composer Wilfrid Mellers places Beethoven as a figure in history and one who made history:

'No work of art can be "explained" by reference to its historical connotations. Every artist self-evidently "reflects" the values and beliefs of his time ... At the same time, any truly creative artist is also making those beliefs. It is true that we cannot fully understand Beethoven without understanding the impulses behind the French Revolution. It is equally true that we cannot fully understand the French Revolution without some insight into Beethoven's music. We can see in his music those elements which are conditioned by his time (for they could not be otherwise) and yet are beyond the topical and local. Beethoven is a point at which the growth of the mind shows itself. He is a part of history: and also of the human spirit making history.'

Wilfrid Howard Mellers and Alec Harman, *Man and his Music*, London, Barrie and Jenkins, 1988, pp. 575–6.

Mellers considers Beethoven's progress along his self-imposed *New Path*:

> 'This process starts in the work which Beethoven began to conceive at Heiligenstadt, though he did not complete it until some years later. His first two symphonies contain anticipations of his later technique, while being based on classical principles. They are insignificant compared with the greatest works of Haydn and Mozart, though fascinating as the creation of a young man of revolutionary genius working within an established tradition. But the Third Symphony is a new kind of music; and we can learn something about the nature of its newness from the sketchbooks in which Beethoven recorded the gradual shaping of his thoughts.
>
> 'Of no composition did he leave more copious annotations than the *Eroica* Symphony, which he was well aware was a key-point in his development — and in that of European music.'

Wilfrid Howard Mellers, *The Sonata Principle (from c. 1750)*, London: Rockliff, 1957, p. 61.

YEHUDI MENUHIN

Although Yehudi Menuhin will be forever associated with the legendary recording he made of the Elgar Violin Concerto (HMV 1932), performed at the age of sixteen, for many it is his association with the Beethoven Violin Concerto that his lasting fame endures. *Menuhin was more than a violinist of course. He has been described as a philoso-*

pher, visionary, humanist, and music's ambassador to the world — he was nominated 'UNESCO Ambassador of Goodwill, 1992'. In conversation with Robin Daniels, the healer and Jungian analyst, Menuhin remarked on the singular nature of making a first-encounter with something very special:

> 'We can never recapture the first hour, the first day, of meeting a loved one or of being introduced to a great work of art, but *deep* acquaintance only comes after many years: so much is yielded which is not apparent in the beginning.
>
> 'The very first time I heard the *Eroica* Symphony, the very first time I heard the *St. Matthew Passion* — they were outstanding moments in my life. I will never forget them. I was amazed that music could throb with such power and meaning, such exaltation.
>
> 'Some of the first encounters has remained. I heard the *Eroica* many times subsequently, conducted by Toscanini and other notable Beethoven interpreters, and then I looked forward to the time when I would conduct it myself, which I did a year or so ago. [Menuhin is referring to sometime in the mid 1970s] Each successive acquaintance brings back something of the first hearing. I am happy to live my life in the friendship of the great works of Beethoven, Bach, Bartók — all the time learning.'

Robin Daniels, *Conversations with Menuhin*. London: Macdonald General Books, 1979, p. 80.

In his Autobiography *Unfinished Journey*, Menuhin recalls

hearing the *Eroica* Symphony for the first time — this was during a visit to Paris:

> 'As might be supposed, Parisian concerts widened and deepened my knowledge of music. Several times we went to the *Opéra Comique*, once or twice the *Opéra* itself, sitting way up in the gallery and finding the experience tremendously exciting. Apart from the opera there were many concerts, of course, but the detail of them is obliterated now by the glory of the *Eroica* Symphony, first heard in the *Salle Gaveau* under Paul Paray's direction. I must have heard more than one Beethoven symphony in San Francisco; I had never heard the *Eroica*, and its meaning, its power, its capacity to move were a revelation. Not being tall enough to sit clear of the velvet-covered balustrade in front of the seats, I lodged my chin on the velvet, and so remained, literally transfixed from start to finish. It was a landmark in my life, balanced a year or so ago by the exaltation of conducting the *Eroica* myself.'

Yehudi Menuhin, *Unfinished Journey*. London: Macdonald and Jane's, 1977, p. 76.

PAUL MIES

Although having a scholarly grounding in mathematics and physics, Paul Mies is better known as a musicologist and, in particular, to Beethovenians, for his study and analysis of the composer's sketches. Writing in a more general capacity, in the *New Oxford History of Music*, Mies positions the length (duration) of the *Eroica* Symphony within the wider context of Beethoven's developing expansive musical-scale and that which he inherited from his predecessors:

> 'Length has its reasons; it is not by chance that the monothematic movements of baroque music are usually short. So it is with the symphonic writing of the eighteenth century. A long work must draw on different, in some respects also ampler, resources in order to avoid boredom and long-windedness. Mozart and Haydn had developed the means suitable to build their immortal masterpieces; Beethoven's stylistic and artistic progress consisted in the expansion and enrichment of these resources and their combination with his own spirit. This step-by-step expansion of old resources, and the employment of new ones, set the seal on Beethoven's unique development, the origins of which are apparent even in his early works. Expansion of resources necessarily led to expansion of forms, though he left their essentials untouched.'

Paul Mies, *Beethoven's Orchestral Works* in: *The Age of Beethoven, The New Oxford History of Music*, Vol. VIII, Gerald Abraham, editor, 1988, pp. 132–33.

ANTON NEUMAYR

Anton Neumayr, a graduate of the Salzburg Conservatory of Music and a doctor of internal medicine, has made clinically informed diagnoses of Beethoven's many illnesses and their influence on his wellbeing and demeanour. Writing of the crisis the composer was undergoing at the period of composition of the *Eroica* Symphony, and other contemporaneous works, he remarks:

> 'From the fall [autumn] of 1802, Beethoven was totally caught up in his artistic activities once more. At practically the same time that he was putting his wounded heart's cries of pain on paper in Heiligenstadt, his pleasant, light-hearted Second Symphony (in D major, Op. 36) was being born, a symphony that does not betray the slightest hint of depression. This work is evidence that the Heiligenstadt Testament fundamentally reflected a fleeting moment when Beethoven's depression had reached its lowest point, and that the act of writing out his thoughts was essentially a conscious acknowledgment, an act of self-therapy by which he sought to free himself from the depression racking his soul. The sunlit, joyous nature of the Second Symphony shows that he attained his therapeutic goals of being able to work steadily again, unencumbered by the course of his hearing difficulties, and of being governed by patience.
>
> 'Dramatic proof that Beethoven's creative powers remained intact is revealed by the fact that he now found time to compose a group of important sonatas — the Violin Sonata in A major (the *Kreutzer*, Op. 37) in 1803, the Piano Sonata in C major (the *Waldstein*, Op. 53) and the *Appassionata* (in F minor, Op. 57) in 1804 — in the same period when he was working on the Third Symphony (the *Eroica*, in E flat, Op. 55) and his Opera *Fidelio*. The mental resilience that enabled him to overcome his depression also

freed enormous impulses that led to the development of a new style in his compositional art.'

Anton Neumayr, *Music and Medicine*. Bloomington, Illinois: Medi-Ed Press, 1994–97, p. 249.

ERNEST NEWMAN

The English music critic and musicologist Ernest Newman has been described as 'the most celebrated British music critic in the first half of the 20th century' (*Grove's Dictionary of Music and Musicians*). He was music critic for the *Sunday Times* for almost forty years. In his many writings and articles he makes occasional reference to Beethoven, including the following:

> 'Fate seems to have shaped [Beethoven] with the conscious and deliberate hand of an artist bending a mass of inchoate material to the realization of his own. It pruned him as a horticulturist prunes a tree, destroying a dozen shoots that one may bear richer fruit. [A reference to Beethoven's tireless rejection of one musical idea in search of a superior one.] We can only dimly speculate on what would have become of him had not disease laid her ugly and terrible hand on him.'

Ernest Newman, *Testament of Music: Essays and Papers*, London: Putnam, 1962, p. 279.

Writing in the *Sunday Times* of 17 February 1929, Newman discussed Beethoven, with reference to the *Eroica* Symphony, in the context of prevailing music criticism:

'The only composer who has been at all adequately studied is Beethoven, the reason being that only in his case have we sufficient documents (his sketch books are particularly valuable) that throw light on the structure of his musical faculty. But even the mind of Beethoven still holds mysteries for us. Personally, I have no further use for the kind of Beethoven criticism that ranges in merely literary fashion over his music, telling us, with more-or-less eloquence, how that music affected the writer, which philosophy, of course he innocently proceeds to attribute to Beethoven himself. My contention is that three-fourths of what is written about Beethoven is "literature", not music. Misled by this or that story from his life, our writers read something into the music that is not really there. They would never have discovered, or thought they had discovered, these things had all the records of Beethoven's life perished the day he had died. They form a certain conception of him from the story of his life, and then innocently proceed to foist that conception upon his music ... Think of all the rhapsodical nonsense, for example, that has been written about the *Eroica* — simply because circumstances have put the idea of a hero into the writer's hands; yet a physiology [Newman's term for the 'intensive study of the music'] of Beethoven's style would show that in the *Eroica* he is merely obeying certain *musical* impulses that are so fundamental in him as to be equally apparent, on analysis, in most other works of his early and middle periods.'

Ernest Newman, *From the World of Music: Essays from The Sunday Times'* London: J. Calder, 1956, pp. 24—25.

MARGARET NOTLEY

The American musicologist and educator Margaret Notley discusses the influence of Beethoven's instrumental music on that of other composers:

> 'Beethoven made instrumental music seem to matter as it had not before. Charles Ives interpreted the "oracle" at the beginning of the Fifth Symphony as "the soul of humanity at the door of the divine mysteries, radiant in the faith that it will be opened — and the human become the divine", because the music apparently struck him, as it has many of the rest of us, with the vividness of revelation. Like the opening of the Fifth Symphony, the fusion of introduction and first theme in the Ninth, the point of recapitulation in the *Eroica*, and the interconnectedness of the C-sharp minor Quartet all have an aura of compelling significance. Ives chose to claim a portion of Beethoven grandeur for American culture and himself by placing the Fifth Symphony's motto at the centre of a theme in the *Concord* Sonata. And, indeed, much of music history after Beethoven reads as a series of engagements — aggressive, inspired, ironic, elegiac — with his greetings and the potential that he had revealed.'

Notley exemplifies her thesis by citing the influence of the *Eroica* Symphony on the music of Arnold Schoenberg:

'For his vast, yet motivically dense one-movement String Quartet in D minor, Op. 7 (completed in 1985), Schoenberg himself cited Beethovenian models in the C-sharp minor Quartet and first movement of the *Eroica*. Schoenberg wrote that the [Beethoven] Quartet had inaugurated "the period of greatly expanded forms", which allowed no breaks between movements yet still encompassed "all the four characters" of tradition. And because the "great expansion" of form in his D minor Quartet required careful organization, he had kept the *Eroica* movement at hand to help him deal with fundamental problems in composition: "how to avoid monotony and emptiness; how to create variety out of unity; how to create new forms out of basic material; how much can be achieved by slight modifications if not by developing variation out of often rather insignificant little formulations".'

Margaret Notley, *With Beethoven-like Sublimity: Beethoven in the Works of other Composers* in: Glenn Stanley editor, *The Cambridge Companion to Beethoven*. Cambridge; New York: Cambridge University Press, 2000, p. 239 and p. 245.

RICHARD OSBORNE

Richard Osborne has written extensively about music and was a former presenter for BBC Radio 3. He contributed the chapter *Beethoven* to Robert Layton's *Guide to the Symphony* from which he has the following to say about the *Eroica* Symphony:

'It is not ... the last two movements, or even the great Funeral March, that makes the *Eroica* Symphony the towering and innovatory thing it is. It is the monumental first movement, and the huge shadows it casts, that give the work its formidable importance and force of character. Certainly, no single symphonic movement seems to have been worked on by Beethoven as assiduously as this ... .'

'Hans Keller once observed that even nowadays, when we hear the opening notes of the work, we realize instinctively that nothing remotely like this had been heard before. We also realize instinctively that we are dealing with music on a huge scale. The first movement of the *Eroica* is the longest opening movement in the cycle of the Nine and the longest of all Beethoven's symphonic movements apart from the Ninth's choral finale. Initially, its sheer length (691 bars) caused Beethoven to have second thoughts about the inclusion of the exposition repeat that runs the grand total up to 846 bars, making the movement half as long again as the first movement of the mighty Ninth Symphony. But whatever contemporary faint-hearts might have preferred, Beethoven ultimately had no choice but to recognize that the movement's vast development, and the unprecedented length and sweep of its Coda, balance out a structure that had the idea of an exposition repeat built into it from the outset. In fact, structural balances apart, it does none of us any harm to hear the Symphony with the repeat in place simply because the exposition itself is so packed with detail and incident. Never before was Beethoven so obviously fired up at the start of a work, so determined to have his say. Equally, it is astonishing how almost every utterance serves the twin aim of advancing the argument at the same time sustaining the structure.'

Richard Osborne, *Beethoven* in: Robert Layton editor, *A Guide to the Symphony*. Oxford: Oxford University Press, 1995, p. 88–89.

HUBERT PARRY

Sir Charles Hubert Hastings Parry was a former pillar of the English musical establishment, occupying the professorship in music at the University of Oxford and later the headship of the Royal College of Music where his pupils included Vaughn Williams, Gustav Holst, Frank Bridge and John Ireland. From his substantial musical output, Parry is best remembered today for his choral song *Jerusalem* and his setting for the Coronation Anthem 'I was glad when they said unto me'. When Parry heard Beethoven's Fifth Symphony for the first time he enthused— adopting the public-school idiom of the period: 'Words cannot express the hopeless gloriousness of this old ruffian! Such a whacker! So tremendously massive!' Of the composer more generally, he remarked:

> '[Beethoven] is one of the few great creators of art whom a man, though he be ever so blessed with musical intelligence, may study for a lifetime and never exhaust.'

Jeremy C. Dibble, *Hubert H. Parry: His Life and Music*,

Oxford: Clarendon Press, 1992, pp. 50—1 and Anthony Boden, *The Parrys of the Golden Vale: Background to Genius*, London: Thames Publishing, 1998, 120—1.

The Austrian-born American writer David Ewen (1907-1985) was the author of many books about classical music, including *Composers of Today, Composers of Yesterday*, and *The Encyclopedia of Musical Masterpieces.* In another of his related works Ewen reproduces an extended article by Parry titled *Beethoven.* In the course of this, Parry writes:

> 'The Third of [Beethoven's] symphonies ... was the result of his feelings on the great questions at issue between kings and aristocracies on the one side, and peoples on the other. He had developed an immense admiration for Napoleon Bonaparte, who seemed to him the very ideal hero of the people. Napoleon's career had not yet arrived at the point when he appeared in his full lineaments as an insatiable conqueror, and the very impersonation of imperial attributes; he was still regarded as the supreme opposite of kings and monarchical traditions; to Beethoven he seemed to be the liberator of down-trodden peoples from old despotisms, and the benefactor who give new laws to the peoples of the world for the peoples' benefit and not for the advantage of despots or privileged aristocracies.
>
> 'In this mood he set about writing a symphony in his honour, and produced by far the grandest and longest and most powerful work of its kind that had ever appeared. It made altogether an epoch in the history of the symphony, for all the greatest works which had appeared before it

> were always mere shadows by its side in point of emotion and breadth and poetical interest. Many had been perfect in respect of artistic workmanship, and balance of beautiful form, but composers of the previous century had never even aimed at such degrees of force or such variety of interest.'

David Ewen, *From Bach to Stravinsky: The History of Music by its Foremost Critics*. New York, Greenwood Press, 1968, p. 123.

LEON B. PLANTINGA
The American musicologist Leon B. Plantinga has made a special study of the music of the later eighteenth and nineteenth centuries. His book writings include *Beethoven Concertos: History* (1999). In his more general survey titled *Romantic Music*, he discusses the *Eroica* Symphony within the context of the period of time that had passed since Beethoven had moved from Bonn to Vienna:

> 'In the works produced during this period of six years, the most salient features of Beethoven's "middle" style were established, and a standard, unassailable in its authority, was set for all composers of large-scale instrumental pieces for the rest of the nineteenth century and beyond. The *Eroica* Symphony, composed in 1803–04, may be considered the first of that series of imposing monuments that so inspired and intimidated Beethoven's followers. Heroic in its physical proportions, this was without precedent in rhythmic energy, in the scope of its developmental

procedures, and in its protracted building of powerful climaxes.'

Leon Plantinga, *Romantic Music: A History of Musical Style in Nineteenth-Century Europe.* New York; London: Norton, 1984, p. 38.

ROMAIN ROLLAND

Notwithstanding his celebrity as a philosopher, dramatist, novelist, essayist, art historian and Nobel Laureate (prize for literature in 1915), Romain Rolland wrote extensively on music and was appointed to the first chair of music history at the Sorbonne in 1903. His passion for music — he was an accomplished pianist — found expression in several studies of Beethoven who for Rolland was 'the universal musician above all the others'. His writings about the composer and his works include: *Beethoven and Handel* (1917); *Goethe and Beethoven* (1930); and *Beethoven the Creator* (1937). Rolland made an extensive study of Beethoven's sketches for the *Eroica* Symphony — styled in his characteristic word-imagery. His text, together with musical illustrations, extends to forty pages from which we quote the following:

> 'Let us brush from our path, first of all, the too simple anthropomorphic explanation that builds on the title — "Bonaparte" — that Beethoven first of all wrote on the Title Page and then tore out. In a mind like that of Beethoven, wholly absorbed in itself, its passions, its combats, and its God, the external world counts merely as a reflection, an echo, a symbol of the interior drama. Moreover, Beethoven is incapable of seeing the life of other beings as it is; his own is

too vast; for him it is the measure of everything; he projects it into everything. Other artists, such as Mozart and Haydn, who are less preoccupied with themselves, find room within themselves for the observation of the external world. Mozart takes other souls to himself: Haydn has a shrewd eye for them, and a roguish touch. Beethoven scarcely ever emerges from himself; but this Self is a universe. Even the exterior nature that he sees becomes immediately incorporated with it, loses its own character, takes the form and the odour of the Beethoven cosmos.'

Rolland, Romain. *Beethoven the Creator.* Garden City, New York: Garden City Pub., 1937, pp. 79—80.

CHARLES ROSEN

Charles Rosen was celebrated for being one of America's foremost pianists and was also respected for his writings on music, notably his much-praised *The Classical Style.* In this he makes reference to the *Eroica* Symphony:

'The first of Beethoven's immense expansions of classical form is the *Eroica* Symphony, finished in 1804 the same year that produced the *Waldstein* Sonata. The Symphony, much longer than any work in that form that preceded it, provoked some displeasure at its first public performance. The critics complained of its inordinate length, and protested against the lack of unity in this most unified of works.

'The public, indeed, seems to have been ill-natured at the first performance and the work immediately divided its hearers into two furiously opposed factions. Not only the bitterness of the criticism, but its nature remind one of more recent attacks on what is thought to be the *avant garde*: one critic wrote, "Beethoven's music could soon reach a point where one would derive no pleasure from it unless well trained in the rules and difficulties of the art, but would rather leave the concert hall ... crushed by a mass of unconnected and overloaded ideas and a continuing tumult by all the instruments".' [Rosen is quoting here from the pages of the contemporary journal *Allgemeine musikalische Zeitung*]

Rosen identified with the perplexity felt by the members of the audience hearing the *Eroica* Symphony for the first time:

'It is understandable that the Symphony was found so difficult, as the extension of the range of hearing in time is remarkable: the dissonant C sharp in the seventh measure finds its full meaning only much later at the opening of the recapitulation, when it becomes a D flat and leads to an F major horn solo; yet the unprecedented scope of modulation in the development is carried out without the slightest diffusion of the sense of tonal unity; above all, the proportions are firmly defined.'

Charles Rosen, *The Classical Style: Haydn, Mozart, Beethoven*, London: Faber and Faber, 1976, pp. 392–94.

GIOACHINO ROSSINI

It had long been the wish of the Italian composer Gioachino Rossini to meet Beethoven whose music, although so radically different to his own, he so much admired. He had first heard string quartets by Beethoven performed when he was in Milan and admired them greatly. He was also familiar with some of the composer's piano compositions. But it was hearing a performance of the *Eroica* Symphony that resolved him to visit Beethoven. 'That music', Rossini relates, 'bowled me over. I had only one thought: to meet that great genius, to see him, even if only once.'

The opportunity finally came in 1822 when Rossini was in Vienna – where his operas were all the rage. Their success was to stir the young Franz Schubert to write his Overture *In The Italian Style*. Rossini was finally able to arrange a meeting with Beethoven through the help of his fellow countryman Giuseppe Carpani – who knew Beethoven and before him Salieri and Haydn, to all of whom he had served as poet and translator.

Of his meeting with Beethoven, Rossini recalls:

> 'As I went up the stairs leading to the poor lodging's in which the great man lived, I had some difficulty in containing my emotions. When the door opened, I found myself in a sort of hovel, so dirty as to testify to frightening disorder.'

Rossini recognised Beethoven from the portraits he had already seen of him. He refers to 'the indefinable sadness spread across all his features' but whose eyes 'though small appeared to pierce you'. Beethoven congratulated Rossini for being the composer of *Il Barbiere di Siviglia* and encouraged him to work at his chosen vocation: 'You

Italians. Your language and your vivacity of temperament destine you for it.'

As recalled by Edmond Michotte, *Richard Wagner's Visit to Rossini* (Paris 1860): and, *An Evening at Rossini's in Beau-Sejour* (Passy), 1858, English translation: Chicago; London: University of Chicago Press, 1982, pp. 40–4, p. 49 and p. 52.

STEPHEN RUMPH

The American musicologist and academic Stephan Rumph positions Beethoven in the context of the politics of his time:

> 'Beethoven was a political composer. Like few other musicians in the Western canon, he stubbornly dedicated his art to the problems of human freedom, justice, progress, and community. Beethoven found his voice with a cantata memorializing the enlightened reforms of Joseph II, and he crowned his public career in Vienna with the Ninth Symphony's hymn to universal brotherhood. No intervening work drew more labour or revisions from him than *Fidelio* (née *Leonora*), the first political opera to remain in the permanent repertory ... The political note in Beethoven's music echoes the cataclysmic times in which he lived ... While Napoleon was gathering laurels in Italy and Egypt, Beethoven was conquering the salons and halls of Vienna, undertaking a deliberate campaign to annex all current musical genres.'

Rumph considers the reputation of the *Eroica* Symphony

may have overshadowed certain of the underlaying musical aspects of the *Pastoral* Symphony:

> 'The touchstone for Beethoven's early ideology remains the *Eroica* Symphony, namesake and glory of the heroic age. A host of political interpretations has marched alongside the Third Symphony for nearly two centuries now. Each generation, from Beethoven's age to our own, has wrung new meaning out of the Napoleonic dedication, the French Revolutionary march, and the "heroic" title. The critic who would join this long parade might well despair of finding any unturned stone, any unbeaten path. Yet one source seems to have escaped attention, a related work that at first seems wholly removed from political concerns – the Sixth Symphony. This mildest offspring of Beethoven's heroic impulse has rested in the shade of its more bellicose siblings, disarming political criticism with its motley country charms. Nevertheless, the *Pastoral* quietly preserves the legacy of the *Eroica*, pointing to a level of meaning more telling than all talk of emperors, battlefields, or even heroes.'

Rumph amplifies his outlook with reference to the contemporary writings of Friedrich von Schiller and the Enlightenment protagonist Jean-Jacques Rousseau – but which are outside the scope of our selection of writings. Returning to a consideration of the *Eroica* Symphony he maintains:

> 'Regarding the *Eroica* from the perspective of 1803, it seems dubious that Beethoven intended

anything even vaguely militaristic. Excepting the funeral march, the thematic material uniformly inhabits the same naïve world as the *Pastoral* ... Of course, the *Eroica* evokes a more violent, dynamic experience of nature than the *Pastoral* — something obviously inspired by all the battlefield narratives. And this leads to a crucial distinction. The tremendous dissonant energies of the *Eroica*, especially in the third movement, do indeed evoke a heroic chaos. But unlike the mood of the Fifth Symphony or *Coriolanus*, this ethos arises not from the nature of the themes, but solely from the manner of their development. The *Eroica* is pastoral in essence, heroic in actions; naïve in matter, sentimental in manner.'

Stephen C. Rumph, *Beethoven after Napoleon: Political Romanticism in the Late Works*, Berkeley; London, University of California Press, 2004, pp. 1–2, p. 58 and p. 76.

CAMILLE SAINT-SAËNS

The French composer, organist, conductor and pianist Camille Saint-Saëns was one of the most remarkable musical child prodigies in history. At the age of five he performed to private audiences and when age ten made his public debut in Paris at the Salle Pleyel. His programme included Mozart's Piano Concerto in B flat, K450 and Beethoven's Third Piano Concerto. Most remarkably, Saint-Saëns played from memory. At the close of the concert he offered to give as an encore any of the Beethoven Piano sonatas! At over the age of sixty he repeated the offer at a concert to the musical elect of Madrid. Towards the end of his long life (86), Saint-Saëns maintained diligent morning practice by performing scales and arpeggios — relieving what he considered to be the tedium by simultaneously reading the morning newspaper that he placed on the piano's music rack!

Adapted, in part, from James Harding, *Saint-Saëns and his Circle*, London: Chapman & Hall, 1965, p. 18.

Saint-Saëns held the Grand Cross of the Legion of Honour that entitled him to be laid to rest with full military honours. This was duly conferred with squadrons of cavalry accompanying the funeral cortège to the muted sounds of the *Eroica's Marcia funebre*.

Brian Rees, *Camille Saint-Saëns: A Life*. London: Chatto & Windus, 1999, p. i.

CLARA SCHUMAN

In her lifetime Clara Schuman was recognised for being one of the most accomplished pianists of her day. She received early instruction from her father who encouraged her to memorize the works she intended to perform in public — something of an innovation for the period. Clara came to public attention during the Vienna concert season 1837–38, when, still only eighteen, she gave a series of recitals that included such challenging pieces as Beethoven's *Appassionata* Sonata. Her marriage to her composer-husband Robert has, perhaps, unjustly, eclipsed Clara's own standing as a composer. On their wedding day Robert gave Clara a diary that now serves musicologists as a form of autobiography of their shared interests and accomplishments in music. (see, for example, Berthold Litzmann editor, Clara Schumann: *An Artist's Life, based on Material found in Diaries and Letters*. London: Macmillan; Leipzig: Breitkopf & Härtel, 2 Vols., 1913.) In her so-called *Marriage Diaries*, Clara records her impressions of hearing the *Eroica* Symphony at a concert given in October 1840:

'Finally, I heard a subscription concert again ... One is truly edified by such a Beethoven Symphony [*Eroica*]; the more I hear it the greater the enjoyment — no music other than this gets all my feelings stirred up. The performance was very good except for a few mistakes in the last movement, and if one missed Mendelssohn it was only visually, since one has grown used to seeing him on the podium ... The last movement of the *Eroica* has always seemed somewhat unclear to me, but that was due to the interpretation, for example, the one I heard in Berlin, where the various entrances of the theme did not merge clearly — this time, however, it all seemed much more understandable to me, particularly because it was executed so very exactly (except for the few mistakes mentioned above).'

Clara's diary entries for 1844 are revealing. Her standing as a pianist is evident when she records (21st November) performing Moscheles's E-flat major Piano Sonata for four hands with Mendelssohn. At the same concert Beethoven's incidental music to Goethe's *Egmont* was performed, disposing Clara to enthuse: 'I cannot describe the impression that this music made on me today! ... Never has this music ... affected me so deeply. Three days later she attended another concert that was directed by Mendelssohn. The principal item on the programme was the *Eroica* Symphony, of which she writes:

'Today I found the [funeral] march the most beautiful, sublime, grand, as always all of *Beethoven*. I have certain feelings for both of these two great masters, *Beethoven* and *Mozart*. [Clara's emphasis] *Mozart* I love tenderly, but *Beethoven* I worship like a god who always remains distant to us, however, who never becomes one of us.'

Gerd Nauhaus editor, *The Marriage Diaries of Robert and Clara Schumann*. London: Robson Books, 1994, p. 14 and pp. 181–82.

MARION SCOTT

Marion Scott studied violin and piano at the Royal College of Music and after graduating founded *The Marion Scott String Quartet*. Her great enthusiasm was to introduce contemporary music to London audiences, particularly that of Frank Bridge, Hubert Parry and Charles Villiers Stanford. However, Scott is primarily remembered today for her contribution to musicology. Her early writings were for such publications as *Music and Letters* and *The Musical Times* with her later, more substantial, researches appearing in *Grove's Dictionary of Music and Musicians*. She became a respected authority on the lives of Haydn and Mendelssohn but it is for her pioneering study of Beethoven with which Marion Scott's name will forever be mostly associated. This was published in 1934 by J. M. Dent & Sons, Ltd. as part of their *Music Masters Series*. It received both critical and public acclaim; testimony to its popularity is that it was republished many times. Through this publication Scott introduced many music lovers, the present writer included, to Beethoven's personal history and the circumstances surrounding the creation of his music. Her thoughtful insights also included reflections on the nature of his music that are still invoked by contemporary writers when discussing the intellectual and musicological perspectives of Beethoven's life and work. The influence of Scott's book may also be found in its subsequent transformations in the *Master Musicians Series* of publications, the first of which was under the authorship of Denis Matthews, and subsequently by Barry Cooper.

Writing of the Third Symphony, Scott gives her reasons for believing the Symphony to be 'heroic':

> 'The *Eroica* Symphony, Op. 55 was ... [Beethoven's] own favourite. The revolution it marked was so great that the distinguished critic, Dr. H. C. Colles, divides Beethoven's career simply into *pre-* and *post-Eroica*.' [Henry Cope Colles was an English music critic for *The Times*, a music lexicographer, and editor of the 3rd and 4th editions of Grove's *Dictionary of Music and Musicians*]
>
> 'In every way the Symphony is heroic. The themes, texture and treatments are superb, and though the movements are extremely long, their proportions are so fine that not one bar could be spared. They follow the order usual in a four-movement symphony: (1) an *allegro*, (2) slow movement, (3) scherzo and Trio, (4) finale; but their poetic contents so transform the scheme that the Symphony presents one of the profoundest problems in music. What Beethoven did was this: he wrote a glorious opening *allegro* and followed it with a funeral march for the slow movement. Thus, by the middle of the Symphony the hero had vanished from the scene. Yet Beethoven still went on, following the funeral march with a shimmering, resilient scherzo, and that in turn by

a set of variations on the dance theme from *Prometheus* [*Die Geschöpfe des Prometheus*, Op. 43] Thus, the Symphony divides, as it were, into two halves — the first noble and broad, weighted with majesty, courage, and grief; the second altogether lighter, brighter, more imponderable.'

In her summation, Scott in unequivocal:

'The *Eroica* Symphony is one of Beethoven's supreme works; it is one of the supreme treasures of the world. It remains to us as a spiritual woven signal for all nations, emblem of man, elate above death.'

Marion M. Scott, *Beethoven: The Master Musicians*. London: Dent, 1940, pp. 159—60 and p. 164.

GEORGE BERNARD SHAW

George Bernard Shaw's fame as a playwright and polemicist has eclipsed his reputation for being a discerning music critic. Eugene Gates, of the Faculty of the Royal Conservatory of Music, Toronto, writes: '[Shaw] was ... the most brilliant British music critic to emerge in the late-nineteenth century. His vision of the ideal critic was not a passive reporter of musical events, but rather a vital and initiating force within the music community.' (*Journal of Aesthetic Education*, Vol. 35, No. 3, 2001) Shaw was committed to the principle of making music criticism both intelligible and entertaining. To this end he invented the persona of *Corno di Bassetto* (in music, the basset horn) to serve as his spokesperson. Shaw's collected writings on music fill no fewer than three sturdy volumes:

Shaw was an accomplished amateur pianist and enjoyed playing piano reductions of Beethoven's symphonies with his sister. From his copious writings, we offer the following selection of abstracts, commencing with his estimation of Beethoven, the man and composer.

In the *Saturday Review* of 14 November 1896, Shaw wrote an article concerning the recently published *Beethoven and his Nine Symphonies* by George Grove (London and New York, Novello, Ewer & Co.). Of Beethoven, Shaw remarks:

> 'Beethoven was the first man who used music with absolute integrity as the expression of his own emotional life. Others had shown how it could be done — had done it themselves as a curiosity of their art in rare, self-indulgent, *unprofessional* moments — but Beethoven made this, and nothing else, his business. Stupendous as the resultant difference was between his music and any other ever heard in the world before his time, the distinction is not clearly apprehended to this day, because there was nothing new in the musical expression of emotion: every progression in Bach is sanctified by emotion; and Mozart's subtlety, delicacy, and exquisite tender touch and noble feeling were the despair of all the musical world. But Bach's theme was not himself, but his religion; and Mozart was always the dramatist and story-teller, making the men and women of his imagination speak, and dramatizing even the instruments in his orchestra, so that you know their very sex the moment their voices reach you. Haydn really came nearer to Beethoven, for he is neither the praiser of God nor the dramatist,

but, always within the limits of good manners and of his primary function as a purveyor of formal decorative music, a man of moods. This is how he created the symphony and put it ready-made into Beethoven's hands. The revolutionary giant at once seized it, and, throwing supernatural religion, conventional good manners, dramatic fiction, and all external standards and objects into the lumber room, took his own humanity as the material of his music, and expressed it all without compromise, from his roughest jocularity to his holiest aspiration after that purely human reign of intense life.'

George Bernard Shaw, cited in: Percy M. Young, *George Grove, 1820–1900: A Biography*, London: Macmillan, 1980, Appendix B.

In his reviews of Beethoven concerts, Shaw makes several references to the *Eroica* Symphony. We cite the most significant of these as they appeared in their chronological sequence. His early music reviews were published in *The Star*, London's foremost evening newspaper. On 15 February 1889, Shaw attended a concert given by the London Symphony Orchestra. Of particular interest is that this was the first time that Shaw wrote under the persona of *Corno di Bassetto*. He was not impressed by the performance of the *Eroica* Symphony:

> 'The first movement of the *Eroica* Symphony was being played; but as usual, it was going haphazard. The band had not really studied it with the conductor; and the conductor was taking his chance with the band ... Now, by this time we all

know the *Eroica* Symphony as well as we know *Hamlet* or *Macbeth*, and I, for one, am tired of scratch performances of it.'

Dan H. Laurence, editor, *Shaw's Music: The Complete Musical Criticism in Three Volumes*, London: Max Reinhardt, the Bodley Head, 1981, Vol. 1, p. 552.

Later in the year, on 13 May, Shaw had occasion to refer to a series of concerts performed in London under the direction of the celebrated Austrian-Hungarian conductor Hans Richter — renowned for his 'monumental' interpretations of symphonic music. The occasion in question coincided with the centenary of the onset of the French Revolution. Shaw responded:

'This week seems to be devoted to celebrating the French Revolution of 1789 which produced such an effect on music that it has never been the same since. I can bring the connection down to this very week; for the first musical product of the Revolution was the *Eroica* Symphony, utterly unlike anything that had ever been heard in the world before.'

Shaw was not able to attend the Richter concert at which the *Eroica* Symphony was performed and, therefore, left no account of it. This did not deter him, however, from expressing — in crushing, inimitable manner — his views, in general, of so-called, 'revolutionary music':

'I meditated on the Revolution music — on its grandioseness, splendidness, neuroseness, and sentationaloseness; on its effort, its hurry, its

> excitement, its aspiration without purpose, its forced and invariably disappointing climaxes, its exhaustion and decay, until in our own day everything that once was most strenuously characteristic of it seems old-fashioned, platitudinous, puerile, forcible-feeble, anything but romantic and original.'

George Bernard Shaw, *London Music in 1888—89:* as heard by *Corno di Bassetto*, London: Constable and Company, 1937, Vol.1, pp. 114—15.

The following year, Shaw heard a further rendering of the *Eroica* Symphony, this time with the Hallé Orchestra under the direction of its founder Sir Charles Hallé. Notwithstanding the celebrity of the conductor and his players, the occasion was marred for Shaw — and, by all accounts, for the rest of the audience — by the intrusive sounds of a military band playing quadrilles at the nearby St. James Restaurant. The experience drew from Shaw a characteristically withering response that duly appeared in the 8 February 1890 edition of *The Star*:

> '[We] came to those eloquent pauses between the last broken chords in the *Eroica* Symphony — pauses during which you can usually hear a pin drop. But last night it would have been necessary to let Cleopatra's Needle drop to overpower the wild strain of brazen minstresly that rushed through the room and double me up in my fancied safety.'

Dan H. Laurence editor, *Shaw's Music:* — see above, Vol. 1, p. 919.

In *The Star* the following week, Shaw gave his impressions of the Hallé's and Sir Charles' interpretation of the *Eroica* Symphony — he was none too satisfied with either:

> 'The *Eroica* Symphony is something besides a tone poem: much of it is excellent abstract music from the Cherubini-Anacreon point of view; and so it went along to the strains of its own funeral march, a very handsome corpse. The truth is that no man can conduct a Beethoven symphony unless his instincts are not only musical, but poetic and dramatic as well. Consequently, as Sir Charles is only a musician, the Manchester Orchestra has yet to experience the delights of really learning a Beethoven symphony.'

Dan H. Laurence, editor, *Shaw's Music:* — see above, Vol. 1, p. 924.

Towards the close of the nineteenth century, Shaw's music reviews appeared in *The World*, a London newspaper established in the mid-eighteenth century. In the issue of 22 February 1893, he reported on a concert given under the direction of the multi-talented Sir George Henschel — celebrated, variously, as composer, baritone, pianist, and conductor. Despite his reputation, his rendering of the *Eroica* Symphony did not measure up to Shaw's exacting standards:

> 'The *Eroica* ... suffered for a few moments in the middle of the last movement by expressive whipping up: otherwise it went admirably, especially in the funeral march, but always excepting the first movement, which we shall hear in its

glory, I suppose, when we get an orchestra of heroes to play it and a demigod to conduct it. Nothing will ever persuade me that Beethoven meant it to begin in a hurry, with the theme stumping along to catch the last train, and the syncopations in the fifth bar coming in like the gasps of a blown pedestrian.'

George Bernard Shaw, *Music in London*, 1890—94. London: Constable and Company Limited, 1932, Vol.2, p. 254.

ROBERT SIMPSON

Robert Simpson was a prolific English composer of eleven symphonies, fifteen string quartets, and four concertos, not to mention a great deal of other music written for various combinations of instruments. During his long service as a BBC producer and broadcaster, he gave talks on his favourite composers including Beethoven, Bruckner, Nielsen and Sibelius, about each one of whom he wrote an informed, scholarly monograph. His thoughts on Beethoven were published as, *Simpson on Beethoven: Essays, Lectures and Talks by R. Simpson, Selected and Edited by Lionel Pike*, 1996. From Simpson's *Beethoven Symphonies*, we quote the following:

'The fact that the *Eroica* is considerably longer than [Symphony] No. 2 is not the only sense in which it is larger. [Donald] Tovey has demonstrated how Beethoven, by introducing a sudden series of remarkable modulations into a very solid fugue in the *Gloria* of the Mass in D, creates a sense of expansion that is in fact caused by a contraction ... something of the kind in the finale of the Second Symphony. It is rather like the experience to be had in a small room when a window is suddenly opened to reveal a vast landscape. It is not necessary to explore the whole to appreciate this particular effect on the imagination; a glimpse is better. Beethoven's mastery of the inspired glimpse and in perfect timing is absolute; if we could count the instances of it in the *Eroica* we should see how much larger is the work than its physical dimensions, huge though they are.'

Robert Simpson, *Beethoven Symphonies*. London: British Broadcasting Corporation, 1970, p. 18.

THOMAS SIPE

In the introduction to his book-length study of the *Eroica* Symphony, Thomas Sipe states:

'The *Eroica* Symphony is one of the most discussed works of Beethoven. Its connection with Napoleon Bonaparte, its unprecedented design, and its powerful emotional impact have continually fascinated critics. Its success forever redefined the potential of symphonic expression, and it may be termed without exaggeration one of the most significant works in the entire history of Western music. Almost two centuries of reception have not dulled its effect [Sipe was writing in the late 1990s]; even if Beethoven's music has become familiar, his accomplishment still astonishes.

'Interpretive approaches to the *Eroica* have

ranged from programmatic accounts of Bonaparte to autobiographical accounts of Beethoven to abstract theoretical observations ... Beethoven's proposed dedication to Napoleon has never been satisfactorily explained [and] Beethoven's political acumen has been consistently neglected or misunderstood ... [The] connection with Bonaparte was profoundly formative for both the concept and structure of the Symphony. The epic-like opening movement, the borrowings from French revolutionary celebrations in the Funeral March, the quotation of a soldier's song in the *Scherzo*, and the allusion to the Ballet *Die Geschöpfe des Prometheus* [*The Creatures of Prometheus*] in the finale all have special "Napoleonic" significance ... Beethoven became disillusioned with Bonaparte the *man*, but never lost faith in the ideals the First Consul had inspired.'

Thomas Sipe, *Beethoven: Eroica Symphony*. Cambridge: Cambridge University Press, 1998, p. ix.

MAYNARD SOLOMON

The American musicologist Maynard Solomon has a reputation for being an authority on Beethoven. His work is characterised by a scholarly presentation of the available evidence and the construction of plausible hypotheses. Positioning Beethoven the Romantic, Solomon writes:

'It is common knowledge that Beethoven was a founder of the Romantic movement in music and that his works influenced most of the romantic composers and were models against which nineteenth-century romanticism measures its achievements and failures ... [During] his own lifetime, Beethoven was widely regarded as a radical modernist, whose modernism was seen sharply to have distinguished him from the classical standards established, in the main, by Mozart and Haydn. Of course, they too had their share of hostile notices before they were elevated to canonical status; but the classicizing critiques of Beethoven were too intense and pervasive to be regarded as merely the usual, provisional resistance to modifications of cultural traditions. His contemporaries – including many of his advocates – saw him as subverting classical principles and procedures, as radical iconoclastic, and eccentric. They did not regard him as an eighteenth-century composer.'

Maynard Solomon, *Beethoven: Beyond Classicism*, in: Robert Winter, and Robert Martin, editors *The Beethoven Quartet Companion*, Berkeley: University of California Press, 1994, p. 59 and pp. 70–1.

Of Beethoven's concept of heroism, as expressed in the *Eroica* Symphony, and his ambiguous relationship with the ideals of Napoleon Bonaparte, Solomon maintains:

'That Beethoven was capable of producing the ultimate musical definition of heroism ... is itself extraordinary, for he was able to evoke a dream of heroism which neither he nor his native Germany nor his adopted Vienna could express in reality. Perhaps we can only measure the heroism of the *Eroica* by the depths of fear and uncertainty from which it emerged.

'Beethoven regarded Bonaparte as an embodiment of enlightened leadership, but, simultaneously, he felt betrayed by Bonaparte's Caesaristic actions. Beethoven's ambivalence mirrored a central contradiction of his age. It is this contradiction that finds expression in the *Eroica* Symphony. The *Eroica* arose from the conflict between enlightened faith in the saviour/prince and the reality of Bonapartism ... As an artist and a man, Beethoven could no longer accept unmediated conceptions of progress, innate human goodness, reason, and faith. His affirmations were now leavened by an acknowledgement of the frailty of human leadership and consciousness of the negative and brutalizing components in all forward-thrusting stages in social revolution.'

In his summation of Beethoven's Op. 55, Solomon states:

'With Beethoven's ... *Eroica* Symphony, Op. 55, we know that we have crossed irrevocably a major boundary in Beethoven's development and in music history as well. The startling and unprecedented characteristics of the *Eroica* — and many of his subsequent major compositions — were to some degree made possible by Beethoven's perception of new possibilities inherent in the flexible framework of sonata form ... Apart from its extra-musical associations, its heroic stance, and its "grand manner", the *Eroica* Symphony marks Beethoven's turning to compositions of unprecedented ambition. He has now chosen to

work on a vastly expanded scale, twice the size of
the symphonic model that he had inherited from
Haydn and Mozart.'

Maynard Solomon, *Beethoven*, New York: Schirmer, 1977,
p. 141, p. 192 and p. 195.

WILLIAM PRESTON STEDMAN

In his survey *The Symphony*, the American academic, musicologist and music administrator William Preston Stedman positions the *Eroica* Symphony in its epochal context within the genre of symphonic composition:

'The *Eroica* represents a change in the basic nature of the symphony, a change that markedly affected the history of the symphony perhaps more than any other single work. While Beethoven's two earlier works gave some indications of the nature of this change, it was the *Eroica* which established a style-norm for his more expansive works. Whether or not Beethoven actually perfected the form of the symphony in the *Eroica* is not pertinent. What is important is that the *Eroica* and Fifth, Seventh and Ninth Symphonies crystalized a concept which has remained more-or-less intact to this date and thus became the single most influential group of symphonies in the history of the genre.

'Several concepts seem to permeate the *Eroica* to a much greater extent than they did the first two symphonies. Thematic material has a greater motivic unity within movements and within groups of themes in a movement. This creates a more highly articulated style than was apparent in the first two symphonies. Motives are easily extracted for further unification of the work in developmental passages. There is also a greater emphasis on counterpoint and imitation to extend and to develop. The contrapuntal development becomes quite complicated, as the double fugue in the second movement exemplifies. All movements are much longer, largely because of extended development, even in codas. The adoption of a much more complex variation style as a movement form in the Third Symphony. While Haydn used variation form for slow movements, Beethoven deemed the form appropriate for either slow or for fast movements.'

William Preston Stedman, *The Symphony*. Englewood Cliffs, New Jersey; London: Prentice-Hall, 1979, pp. 68–69.

MICHAEL P. STEINBERG

The American scholar Michael P. Steinberg is Professor of history, music and German studies at Brown University and was President of the American Academy in Berlin from March 2016 to August 2018. He has written at length about Beethoven, notably in collaboration with fellow American, the musicologist Scott G, Burnham (editors, *Beethoven and his World*, 2000.) In his study of the *Eroica* Symphony, Steinberg recalls the reception the work received in an early performance and how the music critic of the journal *Der Freymüfhinge* deplored Beethoven's manner of achieving 'a certain undesirable originality', and regarded the work's 'inordinate length' to be 'unendurable to the mere music-lover'. To this, Steinberg responds:

'Having no difficulty ourselves of finding the *Eroica* 'beautiful and sublime', we slip easily into a position of feeling superior to this critic. We would do well at this point to remember that we are not likely to find it 'unusual and fantastic' either — which, if so, is very much our loss. When it comes to maintaining a sense of the 'unusual and fantastic' or just of freshness, we are not much helped by conductors, particularly the ones whose attitude of reverence and awe before 'A Great Classic' leads them into *monumental* tempi at which the length of the work easily becomes *inordinate*, if not *unendurable*. Of course, the rare conductor of genius, like Furtwängler or Klemperer, can make a convincing case for a *monumental Eroica*. More valuable by far is the fiery performance — at Beethoven's tempi or something close to them — they can give us an experience like the one the audience in the Theater an der Wien in 1805 must have had, that of an electrifying, frightening encounter with revolution, with a force sufficient to blast doors and windows out of the room. Once in a while that happens, but it is rare. Too rare.'

Michael P. Steinberg, *The Symphony: A Listener's Guide*, Oxford University Press; Reprint edition, 1998, p. 13.

RICHARD STRAUSS

We learn of the high regard in which the youthful Richard Strauss held the *Eroica* Symphony from a letter he wrote to his childhood friend, the Austrian composer and music theorist Ludwig Thuille. In March 1879, when Strauss was just fifteen, he wrote to Thuille to describe a concert he had attended:

> 'At the end came Beethoven's splendid *Eroica* — It is funny how the more often one hears something truly beautiful the more one likes it; but the oftener one hears something bad or mediocre, the more one dislikes it or even finds it quite unpleasant.'

Bryan Gilliam editor, *Richard Strauss and his World*. Princeton, New Jersey: Princeton University Press, 1992, p. 220.

The depth of feeling Strauss felt for the *Eroica* Symphony found its fullest expression at the close of his life. For sometime he had been working on a composition for strings that subsequently found expression in his *Metamorphosen*, for ten violins, five violas, and three double basses. In the closing bars, the basses play the opening of the Marcia Funebre from the *Eroica* Symphony. The piece, that lasts typically for 25–30 minutes, is considered to express Strauss's statement of mourning for Germany's destruction during the war, in particular as an elegy for the devastating bombing of Munich and its Opera House. A few days after finishing *Metamorphosen*, Strauss wrote in his diary:

> 'The most terrible period of human history is at an end, the twelve-year reign of bestiality, ignorance and anti-culture under the greatest criminals, during which Germany's 2,000 years of cultural evolution met its doom.'

Strauss later related how the Beethoven quotation had 'flowed off the end of his pen'. At the foot of the manuscript score he wrote: 'In memoriam'

Kurt Wilhelm, *Richard Strauss: An Intimate Portrait.* London: Thames and Hudson, 1999, p. 263.

PETER TCHAIKOVSKY

Late in life, Tchaikovsky was befriended by the influential patron of the arts Nadezhda von Meck. She was herself a capable pianist, familiar with the classical repertoire and regarded Tchaikovsky as her ideal composer and philosopher-friend. Tchaikovsky wrote a long letter to von Meck from Florence on 16–18 February 1878 in which he enthused on the delights of Florence, telling her that the greatest impression made on him was the Medic Chapel in San Lorenzo. The greatness of Michelangelo prompted Tchaikovsky to find a parallel between him and Beethoven — as others have done:

> 'Here at last I've begun to appreciate Michelangelo's immense genius for the first time. I've begun to recognize a vague kinship with Beethoven.'

Edward Garden and Nigel Gottrei, editors, *'To My Best Friend': Correspondence between Tchaikovsky and Nadezhda von Meck, 1876–1878,* Oxford: Clarendon Press, 1993, pp. 122–3. See also: Jay Leyda and Sergi Bertensson, *The Mussorgsky Reader: A life of Modeste Petrovich Musorgsky in Letters and Documents,* New York: W.W. Norton, 1947, p. 367

In another letter to von Meck, written in 1888, Tchaikovsky enthused:

> 'There is no padding in Beethoven. It is astonishing how equal, how significant and forceful this giant among musicians always remains and how well he understands the art of curbing this vast inspiration, never losing sight of balanced, traditional form.'

Tchaikovsky expressed similar thoughts to those above in a diary entry he recorded sometime in 1888:

> 'Could anyone show me a bar in the *Eroica* — a long symphony — that could be called superfluous, or any portion that could really be omitted as padding? Thus, everything that is long is not too long; many words do not necessarily mean empty verbiage and terseness is not an essential condition of beautiful form. Beethoven, who in the first movement of the *Eroica* has built up a superb edifice out of an endless series of varied and ever-new architectural beauties upon so simple, and seemingly poor, a subject, knows on occasion how to surprise us by the terseness and exiguity of his forms.'

Ferruccio Bonavia, *Musicians on Music*, London: Routledge & Kegan Paul, 1956, p. 262.

DONALD FRANCIS TOVEY

The British musicologist, composer, pedagogue and conductor Sir Donald Francis Tovey is best known for his

Essays in Musical Analysis. They had their origins as programme notes written by him to accompany the concerts given by the Ried Orchestra, Edinburgh — performed largely under Tovey's direction. The *Essays* were published in six volumes with each volume focusing on a particular category of Beethoven's music. Volumes I and II were devoted to the symphonies; Volume III, the concertos; Volume IV, illustrative music, Volume V, vocal music; and Volume VI, supplementary essays. A seventh volume was published posthumously dealing with chamber music. These writings are still respected today for their musicological erudition that Tovey interspersed with passages of wit and mordant humour. His musical analyses seek 'to facilitate the listener's appreciation of [the music's] artistic content and technical merits'. In addition to the *Essays*, Tovey paid tribute to Beethoven and his music in a series of articles that were published in the 1911 edition of the *Encyclopaedia Britannica*. Writing of Beethoven's artistic development, Tovey observes:

> 'The peculiar interest and difficulty in tracing Beethoven's artistic development are that the changes in the materials and range of his art were as great as those in the form, so that he appears in the light of a pioneer, while the art with which he started was nevertheless already a perfectly mature and highly organized thing.'

Donald Francis Tovey, *Ludwig van Beethoven*, in: Michael Tilmouth, editor: *Donald Francis Tovey: The Classics of Music: Talks, Essays, and other Writings Previously Uncollected*, Oxford: Oxford University Press, 2001, p. 333. Tovey's *Beethoven* article originally appeared in the *Encyclopaedia Britannica*, 1914.

In the introduction to his discussion of the *Eroica* Symphony, Tovey asserts:

> 'Much comment has been wasted on the position of the funeral march, and on the *Scherzo* and finale which follow it. One very useful treatise on composition actually cites the *Eroica* Symphony as an example of the way in which the sonata form loads the composer with inappropriate additions to his programme. Such criticism has two aspects, the literary, which concerns the programme, and the musical, which concerns the form. In order to be literary, it is not necessary to be unmusical. Beethoven does not think a symphony a reasonable vehicle for a chronological biography of Napoleon; but he does think it the best possible way of expressing his feelings about hero-worship. Death must be faced by heroes and hero-worshippers, and if what heroes know about it is of any value to mankind, they may as well tell us of their knowledge while they are alive. And the mere courage of battle is not enough; it is the stricken nations whose sorrow must be faced. Afterwards the world revives, ready to nourish heroes for happier times.'

Donald Francis Tovey, *Essays in Musical Analysis*. London: Oxford University Press, H. Milford, 1935—41, Vol.1, pp. 29—30.

Writing of the variations in the fourth movement of the *Eroica* Tovey comments:

> 'Beethoven has given us an extremely interesting case of variation theme which he first developed as an independent work and later worked out, in a form compounded of variations and elements, as the finale of the *Eroica* Symphony. The style and treatment of the variations in the *Eroica* Symphony are far more gorgeous than that of the Pianoforte Variations, Op. 35, but the Pianoforte Variations contain many transformations of the theme that would be entirely unrecognizable as such if they occurred in the Symphony.'

Donald Francis Tovey, *Beethoven*. London: Oxford University Press, 1944, p. 124.

Together with his more substantial publications, Tovey contributed to various journals. In one of these (*The Musical Gazette*, July 1902) he makes reference to Beethoven's creative progress:

> 'With Beethoven, progress seems to start out in all directions and all of them lead to truth. The real fact is that in his case the differences between one work and another are evident in outward form, and the range covered by each work increased with enormous rapidity throughout his career. But his early works certainly do not stand towards the later as exercises to works of art: they are perfect masterpieces of smaller range. What is right for them would be inadequate for later: what is right for the later would be nonsensical in the earlier.'

Michael Tilmouth, *ibid*, p. 677.

In 1975, the American critic and musicologist Joseph Kerman wrote an essay to commemorate the hundredth anniversary of Tovey's birth, titled *Tovey's Beethoven*. In this, he makes a measured critique of the British musicologist's contribution to Beethoven musicology. He writes:

> 'To Tovey ... and I think many naïve listeners [i.e. not musically trained] ... Beethoven's music more than any other suggested links with life experience. Darkness, mystery, fierceness, ghostliness: Beethoven puts words like these into the critic's mouth in a way that Bach and even Haydn and Brahms do not. Beethoven also suggests psychological states of mind.'

In his summing up of Tovey's achievement, Kerman reflects:

> '[In] some sense [Tovey] ... was ... one of the completest musicians who ever lived. Our latest musical dictionary calls him a "musical historian, pianist, composer and conductor".'

Kerman's reference here is to the entry in *Collins Music Encyclopedia*, London and Glasgow, 1959. Kerman adds 'a list which is obviously half as long as it should be: he was also a legendary teacher, a musical analyst, theorist, music critic, and aesthetician'. We should also add that Tovey was an accomplished contributor to radio broadcasts, illustrating his remarks at the piano. Kerman concludes:

> 'Beethoven ... brought out the best in [Tovey], and for him richness, consistency, and completeness, *Tovey's Beethoven* stands out as the most

impressive achievement, perhaps, yet produced by the art of music criticism.'

Joseph Kerman, *Write All These Down: Essays on Music*, Berkeley, California; London: University of California Press, 1994, pp. 155–70.

RICHARD WAGNER

We learn of Wagner's admiration of Beethoven from his biographer, the composer, teacher and writer on music Ferdinand Praeger. His *Wagner As I Knew Him* appeared in 1892 – the first-full length biography of the composer to be published in English. It earned the endorsement of the Wagner enthusiast George Bernhard Shaw but was later criticized for Praeger's alleged misrepresentations. If we place our trust in the less controversial aspects of Praeger's account, we derive the following impressions:

Beethoven's youthful influences on Wagner

> 'Wagner at fifteen was a poet, and the energetic, suggestive music of Beethoven was mentally transformed into living personalities. He has said that he felt as if Beethoven addressed him "personally." Every movement formed itself into a story, glowed with life, and assumed a clear, distinct shape. I do not forget the earlier influence of Weber over him, but then that was more due to emotion than to reason. The novelty of *Der Freischütz*, the freshness of its melodic stream, and the wild imaginative treatment of the romantic story captivated his first affection and enchained it to the last. The whole of his impressions of Beethoven

(whom, by the way, Wagner never saw) were embodied by him in a sketch written for a periodical and entitled, "A Pilgrimage to Beethoven." Although the incidents painted there are not to be taken as having happened to the pilgrim, Wagner, yet the story is clear on one point — the unbounded spell Beethoven exercised over him.'

Praeger continues:

'Beethoven was his daily study. He was carefully storing all the grand thoughts of the great master, but his fiery enthusiasm had not yet come to that burning-point when it should ignite his own latent powers. His acquaintance with the scores of Beethoven has never been equalled. It was extraordinary. He had them so much by heart that he could play on the piano, with his own awkward fingering, whole movements.'

Ferdinand Praeger, *Wagner as I Knew Him*, London; New York: Longmans, Green, 1892, p. 37 and p. 40.

Wagner held the *Eroica* Symphony in high regard. On reading through the score he once remarked to his wife Cosima: 'The only mortal who can be compared with Shakespeare is Beethoven' On a further occasion he enthused:

'I should like to know whether there is any more like this than the point in the *Eroica* where the theme is played in three different keys in succession. That is will, utterly freed and relieved of the weight of individuality. The material is always a limiting factor; one has to think of human beings dancing, resting, drinking, sleeping, and so on — all this ceases here.'

Gregor-Dellin and Dietrich Mack, editors. *Cosima Wagner's Diaries*, Vol. 1, 1869 - 1877 London: Collins, 1978-1980, p. 183 and p. 283.

Wagner's prose works extend to eight substantial volumes, English editions of which appeared in translation over the period 1895—1907 from the hand of William Ashton Ellis (see *Bibliography*) In Volume Three Wagner set out his views on the *Eroica* Symphony from which we cite the following:

'This highly significant tone poem — the master's Third Symphony, and the first work with which he struck his own peculiar path — is, in many respects, not so easy to understand as its name might allow one to suppose; and that precisely since the title *Heroic Symphony* instinctively misleads one into trying to see therein a series of heroic episodes, presented in a certain historico-dramatic sense by means of pictures in Tone. Whoever approaches this work with such a notion, and expects to understand it, will find himself at first bewildered and lastly undeceived., without having arrived at any true enjoyment ... .

'In the first place, the designation *heroic* is to be taken in its widest sense, and in nowise to be conceived as relating merely to a military hero. If we broadly connote by *hero* ... the whole, the full-fledged *man*, in whom are present all the purely-human feelings — of love, of grief, of force

> — in their highest fill and strength, then we shall rightly grasp the subject which the artist lets appeal to us in the speaking accents of his tone-work.'

William Ashton Ellis, *Richard Wagner's Prose Works*: Vol. 3. London: Kegan Paul, Trench, Trübner, 1907, p. 221.

Wagner wrote extensively on the art of conducting. Of his early experience he states:

> 'At Leipzig the orchestra reeled them [symphonies] off like any overture or the entr'acte of a play. One remained completely unmoved by a conductor's readings. The chief classical works were played regularly every winter and the playing was, therefore, smooth and precise. One felt that the orchestra, knowing it all inside out, was enjoying the annual performance of favourites.'

Other of Wagner's youthful recollections were not so positive:

> 'I still remember the critical remarks which in my youth were made about the *Eroica* by older musicians. Dyonis Weber, of Prague, simply treated it as a monstrosity. [Dyonis Weber was a Bohemian composer, conductor and Director of the Prague Conservatory] ... He made his students play the first movement of the *Eroica* in the strict tempo of a Mozart *allegro* ... [The] Symphony is everywhere treated in the same manner [and] the public nowadays receives it with acclaim.'

Wagner protested:

> 'Now, how does the Beethoven *allegro* compare with that? To refer to the boldest example of Beethoven's novelties, how will the first movement of his *Eroica* sound if it is rattled off in the strict *allegro* tempo of a Mozart overture? I ask, does it ever occur to anyone of our conductors to take the tempo of this movement differently from that of a Mozart overture? No, it remains the same throughout from the first bar to the very last!'

Richard Wagner, Wagner *on Conducting*, derived, in translation, from Wagner's *Über das Dirigieren* and cited in: Ferruccio Bonavia, *Musicians on Music*. London: Routledge & Kegan Paul, 1956, p. 150, p. 162 and p. 166. For a more comprehensive study of Wagner, the conductor, see: Richard Wagner, *Wagner on Conducting*, translated by Edward Dannreuther. New York, New York: Dover Publications, 1989.

Wagner appeared before the public, in the role of orchestral conductor, on a number of occasions. Some idea of his manner is conveyed, not very favourably, in a review the Viennese music critic Eduard Hanslick wrote, after hearing Wagner conduct the *Eroica* Symphony at a concert in Vienna sometime in 1872:

> 'The novel element in Wagner's interpretations consists, to put it briefly, in frequent modifications of the tempo within a single movement ... after a very fast beginning of the first movement, for example, he takes the theme (forty-sixth

measure) conspicuously slower, thus disturbing the listener's hardly confirmed establishment of the fundamental mood of the movement and diverting the *heroic* character of the Symphony toward the sentimental. He takes the *scherzo* uncommonly fast, almost presto – a hazardous undertaking even with a virtuoso orchestra ... Were Wagner's principles of conducting universally adopted, his tempo changes would open the door to intolerable arbitrariness, and we should soon be having symphonies "freely adapted from Beethoven" instead of "by Beethoven" ... Wagner approaches conducting as he approaches composing. What suits his individuality and his utterly exceptional talent must be accepted as the one and only universal, true and exclusively authorised artistic law.'

Harold C. Schonberg, *The Great Conductors*. New York: Simon & Schuster 1967, p. 142.

ANTON WEBERN

In 1902 the composer and conductor Anton Webern commenced the study of musicology at the University of Vienna. There, he became enthusiastic about the music of Mozart, Beethoven, Schubert – [the latter] whom he described as 'so genuinely Viennese – and, likewise, composers nearer his own time including Mahler, Wagner, and Wolf. During his studies, Webern kept a diary in which he made the following entry on 6 November, 1904 – following a concert in which the *Eroica* Symphony was performed:

'The genius of Beethoven reveals itself more and

more clearly to me. It gives me an elevated strength – experience, the final experience when one veil after the other is torn away, when his genius shines for me ever more radiantly – and one day the moment will come when I am directly imbued, in brightest purity, with his divinity. He is the comfort of my soul, which searches, cries for truth. I long for an artist in music such as Segantini was in painting. [Giovani Segantini (1858–99) was renowned for his portrayal of grandiose mountain scenery] His music would have to be a music that a man writes in solitude, far away from all turmoil of the world, in contemplation of the glaciers, of eternal ice and snow, of the sombre mountain giants. It would have to be like Segantini's pictures. The onslaught of an alpine storm, the mighty force of the mountains, the radiance of the summer sun on flower-covered meadows – all these have to be in the music, born immediately out of alpine solitude. That man would then be the Beethoven of our day. An *Eroica* would appear again, one that is younger by one-hundred years.'

Hans Moldenhauer. *Anton von Webern: A Chronicle of his Life and Work.* London: Victor Gollancz, 1978, p. 76.

CONRAD WILSON

Conrad Wilson was the music critic for *The Scotsman* newspaper for almost thirty years. His candid, strongly-held views were often at odds with those who attended the concerts he wrote about – the present writer included! Wilson's intentions, however, were never to consciously offend, but always to respond with honesty and integrity to music as he felt it should be understood and performed. In addition to his many concert reviews he published a number of books, from one of which we quote the following:

> 'It was inevitable that Beethoven's *Bonaparte* Symphony, as he originally called it, would gather myths. The truth, equally inevitably, is less romantic than the tale of the disillusioned composer slashing the dedicatee's name from the title page when he heard that Napoleon had proclaimed himself Emperor. Beethoven knew the truth about Napoleon two years before he did the erasing, and restored the name in pencil very soon afterwards. Not until the work was published, a year after the premier, was the title *Eroica* added. Had it all, therefore, just been a gesture?
>
> 'The answer is both yes and no. That Beethoven's views on Napoleon were mixed is not in doubt. That he saw himself as the enlightened musical spokesman for a new century is also clear. His adoption of the *Heroic Style* [italics added] in the works of his so-called middle period was evidence of this. But in some respects he was a composer like any other, which meant that he wanted to advance his career to his own benefit, not least because he was going deaf and knew that his days as a great public pianist were numbered.'

Conrad Wilson, *Notes on Beethoven: 20 Crucial Works*. Edinburgh: Saint Andrew Press, 2003, pp. 31–32.

BEETHOVEN AND VIENNA: GESTATION OF THE *EROICA* SYMPHONY

Several influences had a bearing on the creation origins of the *Eroica* Symphony. In this part of our account we discuss the most significant of these. We commence our discussion with a consideration of Beethoven in Vienna, at the period of gestation of the *Eroica* Symphony, and his growing fame both at home and abroad. We consider how he appeared to his contemporaries, in the formal portraits taken of him and through the anecdotes and descriptions left by those who met and worked alongside him. Central to our narrative is Beethoven's awareness of his deteriorating hearing and of the torment he endured at Heiligenstadt. We discuss his new-found resolve and his triumph over what we describe as his 'dark night of the soul'. We trace his footsteps back to Vienna and identify various locations where he lived and worked. We broaden the scope of our discussion to consider music-making in Vienna and the concert venues available to Beethoven. In this context, we reflect on Beethoven the conductor, perhaps more correctly, Beethoven the *would-be* conductor. We consider the importance to Beethoven of the concepts of self-sacrifice and heroism that found expression in his music to the Ballet *Die Geschöpfe des Prometheus* ('The Creatures of Prometheus') and make reference to other of his compositions charged with inner meaning. We draw to a close with remarks bearing on Beethoven's complex relationship with the ideals of Napoleon Bonaparte and his association with the *Eroica* Symphony.

BEETHOVEN'S GROWING FAME

Alexander Wheelock Thayer, Beethoven's pioneering biographer, writes of the composer in 1803:

> '[Beethoven's] works had already spread to Paris, London, Edinburgh, and had gained him the fame of being the greatest living instrumental composer — Father Haydn, of course, excepted.'

Such was the young composer's celebrity, Thayer states that Beethoven's name alone on a concert programme was sufficient to ensure an audience.[1] His First and Second Symphonies had enhanced his reputation as a composer of large-scale orchestral compositions, and his prowess in the salons of the nobility had further advanced his celebrity for being a virtuoso pianist possessed of unmatched powers of improvisation. In the words of musicologist Clive Brown, 'with each succeeding work he advanced his claim to be the most original young composer of the day'.[2]

In 1802, Beethoven composed the monumental fifteen variations and fugue in E-flat major, Op. 35; they are commonly referred to as the *Eroica* Variations since they are based on the theme of the Symphony's final movement. Two points are worthy of remark. First, Beethoven assigned them an opus number — he had previously composed several other sets of piano variations that he did not consider as belonging to his growing catalogue of major compositions. Second, the Variations were favourably reviewed in the Leipzig-based journal the *Allgemeine musikalische Zeitung*. Significantly, in recognition of Beethoven's growing fame as a composer, the editors incorporated an engraving of his portrait on the journal's cover — an honour ordinarily reserved for artists of acknowledged stature.[3]

Beethoven was establishing a reputation in France. In the summer of 1803, Sébastien Érard arranged for one of his finest pianofortes to be delivered to the composer from his workshop in Paris. Beethoven's new instrument, which is preserved today in Vienna's *Kunsthistoriches Museum*, is triple-strung and equipped with four foot-pedals, namely, a lute stop, sustaining pedal, *sourdine* (mute) and *una corda* (soft pedal).[4] Of greater significance to Beethoven was the innovation of a more extended compass. A number of commentators believe the *Waldstein* Piano Sonata's 'unprecedented grandeur of manner' and 'added brilliance of tonal expression' may be attributed directly to Beethoven benefitting from Érard's technical innovations.[5] Sketches for the *Waldstein* Sonata co-exist alongside those for the *Eroica* Symphony in the so-called Landsberg 6 sketchbook (see later).[6]

In social terms, Érard's gift placed Beethoven amidst the musically-minded members of the newly established French Republic. Around 1803, the period of composition of the *Eroica* Symphony, Beethoven in fact gave serious consideration to relocating to Paris. He had now worked hard for more than ten years in Vienna and, although benefiting from the support of patrons, he was, like Mozart before him, without a permanent appointment such as that of kapellmeister. For his income, he had to rely largely on the sale of his compositions. As Thomas Sipe remarks:

> 'Beethoven may have believed he could improve his chances for a permanent appointment in Vienna, or elsewhere, by cultivating new ties with Parisian audiences.'[7]

PORTRAITS

Beethoven's portrait has been mentioned. We give consideration next as to how Beethoven was portrayed around the period of composition of the *Eroica* Symphony.

JOSEPH MÄHLER

A measure of Beethoven's growing fame is indicated by the circumstance of him being persuaded to have his portrait painted by Joseph Mähler. He was introduced to the composer by Stephan von Breuning, his friend from their days together in Bonn. Years later Thayer became acquainted with Mähler from whom he derived the following account that took place in the autumn of 1803:

> 'Soon after Beethoven returned from his summer lodgings to his apartment in the theatre building [where he was then residing], Mähler, who had recently arrived in Vienna, was taken by Breuning thither to be introduced. They found him busily at work finishing the *Eroica* Symphony. After some conversation, at the desire of Mähler to hear him play, Beethoven,

> instead of beginning an extempore performance, gave his visitors the finale of the new Symphony; but to close, without a pause, he continued in free fantasia for *two hours*, "during all which time", said Mähler to the present writer, "there was not a measure which was faulty or which did not sound original".'[8]

Mähler portrayed Beethoven in an Arcadian setting striking a lyre, in the background is a temple of Apollo. Although this portrait situates Beethoven in a somewhat idealised pastoral setting, the artist is not considered to have sacrificed his appearance in striving for Romantic effect. For his portrait Beethoven wore a blue tailcoat and white neckerchief, then both fashionable.

> 'It can be assumed that this is a good painting of Beethoven's physiognomy and expression, and that the painter has captured a lot of Beethoven's character while he was young and expressed it very well through this vivid expression and the concentrated look.'[9]

The painting remained in Beethoven's possession until his death. Mähler's depiction of Beethoven reached a wider public audience through a later lithograph of it that was made by Joseph Kriehuber. Today, the painting is located in the Beethoven Memorial House — the Pasqualati Haus in Vienna.

ISIDOR NEUGASS
A few years later, the Berlin artist Isidor Neugass took the composer's likeness. Judging by his portrait Beethoven was then taking care with his appearance — unlike later in life.

Neugass chose to depict Beethoven in a half-length portrait that was fashionable at the time. The closely cropped hair, as depicted in the painting of the composer by Joseph Mähler, is transformed in Neugass's depiction into a stylish *bouffant*. Around his neck is suspended a double lorgnette to assist his reading — Beethoven being somewhat short sighted. There are two versions of the painting: one version originates from the Lichnowsky family and is said to have been made, according to the family tradition, by the order of Beethoven's then patron Prince Karl von Lichnowsky; the second version was made for the aristocratic Brunswick family with whom Beethoven was on familiar and affectionate terms.[10]

Throughout the nineteenth century, Beethoven's image appeared in numerous engravings and lithographs, frequently in association with one or other of his compositions. In the case of the *Eroica* Symphony, Roberto Hoffmann depicted the composer as stern-looking and wind-swept.[11] Alois Kolb also adopted the composer's image portraying him, somewhat trance-like, for the cover of the periodical *Illustrirte Zeitung* — Germany's first illustrated magazine.[12]

ANECDOTES: DESCRIPTIONS OF BEETHOVEN

According to contemporary accounts of Beethoven, the formal, painterly representations of him are at variance with the realities of how he appeared in everyday life. For example, his piano pupil relates:

FERDINAND RIES

'In his manner Beethoven was very awkward and helpless; and his clumsy movements lacked all grace. He seldom picked up anything with his hand without dropping or breaking it. Thus, on several occasions, he upset his ink well into the piano which stood beside his writing desk. No furniture was safe with him; least of all a valuable piece; all was over-turned, dirtied and destroyed. How he ever managed to shave himself [with a cutthroat razor] is hard to understand, even making allowances for the many cuts on his cheeks.'[13]

JOSEF AUGUST RÖCKEL

The tenor Josef August Röckel has left an account of Beethoven that is consistent with Ries's recollections. Röckel sang the role of Florestan in the composer's Opera *Fidelio*, much adapted from its earlier version *Leonora* – but only after many entreaties and supplications by Beethoven's well-meaning friends. Röckel, who was one of them. called on Beethoven to receive his copy of the music and has left the following description of his living quarters:

> 'I entered the place consecrate to supreme genius. It was almost frugally simple and a sense of order appeared never to have visited it. In one corner was an open piano, loaded with music in the wildest confusion. Here, on a chair, reposed a fragment of the *Eroica*. The individual parts of the Opera with which he was busy lay, some on other chairs, others on and under a table which stood in the middle of the room. And, amid chamber music compositions, piano trios and symphonic sketches, was placed the mighty bathing apparatus with which the Master was laving his powerful chest with the cold flood.'[14]

GEORG JOSEPH VOGLER

The account of an evening in the home of Josef Sonnleithner — librettist for Beethoven's opera *Fidelio* — connects us with Beethoven the pianist. Until his hearing deteriorated, as remarked, Beethoven's powers of improvisation were regarded as being without equal. However, sometime in 1803 Beethoven took part in a pianistic contest with Georg Joseph Vogler in which he may not have emerged the victor. Vogler was a theorist, organist, pianist and composer and improvised on a theme given by Beethoven who in turn improvised on a theme of Vogler's. A guest at the event later recorded in his diary that although he was greatly impressed by Beethoven's improvisation, it had not aroused in him 'the enthusiasm inspired by Vogler's learned playing'. Doubtless Beethoven's flights of fancy and departures from pianistic convention had proved too much for the guest in question?[15]

IGNAZ PLEYEL

An evening with French army officers

A further recollection from 1805 is of interest and allows us to introduce Beethoven's most prodigiously gifted piano pupil Carl Czerny. French soldiers occupied Vienna in 1805 and placed the city under military occupation. This coincided with the premier of Beethoven's Opera *Leonora-Fidelio* in November. It was considered a failure; much of the audience consisted of French military officers who had little interest in German opera and some of whom behaved disruptively. According to Czerny's account, despite these events, Beethoven does not appear to have borne those who appreciated music any ill will. He recounts:

> '[Beethoven] was on one occasion visited by several officers and generals who were musically

inclined. He played them Gluck's *Iphigénie en Tauride* (*Iphigenie in Tauris*) from the score, and they sang the aria and choruses not at all badly.'

The next part of Czerny's account is of particular interest:

'I asked [Beethoven] for the score and wrote out the piano arrangement at home, putting down, as exactly as possible, what I had heard him play [Czerny was still only fourteen years old]. I still have my arrangement. My skill in arranging orchestral works dates from that time, and Beethoven was always completely satisfied with my transcriptions of his symphonies, etc.'

Beethoven clearly placed his trust in Czerny and sometime later asked him to make a piano transcription of the score to *Fidelio*. After the composer's death Czerny brought out piano-duet arrangements of all the composer's nine symphonies.[16]

Baron Louis Trémont

In 1809, Baron Louis Trémont, a French nobleman, met Beethoven. He was a young man at the time and several years later recalled:

'I admired [Beethoven's] genius and knew his works by heart ... he arranged several meetings with me during my stay in Vienna, and would improvise an hour or two alone for me ... I fancy that to these improvisations of Beethoven's I owe my most vivid musical impression. I maintain that unless one had heard him improvise well and

> quite at ease, one can but imperfectly appreciate the vast scope of his genius.'[17]

Trémont relates how he talked at length with the composer: 'Then we would talk philosophy, religion, politics, and especially Shakespeare, his idol.' The Baron further recalled:

> 'The greatness of Napoleon preoccupied him and he often spoke to me about it. I observed, he admired Napoleon's ascent from such a low beginning. It suited his democratic ideas.'

Trémont recalls Beethoven saying: 'I have always ardently desired to see France, but that was before France acquired an Emperor. Now, I have lost my inclination.' (see later)[18]

DEAFNESS – HEILIGENSTADT – NEW RESOLVE

Beethoven received medical advice from the physician Dr. Gerhard von Vering — a senior, and distinguished, army medical officer. He had treated the composer with some success for abdominal pains but had made no progress in alleviating a hearing condition that was worsening. Beethoven became dissatisfied with Vering and in November 1801 he wrote to his old friend Franz Gerhard Wegeler seeking his advice. In particular he wanted his opinion concerning Dr. Johann Schmidt, a physician of considerable repute, a professor of anatomy and, congenial to Beethoven, an accomplished violinist.[19] In the winter of 1801–2 Beethoven placed himself under Schmidt's care. Schmidt appears to have considered a period of peace and tranquillity would be of benefit to the composer; he suggested somewhere in the countryside away from Vienna's bustle and activity.

We pause for a moment in our narrative to remark on the manner in which the plight of Beethoven, the deaf composer, seized the popular imagination in the nineteenth century. This is nowhere more evident – albeit somewhat melodramatically – than in the portrayal of Beethoven by the distinguished actor Sir Beerbohm Tree. He played the role of Beethoven – anguished and despairing – at His Majesty's Theatre, London. *The Graphic* illustrated weekly newspaper for 27 November 1909 depicted a scene from a play about the composer by René Fauchois. The cover illustration, by the artist Steven Spurrier, portrays Beethoven in a state of torment at not being able to hear the sounds of his music. His patron Karl Lichnowsky, and others, look on in manifest despair. The caption to the cover reads: "The play by René Fauchois, adapted by Mr. Louis Napoleon Parker, was produced on November 25, with Sir Herbert Tree as the great composer. This picture represents the moment when Beethoven realizes he is becoming deaf – the greatest tragedy for a master of sound."[20]

Returning to our remarks about Beethoven and his physicians, in response to Schmidt's encouragement, in April 1802 Beethoven departed Vienna to take up residence in a modest property at Heiligenstadt, a secluded village some two miles north of the city. Beethoven's rooms offered the composer sight of the Danube, the fields round about, and the more distant panorama of the Carpathian Mountains. Something of the enchantment of this location is conveyed in a watercolour study of the village and its surroundings that is preserved today in Vienna's Kunsthistorisches Museum.[21]

> 'This was the house, this summer, and these the scenes in which the composer wrought out the conceptions that during the past five years had

been assuming form and constancy in his mind
... and which we know as the *Eroica* Symphony.'[22]

Confirmation that Beethoven was working at this address in the summer of 1803, is evident from a letter he sent to Ferdinand Ries requesting: 'Go to Stein and find out whether he can't send out an instrument to me here — against payment — I'm afraid of having mine brought out here.'[23] Beethoven may be referring here to his new piano that he had just received from Sébastien Érard. Matthäus Andreas Stein was the younger brother of Nanette Streicher and had just started his own business as a pianoforte maker in Vienna in 1892. Today, the house where Beethoven lived and worked in the summer of 1803 is known as the *Eroicahaus* — 92 Döblinger Hauptstrasse.

Returning only occasionally to Vienna, Beethoven's social sacrifice was considerable, isolating him from his brother, his closest friends and contact with the circle of distinguished families to whose various lady-members he was then giving piano lessons. Moreover, such isolation was probably counterproductive. To quote Thayer once more: 'It gave him too many lonely hours in which to brood over his calamity ... and the benefit to his hearing proved to be small or none.'[24]

Beethoven gave expression to his despondency in the so-called *Heiligenstadt Testament*. This document, in effect a letter to his brothers Carl and Johann, recounts his despair over his worsening deafness. Given the poignancy that pervades the document, a parallel is to be found in the lines of John Keats, whose awareness of his impending mortality disposed him to write, 'I have fears that I may cease to be/Before my pen has gleaned my teaming brain'.[25] Significantly, towards the close of his text, Beethoven affirms his resolve to overcome his misfortune in order to complete his artistic destiny. His *Testament* may, in the Aristotelian sense, have helped him to purge his emotions and, through his art, find renewal and restoration — what Barry Cooper has described as 'a kind of ceremonial burial'.[26]

Beethoven eventually passed through his 'dark night of the soul', emboldened by his indomitability of spirit and self-belief and with the realization that his 'inner ear' — his precious compositional faculty — was still intact. Saint John of the cross speaks of 'darkness' representing the hardships and difficulties encountered in life. We take the generic meaning of his words to signify Beethoven's triumph over his feelings of depression and the isolation he felt imposed by his encroaching deafness. He returned to Vienna, not with his hearing restored but, to quote Cooper once more, 'with his spirit revived and ready to break new ground in the development of his art'.[27]

The physician and musicologist Anton Neumayr studied the medical histories of Haydn, Mozart, Beethoven and Schubert. Considering the period when Beethoven was in self-imposed isolation at Heiligenstadt, Neumayr writes of Beethoven 'putting his wounded heart's cries of pain on paper'. Neumayr is referring of course to the *Heiligenstadt Testament*.[28]

After considering the available evidence, bearing on Beethoven's deafness, Neumayr suggests he could probably hear relatively well until about 1806. By this time, though, he was apparently experiencing difficulties in conducting. He cites the recollections of the cellist Jan Doležlálek who recalls how during rehearsals for the *Eroica* Symphony, sometime in 1804, it was apparent Beethoven was not able to hear the wind instruments distinctly enough. The extent to which Beethoven's hearing continued to fail is revealed by the further recollections of the horn player Johann Friedrich Nisle. When visiting Beethoven, sometime in

1808, he noticed how 'the servants had to ask him to speak louder because the master did not hear well'. On this occasion, however, Beethoven had his back to his visitor at first and was unable to follow the spoken words from his visitor's lips. Nisle states:

> 'When [Beethoven] sat directly facing the person to whom he was talking, he was able to carry on a conversation – as the playwright Franz Grillparzer also reported from the same year.'

In his summation of the tribulations Beethoven experienced at Heiligenstadt, Neumayr suggests:

> 'The mental resilience that enabled him to overcome his depression also freed enormous impulses that led to the development of a new style in his compositional art.'

As evidence of his spirit being unbowed and of his creativity being undiminished, Neumayr asserts:

> 'Dramatic proof that Beethoven's creative powers remained intact is revealed by the fact that he now found time to compose a group of important sonatas – the Violin Sonata in A minor, the *Kreutzer*, Op. 47 in 1803, and the Piano Sonata in C major, the *Waldstein*, in F minor, Op. 57 in 1804 – in the same period when he was working on the Third Symphony, The *Eroica*, Op. 55.'[29]

The American musicologist and Beethoven authority Maynard Solomon suggests the closing words of the *Heiligenstadt Testament* – "Thus I bid thee farewell" – imply that a biographical connection may be found between the *Eroica* Symphony and other of the composer's emotionally-charged, meditative compositions:

> 'The *Heiligenstadt Testament* is a leave-taking, which is to say a fresh start. Beethoven here enacted his own death in order that he might live again. He recreated himself in a new guise, self-sufficient and heroic. The *Testament* is a funerial work, like the *Joseph Cantata* and *Christ on the Mount of Olives*. In a sense it is the literary prototype of the *Eroica* Symphony, a portrait of the artist as hero, stricken by deafness, withdrawn from mankind, conquering his impulses to suicide, struggling against fate to find, "but one day more of pure joy" [quoted from the *Testament*]. It is a daydream compounded of heroism, death, and rebirth, a reaffirmation of Beethoven's adherence to virtue and to the categorical imperative.'[30]

Barry Cooper writes in a similarly affective manner, and suggests Beethoven's return from Heiligenstadt 'marked a new beginning' and from this time he proposes 'there is a distinctive change in the nature of his output':

> '[The] works written immediately after Heiligenstadt can be seen as more profoundly innovative, pointing in new directions and moving much further away from the legacy of Haydn and Mozart. The first works conceived after Heiligenstadt are extremely important in this respect: the Oratorio *Christus am Ölberge* ('Christ on the Mount of Olives') and the *Eroica* Symphony, both of which had deep personal significance.'[31]

Beethoven had earlier resolved in his music 'to make a fresh start' and 'to take a new path'.[32] Consistent with his resolve, and after giving expression to his innermost thoughts in the *Heiligenstadt Testament*, he returned to Vienna and resumed his negotiations with Breitkopf and Härtel. On 18 October 1802 he wrote enthusiastically to the publisher:

> 'I have composed two sets of variations ...Both sets are worked out in quite a *new manner*, and each in a *separate and different way* ... I assure you that you will have no regrets in respect of these two works — Each theme is treated in its own way and in a different way from the other one. Usually, I have to wait for other people to tell me when I have new ideas, because I never know myself. But this time — I myself can assure you that in both these works *the method is quite new so far as I am concerned.*'[33] [Beethoven's emphasis]

As one commentator has remarked:

> 'Beethoven's insistence on the novelty-value of the two variation-sets was no mere piece of salesmanship: both show a wilful determination to be original from the very outset.'[34]

Beethoven was clearly proud of his new compositions since, as remarked earlier, he assigned to both of them an opus number; first set Op. 34, consisting of six variations, and the second, Op. 35, consisting of fifteen variations and fugue. These are the *Eroica* Variations, so-called since they share the same theme Beethoven used for the finale of the *Eroica* Symphony.

RESIDENCES

BEETHOVEN AND VIENNA:
THEATER AN DER WIEN

Early in 1803, Beethoven and his brother Caspar Carl (Kaspar Karl) were provided with living quarters at the recently opened Theater an der Wien; Carl was then acting as Beethoven's business manager. The rooms were made available to them by the theatre's founder Emmanuel Schikaneder — remembered today for his collaboration with Mozart and *Die Zauberflöte*. As an incentive for his free accommodation, it was intended Beethoven would fulfil the role of putative composer in residence, notably of opera and vocal works for the stage. With this in mind, Schikaneder invited Beethoven to compose an opera for his new theatre titled *Vestus Feuer* ('The Vestal Flame'), a classical subject set in Roman times for which Schikaneder was to provide the libretto. Beethoven was initially attracted to the subject and its sentiments of love and forgiveness. During the closing months of 1803 he completed some 275 bars of more-or-less full score before becoming dissatisfied with Schikaneder's text.[35]

On 4 January 1804, Beethoven wrote to Johann Friedrich Rochlitz, the influential writer and editor of the Leipzig *Allgemeine musikalische Zeitung*:

> 'I have finally broken with Schikaneder ... Just picture to yourself a Roman subject (of which I have been told neither the scheme nor anything else whatever) and language and verses such as could proceed only out of the mouths of our Viennese apple women.'[36]

The abandoned music for *Vestus Feuer* survives today as

Hess 115 with a performing time of about ten minutes. Although the experience vexed Beethoven – he claimed he had lost six months working on the project (an exaggeration) – the dramatic nature of the music gave added depth of feeling to his developing musical language. This would become even more apparent when he shortly turned his attention to setting Joseph Sonnleithner's German translation of Bouilly's *Leonora*. In particular, he adapted the aria 'O namenlose Freude' ('O nameless joy') from *Vestus Feuer* and gave it enduring value in duet-form in his Opera *Fidelio*.

MÖLKERBASTEI

On 14 July 1804, Beethoven wrote once more to Ferdinand Ries asking him 'to find better rooms'. He was dissatisfied with the accommodation provided for him at the Theater an der Wien and advised Ries: 'I should very much like to have rooms in a large quiet square or on the Bastei.'[37] Ries duly obliged and secured rooms for his teacher on the fourth floor of the Mölkerbastei, an imposing residence situated on what were then the city's outer defensive ramparts. Beethoven moved there in October and so began a long association with the property; he lived at this address intermittently until 1815. His rooms afforded views over his beloved *Wienerwald* (the Vienna Woods) and the Glacis, an expanse of open meadow which then surrounded Vienna and which bordered on the Bastei. The building was known in Beethoven's day as the Pasqualati House because of its association with the owner, Baron Johann Baptiste von Pasqualati. Although Beethoven moved out on several occasion, Pasqualit was good-natured enough to say: 'The lodgings will not be rented; Beethoven will come back.'[38]

MUSIC-MAKING IN VIENNA: CONCERT VENUES

THEATER AN DER WIEN

The theatre owed it origins to the enterprise of the impresario Emmanuel Schikaneder, remembered for his collaboration with Mozart for providing the libretto to his Opera *The Magic Flute*. The theatre opened in June 1801 and was considered to be one of the best equipped theatres of its kind; the music correspondent of the *Allgemeine musikalische Zeitung* declared it to be 'the most comfortable and satisfactory in the whole of Germany'. As we have seen, Beethoven occupied rooms in the theatre, at Schikaneder's invitation, during part of the period he was composing his Opera *Fidelio*.

The theatre was a favourite of Beethoven's and was the venue for the following premieres of his works:

5 April 1803: Second Symphony, Third Piano Concerto and the Oratorio *Christ on the Mount of Olives*
7 April 1805: Third Symphony, *Eroica*
20 November 1805: First version of Fidelio
23 December 1806: Violin Concerto
22 December 1808: Fifth and Sixth Symphonies, Choral Fantasy and the Piano Concerto No. 4.[39]

REDOUTENSAAL

Masked balls were held at the Redoutensaal of the Hofburg. It provided a large room with a typical orchestra of some forty players and a smaller room able to accommodate about twenty players. Mozart had written dance music for these functions in the last years of his life and in 1792 Haydn contributed twelve German Dances and Minuets. In 1795 Beethoven, as his pupil, made his début at the Redoutensaal as a composer of orchestral music with his own dance music.[40]

THEATER AM KÄRNTNERTORTHEATER

The Kärntnertortheater was known as the *Kaiserliches und Königliches Hoftheater zu Wien* (Imperial and Royal Court Theatre of Vienna). Mozart's Piano Concerto K. 503 received its premier there in 1787 as did Beethoven's *Fidelio* in 1814 (in its present-day form) and his Ninth Symphony in 1824. The Kärntnertortheater was a small theatre, even compared with the Burgtheater. It had only three galleries with seats, its upper two floors being provided with benches and space for standing. When full to capacity it may have housed an audience of about a thousand. Musicians at the Kärntnertortheater were paid less than their counterparts at the Burgtheater. String and wind players received a mere 125 florins. To place these figures in context, it has been estimated that during his years in Vienna (1781–91) Mozart's income fluctuated between 800 and 3,800 florins. He lived in relatively spacious apartments that cost him some 460 gulden — broadly interchangeable with the florin.[41]

AUGARTEN

Vienna's Augarten provided a venue for informal daytime concerts. A further venue was the University's *Festsaal* that was used by the *Gesellschaft der* Musikfreunde before they had their own hall. Vienna, as Europe's leading musical city, enjoyed a flourishing operatic tradition. So-called 'rescue' dramas were fashionable and were a source of stimulus to Beethoven in the composition of his only work for the lyric theatre *Leonora/Fidelio*. Beethoven was fortunate insofar as his most wealthy patrons, such as the Princes Lobkowitz and Lichnowsky and Count Razumovsky, maintained high standards of chamber music in their own salons. Touring virtuosi were sought after in these venues to showcase their skills. Beethoven himself was obliged to take part on occasions in pianistic contests against such would-be rivals as Joseph Johann Baptist Wölfl (Woelfl) and Daniel Gottlieb Steibelt.[42]

The Augarten was situated on the far side of Vienna's suburb called Leopoldstadt. It featured a landscaped garden, making it a fashionable venue in which concert-goers could promenade in summer. There were usually twelve concerts each season that took place at the early hour of seven o'clock on Saturday mornings — doubtless by way of seeking relief from Vienna's oppressive summer heat. Haydn often attended the Augarten concerts. In its October issue of 1800, the correspondent of the *Allgemeine musikalische Zeitung* wrote:

> '[The orchestra] consisted mostly of amateurs, except for the wind instruments and the double basses. Even ladies of the highest nobility were to be heard. The auditorium was very brilliant, and everything went off with order and with decorum.'

Of the standard of performance, the correspondent remarked:

> 'The concertos are seldom well accompanied: but the symphonies go better ... the room is very good, but the orchestra is badly placed ... without being raised up.'[43]

Beethoven played at the Augarten on 24 May 1803. He accompanied the violinist George Polgreen Bridgetower in the première of the *Kreutzer* Sonata, Op. 47. It was originally composed with Bridgetower in mind but Beethoven later dedicated it to Rudolphe Kreutzer — from which its name derives — as a consequence of Beethoven falling out with Bridgetower. The next year Beethoven conducted a concert at the Augarten which included his Second Symphony and the Piano Concerto in C minor, Op. 37. The solo part was played by the composer's pupil, Ferdinand Ries who relates:

> 'Beethoven had given me his beautiful Concerto in C minor, Op. 37 in manuscript so that I might make my first public appearance *as his pupil* with it.' [Ries's italics]

With a touch of pride Ries adds: 'I am the only one who ever appeared as such while Beethoven was alive.'[44]

It is not clear here whether Ries is making explicit reference to the performance of the C minor Concerto. The point being that Beethoven's other piano pupil, Carl Czerny, rendered a similar service to that by Ries when he performed the *Emperor* Piano Concerto at a concert on 12 April 1818 — Beethoven being too deaf by then to play the work himself. The concert in question was planned to take place in July as part of the Augarten concert series. Beethoven himself was to conduct with Ignaz Schuppanzigh as leader of the orchestra. Schuppanzigh was an excellent violinist and had some responsibility for organizing the Augarten concerts.

TONKÜNSTLER-SOCIETÄT —
THE SOCIETY OF MUSICIANS

The most important public concerts in Vienna were those of the so-called Tonkünstler-Societät — the Society of Musicians — whose biannual concerts two at Easter and two at Christmas raised money for the Society's Widows and Orphans. Beethoven made his first public appearance at the Easter Concert of 1795 when he performed his Piano Concerto in B-flat major, Op. 19. For these concerts, the Society rented Vienna's Burgtheater that could accommodate large orchestras. Haydn had a close association with the Burgtheater with his Oratorios and Beethoven performed at the Burgtheater's Easter concert on 2 April 1798.[45]

LIEBHABER CONCERTE

In 1807 and 1808 a series of twenty concerts were given in Vienna known as the Liebhaber Concerte — 'Music-Lover's Concert'. One of the concerts' principal sponsors was Beethoven's patron Prince Lobkowitz. On 2 February the *Eroica* Symphony was performed together with the composer's Overture to Heinrich von Collin's drama *Coriolan*. Beethoven is known to have attended this concert together with his benefactor the Archduke Rudolph. A measure of Beethoven's celebrity is that ten of these concerts included his works. In addition to two performances of the *Eroica* Symphony other works by Beethoven included, Symphonies One and Two, the Piano Concerto No. 1, and the Overture to *The Creatures of Prometheus*.[46]

The Liebhaber-Concerte were sponsored by Johann von Häring, a banker who was recognised for being one of Vienna's foremost amateur violinists; he had the distinction of performing chamber music with Mozart. A measure of his financial and musical standing is that he possessed instruments by Amati, Guarneri, and Stradivarius. Häring made a significant contribution to Viennese musical life and was elected Director (Leader) of the orchestra when the Liebhaber-Concerte commenced. A number of these concerts were also directed by the celebrated violinist Franz

Clement, known to Beethovenians for premiering his Violin Concerto. In the opening concert season 1807–08, Clement directed performances of Beethoven's First, Second, and Fourth Symphonies as well as his First Piano Concerto. From Thayer we learn:

> 'The audiences were composed exclusively of the nobility of the town and foreigners of note, and among these classes the preference was given to the cognoscenti and amateurs ... [In] twenty meetings, symphonies, overtures, concertos, and vocal pieces were performed zealously and were received with general approval.'[47]

BEETHOVEN'S ORCHESTRA

In his pioneering English-language study *Beethoven*, the American-based, German music critic and musicologist Paul Bekker considers the composer's orchestration:

> 'Blend of tone was not the root idea of Beethoven's method of orchestral composition. His instrumentation is in the first place idealistic rather than practical. The sensuous effects of tone were a secondary consideration with him. He used each colour as a means of symbolic expression. He personified an instrument, and this personal character remained, even when lost in the impression produced by the whole. Beethoven's orchestra is the sum of such individuals, a republic of instruments, and the different "personalities" are displayed and interact in a fashion so marvellous and enchanting (the many working together at the will of one) that the total

impression does not absolutely correspond with the requirements of the tone-sense.'

Becker acknowledged Beethoven's debt to his teacher Haydn, but also recognised their very different styles of orchestration:

'Beethoven's model for his individual treatment of instruments was Haydn. Haydn, in contradistinction to Mozart, did not regard the orchestra as a great unit in which the colours of the separate instruments might be prismatically split off. Like Beethoven, he thought of it as an ensemble of instruments, as used in chamber music, a collection of entities. He had, however, extraordinary skill, cultivated to perfection, in subordinating the individual instrument at given moments to the whole. Beethoven lacked Haydn's enforced education in such adroitness. He was more ruthless, and his ruthlessness increased with age.'[48]

Donald Tovey writes in characteristically trenchant terms about Beethoven's orchestration:

'Beethoven enlarged the range of orchestral thought more than any other composer between Gluck and Wagner. The circumstances of his deafness made him the victim of some miscalculations: and pedantic views of orchestration lead many critics to exaggerate these ... Two things must be learnt by everybody who wishes to understand Beethoven: first, that errors of calculation are not the same things as errors of imagination; secondly, that a symphony is not an opera. Beethoven's errors of calculation are no greater than those of any composer who has not been able to hear a rehearsal of his work ... Errors of imagination do not exist in Beethoven's art ... Compared with Mozart's, Beethoven's scoring is rough, redundant, and capricious. But Beethoven's ideas are not Mozart's and can be expressed neither in Mozart's scoring nor in Wagner's scoring.'[49]

There was no such thing as a Beethoven orchestra *per se*. The size and combination of the instruments of a Beethoven's orchestra varied considerably. His orchestration and his orchestra expanded alongside his growing imagination. His typical orchestra consisted of strings with two each of flutes, oboes, clarinets, bassoons, trumpets, horns, and timpani. Over time this combination was modified as follows:

Symphony No. 1, *Andante* without second flute
Symphony No. 2, *Larghetto* without trumpet
Symphony No. 3, third horn added
Symphony No. 4, one flute
Symphony No 5, three trombones (first use of), piccolo, and double bassoon
Symphony No. 6, trombones and piccolo — used in the *Storm* — solo cellos in the *Andante Battle* Symphony, piccolo, triangle, cymbals, bass drum, three trombones and — 'off stage' — two great drums, two rattles, four trumpets, and military drums
Symphony No. 7, a reversion to the 'standard' orchestra

> Symphony No. 8, second movement without timpani and trumpets, and
>
> Symphony No. 9, three trombones, double bassoon, piccolo, triangle, cymbals, bass drum, with four solo voices and chorus.[50]

Writing about the subscription concerts that Beethoven gave in Vienna in 1807–08, Otto Biba writes:

> '[The] following orchestra was employed: 13 first violins, 12 second violins, 7 violas, 6 cellos, 4 double basses, and a single compliment of woodwind. Orchestral works by Beethoven included his first four symphonies and were played ten times in these performances. We must therefore assume that Beethoven approved of an orchestra of this size with 55 musicians ... Eighteen of the musicians were professionals and the rest dilettantes.'[51]

At the period of composition and performance of the *Eroica* Symphony, there was no official resident orchestra in Vienna. The orchestras associated with the city's theatres provided the basis for public concerts. Certain of Vienna's noble families maintained orchestral ensemble, but these were strictly reserved for private performance in their great salons. By way of illustration, in 1808 the orchestra in the Theater an der Wien consisted of 12 violins, 4 violas, 3 cellos, 3 bases, 2 each of flutes, oboes, clarinets, horns and trumpets and timpani. But in 1815, in the Redoutensaal, the strings comprised 36 violins, 14 violas, 12 cellos and 17 double bases. Musicologist Anne-Louise Coldicott remarks:

> 'As the time went on large orchestras became

increasingly normal: in 1817 the Tonkünstler-Societät performed *Christus am Oelberg* with 20, 20, 8, 7, 6, 4 [of the above combination] — and woodwind doubled or trebled, and in 1824 the Ninth Symphony was performed by 24 violins, 10 violas, 12 cellos and 12 bases.'

The sound and balance of an early nineteenth-century orchestra would be different to that of today's. Coldicott suggests:

'Overall the wind were louder and more piercing than the strings; oboes were louder and more penetrative, bassoons produced a more vital sound, and only the flutes, made of wood, were softer than present-day instruments. The strings were softer due to their gut strings and their different manner of articulation dictated by contemporary bows.'[52]

The violinist and Professor of Applied Musicology Clive Brown provided the introductory notes to the recordings of Beethoven's early symphonies recorded Sir Roger Norrington — known and respected for his historically-informed performances. In these Brown outlines the ways in which Beethoven's orchestra differed to that of today:

'This is strikingly true of the sounds of the individual instruments and their effects in combination: brass instruments were valveless, woodwind had fewer keys and were more sharply differentiated from one another in tone and quality than their modern counterparts, while the skin-covered timpani made a particularly distinct sound. Members of the violin family ... continued to be strung with gut until the end of eighteenth century, giving a clearer articulation and brighter sound. The bow too was in a transitional stage ...'. [Brown's reference to wind instruments being valveless, had particular significance for Beethoven's writing for the horn in the *Eroica* Symphony]

Brown reminds us how the balance of Beethoven's orchestra was weighted in favour of the wind instruments:

> 'Instead of the usual eight to ten desks of first violins [as in] a modern symphony orchestra, most early nineteenth-century German orchestras had only three or four desks ...'.

When string numbers were increased, as for example for festive performances, it was usual to supplement the wind instruments. The subtle nuances of musical style must have differed from the sounds we expect from today's orchestra. Additionally, Brown remarks:

> '[There] is no doubt, for instance, that throughout most of the nineteenth century there was a totally different attitude towards vibrato which materially affected the orchestral sound. It was virtually unknown on wind instruments, while on strings it was used only as an occasional ornament, and even here it tended to be a soloist's rather than a player's device.'

When Beethoven was at work on the *Eroica* Symphony, it was still the practice for the orchestra to be directed by the leader of the strings or for the orchestra to be conducted from the harpsichord or piano. Beethoven's violinist-contemporaries Ignaz Schuppanzigh and Franz Clement were recognized *concertmeister* who controlled the orchestra in the role of violin-leader, when a *kapellmeister* was not playing at the keyboard. The former of these was described by the Austrian conductor and composer Ignaz von Seyfried as being 'a natural-born and really energetic leader of the orchestra'. [Thayer, first edition, Vol.1, p. 238] Notwithstanding the musicianship of such accomplished performers as Schuppanzigh and Clement, Brown suggests:

> 'One consequence of directing an orchestra from the first violin or keyboard was that performances must almost entirely have lacked the wider variety of nuance and tempo modifications which were later to be considered the hallmarks of a conductor's interpretation: the old system inevitably necessitated a constant pulse in the music.'

Brown, a champion of authentic performance, enthuses:

> 'The net results of reviving the instruments and performance practices of Beethoven's period are a brighter, clearer sound, sharper contrasts, and uncomplicated, rhythmic performances.'[53]

Roger Norrington endorses these views in his own summation of the virtues of authentic performance:

> 'Every single instrument was subtly different from today's equivalent, and each was perfectly adapted to the world of Classical music. The

strings, cleaner but more plaintive, articulate easily and expressively. The woodwind each has an individual colour, creating character and clarity of ensemble within the section. The horns' hand-stopped notes give a vivid, dramatic variety to their playing, while the tympani, small and beaten with hard sticks, sound as if they have come straight from the field of Waterloo. This sheer variety of sound is essential to Beethoven, who was using a full orchestra that had recently matured under the hands of Haydn and Mozart.'[54]

BEETHOVEN AS CONDUCTOR

Although Beethoven had played the viola as a young man in the Elector's Orchestra at Bonn, he was not a sufficiently proficient string player to direct an orchestra with the violin — in the manner of his violinist-contemporaries Ignaz Schuppanzigh and Franz Clement. Moreover, Beethoven held no appointment as *kapellmeister* either at Bonn or at Vienna. He took charge occasionally of performances of his own works, but had no routine experience of conducting as such. Furthermore, he did not have the benefit of travelling far afield to hear orchestras outside of Vienna. In performances of his concertos he endeavoured to supervise the performance from the piano, but often with little control over the orchestra.[55]

Even allowing for his hearing deficiency, when Beethoven did conduct the orchestra he appears to have been somewhat idiosyncratic and not very clear with his directions. Ries recalls an occasion when he was conducting his *Eroica* Symphony and threw the orchestra out so badly in the first movement that it was necessary to restart it.[56] A contemporary account of Beethoven conducting appeared in the Journal *Cäcilia — Cecilia*, patroness of musicians — of the Mainz publisher Schott's and Sons. The contributor stated:

> 'Our master could not be presented as a model in respect of conducting, and the orchestra always had to have a care in order not to be led astray by its mentor; for he had ears only for his composition and was ceaselessly occupied by manifold gesticulations to indicate the desired expression. He often made a downbeat for an accent in the wrong place. He used to suggest a *diminuendo* by crouching down more and more, and at a *pianissimo* he would almost creep under the desk. When the volume of sound grew he rose up as if out of a stage-trap, and with the entrance of the power of the band he would stand upon the tips of his toes almost as big as a giant, and waving his arms, seemed about to soar upwards to the skies. Everything about him was active ... When he observed that the players would enter into his intentions and play together with increasing ardour, inspired by the magical power of his creations, his face would be transfigured with joy.'[57]

Commenting on the years between 1800 and 1805, when Beethoven retained some hearing, Seyfried describes Beethoven's manner when conducting terms similar to the foregoing:

> 'Our Beethoven was not one of those fastidious composers whom no orchestra could please; sometimes he was too lenient, and would not even repeat passages which went badly at the

rehearsal; "It will go better next time", he would say. But he was most particular about expression, the small *nuances*, the numerous alterations of light and shade, and the frequent passages in *tempi rubato*, all of which he was, however, quite ready to discuss with anyone. When he saw that the performers entered into his ideas, played together with increasing spirit, and captivated by the magic of his music were carried away by enthusiasm, then his face would grow bright, and with pleasure beaming from every feature, and an agreeable smile, he rewarded the successful achievement with a thundering "Bravi tutti".'[58]

In December 1813, Louis Spohr took part as violinist in a performance of Beethoven's Seventh Symphony. Although he had been alerted to the composer's style of conducting, what he witnessed with his own eyes still surprised him:

'Beethoven had accustomed himself to indicate expression to the orchestra by all manner of singular bodily movements. So often as a *sforzando* occurred, he tore his arms, which he had previously crossed upon his breast, with great vehemence asunder. At *piano* he crouched down lower and lower as he desired the degree of softness. If a *crescendo* then entered he gradually rose again at the entrance of the *forte* ... It was obvious that the poor man could no longer hear the *piano* of his music.'[59]

Deafness would eventually deprive Beethoven completely of the facility to conduct an orchestra effectively. His inability to hear the orchestra at all, at the premier of his Ninth

Symphony — and its moving consequences — has become part of musical legend.[60]

BEETHOVEN AND HEROISM

Having drawn a portrait of Beethoven and having established him within the musical milieu at the period when he was embarking upon the composition of the *Eroica* Symphony, we now briefly consider some of the social and political influences that helped to shape his musical outlook and which were to find expression in the *Eroica* Symphony itself.

Beethoven's adolescence in Bonn corresponded with a period of significant social and political change. The Elector in Bonn, Maximilian Franz, was musically inclined and supported Enlightenment ideals in the arts and education. Beethoven had in fact intended to dedicate his First Symphony to Maximilian but his patron died before it was completed. With the founding of the University of Bonn, in 1785, the youthful Beethoven became aware of the teachings of writers and philosophers that helped to shape his own political and intellectual outlook — in particular his lifelong intolerance of tyranny, injustice and oppression. As Cooper remarks: 'The seeds of *Fidelio*, *Egmont*, and the Napoleonic elements of the *Eroica* were sown in Bonn.'[61]

Utopian currents in the late eighteenth century revolved around the concept of the enlightened leader, the highminded noble figure who would, in the words of Maynard Solomon, 'dissolve the tangled problems of the relations between masters and men'. Such figures, as just remarked, with whom Beethoven would identify in his Opera *Fidelio*, the *Eroica* Symphony and the incidental music to *Egmont* and *Coriolanus*.

Ideas about the rights and values of man, arguments against tyranny, and praise of virtue were Enlightenment themes that began to find expression in writings and works for the theatre. The Italian musicologist Giorgio Pestelli argues these influences imparted to some genres of music, notably opera, a revolutionary flavour. He cites an early anticipation of this in Figaro's defiant 'Se vuol ballare signor contino', from Mozart's *The Marriage of Figaro* – on learning of the Count's ploys to exercise his newly reasserted feudal rights of *Droit du seigneur*. He also notes the more general prevalence in music of *sturm und drang*, characterised by feelings of action and emotional unrest, imparted by the use of unisons, minor keys and *sforzatos* – marked *fortissimo decrescendo* in which the instruments are directed to play *sforzando*.[62]

Beethoven, the democrat, identified with those who were no longer prepared to serve the aristocracy as servants did their masters. Rather, whilst recognizing his reliance on patronage, he sought to preserve aristocratic ideals through the notion of the enlightened ruler, free of oppression and tyranny.[63] William Kinderman considers indications of what he describes as 'Beethoven's psychological realignment[64]', and his resolve to overcome the misfortune of deafness, is evident in compositions that preceded the *Eroica* Symphony. We next discuss some of these.

Joseph Cantata

When the youthful Beethoven learned of the death of the Holy Roman Emperor Joseph II, on 20 February 1790, he set about writing a commemorative piece, the Joseph Cantata, WoO 87. It remained unpublished in the composer's lifetime and only came to light at an auction of scores in 1884.[65] In a letter to the music critic Eduard Hanslick,

Brahms remarked how it was 'Beethoven through and through!' He referred to:

> 'The noble pathos, sublime in its feeling and imagination; the intensity, perhaps violent in its expression ... characteristics which we may observe in his later works.'

The Cantata helped to shape Beethoven's musical vocabulary, his use of motifs and the adoption of dramatic ideas. Solomon suggests: 'The death of a hero, as a great man, had found expression in the Joseph Cantata and was to become a prime component of Beethoven's vocabulary.' It found further expression in the slow movement of the Piano Sonata, Op. 26 (Funeral March on the Death of a Hero); *Christ on the Mount of Olives*; *Leonora/Fidelio*; the incidental music to Goethe's *Egmont*, Op. 85; and, quintessentially, the *Eroica* Symphony ('Composed to Celebrate the Memory of a Great Man').[66]

THE MYTHOLOGICAL LEGEND OF PROMETHEUS

Beethoven composed ballet music titled *Die Geschöpfe des Prometheus* ('The Creatures of Prometheus'), Op. 43, in collaboration with the Italian dance master Salvatore Viganò. Today, the music is seldom performed in full but a theme from one of its scenes endures in the final movement of the *Eroica* Symphony. More generally, some commentators consider the libretto to the Ballet to be nothing less than a covert programme for the *Eroica* Symphony. Beethoven identified with Viganò's choreography, its implicit symbolism, and his interpretation of the classical tale of Prometheus as the defiant champion of humanity — compatible with the spirit of the Enlightenment.

Prometheus was the ennobler of humankind through

his gifts of knowledge and art, fashioned from the fire that he stole from the gods — and for which he had to endure lasting punishment. Beethoven's and Viganò's version of the legend does not, however, include the torment that Prometheus had to endure. Zeus had Prometheus chained helplessly to a rock to ensure that each day an eagle would descend to consume his liver — only for it to heal the following night to enable the punishment to be repeated.

Beethoven had not yet written a work for the stage and his preparedness to do so may have been given impetus by his wish to be recognised by Vienna's Imperial Court as a composer of large-scale dramatic works. It has been suggested, the request for Beethoven's participation in the Ballet may have come from Marie Theresa herself. We recall the composer's Septet was written in 1799 and was first performed with great success a year later at a concert in the Court Theatre in Vienna, together with the First Symphony. It was published in 1802 and was dedicated to the Empress Maria Theresa. Evidence of the Court's involvement in the promotion of the Ballet is found in the correspondence of Caspar Joseph Erbel, manager of the publishing firm Hoffmeister & Company in Vienna. On 7 March 1801 he wrote to his associates at Hoffmeister & Kühnel that Beethoven had received an urgent commission from the Empress 'which would keep him busy from all other work for the next two weeks'.[67]

Beethoven was fortunate to have Salvatore Viganò as his fellow collaborator in their interpretation of *The Creatures of Prometheus*. Viganò was himself an accomplished dancer who had studied music with his uncle, Luigi Boccherini. He had appeared on the stage in Venice and had performed at the Coronation Festivities of Charles IV of Spain. In modern-day terms, he was a box-office attraction.

A poster announced the premiere of the Ballet on 28 March 1801. It included a synopsis of the allegorical text and a summary of the classical myth in which Prometheus, finding mankind in a state of ignorance, improved their state, as remarked, by means of science and the arts. Prometheus could be seen as none other than Marie Theresa, patron of music, honoured by demonstrating the importance to human life of music, drama, and dance.

In the Ballet, statues come to life and are made responsive to all the passions of human life through the power of harmony; Prometheus leads them to the god Apollo; scenes unfold involving the gods Pan and Bacchus; a mythological pageant takes place with dancers adorned in splendid costumes. The music to accompany the depiction of Parnassus – home of the Muses– includes an *adagio* followed by an *Andante quasi Allegretto* with solos for flute, clarinet, bassoon, and prominent solos for cello and harp – Beethoven's only solo for the harp. A violent thunderstorm ensues – anticipating, by several years, that which occurs in the composer's *Pastoral* Symphony.[68]

Although music critics considered the Prometheus subject 'too learned for a ballet', it was well received by the public and was given more than twenty performances in the 1801–02 music season. Cooper considers the mythological subject appealed to Beethoven insofar as it enabled him to give expression to the idea of suffering – that of Prometheus. He regards the work as being one of the earliest in which he portrayed heroism 'more-or- less explicitly'.[69]

At the close of the nineteenth century, Sir George Grove wrote at length about Beethoven's nine symphonies. In his discussion of the *Eroica* Symphony, he comments on Beethoven's susceptibility to the influence on music of revolutionary ideas, stating:

'[Beethoven] had not [yet] openly acknowledged this in his music. Prometheus was a not unsuitable hero for a work that may have been full of revolutionary ideas, though invisible through the veil of the Ballet. Perhaps the melody which he employed in this finale, and elsewhere twice outside his Ballet, may have had to him some specially radical signification. At any rate, his first overt expression of sympathy with the new order of things was the *Eroica*. And a truly dignified expression it was.'[70]

Grove's reference to 'elsewhere twice outside his ballet' requires a few words of explanation: The finale to *The Creatures of Prometheus* takes the form of a rondo that adopts a theme that appears to have held particular appeal to Beethoven. He used it in the seventh of his twelve Contradances, WoO 14 and the Piano Variations, Op. 35 – The *Eroica* Variations – to which we have made previous reference. Some commentators consider the libretto of *The Creatures of Prometheus* to be no less than a hidden programme to the *Eroica* Symphony. William Kinderman also finds a connection between Beethoven's personal circumstances and the Symphony:

'The overall narrative progression of the four movements of the Symphony outlines a sequence – struggle, death, rebirth, apotheosis. The parallel with Beethoven's own despair, thoughts of suicide, and discovery of his new artistic path is scarcely accidental ... What Beethoven explores in the *Eroica* are universal aspects of heroism, centring on the idea of a confrontation with adversity leading ultimately to a renewal of creative possibilities.'[71]

VICE-ADMIRAL HORATIO NELSON AND GENERAL SIR JAMES ABERCROMBIE

Various conjectures circulated in Beethoven's lifetime, and beyond, as to the inspirational source for the Funeral March in the *Eroica* Symphony. Both Lord Nelson and General Abercrombie were suggested as possible models for the heroic figure enshrined within the *Eroica* Symphony. In 1852, Dr. Andreas Bartolini — Beethoven's physician and medical advisor between 1806 and 1816 — informed Mozart's biographer Otto Jahn that the first idea came to Beethoven on hearing of Bonaparte's expedition to Egypt and the rumour of the death of Nelson at the Battle of Abukir Bay.[72] Nelson, although recovering from wounds from a previous conflict, was, of course, mortally wounded some years later at the Battle of Trafalgar.[73]

In composing the Funeral March to the *Eroica* Symphony, Beethoven is said to have been further influenced by the account Bartolini is alleged to have given of General Sir James Abercrombie; he had died of his wounds following the Battle of Alexandria in 1801. As Thomas Sipe concludes: 'Because they lack any supporting evidence, and were reported second-hand, the contradictory reports stemming from Bartolini should be regarded as purely anecdotal.'[74]

GENERAL JEAN BAPTISTE BERNADOTTE

In 1798, Bernadotte was appointed to the post of Ambassador of the French Republic to the Austrian Court. From Anton Schindler we learn:

> 'His salon was frequented by distinguished persons of all ranks among whom was Beethoven, who had already expressed great admiration for the First Consul of the Republic [Napoleon Bonaparte].'

Schindler adds:

> 'The suggestion was made by the General that Beethoven should honour the greatest hero of the age in a musical composition. The idea soon became a reality which the master, having battled with his political scruples, gave to the world under the title *Sinfonia Eroica*.'

Schindler was a child in 1798 and, doubtless, relied on the accounts of others when he wrote his Biography of Beethoven many years later. Schindler is known in his account of the composer to have made errors of fact and his record of events, in which he was not a direct participant, are considered to be not always trustworthy. In the present case, it is known that Bernadotte was obliged to relinquish his post and to leave Vienna in 1798, only a few months after his arrival – and years before Beethoven started work on the *Eroica* Symphony. Peter Clive, the punctilious chronicler of Beethoven's contemporaries, observes:

> 'The overall credibility of Schindler's statement is seriously impaired by his placing the whole sequence of events in the year 1804, whereas Bernadotte's appointment in Vienna was ... limited to a few weeks in 1798; he had left the city several years before 18 May 1804, the day on which Napoleon was proclaimed Emperor. Many scholars ... have been reluctant to take Schindler's word in this matter, in view of the faulty chronology of his account and his well-established untrustworthiness as a source. There is also the fact that five years were to elapse between Bernadotte's

presence in Vienna and Beethoven's first sketches for the [*Eroica*] Symphony.'[75]

Bernadotte's untimely departure from Vienna was on account of his tactlessness; he impudently wore the French revolutionary tricolour in his hat and, more provocatively, had the tricolour displayed from the ambassador's balcony — thereby, provoking civil unrest. A measure of the tension prevailing in Vienna, as early as 1794, can be judged by remarks Beethoven made in a letter he sent on 2 August of that year to the publisher Nikolaus Simrock in Bonn. He informed him:

> 'Here various *important* people have been locked up; it is said that a revolution was about to break out ... People say that the gates leading to the suburbs are to be closed at 10.00 p.m. The soldiers have loaded their muskets with ball. You dare not raise your voice or the police will take you into custody.'[76]

Turning to later events:

On 22 December 1822, Beethoven was made a Member of the Swedish Royal Academy of Arts and Sciences. A year later he was elected to Membership of the Royal Academy of Music, Stockholm. On 1 March 1823, Beethoven expressed his appreciation in a letter to the Academy, written in French in another hand — possibly that of his Nephew Karl — and signed by Beethoven: 'C'est avec bien plaisir ... que je recoit l'hommage que l'Accademie royale suédoise de Musique rend à mes médiocres mérites.'[77] On the same day, possibly prompted by this circumstance, Beethoven also wrote to Bernadotte.

In 1810 Bernadotte commanded in the Netherlands

and was offered the crown of Sweden as Karl XIII, later Karl XIV. Accordingly, in his letter, Beethoven addressed Bernadotte as 'King Karl XIV' and expressed to him the pleasure he had received in being made a member of the Swedish Royal Academy of Music. He recalled Bernadotte's meeting with him in Vienna, some twenty-five years earlier: 'Le présence de Votre Majesté à Vienne, et l'intérêt qu'elle prit avec quelques Seigneurs de sa suite à mes médiocres talents, s'est profondement grave dans mon coeur'. Significantly, though, Beethoven makes no reference to the *Eroica* Symphony or Bernadotte's alleged role in bringing it about.[78]

BEETHOVEN AND NAPOLEON BONAPARTE

Anton Schindler writes:

> 'Beethoven's admiration of Napoleon was not based so much on that general's countless military victories as on his success in bringing, within a few years' space, political order out of the chaos of a bloody revolution. And the fact that this new order was founded on republican principles, even if they were not dictated by the First Consul himself, they could only raise Bonaparte and the new regime in Beethoven's estimation. For Beethoven already had republican sympathies, personally inclined as he was towards unimpeded freedom and independence.'[79]

Ferdinand Ries writes in similar vein:

> 'In the year 1802, Beethoven composed his Third Symphony (now known by the title of

Sinfonia Eroica) in Heiligenstadt, a village an hour and a half distant from Vienna. In writing his compositions Beethoven often had some special subject in mind, though he often laughed and scolded me about musical tone-paintings, especially those of a more trifling nature ... In the Symphony Beethoven had thought of Bonaparte, but Bonaparte when he was still First Consul. At that time Beethoven held him in the highest esteem and compared him to the great consuls of ancient Rome. I myself, as well as other intimate friends of his, have seen this Symphony. Already scored, lying on his table, with "Bonaparte" at the very top of the Title Page, and at the very bottom "Luigi van Beethoven", without another word. How and wherewith the gap was to be filled in I do not know.'[80]

More generally Ries states:

'The initial idea for a large-scale piece often lay dormant for years before Beethoven began to work it out. It is possible, however, that one of Beethoven's moods (they were always chopping and changing) was responsible for the connection with Napoleon [and the Third Symphony].'[81]

At the period of composition of the *Eroica* Symphony, Bonaparte was perceived as a champion of freedom and a latter-day hero – a modern-day Prometheus. *The Peace Almanac* of 1803 described Napoleon as the 'lion of the valley' and the 'tiger of the mountains'. It compared him to Alexander the Great and stated 'he had the unconditional protection of the Gods'.[82]

In 1802 an event occurred that reveals something of Beethoven's ambivalent response to the revolutionary fervour then engulfing much of Europe. He received a letter from his Leipzig publisher Franz Anton Hoffmeister concerning a rather unusual potential commission. Hoffmeister had received a suggestion from a lady admirer of Beethoven's music – her name has not come down to us. She had proposed to Hoffmeister that Beethoven should write a *Revolutionary Sonata* (her description); furthermore, this would be at her expense.

Beethoven's response to Hoffmeister, sent from Vienna on 8 April, was initially somewhat tetchy. He expostulated: 'Has the devil got hold of you gentlemen? – that *I should compose such a sonata.*' [Beethoven's italics] He concedes, such a composition might have been credible 'at the time of the revolutionary fever' – a reference to the grip with which Bonaparte had seized Europe, and, for a period, his own imagination – but now, he intimated, times had changed. Later in the letter though he began to warm to the lady's suggestion – but with reservations. He agreed to write a sonata for his admirer but on the following conditions: the work would be conceived from an '*aesthetic* point of view' [Beethoven' italics]; he would adopt her suggested plan of keys (illustrating how amenable Beethoven was prepared to be on occasions in response to a commission); and, finally, he would charge the handsome fee of 50 ducats. For all of this, Beethoven stipulated, the lady in question could keep the sonata for her own enjoyment for one year – provided she did not publish it. Thereafter, the copyright would revert to Beethoven as was then the custom. Nothing, however, came of these proposals.[83]

Not only 'had times changed', to quote Beethoven, but so had his attitude to Bonaparte – on hearing he was proclaimed Emperor. Ries recalls this moment in an incident that has passed into musicological legend:

> 'I was the first to announce to him the news that Napoleon had declared himself Emperor, whereupon he flew into a rage and cried: "Then he, too, is nothing but an ordinary mortal! Now he also will tread all human rights underfoot, will gratify only his own ambition, will raise himself up above all others and become a tyrant!" Beethoven went to the table, took hold of the Title Page [of the *Eroica* Symphony], tore it off and flung it on the ground.'[84]

Schindler gives the following account of this incident:

> 'The fair copy of the score [of the *Eroica* Symphony], with the dedication to the First Consul of the French Republic inscribed simply 'Napoleon Bonaparte' on the Title Page, was ready to be given to General Bernadotte, who was to send it to Paris, when the news reached Vienna that Napoleon had allowed himself to be proclaimed Emperor of the French. It was Count Lichnowsky and Ferdinand Ries who brought the news to Beethoven. No sooner had the composer heard it than he seized the score, tore out the Title Page and, cursing the "new tyrant", flung it on the floor.'

Schindler's assertion that Bernadotte was to take a copy of the *Eroica* Symphony to Paris is inconsistent with the chronological evidence; as remarked, General Bernadotte had departed Vienna years before in 1798. Of subsequent events Schindler states, more reliably:

> 'It was a long time before the friends of the democracy-loving composer were able to calm his righteous anger, but finally his passions gave way to quieter reflections on what had occurred. In the end he consented to the publication of the work under the title *Sinfonia Eroica* with the sub-title: *composta per festeggiare il sovvenire di un gran Uomo* ['composed to honour the memory of a great man'].[85]

With regard to the dedication of the *Eroica* Symphony, Beethoven subsequently transferred his allegiance from Napoleon to his patron Prince Lobkowitz. We discuss this, and the related circumstances, in the following section of our text. For the present we note Solomon's circumspect observation:

> 'The strained relations between Austria and France, at this period, meant it would have been imprudent of Beethoven to have retained any overt association with Bonaparte on the Title Page of the Third Symphony. On a personal level, it would have imperilled his relationship with his patron Prince Lobkowitz and, more threateningly, could have rendered him liable to reprisals by the State for giving expression to anti-Austrian sentiments. We recall how his *Opera Fidelio* – adapted from a post French revolutionary drama – initially fell foul of the public censor and had to have its setting removed to Spain.'[86]

Beethoven's ambivalent association with Bonaparte did not deter him from giving serious thought to accepting an offer to join the Court of Jerome Bonaparte, the future King of Westphalia, in the capacity of his Kapellmeister.

On 1 November 1808, Napoleon's younger brother Jérôme — recently installed as the King of Westphalia — invited Beethoven, through the diplomatic offices of his High Chamberlain, to consider an offer of appointment as his Senior Kapellmeister in Kassel. Despite the somewhat archaic-sounding title, the post held distinct attractions for Beethoven. His duties would not be onerous; he would merely be required to play for Jérôme's personal pleasure and to conduct occasional concerts. Moreover, he was offered a salary of 600 gold ducats (the equivalent of about 4000 gulden/florins or 200 pounds sterling) and an additional 150 ducats for travelling expenses.[87]

Beethoven was attracted by the invitation and was disposed to accept it. On 24 November he wrote in enthusiastic terms to his new confident and general factotum Baron Gleichenstein:

> 'I have received the offer of a fine appointment as Kapellmeister to the *King of Westphalia*. I am to be paid handsomely — I have been asked to state how *many ducats* I should like to have — and so forth.'

He closed the letter by asking Gleichenstein for a meeting to seek his advice.[88]

News of Beethoven's intended departure duly reached the ears of a privileged inner-circle that included the Archduke Rudolph, Prince Ferdinand Kinsky and Count Franz Joseph Lobkowitz. In order to secure Beethoven's continuing presence in Vienna, they resolved to take immediate action and collectively agreed to settle upon

Beethoven an annuity of 4000 gulden/florins — the equivalent offered to him by Jérôme Bonaparte. Part of their Contract reads:

> '[The] undersigned have made the decision to place Herr Ludwig van Beethoven in a position where the most pressing circumstances shall not cause him embarrassment or impede his powerful genius.'

Despite this promised financial support, Beethoven did not secure the title he so much cherished, namely, that of *Imperial Kapellmeister*.[89] Thayer remarks that the three signatories to Beethoven's Annuity Contract were doubtless motivated to assist the composer on the grounds: 'What an inexcusable, unpardonable disgrace to Vienna would be the departure of Beethoven under such circumstances!'[90]

We take leave of Beethoven, and his complex relationship with Napoleon Bonaparte, with a recollection of Carl Czerny. From him we learn:

> 'In 1824 I went on one occasion with Beethoven to a coffee shop in Baden. There were several newspapers on the table. In one of them I read an announcement of Walter Scott's biography of Napoleon. "Napoleon", [Beethoven] said. "I could not tolerate him before. Now I think quite differently".'[91]

On hearing news of Napoleon's death on St. Helena on 5 May 1821, Beethoven is said to have remarked: 'I have already composed the proper music for that catastrophe.' It is to the creation origins of the music in question — the

Eroica Symphony – that we consider in the next part of our account.

1. *Elliot Forbes editor, Thayer's Life of Beethoven, 1967 p. 327.*
2. Clive Brown, Introduction to *Ludwig van Beethoven, Beethoven: Symphony No. 1 and 2,* The Academy of Ancient Music conducted by Christopher Hogwood.
3. Robin Wallace, 1986, p. 11.
4. See: Derek Melville, *Beethoven's Pianos* in, Denis Arnold and Nigel Fortune, editors, 1973, pp. 50–51; Leon Plantinga, 1999, Plate 6; and Ernest Closson, *History of the Piano*, translated by Delano Ames and edited by Robin Golding, 1947, plate 27.
5. *See for example: Denis Matthews, 1967, p. 32 and Denis Matthews, 1972, pp. 176–7.*
6. In 1817 the English piano maker John Broadwood made a similar gift of one of his firm's finest pianos. It was a considerable advance upon the Érard with a thicker soundboard, larger hammers, and sonorous bass – all well suited to the grandeur of Beethoven's later keyboard music. Doubtless Érard's and Broadwood's solicitude of Beethoven was, at least in part, motivated by a commercial impulse.
7. Thomas Sipe, 1998, p. 48.
8. Elliot Forbes editor, *Thayer's Life of Beethoven*, 1967 p. 337.
9. Derived from the text to Beethoven House Library Document HCB B 1. See also: Beethoven House Digital Archives, Document B 2388, *Beethoven Gallery* and H. C. Robbins Landon, 1992, plate. 6.
10. A facsimile reproduction of the Neugass portrait, with accompanying historical information, can be seen at the Beethoven House, Digital Archives, Library Document B 1093 and Library Document B 1925. See also: H. C. Robbins Landon, 1992, plate 7.
11. Beethoven House, Digital Archives, Library Document, B. 1878.
12. *Ibid*, Library Document, B 2472.
13. Ferdinand Ries in: Oscar George Theodore Sonneck, 1927, p. 58.
14. Josef August Röckel in Oscar George Theodore Sonneck, 1927, pp 64–65.
15. See: Beethoven House, Digital Archives, Library Document, B 937 and Peter Clive, 2001, pp. 381–82.
16. As recalled by Carl Czerny in: Paul Badura-Skoda, 1970, p. 14. See also: Elliot Forbes, 1967, p. 391.
17. Paul Nettle, 1975, pp. 278–80 and Thayer-Forbes, 1967, p. 466.
18. Quoted from Trémont's Diary by Christpher T. George, *Journal of the International Napoleonic Society*, December, 1998, p. 3 and pp. 5–6. For a fuller account of Beethoven's meeting with Trémont, see: Oscar George Theodore Sonneck, 1927 p. 74.
19. Emily Anderson, 1961, Vol. 1, Letter No. 54, pp. 66–9 and Peter Clive, 2001, p. 318 and p. 379. Beethoven showed his appreciation for the care and attention Schmidt bestowed upon him by dedicating to him his own arrangement of his celebrated Septet, Op. 20, for piano, clarinet or violin, and 'cello, Op. 38.
20. The illustration can be seen by accessing 'Sir Beerbohm Tree, Beethoven' on the internet.

21 For a reproduction of the watercolour, see: Leon Plantinga, 1999, Plate 4. The illustrator, known to art historians as Johann Peter Lyser (real name Ludwig August Burmeister), created a sketch-impression of Beethoven as he may have appeared when walking the highways and byways of the countryside. Although created largely from his imagination – Lyser probably never met Beethoven – it effectively captures his profile and determined gaze. See: Beethoven House, Digital Archives, Library Document B 888. Lyser also drew a sketch profile of the composer's head that was later reproduced lithographically. Although the artist has taken liberties – Beethoven looks distinctly unshaven and windswept – as Carl Dalhaus observes (his study being one of several sources reproducing the image), the significance of the portrait lies in that 'it represents the romantic image of Beethoven: the image of the revolutionary, the genius unconcerned with externals'. Carl Dahlhaus, 1991, plate 14.

22 Elliot Forbes editor, *Thayer's life of Beethoven*, 1967, p. 335.

23 Emily Anderson editor and translator, 1961, Vol. 1, Letter No. 80, p. 95.

24 Elliot Forbes editor, *Thayer's Life of Beethoven*, 1967, pp. 303–6.

25 John Keats, '*When I have fears that I may cease to be*'. Keats wrote his lines, in part prompted by the deaths of members of his family, but also in recognition of the malign influence of the consumption that gripped him and sent him to the grave at the tragically early age of twenty-five.

26 Barry Cooper, 2000, p. 121.

27 *Ibid*, p. 121.

28 The *Heiligenstadt Testament* takes the form of a letter that was intended for his brothers Carl and Johann. It was, however, never made known to them. Beethoven kept the document among his private papers where it was not discovered until March 1827 following his death. It was published later that October by Anton Schindler and Stephan von Breuning.

29 Anton Neumayr, 1994–97, p. 225, p. 249 and pp. 253–54.

30 Maynard Solomon, *Beethoven* (paperback edition),1979, p. 121.

31 Barry Cooper, 2000, pp. 122–23.

32 Beethoven wrote the words quoted in his sketchbook and revealed his intentions 'to make a fresh start' to his friend the mandolin player Wenzel Krumpholz. As related in: Ludwig Nohl, 1880, p. 48.

33 Emily Anderson editor and translator, 1961, Vol. 1, Letter No. 62, pp. 76–77.

34 Liner notes to accompany the Hyperion recording of the Variations by the pianist Llyr Williams.

35 For a discussion of *Vestus Feuer* and its place in Beethoven's developing musical language, see: Barry Cooper, 1990, p. 119; 1991, p. 276; and 2000, pp. 134, 137, and 149.

36 Emily Anderson editor and translator, 1961, Vol. 1, Letter No. 87a, p. 105.

37 *Ibid*, Letter No. 92, p. 111.

38 Elliot Forbes editor, *Thayer's Life of Beethoven*, 1967 pp. 356–57.

39 For reference to the Theater an der Wien in the wider context of music making in Vienna, in the early nineteenth century, see Otto Biba, *Concert life in Beethoven's Vienna* in: Robert Winter editor, *Beethoven, Performers, and Critics*, 1980, pp. 77–91.

40 H. C. Robbins Landon, 1977, pp. 33–34.

41 Quoted, with adaptations, from Mary Sue Morrow, 1989, pp. 71–81, and

pp. 113—15. Morrow's account of Vienna's principal theatres includes seating plans and contemporary engravings of both their exteriors and interiors.
42 For a comprehensive study of concert life in Beethoven's Vienna see Anne-Louise Coldicott, *Beethoven's Musical Environment* in: Barry Cooper, 1991, pp. 87—91.
43 H. C. Robbins Landon, 1977, pp. 33—34.
44 Elliot Forbes editor, *Thayer's Life of Beethoven*, 1967 p. 355.
45 H. C. Robbins Landon, 1977, pp. 33—34.
46 For contextual information see: Theodore Albrecht editor and translator, 1996, Vol. 1, Letter No. 128, pp. 197—99.
47 Elliot Forbes editor, *Thayer's Life of Beethoven*, 1967 p. 428.
48 Paul Bekker, 1925, pp. 156—57.
49 Donald Francis Tovey, 1944, pp. 79—80.
50 Adapted from: Paul Mies, *Beethoven's Orchestral Works* in: *The Age of Beethoven, The New Oxford History of Music*, Vol. VIII, Gerald Abraham editor, 1988, pp. 122—23.
51 Otto Biba, *Concert Life in Beethoven's Vienna*, in: Robert Winter editor, *Beethoven, Performers, and Critics: The International Beethoven Congress*, Detroit, 1977, 1980, p. 88.
52 Anne-Louise Coldicott, *Performance Practice in Beethoven's Day* in: Barry Cooper, *The Beethoven Compendium: A Guide to Beethoven's Life and Music*, 1991, pp. 284—85.
53 Clive Brown, Introduction to *Ludwig van Beethoven, Beethoven: Symphony No. 1 and 2*, The Academy of Ancient Music conducted by Christopher Hogwood.
54 Roger Norrington, Liner notes to *Beethoven, Symphonies 1 & 6*, The London Classical Players, EMI CDC 7497462, 1988.
55 For a discussion of Beethoven the conductor see: Adam von Ahnen Carse, 1948, pp. 306—7.
56 Franz Wegeler, *Remembering Beethoven: The Biographical Notes of Franz Wegeler and Ferdinand Ries*, 1988 (reprint), pp. 68—69.
57 Quoted in: Elliot Forbes editor, *Thayer's Life of Beethoven*, 1967, pp. 371—72.
58 Ignaz von Seyfried, as recounted in: Ludwig Nohl, *Beethoven Depicted by his Contemporaries*, 1880, pp. 49—56 and Oscar George Theodore Sonneck, *Beethoven: Impressions of Contemporaries*, 1927, pp. 35—46.
59 Louis Spohr quoted in: Elliot Forbes editor, *Thayer's Life of Beethoven*, 1967 pp. 565—66.
60 The first performance of the Ninth Symphony was conducted by Michael Umlauf, with Beethoven standing by side. At the close of the work, due to his deafness, he could not hear the applause. According to one account, Unger had to turn the composer to face the audience as they hailed him with standing ovations.
61 Barry Cooper, 2000, p. 14.
62 Giorgio Pestelli, *Music and the French Revolution* in: *The age of Mozart and Beethoven*, 1984, p. 175.
63 With acknowledgement to Maynard Solomon, 1977, p. 39.
64 William Kinderman, 1997, pp. 87—90
65 The Joseph Cantata was premiered in November 1884, fifty-seven years after the composer's death and almost a hundred years since its composition.

The score was published in 1888 as a supplement to Beethoven's *Complete Works*. Today it has the Catalogue No. WoO 87.
[66] Maynard Solomon, 1977 p. 79.
[67] Derived from: John A. Rice, *Empress Marie Therese and Music at the Viennese court*, 1792—1807, 2003, pp. 248—50.
[68] Thomas Sipe, 1998, pp. 13—14.
[69] Barry Cooper, 2000, pp. 98—100.
[70] George Grove, 1896, p. 52.
[71] William Kinderman, 1997, pp. 87—90.
[72] H. C. Robbins Landon, 1970, p. 91.
[73] For a discussion of Nelson's Victory over the French at the Battle of the Nile (Abukir Bay), see: Terence M. Russell, Ashgate (2001) and History Press (2005).
[74] Thomas Sipe, 1998, p. 33.
[75] Peter Clive, 2000, pp. 27—29. See also, Thomas Sipe, 1998, p. 31.
[76] Emily Anderson editor and translator, 1961, Vol. 1, Letter No. 12, pp. 17—18.
[77] Emily Anderson editor and translator, 1961, Vol. 3, Letter No. 1149, p. 1011.
[78] *Ibid*, Letter No.1150, pp. 1012—13.
[79] Anton Felix Schindler, edited by Donald W. MacArdle and translated by Constance S. Jolly from the German edition of 1860, 1966, p. 112.
[80] Franz Wegeler, Remembering Beethoven: The Biographical Notes of Franz Wegeler and Ferdinand Ries, 1838/45, reprint, 1988, pp. 67—68. Ries's account is also reproduced in: Oscar George Theodore Sonneck, 1927, pp. 53—55.
[81] Quoted in: Paul Badura-Skoda, Carl Czerny: *On the Proper Performance of all Beethoven's Works for the Piano*, 1970, p. 8 and p. 13.
[82] Quoted in: Thomas Sipe, 1998, p. 46.
[83] Emily Anderson editor and translator, 1961, Vol. 1, Letter No. 57, pp. 73—74.
[84] See endnote 76.
[85] Anton Felix Schindler, edited by Donald W. MacArdle and translated by Constance S. Jolly from the German edition of 1860, 1966, pp. 115—16.
[86] Maynard Solomon, 1977, p. 137.
[87] Elliot Forbes, editor, *Thayer's Life of Beethoven*, 1967, p. 442 and Peter Clive, 2001, pp. 39—40. Denis Matthews makes the interesting observation that although the title of Kapellmeister was becoming somewhat antiquated, in the first decade of the nineteenth century, it may have had a particular resonance for him. His grandfather had held such an appointment, and this, combined with childhood memories, may, Matthews suggests, have exerted an influence on his subconscious mind.
[88] Emily Anderson, 1961, Vol. 1, Letter No. 170, p. 200. Beethoven opens his letter to Gleichenstein with the salutation 'Dissolute Baron' — a characteristic example of the word play he inflicted on his close friends and associates.
[89] The wording of the Contract is reproduced in full in: Theodore Albrecht, translator and editor, 1996, Vol. 1, Letter No. 134, pp. 205—6.
[90] Elliot Forbes, editor, *Thayer's Life of Beethoven*, 1967, pp. 453—9.
[91] Paul Badura-Skoda, *Carl Czerny: On the Proper Performance of all Beethoven's Works for the Piano*. Universal Edition: A. G. Wien, 1970, p. 8 and p. 13. Walter Scott's biography was duly published as: *The Life of Napoleon Buonaparte, Emperor of the French. With a Preliminary View of the French Revolution*. By the Author of "Waverley," &c. In Nine

Volumes. Vol. I [II-IX]. Edinburgh: Printed by Ballantyne and Co. for Longman, Rees, Orme, Brown, & Green, London; and Cadell & Co., Edinburgh 1827. Reference is also made to these events in Elliot Forbes editor, *Thayer's Life of Beethoven*, p. 920.

CREATION ORIGINS

The period between Beethoven turning his mind to the composition of the *Eroica* Symphony and its eventual publication – its 'creation origins' – was protracted and took several twists and turns. Here, we trace the events and circumstances in question. To assist the reader's assimilation, our text is presented under the following headings: Beethoven's compositional process; the sketches and sketchbooks used by Beethoven; the autograph score – more correctly Beethoven's copy of the score; Beethoven's negotiations with publishers – and those made on his behalf; the Title Page and its significance relating to the *Eroica* Symphony's eventual dedicatee; Beethoven's tempo indications – and their implications for contemporary performance; and, finally, the publication of the *Eroica* Symphony.

BEETHOVEN'S COMPOSITIONAL PROCESS

For the reader unfamiliar with Beethoven's manner of composing — his 'compositional process' — we provide the following introductory remarks. Donald Tovey states:

> 'No artist has left more authoritative documentary evidence as to the steps of his [creative] development than Beethoven. His sketches and compositional drafts cover the so-called 'three-periods' of his career, and give insights into the origins of many of his most important works; throughout, the same level of rigorous self-criticism, integrity and tireless search for "perfection" is evident ... The number and triviality of Beethoven's preliminary sketches should not ... be taken as evidence of a timid and vacillating spirit. But if we regard his sketches as a diary, their significance becomes inestimable.'[1]

Gustav Nottebohm, the Viennese pianist, composer and pioneer in the study and decipherment of Beethoven's sketchbooks, remarks:

> '[In] spite of this unsystematic procedure it is evident that as a rule Beethoven was clear about his objectives from the start; he remained true to his original conceptions, and once an idea was grasped, he carried it through to the end ... We may seek [in the sketchbooks] the artist himself, in the unity of his whole character and spirit, and in the harmony of his inner powers.'[2]

In his scholarly commentary to Beethoven's sketchbooks, Alan Tyson suggests they may have performed 'a special function for him in maintaining his morale as well as in facilitating his creative processes'. They did indeed become indispensable to him and at times, when his working method came up in conversation, he was given to quoting from Schiller's *Joan of Arc*: 'Without my banner I dare not come.'[3] Remarks attributed to Beethoven, in conversation with the violinist-composer Louis Schlösser — and later recorded by Ignaz von Seyfried with whom Beethoven was on friendly terms — record him saying:

> 'I make changes, and reject and try again until I am satisfied. Then the breadth, length, height and depth begin in my head, and since I am conscious of what I want the underlying idea never deserts me.'[4]

From his days in Bonn, Beethoven adopted the habit — he called it 'his bad habit' — of recording his musical thoughts on oblong sheets of paper, folded about the middle to yield pages measuring about eight by five inches (twenty by thirteen centimetres). A collection of these sheets then formed the basis of a pocket sketchbook that could serve him on his country walks, enabling him to jot down tentative ideas as they entered his head, or, as Alan Tyson figuratively puts it, 'the honey that the bee had gathered in the meadows'.[5] When back home, Beethoven would transfer his ideas, initially recorded in pencil, onto ruled sheets of manuscript paper that formed the basis for his desk sketchbooks.[6]

The British music scholar Nicholas Cook comments on the 'enormous repertoire of compositional sketches and other materials' Beethoven has bequeathed to musicologists as a consequence of his working method — putting his thoughts down in sketch form as distinct from working directly at the piano. This process, he suggests, was Beethoven's way of 'using paper to improvise'. Beethoven would write something down, perhaps, as remarked, when out on one of his walks in the country — which he found so stimulating to his personal wellbeing and creativity — and then, back at his writing desk, he would, in Cook's memorable phrase, 'let the paper speak back to him'.[7]

In their study of Beethoven's autographs upon which he worked in the later phase of his compositional process, Hans Conrad Fischer and Erich Kock comment:

> 'Beethoven's autograph compositions nearly always showed various preliminary studies and sketches of settings ... First, he noted down the melody on a sketch sheet. This melody might be altered many times but the main framework of the movement was sketched out ... Beethoven transferred the sketch to large [score] sheets containing [twelve or] sixteen [ruled] staves which were divided across the page into three bars. He drew in additional bar lines as he needed them. As the drama of the music increased, so he would increase the speed at which he wrote and the bar lines would get closer together. With a bracket, called an accolade, Beethoven combined a set of twelve staves into a scoring system for the twelve instruments that he envisaged for [the] movement. He later wrote in the parts of the remaining instruments, thus building up the instrumentation to the full orchestra. At the same time, he redrafted complete passages. Corrections in ink, and red pencil were [frequently] superimposed on one another in the score.'[8]

Beethoven authority Barry Cooper discusses the role played by words in the composer's compositional process:

> 'In addition to purely musical symbols, the sketches frequently contain other symbols or ordinary words. Words ... occur where Beethoven is planning the formal scheme of a work or movement. Such plans usually contain a mixture of musical notes and words. A good example is the first sketch draft of the finale of the *Eroica* Symphony, where the remarks concerning form ('principio', 'Var'), texture ('Fuge'), key ('dope in 'Es'), tempo ('un poco adagio'), and instrumentation ('Clarinetto solo', 'Corno solo'), are interspersed with fragments of thematic material ...'.[9]

At the conclusion of his pioneering English-language study of Beethoven's sketches (1929), musicologist Paul Mies wrote:

> 'The study of the *Eroica* sketches shows us with what precision Beethoven balanced the several parts of the Symphony; we see how the growth of one section is directly followed by an increase in an adjoining section; the changing of one part involves that of another, and the later portions of the work develop out of the earlier.'[10]

THE *EROICA* SKETCHES

Beethoven sketched preliminary ideas for the *Eroica* Symphony in the autumn of 1802. He worked more actively on the composition in the summer of the following year and by

1804 it was sufficiently complete to be heard in rehearsal. We consider the successive stages in this creative process with reference to the sketchbooks Beethoven used at this time.

WIELHORSKY SKETCHBOOK

Beethoven made use of the so-called Wielhorsky Sketchbook during 1802–03. Today it consists of 87 leaves, 174 pages, that contain sketches for a putative version of the *Eroica* Symphony (see following) together with those for the Piano Sonata in E-flat major, Op. 31, No. 3, *Christus am Ölberge* (*Oelberge*), and the *Kreutzer* Violin Sonata. It originally came into the possession of the daughter of the Russian Countess Rosalia Rzewuska, sometime in 1832, and was later acquired in the 1850s by Count Mikhail Wielhorsky from whom the sketchbook derives its name. Fittingly, it is now preserved in the Glinka Museum for Musical Culture in Moscow. The sketches for the *Eroica* Symphony are early ideas that are found at pp. 44–45.[11]

Lewis Lockwood asserts the Wielhorsky orchestral sketches 'played a decisive role in the composition of the *Eroica*'.[12] These sketches date from about October 1802 and are therefore contemporaneous with the Heiligenstadt Testament to which we have made previous reference; they follow the *Prometheus* Variations, Op. 35. Cooper considers the orchestral sketches represent 'a plan for a great new symphony in E flat' that he describes in the following terms:

> 'The details are very different from the *Eroica*: there is a slow introduction; the second movement is an adagio in C major; the third movement is a "Menueto serioso", followed by a Trio in G minor; and the themes are unrecognizable. Yet

some melodic fragments resemble ideas in the *Eroica*, and the similarity grows stronger during the detailed sketching on the second page. Most strikingly, there is a sketch for a finale, and it must be assumed that Beethoven had already decided to incorporate the theme from *Prometheus* that he had just used for the variations sketched on the previous pages ... Thus, Beethoven's initial idea was for a grand and heroic Promethean Symphony, whether or not Napoleon was involved.'[13]

LANDSBERG 6 – THE EROICA SKETCHBOOK

Beethoven resumed work on what was to become the *Eroica* Symphony in 1803. In his working out, he made use of the so-called Landsberg 6 Sketchbook that he used from May-June 1803 until March-April 1804. Landsberg 6 was purchased by Ludwig Landsberg, sometime in the 1840s, after which in 1862 it was purchased by the Berlin Royal Library. It was formally in the possession of the Preussische Staatsbibliothek, Berlin but after the Second World War it was removed to the Biblioteka Jagiellońska in Kraków. Through its association with the *Eroica* Symphony, Landsberg 6 is more colloquially known as the *Eroica* Sketchbook.

The *Eroica* is well represented, sketches for it being found in the first part of the sketchbook as follows: First movement, pp. 4–5, 7, 10–18, 20–23, 26–27, 30–41; Second movement, pp. 6, 9, 19, 42–43, 48–56, 61, 92; Third movement (*scherzo*), pp. 10, 36, 42, 60–61, 64–67; Third movement (*Trio*), pp. 27, 42, 60–61, 65, 68–69; Fourth movement, pp. 70–85, 88–91. As can be seen, a survey of the pagination sequence reveals Beethoven moving from one movement to the other, following the dictates of his imagination. Interposed between the four movements are putative ideas for the *Pastoral* Symphony that were already formulating in his mind. Also Illustrative of Beethoven's creativity, and his disposition to turn his mind form one composition to another, are related sketches for the *Waldstein* Piano Sonata, Op. 53, music for the Opera *Leonora* (later *Fidelio*), Triple Concerto, Op. 56, early ideas for the Fifth Symphony, Op. 67, and revisions for *Christus am Ölberge*, Op. 85.[14]

The ideas set forth in the *Eroica* Sketchbook — musical and intellectual — have earned the admiration of many musicologists. Eliot Forbes, editor of Alexander Thayer's *Life of Beethoven*, writes: 'The great accomplishment of the year 1803 had been the writing of the Symphony No. 3.'[15] Thomas Sipe detects a 'sense of intense creative excitement throughout the entire sketchbook'. [16] In more formal terms, Barry Cooper describes Beethoven's melodic sketch process as 'a kind of growth, with the themes tending to acquire more notes (particularly purely decorative ones and connecting notes between phrases) and less regular rhythms, moving away from the obvious and predictable towards something more original and unexpected'.[17] Richard Osborne discusses the level of imagination revealed in Beethoven's sketches:

> 'Examine the sketches and you will see the sweep of Beethoven's imaginative vision — how, at quite an early stage, the melody's dissonant C sharp in bar 7 of the Symphony is already linked to the C sharp [= D flat] in the visionary bridge from development to recapitulation at what will eventually be bar 418. At that time, Beethoven had no more idea of how to cross the space between than a mountaineer contemplating a distant col

from the valley beneath; and, indeed, he wrote out the skeletal development of the movement on a single stave many times before the whole enormous structure fell finally into place.'[18]

Romain Rolland made an extensive study of Beethoven's sketches for the *Eroica* Symphony — styled in his characteristic word-imagery. His text, together with musical illustrations, extends to forty pages and bears eloquent testimony to Beethoven exploring and rejecting musical ideas. We quote the following:

FIRST MOVEMENT:
'We observe that the first long sketch, which at one stroke projects the whole design of the first movement, hollows out the river bed, draws with sure and heavy line the contour of the summit, the melodic peaks, the succession of lights and shades, the sequence of the modulations ... Beethoven has thus received, from the very first instant, the revelation as a whole, the impulse and the general atmosphere of the first part of the movement. But if the weighty machine is now posed on the rails, and endued with its essential organs, the themes and principal motives of its first half, begins to move, all the rest is still to find; the second half of the first movement is still a haze; and even in the first half how heavy this hangs on the workman's heart! Later on, his lucid economy of the elements he is employing will make him reserve this athletic motive for the combat of the second part ... What stupendous agitations, what stampings and tramplings, Beethoven must have

erased from his idea! Sometimes the second sketches increase the chaos by the very act of trying to win free of it, and it is only in the last ones, after the ultimate rigours of criticism and after a furious tension, that the artist achieves the broad, continent, flawless line. The combat is all the more exhausting because Beethoven, quitting the inspired opening, pierces to the tangled heart of the movement, stripping from it, shred by shred, the most exquisite details of expression.'

SECOND MOVEMENT:
'If ever a melody has seemed inspired, if ever a phrase has seemed to find its appointed line at the first attempt, if any work of art conveys the impression that it could never have been written otherwise, that not a single one of its accents or inflections could be changed, for they are part of it from all eternity, it is the principal motive of this Funeral March. Yet the sketchbook shows that Beethoven reached it only by slow stages, painfully, sweating blood and tears.'[19] [20]

AUTOGRAPH SCORE
We recall, from our earlier account, how Ferdinand Ries relates he saw a copy of the autograph score of the *Eroica* Symphony lying upon the composer's table. The word 'Buonaparte' [sic] was indicated at the top of the title page, and, and at the bottom 'Luigi van Beethoven'. Ries was with Beethoven frequently at this time, both as his piano pupil and as his assistant. Regarding Beethoven's attitude to his scores, once they had served their purpose, he recalls:

'Beethoven attached no importance to his autograph compositions. In most cases, once they had been engraved, they lay about in an adjoining room or in the middle of his workroom scattered over the floor among other music. I have often put his music in order, yet, when Beethoven was looking for something, everything was turned upside down again. I could at that time have carried off all those original autograph compositions of his which had already been engraved, and had I asked him for them. I am sure he would have given them to me without a moment's hesitation.'[21]

We further recall from Ries how Beethoven flew into a rage, on learning Bonaparte had been proclaimed Emperor, tearing the title page from the manuscript score — bearing Bonaparte's name — and trampling it on the floor. Ries is here referring to the *original* autograph score of the *Eroica* Symphony. This is now lost — perhaps for the reasons to which Ries alludes? Beethoven's own copy of the score has, however, survived. Scholars have dated this from the first months of 1804 and it was from this copy of the score that an early set of parts was derived.[22] It was auctioned at the sale of the composer's effects following his death in 1827 It was listed as item 'No. 144, *Fremde Abschrift der Sinfonia Eroique in Partitur mit eigenhändigen Ammerkungen*' — with an estimated value of 3 florins. It sold for 3 florins and 10 kreuzer, about 3 francs, to Joseph Dessauer — a Viennese composer of songs.[23] In 1870, Dessauer presented the score to the Gesellschaft der Musikfreunde with whom it remains today as one of their treasured possessions.[24]

In its final form Beethoven's score exceeded in magnitude that of any other symphony to date. It comprises: First movement, *Allegro con brio*, 691 bars; Second movement, *Marcia funebre*, 247 bars; Scherzo, *Allegro vivace*, 397 bars; and Finale, *Allegro molto*, 473 bars. When Sir George Grove examined the score in the nineteenth century, he described it as having an oblong (landscape) format measuring 33 cm by 24 cm.

Although Beethoven's score is not the original autograph, it is valued for containing many emendations and corrections by Beethoven. In this connection, the German musicologist and Beethoven scholar Sieghard Brandenburg has made a detailed study of the surviving copy of the score and elucidates:

> 'The copyist was extremely careless, according to the evidence presented in the *Eroica* score. He omitted numerous accidentals, dynamics, staccatos, ties, and slurs, and often noted the slurs and dynamics vaguely or incorrectly. However, in a way we have to be grateful that he was a "very indifferent worker", to use Beethoven's words, since his errors forced Beethoven to review the score and enter countless corrections. [see later letter to Härtel of 16 January 1805] The corrections, found on almost every page of the score, were largely made in black ink as well as red crayon and pencil ... Beethoven's corrections solve several textual problems and thus increase greatly the value of the score, which is the most important source for the Symphony.'[25]

A list of errors in the first edition of the *Eroica* Symphony was subsequently published in the 18 February 1805 edition of the *Allgemeine musikalische Zeitung*. This identified wrong notes and significant errors, for example, in the second horn part. These disposed the *AmZ* correspondent to remark: 'The engraving is clear and beautiful, but unfortunately not entirely correct.'[26]

Beethoven's copy of the score bore the modified title: SINFONIA GRANDE / *Intitulata Bonaparte* / Del Sigr / Louis van Beethoven / Geschrieben auf Bonaparte / Sinfonia [No.] 3, Op. 55.[27]

This copy of the score did not escape the composer's wrath since he effaced the word 'Bonaparte' with such vigour that he tore a hole in the paper!

BEETHOVEN'S NEGOTIATIONS WITH PUBLISHERS

Beethoven's correspondence extends to several volumes and many of his letters concern his negotiations with publishers.[28] Although Beethoven's younger brother Carl (Caspar Karl) and Ferdinand Ries — and later in life his nephew Karl— assisted Beethoven with the business side of getting his symphonies published — and other compositions — he nevertheless found the process burdensome and a distraction from what he enjoyed most of all, composing. His feelings on the subject are evident from a letter he wrote in January 1801 to the publisher Franz Anton Hoffmeister in Leipzig. He closed his letter remarking, 'Well that tiresome business has now been settled', by which he meant the time-consuming procedures he had to transact with Hoffmeister to see some of his works in print. Beethoven calls it 'tiresome' because, he would like 'such matters to be differently ordered in this world'. He goes on to say:

> 'There ought to be in the world *a market for art* [Beethoven's italics] where the artist would only

have to bring his works and take as much money as he needed.'

He laments how he has to be both an artist and 'to be to a certain extent a business man as well, and how can he manage to be that — Good Heavens!'[29]

With the foregoing in mind, we trace the negotiations made with various publishers by Beethoven, and others on his behalf, in order to bring about the publication of the *Eroica* Symphony.

1803

Between 1802 and 1806 Carl helped Beethoven with his business affairs and his negotiations with publishers. On 21 May, he wrote to the Leipzig publisher Breitkopf and Härtel to offer his publishing house his brother's recently composed Overture to the Ballet *The Creatures of Prometheus* — for which he requested 25 ducats. More significantly he added he had 'a new symphony' — taken to be a reference to the *Eroica* — about which he sought the publisher's opinion.[30]

On 6 August Beethoven's piano pupil Ferdinand Ries, then acting as his teacher's secretary-assistant, wrote on his behalf to the publisher Nikolaus Simrock in Bonn. He offered several recently composed works adding, tantalisingly, 'Beethoven is now writing two symphonies, one of which is practically finished'. The symphony in progress is thought to refer to the *Eroica*, and the one 'practically finished' to be the Second Symphony, Op. 36. Following its first performance on 5th April, Beethoven set about making revisions to the score before its eventual publication the following year in March 1804.

Ries closes his letter with a remark of some significance:

> 'Beethoven will now remain here at most another year and a half. Then he is going to Paris, which I am extraordinarily sorry about. Even though I told him, in jest, that he would have to take me along as his pupil and treasurer.'

As we have already noted, Beethoven had entertained thoughts of leaving Vienna for some time, in the hope his music would be better appreciated in Paris. In the event, he appears to have cast of his slough of despondency, buoyed-up by his burgeoning success as a composer and the growing demand for his work, closer to home, by several publishers.[31]

A letter of 20 September to Beethoven from Gottfried Christoph Härtel is also of particular interest. It sheds lights on the challenges facing legitimate publishers in an era when they did not have the protection of copyright. Since the death in 1800 of G. G. Breitkopf, son of the founder of the publishing house Bernhard Breitkopf, Gottfried Härtel had taken over responsibility for the publishing firm, known as Breitkopf and Härtel, Leipzig and had been negotiating with Carl regarding the publication of Beethoven's Violin Sonata, Op. 47 and the Piano Sonatas, Op. 49, among others. Regarding the terms Carl was seeking for these works, Härtel responded:

> 'Any legitimate publisher of your works is now uncertain to see in advance that the works, which he takes from you for an agreed-upon fee, are [pirate] reprinted not only in Bonn [Nikolaus Simrock], Offenbach [Johann André], and by several other German and French publishers ... It is these circumstances ... [that] make it impossible for a dealer, situated in the middle of Germany, to offer you terms that you find agreeable.'

Despite his caution, Härtel concluded his letter on a more positive note:

> 'On the other hand, should you once again produce a piano concerto or a symphony, and be inclined to entrust it to us for publication, we ask that you let us know your terms.'[32]

On 14 October, Carl replied to Härtel's letter of 20 September, stating:

> 'I can in part fulfil your wish. You can have one or two symphonies, or a symphony and concertante for piano, violincello and violin with full orchestra [possibly a reference to the Triple Concerto, Op. 56].'

For one of the symphonies with the concerto, Carl wanted 700 florins. The symphonies referred to are the Second, Op. 36, then in the final process of revision, and the Third, Op. 55, on which Beethoven was still at work.[33] On 22 October it was Ferdinand Ries who once more corresponded on Beethoven's behalf, this time to Nikolaus Simrock in Bonn. From what he had to say it appears Beethoven's anger towards Bonaparte had mollified somewhat:

> '[Beethoven] wants to sell you the Symphony [Op. 55] for 100 gulden. In his opinion it is the greatest work that he has yet written. Beethoven played it for me recently, and I believe that Heaven and Earth will tremble when it is performed. He is very much inclined to *dedicate* it

[italics added] to Bonaparte, but because [Prince] Lobkowitz wants to have it for half a year, and will give 400 [gulden] [for the privilege], then he will *entitle* it [italics added] "Bonaparte".'[34]

The inference from this part of the letter is that in October 1803 Beethoven had intended to *dedicate* the Symphony to Bonaparte but, with the realization of securing a handsome fee for its use from his patron Prince Lobkowitz, he was prepared to simply assign the *title* of the work to the French Consul. In the event, as we shall see, Bonaparte received neither the dedication to, nor the title of, the *Eroica* Symphony. As Maynard Solomon remarks: 'Beethoven disposed of Bonaparte twice — once in composing the Symphony and again in removing his name from the title.'[35]

Beethoven's financial arrangement with Prince Lobkowitz was typical at this period of the relationship between composer and patron. It conferred on the latter the initial performance-rights of the composition he wished to support and with which he wished his name to be associated — a form of immortality! As we shall in due course relate, Lobkowitz ultimately became the dedicatee of the *Eroica* Symphony.

The correspondence with publishers for 1803 closed on 11 December when Ries wrote once more to Nikolaus Simrock who was still considering whether to publish the *Eroica* Symphony. However, he wanted certain proprietorial reassurances that disposed Ries to write: 'Beethoven will absolutely not sell his new Symphony and will reserve it for his tour, for which he is also composing another new one.'[36]

Beethoven had been contemplating undertaking a foreign tour for some time. Perhaps, whilst still in possession of some hearing, he had hopes of repeating the success of the concert tour he had made early in 1796 when he journeyed to Prague in the company of his patron Prince Lichnowsky; Mozart had made a similar trip — remembered today through its association with his *Prague* Symphony, K. 504. Beethoven interrupted his 1796 tour with a brief return to Vienna after, which he departed for Leipzig, Dresden, and Berlin where he gave a number of concerts. His new projected tour, however, did not materialize. Regarding Ries's reference to 'another new [symphony]', this can be taken to refer to the *Pastoral* Symphony, Op. 60 that Beethoven already had in hand — further testimony to his extraordinary creativity.

1804

The following year we learn indirectly of a performance of the *Eroica* Symphony from a letter written on 11 June by Anton Wranitsky to Prince Lobkowitz's Cashier. Wranitsky was Lobkowitz's concertmaster (orchestral leader) and conductor and acted on behalf of freelance musicians who were hired on occasions to supplement the Prince's regular, but small, orchestra. Rehearsals of the *Eroica* Symphony, essentially trial readings, had taken place in Lobkowitz's Vienna palace in the great salon, known today as the *Eroica-Saal*. These possibly occurred at the close of May or, more certainly, in early June and Wranitsky was requesting payment for the musicians who had taken part in the performances. He had hired the services of: 4 violins, 2 violas, 2 double basses, 2 oboes, 2 clarinets, 2 bassoons, 2 flutes, 2 horns (to which a third was added), 2 trumpets, and 1 timpani. Each player received 2 florins. With these resources, the *Eroica* Symphony must have made a sonorous effect in the marble-clad walls of the *Eroica-Saal*.[37]

On 26 August, Beethoven himself wrote to Breitkopf

and Härtel to inform him of the progress he was making with several compositions:

> 'You can have: my Oratorio [*Christus am Ölberge*] – a *new grand symphony* [*Eroica*] [Beethoven's italics], a concertante [concerto] for violin, violincello and pianoforte with full orchestra [Triple Concerto, Op. 56 later dedicated to Prince Lobkowitz], and three new sonatas for pianoforte solo [*Waldstein*, Op. 53; Op. 54; and *Appassionata*, Op. 57].'

Beethoven informed Härtel, if he wanted to publish these works he must let him know how long it would take since, he added, 'It is my most earnest desire that the first three works at any rate should appear as soon as possible, we could fix the time in writing'. Of particular significance in this letter is the following passage:

> 'The title of the Symphony is really *Bonaparte*; and in addition to all the other usual instruments it has the compliment of three horns. [an innovation] I think it will interest the musical public.'

Also of significance is Beethoven's request: 'I should like you to publish the Symphony *in score* [Beethoven's italics] instead of engraving the [instrumental] parts.' At the period in question, the publication of large orchestral pieces in their individual orchestral parts, without full score, was the norm. Beethoven's request may be taken as an indication of the importance he attached to his new creation. His request was not, however, fulfilled. The 'official' publication of the *Eroica* Symphony, in full score, had to wait until 1822 when it appeared as such in an edition by Nikolaus

Simrock — an 'unofficial' pirate edition preceded this. (see later)

Beethoven offered the set of compositions mentioned above for a fee of 2,000 gulden (c.f. florins), remarking:

> 'I assure you on my honour that in the case of some individual works, such as, for instance, [the] sonatas, I am really the loser, seeing that people give me up to 60 ducats for a single sonata for pianoforte solo. I beg you not to think that I am bragging.'[38]

From the foregoing it is evident that in August 1804 Beethoven was still unsure whether to restore the association of Bonaparte with the *Eroica* Symphony.[39]

Härtell responded promptly to Beethoven on 30 August. His letter further reveals the challenges confronting publishers at this time. He opens: 'We highly esteem and value your kind application to us concerning the four works that you have produced.' Härtell is referring here to the piano sonatas to which Beethoven makes reference and had assumed that the three sonatas mentioned were in fact a single opus — as was typical in eighteenth-century terms. Härtell proudly described his music engraving and publishing house as being well organized and capable of producing large works in considerable numbers. He regretted, though, that his business was not in a position at present to fulfil the composer's requirements. He explained: 'The reason for this is that sales in Germany have been greatly diminished by pirate printings'. He gave the following illustration:

> 'We have had this experience with Mozart's *Requiem* and *Don Giovanni*, Handel's *Messiah*,

Haydn's *Masses* and similar works which caused us too great a loss ...'.

Härtell tried to be accommodating and concluded:

'If only your proposals are made in one manner or another that does not make the publication of these works impossible for us, then they shall be prepared and distributed very quickly.'[40]

The following month Härtel himself revealed he too was not above entering into a certain amount of *légerdemain* with his fellow publishers. On 4 September 1804, he wrote to the London publisher Muzio Clementi, without Beethoven's knowledge or consent, proposing they should both bring out the composer's new Piano Sonatas Opp. 53, 54 and 57, together with the *Eroica* Symphony and the Triple Concerto, but not the Oratorio since Härtel considered, 'It will be of no utility to us both'. A feature of this somewhat nefarious undertaking was they would together bear their respective publishing costs and then benefit from the joint publication rights in England.[41]

Concerning the foregoing, it is probable that Härtel had suggested some form of financial undertaking with Muzio Clementi earlier in the year for the following reason. On 10 June 1804, Clementi had written to the innovative London piano maker William Frederick Collard – famed for his improvement of the working-action of the piano. Clementi entertained hopes that he himself would soon secure the publication rights of certain of Beethoven's works that were still in manuscript form. He states how he hoped to secure the compositions 'at a tolerably easy rate'. He was aware that in his dealings with publishers, Beethoven could be 'very exorbitant'. This remark is undoubtedly an allusion not to Beethoven *per se* but to his brother Carl, who was prone to demand excessive prices for his brother's works. Clementi's next remark, however, can only have been made with Beethoven in mind: 'He is well, by a miracle, for he quarrels with almost every living creature.'[42]

On 10 October Carl wrote to Härtel once more on his brother's behalf urging him to consider publishing the *Eroica* Symphony together with the Triple Concerto and the three Piano Sonatas. The latter, he insisted, should be published separately and not under a single opus number. He appears to have reduced the asking price — most unusual for Carl — to 1,100 gulden (florins) but insisted 'my brother gets much more for similar compositions'.[43]

Carl's revised offer for the sale of the works in question proved acceptable to Härtel who wrote to Beethoven on 3 November: 'We shall agree to the price [1,100 florins in Viennese currency], and it will give us pleasure to renew our association with you thereby.' On receipt of the manuscripts, Härtel — somewhat optimistically — hoped to publish all five compositions 'within eight or nine weeks'.[44]

On 24 November, Carl confirmed with Härtel that Beethoven was agreeable to his terms and gave an undertaking to mail manuscript copies of the various compositions in a sequence so that they could be published one after the other. He suggested sending the Piano Sonata Op. 53 and Triple Concerto, Op. 56 within two weeks. Two weeks later, he proposed sending the two further Piano Sonatas Op. 54 and Op. 57 and that the *Eroica* Symphony, Op. 55 would follow two weeks after that. Carl explains, that by delivering these compositions in succession it would ensure their negotiations would run more smoothly. He stated this was necessary since only one copyist was available to whom they could entrust the work; Beethoven was endlessly vexed by the careless work of errant copyists. Furthermore, Carl explained how busy Beethoven was working on his Opera. *Fidelio*, Op. 72 and, thereby, 'had little time to oversee so many business transactions'.[45]

On 4 December Härtel confirmed with Beethoven he had received Carl's letter of the previous month and 'very gladly' looked forward to receiving the compositions. However, mindful of his previous losses, occasioned through the subterfuges of rogue publishers, he requested Beethoven's authorisation to the exclusive propriety — publication rights — 'to ward off German as well as French and English pirate printing'.[46]

1805

On 16 January the following year, Beethoven confirmed the manuscript of the *Eroica* Symphony had now been despatched: 'In it you will find the Symphony.' As agreed, he also offered the Piano Sonatas Op. 53 and Op. 54. He complained 'of having many difficulties'. He remarked that his health was always weaker in the winter and that checking through the work of his copyists was 'far less enjoyable than composing'. Moreover, he complained this work was slow since one of his copyists was 'a very indifferent worker', requiring him to correct much of his work.[47]

On 12 February, Carl assisted Beethoven once more. What he has to say reveals how, when Beethoven was still in possession of his hearing, he was prepared to modify his scores having heard his music in performance. Carl informed Härtel:

> 'At first, before he had yet heard the [*Eroica*] Symphony, my brother believed it would be too long if the first part [the exposition] of the first movement were repeated, but after several per-

formances he found it disadvantageous if the first part was not repeated.'

Carl also reiterated Beethoven's request for the Symphony to be printed 'the way the Haydn symphonies were in Paris [Nos. 90—93, 95 and 98], in a small-format score, so that any connoisseur who wants to may buy one'. By this date, Beethoven had heard the *Eroica* Symphony performed at least four times: twice at rehearsals in May—June 1804, and at the semi-private performances at Prince Lobkowitz's Saal in December 1804 and on 23 January 1805. It still awaited it first public performance though at the Theater an der Wien later in the year on 7 April. Of related interest is Carl's suggestion to Härtel that he should try to forestall pirate copies of the Symphony from being issued, and unlawful arrangements of it being made. He suggested the publisher should issue his own piano arrangement and one for string quartet or quintet. Carl reassured Härtel if he did not have anyone available to undertake the work he could recommend Carl Möser of Vienna.[48] Möser was an accomplished violinist and a skilful arranger of large-scale works for piano or smaller ensembles.

On 18 April, Carl wrote again on his brother's behalf. He apologised for the delay in sending Härtel the promised manuscripts and sought to exonerate his brother by explaining he did not have available a copyist 'familiar with [his] handwriting'. The decipherment of Beethoven's musical notation, with its numerous emendations, posed endless challenges to the composer's long-suffering copyists and were the cause of frequent caustic exchanges. Beethoven pledged the *Eroica* Symphony would be ready 'definitely ... in two-months' time'.

Beethoven urgently requested production of the works already sent — the Symphony, Op. 55 and the Piano Sonatas Op. 53 and 54 — should commence. He suggested being paid part of the agreed sum in advance (700 gulden) and the remainder (400 gulden) once he had delivered the other works he had promised (Sonatas Op. 56 and Op. 57). This suggestion may have been at Carl's instigation, since he was known to publishers for striking hard bargains. In much the same vein the letter continues:

> 'Should these conditions relating to both the early publication and to the method of payment not be acceptable to you ... and should you not be able to give me a definite promise that they will be fulfilled, then, although this would be unpleasant for me, I should have no option but to break off our negotiations and demand the immediate return of the works you have already received.'[49]

Härtel appears to have lost patience with Beethoven's tardiness. On 21 June he complained:

> 'Approximately nine months have passed since your first negotiation with us concerning the five new works you offered us, without reaching our goal, although we granted your demands at once ... Although our esteem for your art remains great, and out wish has always been to acquire your new works for our publishing house, this dubious situation has become very unpleasant for us in the long run.'[50]

Accordingly, Härtel relinquished the right to the publication of the *Eroica* Symphony and likewise the other works he had undertaken to bring out. In more conciliatory fashion, Hartel restated it would still give him 'honour and pleasure' to publish his further new works subject, however, to

Beethoven fulfilling more stringent business arrangements.

Beethoven responded to Härtel's letter of 21 June, this time in his own hand (his letter in undated). He asserted the fee he was asking was lower than he would normally receive for such compositions and he could not accept a lower fee. He therefore requested the return of the manuscripts he had already sent.[51]

Thereby, Beethoven terminated his protracted negotiations with Härtel's publishing firm. They would not be resumed for some years — but profitably so. Between 1809 and 1812 Härtel published the Fifth and Sixth Symphonies, the Cello Sonata, Op. 69, the Piano Trios, Op. 70, and the Fifth Piano Concerto, Op. 73.

1806

Beethoven had to wait until the October 1806 to see the *Eroica* Symphony in print. It was eventually published by the Vienna publisher the Kunst- und Industrie-Comptoir, also known by its French title as the Bureau des arts et d'Industrie (Bureau d'arts et d'Industrie) and in Germany, Kunst- und Industrie-Comptoir zu Wien. The Vienna-based publisher became Beethoven's principal publisher for the years 1802–08, eventually including some forty first editions of the composer's works in their catalogue. Aside from publication of the *Eroica* Symphony, the year 1808 was particularly memorable for both Beethoven and the Kunst- und Industrie-Comptoir. It saw publication of the Fourth Symphony, Fourth Piano Concerto, the three *Razumowsky* String Quartets, and the Overture *Coriolan*.

In 1806, by which time the *Eroica* Symphony was being performed in public, Beethoven had occasion to complain to Gottfried Härtel about an adverse review of the *Eroica* Symphony that had appeared in the *Leipziger Allgemeine musikalische Zeitung*. This was published by Härtel's firm and Beethoven, somewhat unjustly, held Härtel personally responsible for the journal's contents. The editor was in fact Johann Friedrich Rochlitz, a respected music critic and musicologist. Beethoven fulminated:

> 'I hear that in the Musikalische Zeitung someone has railed violently against the Symphony which I sent you last year and which you returned to me. I have not read the article [Beethoven's emphasis]. If you fancy that you can injure me by publishing articles of that kind, you are very much mistaken. On the contrary, by so doing you merely bring your journal into disrepute, the more so as I have made no secret whatever of the fact that you returned to me that particular Symphony together with some other compositions.'

Beethoven concluded on a conciliatory note:

> 'Be so kind as to give my compliments to *Herr von Rochlitz*. I trust his angry feelings towards me will have subsided a little ... Should I ever go to Leipzig, I am convinced that we should certainly become good friends, *without prejudice to or disparagement of his criticism.*'[52]

Years later, on a visit to Vienna, Rochlitz did indeed meet Beethoven (and Franz Schubert) and established a cordial relationship with him.

To conclude this section of our discussion, we look a few years beyond 1806. Between 12 November 1807 and 27 March 1808, some twenty concerts were given in Vienna by the newly formed *Gesellschaft von Musikfreunden*. Ten of the concerts included Beethoven Symphonies: Nos. One,

Two, and Three were each performed twice alongside his Piano Concerto No. 1, and the Overture *Coriolan* — also performed twice. For these performances an orchestra of 55 players assembled who included the violinist Franz Clement — remembered for premiering of Beethoven's Violin Concerto on 23 December 1806 at the Theater an der Wien.

DEDICATEE

We have seen, Beethoven initially considered dedicating the *Eroica* Symphony to Napoleon or, at least, associating his name with the title of the work so as to celebrate the ideals he perceived were associated with him. Matters changed, not least when his patron Prince Lobkowitz offered him the princely sum (Beethoven-style pun intended) of 400 ducats for exclusive rights to the work — and possibly an additional sum to secure the dedication. So, it was that Lobkowitz received the dedication — and immortality thereby.[53]

Joseph Franz Maximilian — 7th Prince of Lobkowitz, to give him his full name and title, is remembered in musicology for many reasons. He was an excellent violinist and cellist and a trained singer. He adapted the largest room in his Viennese mansion, the Palais Lobkowitz, into a concert hall — today known as *The Eroica Hall* — where the *Eroica* Symphony was first rehearsed. Lobkowitz actively promoted new music and was a founder member of the Gesellschaft der Musikfreunde. His contribution to Beethoven's annuity, to persuade him not to leave Vienna to take up the post of Kapellmeister at the Court of Jérôme Bonaparte, as has been mentioned.

In addition to the dedication of the *Eroica* Symphony, Beethoven conferred on Lobkowitz the dedications to his

String Quartets, Op. 18, the Triple Concerto, the Fifth and Sixth Symphonies, both jointly with Count (later Prince) Razumovsky and the String Quartet Op. 74, The *Harp*.

TITLE PAGE
The first edition of the Symphony, published in 1806 by the Kunst- und Industrie-Comptoir bears the following title:

> 'SINFONIA EROICA composta per festigiare il Souvenire di un grand Uomo, e dedicate a Sua Altezza Serenissima il Principe di Lobkowitz da Luigi van Beethoven, Op. 55, No. III delle Sinfonie.'[54]

Beethoven responded to the work being very long by having the following words appended to the first violin part:

> '*Questa Sinfonia essendo scritta apposta più lunga della solite, si deve eseguire più vicino al principio ch'al fine di un Academia, e poco doppo un Overtura, un' Aria, ed un Concerto; accioche, sentita troppo tardi, non perda per l'auditore, già faticato dalle precedenti produzioni, il suo proprio, proposto effetto.*'

> 'This Symphony, being purposely written at a greater length than usual, should be played nearer the beginning than the end of a concert, and shortly after an Overture, an Air, and a Concerto; lest, if it is heard too late, when the audience are fatigued by the pervious pieces, it should lose its proper and intended effect.'[55]

BEETHOVEN'S TEMPO INDICATIONS

With the advent of Johann Nepomuk Maelzel's new instrument (1816–17), Beethoven seized upon its potential as a means of securing reliable tempi for the performance of his works. A report in the *Wiener Vaterländische Blätter* (*Vienna Patriotic Periodical*) stated:

> 'Herr Beethoven looks upon this invention as a welcome means with which to secure the performance of his brilliant compositions in all places in the tempos conceived by him, which to his regret have so often been misunderstood.'[56]

The principal feature of the metronome is an oscillating pendulum that had been developed by the Amsterdam mechanic Nikolaus Winkel. Maelzel added a calibrated scale to Winkel's pendulum that could be regulated to set the tempo required for a particular piece of music. Today, it is an indispensable part of a music-teacher's pedagogical armoury.

On 17 December 1817, the *Allgemeine musikalische Zeitung* published a list of 'the tempos for every movement of the symphonies of Herr L. v. Beethoven as determined by the composer using Maelzel's metronome'. Beethoven also had a pamphlet printed by the publisher Sigmund Anton Steiner that gave his suggested metronome markings for the string quartets that he had composed to date, namely, Opp. 18, 59, 74 and 95 and also included markings for his first eight symphonies.[57] Steiner had met Beethoven sometime in 1803. His publishing house specialised in printing sheet music and lithography and his premises became an informal meeting place for Beethoven and his friends.[58]

Beethoven's enthusiasm for the metronome is conveyed in a letter he wrote sometime in November 1817 to Ignaz

Franz von Mosel; Mosel, a composer, violinist and writer on music, arranged and conducted the first concert given by the Gesellschaft der Musikfreunde. In his letter, Beethoven enthused:

> 'I am heartily delighted to know that you hold the same views as I do about our tempo indications which originated in the barbarous ages of music. For, to take one example, what can be more absurd than *Allegro*, which really signifies *merry*, and how very far removed we often are from the idea of that tempo. So much so that the piece itself means the *very opposite of the indications* ... As for me, I have long been thinking of abandoning those absurd descriptive terms, *Allegro*, *Andante*, *Adagio*, *Presto*, and Maelzel's metronome affords us the best opportunity of doing so. I now give you *my word* that I shall *never again* use them in any of my new compositions.'[59]

A further measure of Beethoven's wish to have his orchestral works performed at what he considered to be the 'correct' tempi is evident in a further letter he wrote to the Mainz publisher Bernhard Schotts in December 1826 regarding his *Choral* Symphony:

> 'The metronome markings will be sent to you very soon. Do wait for them ... [I] have received letters from Berlin informing me that the first performance of the Symphony was received with enthusiastic applause which I ascribe to the metronome markings.'

He closes with a typical Beethovenian epithet: 'We can scarcely have *tempi ordinari* any longer, since one must fall into line with the ideas of unfettered genius.'[60]

Beethoven's metronome markings divide opinion today; some orchestral conductors consider they set too fast a tempo. It has been suggested the reason for this is that Beethoven, confined by deafness to an inner world of *imagined* sound, ascribed quicker markings to his music than he would have if he had the benefit of experiencing his music *in performance*. Writing of contemporary attitudes to orchestral tempi, musicologist Anne-Louise Coldicott remarks:

> 'The 1980s were a period of striving towards historical accuracy in performance. In orchestral music this manifested itself in the use of smaller forces and, more radically, of period instruments.'

Coldicott cites the innovations of:

> '*The Hanover Band* (without a conductor), *The London Classical Players* under Roger Norrington, and *The Academy of Ancient Music* under Christopher Hogwood. One of the most interesting aspects [raised in their interpretations] is the question of tempo. In a desire to respect Beethoven's metronome markings, these performances are generally faster than we have come to expect, and in apparent accordance with the practice of Beethoven's time there is much less flexibility.'

Distinguishing between the interpretations of these three sets of players, Coldicott further remarks:

> '[There] are considerable variations in the size of the orchestra, the types of instruments used, and the degree of control and sophistication imposed by the conductors. All display a refreshing transparency of texture and transmit a certain exhilaration.'

This is a case, as Coldicott concludes, quoting the American musicologist, Richard Truscin, of 'restating rather than restoring "literalism".'[61] Sir Roger Norrington, known for historically-informed performances of Classical music, expresses the viewpoint:

> 'Beethoven inherited a whole series of traditional speeds, including an *allegro* which was not very fast and an *andante* which was by no means slow. He is most insistent on the importance of using a metronome (partly, no doubt, because his deafness prevented him from directing performances). In virtually every case his metronome marks tally with an eighteenth-century understanding of tempo indications.'[62]

Jonathan Del Mar has undertaken a scholarly study of the scores to Beethoven's symphonies and has words of caution concerning the too literal interpretation of the composer's metronome indications. He questions how much patience Beethoven may have had when he sent off his suggested tempo indications, in 1817, for publication in the *Allgemeine musikalische Zeitung*.[63] In this context, we make two related observations. Beethoven's eyesight was rather poor; he often complained about this in his letters. This raises the question as to how accurately he could read the fine graduated scale on his metronome. Additionally, it is known, once more from his correspondence, that his metronome was sometimes broken!

Between June and July 1990, the Austrian conductor Nikolaus Harnoncourt recorded Beethoven's Second and Fifth Symphonies. Mindful of Harnoncourt's reputation for 'historic performance-practice', he was asked about his approach to the interpretation of the composer's orchestral music by professor Hartmut Krones — Head of the Department of Musical Studies and Performing Practice at the Vienna College of Fine Arts. Krones raised the question of what he referred to as 'one of the most controversial issues in the whole of Beethoven interpretation', namely the composer's original metronome markings. Harnoncourt responded:

> 'When I read Beethoven's scores without actually playing them, I arrive at almost the same metronome markings as he did. However, a tempo measured as the same can vary greatly in effect according to the circumstances — the size of the orchestra here is just as decisive as the size and resonance of the hall. The tempo, as measured in one's mind, is certainly the fastest of all; with just a piano or string quartet, I am still very close to my "imagined tempo", but with a huge orchestra I may find I have to move away from it. Perhaps it depends on whether one is playing in the morning, afternoon or evening: the pulse-frequency and the attitude of musicians and audience alike is different every time. If you fail to take all these factors into account and simply judge tempo with a metronome, then this is inhuman and unreal. But, notwithstanding, Beethoven did mean his tempi as he wrote them down. One just has to modify them all the time, and nobody knew how to do that better then Beethoven himself.'[64]

PUBLICATION

At the close of eighteenth century it was customary to publish orchestral music in parts. Instrumental pieces were typically played under the direction of a violin-leader who was guided solely by the first-violin part before him. The well-established structure and orchestration of late eighteenth-century works enabled the music to be faithfully interpreted in this way without recourse to a full score. However, with the advent of the later symphonies of, for example, Haydn and Mozart, and, more notably, those of Beethoven, the need for the players to be directed by a conductor, following a full score, became more evident. Prior to their publication in score, symphonies could be conducted from manuscript copies of the full score – borrowed from the musical archives of such publishers as Hoffmeister and Kühnel and Breitkopf & Härtel.[65]

Beethoven's first six symphonies were initially published in parts only; full score editions followed some four to fifteen years after the publication of the parts:

First Symphony, parts in 1801 and score in 1809
Second Symphony, parts in 1804 and score in 1808
Third Symphony, parts in 1806, and score in 1809
Fourth Symphony, parts in 1808 and score in 1823
Fifth Symphony, parts in 1809 and score in 1826,
Sixth Symphony, parts in 1809 and score in 1826.

The first editions of Symphonies Nos. 7–9 were published concurrently in parts *and* full score.[66]

A set of manuscript parts for the *Eroica* Symphony is in possession of the Gesellschaft der Musikfreunde; eleven of an original set of eighteen parts have survived. These include parts for the flute, oboe and clarinet. These parts were corrected by Beethoven and his pupil Ries relating to considerations of markings for dynamics, tempo, slurs and staccato. Other textual corrections were added by performers during the nineteenth century.[67]

We have seen, the first edition of the *Eroica* Symphony was published in parts in October 1806 by the Kunst- und Industrie-Comptoir. This was despite Beethoven's request to have the work published in full score; perhaps the publisher considered the financial outlay to much of a risk? Between 1807 and 1809 the parts were reprinted with various corrections made by Beethoven.

Meanwhile, in England, the London-based publishers Cianchettini & Sperati were some years ahead of their German counterparts in bringing out full-score editions of Beethoven's symphonies — and those of other celebrated composers. In May 1807, under the patronage of the Prince of Wales, in the pages of *The New Musical Magazine, Review, and Register*, they invited subscriptions for 'A compleat collection of Haydn, Mozart and Beethoven symphonies in score'. Two numbers appeared in the months of November and December until the enterprise ceased publication in 1809. Nevertheless, these editions incorporated Beethoven's first three symphonies. The Cianchettini & Sperati Beethoven full-scores were derived — cobbled together — from the editions of the parts of the compositions that had already appeared on the continent. A plan to publish a complete Edinburgh edition was commenced but was not brought to completion. Needless to say, all of this was without Beethoven's knowledge — nor did he gain financially from the venture.[68]

Some of Beethoven's works had appeared in full score fairly early in the century. *Christus am Oelberg* led the way in 1811, followed by the Mass in C during the following year, both by Breitkopf and Härtel at Leipzig. *Wellington's Victory* came out as a lithograph score in 1816 by Steiner of Vienna and the *Choral* Symphony appeared in score with vocal parts in 1826, likewise the great Mass in D in 1827 – both at Schott's of Mayence.

On 13 May 1822, Nikolaus Simrock in Bonn wrote to Beethoven urging him to make progress with the completion of the *Missa Solemnis* for which he had paid 100 Louis d'or. In the course of his letter, Simrock adds: 'For the present I have undertaken to publish your six Symphonies [i.e. Nos. 1–6] in full score.' He gives the reason:

> '[I] wanted to dedicate to my worthy old friend a worthy monument, and I hope you will be satisfied with the edition, since I have done my utmost for it!'[69]

The scores of the First and Second Symphonies appeared in 1822 followed by that of the *Eroica* Symphony a few months later and that of the Fourth Symphony in 1823. In the event, notwithstanding his expressed intentions, Simrock never published the scores of the Fifth and Sixth Symphonies. They were published by Breitkopf & Härtel in 1826.

Commencing in 1862, Breitkopf & Härtel published a complete edition (*Gesamtausgabe*) of Beethoven's works that included full-score editions of the symphonies. Beethoven had cherished such an undertaking in his lifetime – perhaps being influenced by his awareness of such an edition of Handel's music with which he had become familiar and which he so greatly admired. He even envisaged adding new works to fill the gaps in his output.

---

[1] Donald Tovey, *Ludwig van Beethoven* in: *The Classics of Music*, Michael Tilmouth editor, 2001, pp. 333-4.

[2] Gustav Nottebohm, 1979, (translation and reprint) pp. 4–7.

[3] Alan Tyson, *Sketches and Autographs*, in: Denis Arnold, and Nigel Fortune, editors. *The Beethoven Companion*, 1973, pp. 443– 58.

4. Quoted by Peter Clive, 2000, p. 318.
5. Alan Tyson, *Commentaries to Beethoven's Sketches*, 1963.
6. For a modern-day interpretation of how Beethoven may have appeared, when working at his desk, see the illustration by the artist-sculptor Donna Dralle reproduced on the website, *The Unheard Beethoven* to the text, *The Creatures of Prometheus*.
7. Nicholas Cook, in: Michael Oliver, *Settling the Score: A Journey Through the Music of the Twentieth Century*. London: Faber and Faber, 1999, p. 224.
8. Hans Conrad Fischer and Erich Kock. 1972, pp. 96–107.
9. Barry Cooper, 1991, pp. 97–98. This text incorporates several musical illustrations.
10. Paul Mies, 1929, reprint, 1969, p. 187.
11. Douglas Porter Johnson, editor, 1985, pp. 130–35. See also, Peter Clive, 2000, p. 301.
12. Lewis Lockwood editor, *Beethoven Essays: Studies in Honor of Elliot Forbes*, 1984 quoted by Thomas Sipe, 1998, pp. 21–28.
13. Barry Cooper, 2000, pp. 129–30.
14. Douglas Porter Johnson editor, 1985, pp. 137–45.
15. Elliot Forbes editor, *Thayer's life of Beethoven*, 1967, pp. 348–49.
16. Thomas Sipe, 1998, pp. 25–26.
17. Barry Cooper, 1900, p. 152.
18. Richard Osborne, *Beethoven* in: Robert Layton editor, *A Guide to the Symphony*, 1995, p. 89.
19. Romain Rolland, 1937, pp. 65–69 and p. 89.
20. Four of Beethoven's draft sketches for the first movement have been realised in audible form. They include familiar exposition material with ideas for different opening chords. The playing time is nine minutes. Similar recordings have also been made from sketches for the first movement. These contain familiar rhythms with some unfamiliar melodic explorations and themes for a fugato. Their performing time is four minutes. See: website, *The Unheard Beethoven, Draft for the Third Symphony, Op. 55*.
21. Ferdinand Ries as recollected in: Oscar George Sonneck, 1927, p. 57.
22. Thomas Sipe, 1998, p. 26.
23. George Grove, 1896, p. 55.
24. For further details of the circumstances relating to Beethoven's copy of the score to the *Eroica* Symphony, see: Elliot Forbes editor, *Thayer's life of Beethoven*, 1967, pp. 348–50 and Maynard Solomon, 1977, pp. 132–3.
25. Sieghard Brandenburg editor, *Haydn, Mozart, & Beethoven: Studies in the Music of the Classical Period: Essays in Honor of Alan Tyson*, 1998, pp. 184–88.
26. *Ibid*.
27. See: Jonathan del Mar, *Critical Commentary to Symphonie Nr. 3 in D-dur*, Bärenreiter Kassel, Basel, undated. For a facsimile reproduction of the Title Page, see: Barry Cooper, *Beethoven Compendium*, 1991, plate 27. For a commentary on Beethoven's handwriting and the style of notation he adopted in his autograph score, see p. 176 and the subsequent illustrations.
28. For many years the English-language standard work of reference has been that

of Emily Anderson editor and translator, *The Letters of Beethoven*. London: Macmillan, 3 vols.,1961. Between 1996 and 1998, seven volumes of the Beethoven Haus, Bonn edition were published by G. Henle Publishers in Munich under the title *Ludwig van Beethoven. Briefwechsel. Gesamtausgabe*. Volumes 1–6, Letters from 1783 to 1827; and Volume 7, Index.

[29] Emily Anderson, 1961, Vol. 1, Letter No. 44, pp. 47-8. For a facsimile reproduction of this letter see: Beethoven House, Digital Archives, Library Document, NE 160.

[30] Theodore Albrecht editor and translator, 1996, Vol. 1, Letter No. 59, pp. 102–03.For a facsimile reproduction of this letter see: Beethoven House, Digital Archives, Library Document, HCB Br 304.

[31] Theodore Albrecht editor and translator, 1996, Vol. 1, Letter No. 65, pp. 110–11.

[32] *Ibid*, Letter No. 65, pp. 116–17.

[33] *Ibid*, Letter No. 70, pp. 118–19.

[34] *Ibid*, Letter No. 71, pp. 119–121.

[35] Maynard Solomon, 1977, p. 141.

[36] Theodore Albrecht editor and translator, 1996, Vol. 1, Letter No. 75, pp. 125–27.

[37] *Ibid*, Document No. 81, pp. 135–38.

[38] Emily Anderson editor and translator, 1961, Vol. 1, Letter No. 96, pp. 115–17. For a facsimile reproduction of this letter see: Beethoven House, Digital Archives, Library Document, HCB Br 63.

[39] See: Maynard Solomon, 1977, p. 132.

[40] Theodore Albrecht editor and translator, 1996, Vol. 1, Letter No. 83, pp. 140–41.

[41] *Ibid*, Letter No. 84, p. 142.

[42] *Ibid*, Letter No. 80, pp. 133–8.

[43] *Ibid*, Letter No. 86, pp. 144–45. For a facsimile reproduction of this letter see: Beethoven House, Digital Archives, Library Document, HCB Br 309.

[44] Theodore Albrecht, translator and editor, 1996, Vol. 1, Letter No. 87, pp. 146–47.

[45] *Ibid*, Letter No. 91, pp. 149–50. For a facsimile reproduction of the letter see: Beethoven House, Digital Archives, Library Document, HCB Br 310.

[46] Theodore Albrecht, translator and editor, 1996, Vol. 1, Letter No. 92, p. 151.

[47] Emily Anderson editor and translator, 1961, Vol. 1, Letter No. 108, pp. 129–30.For a facsimile reproduction of this letter see: Beethoven House, Digital Archives, Library Document, HCB Br 64.

[48] Theodore Albrecht, translator and editor, 1996, Vol. 1, Letter No. 98, pp. 158–60.For a facsimile reproduction of this letter see: Beethoven House, Digital Archives, Library Document, HCB Br 312.

[49] Emily Anderson editor and translator, 1961, Vol. 1, Letter No. 111, pp. 132–33.For a facsimile reproduction of this letter see: Beethoven House, Digital Archives, Library Document, HCB Br 66.

[50] Theodore Albrecht, translator and editor, 1996, Vol. 1, Letter No. 104, pp. 164–65.

[51] Emily Anderson editor and translator, 1961, Vol. 1, Letter No. 118, pp.

137—38. For a facsimile reproduction of this letter see: Beethoven House, Digital Archives, Library Document, HCB Br 65.
[52] Emily Anderson editor and translator, 1961, Vol. 1, Letter No.134, pp. 152—53. For a facsimile reproduction of this letter see: Beethoven House, Digital Archives, Library Document HCB Br 67.
[53] For contextual discussion, see: Barry Cooper, 2000, p. 141.
[54] Wilhelm Altmann, Preface to: *Symphony No. 3*, Dover Publications, 1976 (reprint).
[55] George Grove, 1896, p. 56.
[56] Elliot Forbes editor, *Thayer's Life of Beethoven*, 1967 p. 544.
[57] Anne-Louise Coldicott, *Performance Practice in Beethoven's Day* in: Barry Cooper, 1991, pp. 280—09.
[58] For a facsimile reproduction of an engraving of Sigmund Anton Steiner, combined with contextual information, see: Beethoven House, Digital Archives, Library Document, B. 184.
[59] Emily Anderson editor and translator, 1961, Vol. 2, Letter No. 845, p. 727. See also: Carlos Chávez *Musical Thought*, 1961. From 1958-59 Chávez was the Charles Eliot Norton professor at Harvard University and in his Fifth Lecture he quoted Beethoven's letter to Ignaz Franz von Mosel with contextual commentary.
[60] Emily Anderson editor and translator, 1961, Vol. 3, Letter No. 1545, p. 1325.
[61] Anne-Louise Coldicott, *Performance Styles Since Beethoven's Day* in: Barry Cooper, *The Beethoven Compendium: A Guide to Beethoven's Life and Music*,1991, pp. 300—02.
[62] Roger Norrington, Liner notes to *Beethoven, Symphonies 1 & 6*, The London Classical Players, EMI CDC 7497462, 1988.
[63] Jonathan del Mar, *Critical Commentary to Symphonie Nr. 2 in D-dur*, Bärenreiter Kassel, Basel, undated.
[64] Introductory notes to the recording of Beethoven's Symphony No. 2 by the Chamber Orchestra of Europe, conducted by Nikolaus Harnoncourt, June—July, 1990.
[65] Jonathan del Mar, *Critical Commentary to Symphonie Nr. 2 in D-dur*, Bärenreiter Kassel, Basel, undated.
[66] Wayne M. Senner, Robin Wallace and William Meredith editors, 1999, Vol. 1, p. 171.
[67] Sieghard Brandenbugh editor, *Haydn, Mozart, & Beethoven: Studies in the Music of the Classical Period: Essays in Honor of Alan Tyson*, 1998, p. 184—88.
[68] Pamela J. Willetts, 1970, pp. 26—27. For a facsimile reproduction of the title page to Cianchettini & Sperati's English editions of the projected compete editions of Haydn's, Mozart's and Beethoven' Symphonies, see: Beethoven House, Digital Archives, Library Document, HCB C Md 44. The title page for the *Eroica* Symphony is reproduced as: HCB C Md 2.
[69] Theodore Albrecht editor and translator, 1996, Vol. 2, Letter No. 285, pp. 203—04. See also: Elliot Forbes editor, *Thayer's Life of Beethoven*, 1967 p. 817.

RECEPTION HISTORY

The *Eroica* Symphony was first heard in a number of private performances under the auspices of Beethoven's patron Joseph Franz Maximilian, the seventh Prince of Lobkowitz. These first performances were, in effect, trial rehearsals that enabled Beethoven to give further consideration to the scoring of his new and monumental composition. The first public performance took place in the Theater an der Wien on Sunday evening, 7 April 1805. We trace these events in this part of our discussion, and those others bearing on the early reception of the *Eroica* Symphony. These include: Beethoven's first public appearance as a composer of large-scale orchestral compositions; the progressive reception of the *Eroica* Symphony in the first two decades of the nineteenth century; the extent to which this pioneering creation divided opinion, amongst even the enlightened musical cognoscenti of the day; the better understanding of the music made possible through the genre of piano transcriptions of the score and adaptations of it for various instrumental ensembles; and we conclude with the wider reception of the *Eroica* Symphony in France and England.

FIRST PERFORMANCES

1803

On 26 March and 30 March, the Wiener Zeitung announced: 'On the 4 April, Herr Ludwig van Beethoven will produce a new Oratorio set to music by him, Christus am Ölberge in the Theater-an-der-Wien.' The other works performed were the First and Second Symphonies and the Piano Concerto in C minor, Op. 37. The concert actually took place on 5 April and was Beethoven's first public appearance as a dramatic vocal composer. It also provided an opportunity for the leading music critics of the day to express their opinions of Beethoven the symphonist. The concert — Beethoven's benefit concert — was a financial success and yielded him 1800 florins. The reviews of the music performed though were somewhat mixed.

A short report in the journal Der Freymüthige recoded:

> 'True, the two symphonies and single passages in the Oratorio were voted very beautiful, but the work in its entirety was too long, too artificial in structure and lacking expressiveness especially in the vocal parts.'

The music correspondent of the Zeitung für die Elegante Welt was of the opinion:

'[The] First Symphony was better than the later one [Op. 36] because it developed with a lightness and is less forced, while in the Second the striving for the new and surprising is already more apparent. However, it is obvious that both are not lacking in surprising and brilliant passages of beauty.'

The writer in the Allgemeine musikalische Zeitung was mostly captivated by the Oratorio, and disposed him to predict:

'It confirms my long-held opinion that Beethoven in time can effect a revolution in music like Mozart's. He is hastening towards this goal with great strides.'[1]

Through June until October, Beethoven worked on the *Eroica* Symphony in anticipation of having the composition performed the following year.

1804

We have seen, Beethoven's patron Prince Lobkowitz received the dedication to the *Eroica* Symphony and paid the composer a handsome emolument for the privilege of retaining possession of the music, for a period, for his personal enjoyment. Accordingly, the work was performed privately on a number of occasions at his Vienna residence. The first of these took place in June 1804. These early performances undoubtedly included the extended repeat section in the first movement, concerning the inclusion of which Beethoven vacillated for some time.

Ferdinand Ries recalls at one of these rehearsals, when

Beethoven was conducting, the persistent syncopations in the development section of the first movement 'so completely put out the orchestra that it had to begin again from the beginning'.[2] It was during one of the June rehearsals that the much-reported Ries 'horn-incident' occurred. Beethoven's biographer Alexander Thayer recalls the incident:

> 'In the first Allegro occurs a mischievous whim (böse laune – 'bad mood') of Beethoven for the first horn; in the second part, several measures before the theme recurs in its entirety, Beethoven has the horn suggest it is a place where two violins are still holding a second chord. To one unfamiliar with the score, this must sound as if the horn player had made a miscount and entered at the wrong place. At the first rehearsal of the Symphony, which was horrible, but at which the horn player made his entry correctly, and, thinking that a blunder had been made, [Ries] said: "Can't that dammed hornist count? – it sounds infamously false!. I think I came pretty close to receiving a box on the ear. Beethoven did not forget [my] slip for a long time".'[3]

In his study Ideas and Music, Martin Cooper discusses the element of surprise in music. He suggests this may be achieved, for example, by a sudden sforzando or an unexpected transition to a distant key 'in fact the dramatic interruption of the normal, continuous flow of the musical discourse'. Turning to Beethoven, Cooper reminds us: 'Beethoven was to make surprise of all kinds one of the salient features of his style.' He cites the moment in his Opera Fidelio when the sudden sounding of a trumpet on the battlements — a coup de théâtre — announces the arrival of the Governor of prisons and with it the subsequent release of the wrongfully imprisoned Florestan. Cooper also makes reference to the early horn entry in the Third Symphony:

> 'The most famous of all Beethoven's surprises is the false horn-entry in the first movement of the *Eroica*. But no one would claim this is one of the beauties of the work; it is rather like the characteristic wart or mole on a great man's face.' [The countenance of the aged Franz Liszt comes to mind.][4]

It is thought Lobkowitz may have supported other early performances of the *Eroica* Symphony in which Beethoven himself did not participate. These may have been associated with his close friend Louis Ferdinand, Prince of Prussia and the youngest brother of Frederick the Great. Beethoven had made his acquaintance when on his concert tour in Berlin in 1796. Prince Ferdinand was a gifted musician and composer but whose vocation, was military service. He arrived in Vienna on 8 September 1804 to witness the manoeuvres of the Austrian army; his intentions were to promote an alliance between Austria and Prussia against Napoleon. A few days later, on his return from Prussia, he visited Lobkowitz at his palace in Roundice (Raudnitz) in Bohemia. Apparently, Lobkowitz still had possession of a copy of the parts for the *Eroica*. Thayer, citing Beethoven's physician Dr. Schmidt, states:

> To give [Ferdinand] a surprise, the new, and of course to him utterly unknown Symphony, was played to the Prince, who "listened to it with tense attention which grew with every movement". At

> the close, he proved his admiration by requesting the favour of an immediate repetition, and, after an hour's pause, as his stay was too limited to admit of another concert, a second.'[5]

Ferdinand was a gifted pianist who had so impressed Beethoven that it was to him he dedicated his Third Piano Concerto. Concerning the events at Lobkowitz's country residence, Thayer contends: '[Prince Ferdinand] was, therefore, well placed to appreciate and make a sound judgement of Beethoven's new and revolutionary music.'[6] Regrettably, shortly after departing from his host, Ferdinand lost his life in combat, leaving his promise as a gifted composer unfulfilled. His gifts, however, did not go unrecognized. Robert Schumann, for example, described Louis Ferdinand as 'that most Romantic of all princes'.

1805

In the winter of 1803–04, the two Viennese bankers, Baron Andreas Fellner and his son-in-law Joseph Würth, gathered together a group of largely dilettante musicians to give Sunday-morning concerts. Their programmes consisted of works for full orchestra and were directed by the violinist Franz Clement, then director of concerts at the Theater an der Wien. The orchestra had already given performances of the composer's First and Second Symphonies and, enterprisingly, they undertook a performance of the challenging *Eroica* Symphony. The music critic of the Allgemeine musikalische Zeitung was present at the concert and expressed his views of the composition in the AmZ issue of 13 February 1805:

> 'An entirely new symphony by Beethoven (to be distinguished from the Second which was

published sometime ago by the Kunst- und Industrie-Comptoir) is written in a completely different style. This long composition, extremely difficult of performance, is a tremendously expanded, daring and wild fantasia. It lacks nothing in the way of startling and beautiful passages, in which the energetic and talented composer must be recognised; but often it loses itself in lawlessness. The Symphony begins with an Allegro in E flat that is vigorously scored; a Funeral March in C minor follows which is later developed fugally. After this comes an Allegro Scherzo and a finale, both in E flat. The reviewer belongs to Herr Beethoven's sincerest admirers, but in this composition he must confess that he finds too much that is glaring and bizarre, which hinders greatly one's grasp of the whole, and a sense of unity is almost completely lost.'[7]

George August von Griesinger was an official in the Saxony embassy in Vienna who came to know Beethoven in 1802 and played an important part in the composer's early business dealings with the music publisher Breitkopf & Härtel. Through his high-level connections, Griesinger appears to have gained access to the salons of Vienna's nobility, including that of Prince Lobkowitz. In a letter to a correspondent in Leipzig, of 13 February 1805, Griesinger wrote:

'This much I can ... assure you; that the [*Eroica*] Symphony has been heard at Academies at Prince Lobkowitz's and at an active music-lover's named Würth, with much applause. That it is a

> work of genius, I hear from both admirers and detractors of Beethoven. Some people say that there is more in it than Haydn and Mozart, that the Symphony-Poem has been brought to new heights! Those who are against it find that the whole lacks rounding out; they disapprove of the piling up of colossal ideas.'[8]

The performance in question probably took place on 20 January 1805.[9] It has been suggested that since the Fellner-Würth orchestra consisted largely of amateur musicians, their performing the *Eroica* Symphony may have proved too challenging for them, which may account for the indifferent rendering of the music.[10] It was as a result of hearing these early performances of the *Eroica* that Beethoven finally decided to reinstate the extensive repeat section to the first movement. As we have seen, in the earlier part of our account, on 12 February Carl van Beethoven wrote to the publisher Gottfried Härtel, on behalf of his brother, to inform him, 'after several performances he found it disadvantageous if the first part was not repeated'.[11]

In 1843, many years after the first performance of the *Eroica* Symphony, the pianist-composer Hieronymous Payer recalled the response to the music in an issue of the Wiener Musik-Zeitung. He relates: '[This] new symphony, then so difficult, so new, original, strange in its effects and of such unusual lengths, did not please.'[12]

The first really public performance of the *Eroica* Symphony took place in the Theater an der Wien on Sunday evening, 7 April 1805, where it opened the second part of the concert. This was given for the benefit of the conductor-director of the orchestra Franz Clement. The programme announced:

> 'A new Grand Symphony in D sharp [according to the German designation of E flat] by Herr Ludwig van Beethoven, dedicated to his Serene Highness Prince Lobkowitz.'

This was the occasion when, according to the recollections of Beethoven's pupil Carl Czerny, someone called out from the gallery: 'I'll give another kreuzer [the admission charge] if the thing will stop!'.[13]

Beethoven's biographer Anton Schindler's remarks on the *Eroica* Symphony being designated as in the key of 'D sharp':

> 'When the composer conducted performances of the *Eroica* Symphony in 1805 and 1806, the programme always indicated the key, quite properly as E-flat major. The term "E flat" for a piece of music written in three flats was, however, then unknown in Vienna, and perhaps elsewhere as well ... When the musicians received their printed parts of the work, they made haste to ignore Beethoven's innovation and for all subsequent performances to use the term D sharp – this was the indication used by Haydn and Mozart ... Even in the 1820s, the designation D sharp was still used for the key of E flat.'[14]

The Allgemeine musikalische Zeitung announced the first public performance of the *Eroica* Symphony would be conducted by Beethoven on 7 April and later reported the impression it had made on the public in its issue of 18 April:

> 'Truly this new work of Beethoven's contains

some grand and daring ideas, as one might expect from the powerful genius of the composer, and shows great strength as well. But the Symphony would be all the better — it lasts a whole hour — if Beethoven could reconcile himself to making some cuts in it and to bringing into the score more light, clarity, and unity — virtues that were never absent from the symphonies in G minor and C minor of Mozart, and those in C and D of Beethoven ... Here, in place of the andante, there is a funeral march in C minor, which develops fugally, but this fugue is completely lost and confused in the way it is handled. Even after several hearings it eludes the most sustained attention, so that the unprepared connoisseur is really shocked. As a result, this Symphony was anything but enjoyed by the greater part of the audience.'[15]

On 26 April, the music correspondent of the Berlin journal Der Freimüthige — described as being 'for serious and impartial readers' — included an article that purported to explain how the *Eroica* Symphony had divided critical musical opinion:

ADVOCATES:
'Beethoven's particular friends assert that it is just this Symphony which is his masterpiece, that this is the true style for high-class music, and that if it does not please now, it is because the public is not cultured enough, artistically, to grasp these lofty beauties; after a few thousand years have passed [!] it will not fail in its effect.'

OPPOSITION:

'Another faction denies that the work has any artistic value and professes to see in it an untamed striving for singularity which had failed, however, to achieve in any of its parts beauty or true sublimity and power. By means of strange modulations and violent transitions, by combing the most heterogeneous elements, as for instance when a pastoral in the largest style is ripped up by the basses, by three horns, etc., a certain undeniable originality may be achieved without much trouble; but genius proclaims itself not in the unusual and fantastic, but in the beautiful and the sublime. Beethoven himself proved the correctness of this maxim in his earlier works.'

THIRD PARTY:

'The third party, a very small one, stands midway between the others — it admits that the Symphony contains many beauties, but concedes that the connection is often disrupted entirely, and that the inordinate length of this longer, and perhaps most difficult of all symphonies, wearies even the cognoscenti, and is unendurable to the mere music-lover; it wishes that H. v. B. would employ his acknowledgedly great talents in giving us works like in his Symphonies in C [Op. 21] and D [Op. 36], in his Septet in E-flat [Op. 20] ... and others of his early compositions which have placed B. forever in the ranks of the foremost composers. It fears, however, that if Beethoven continues on his present path both he and the public will be the sufferers. His

> music could soon reach the point where one would derive no pleasure from it, unless well trained in the rules and difficulties of the art, but rather would leave the concert hall with an unpleasant feeling of fatigue from having been crushed by a mass of unconnected and overloaded ideas and a continuing tumult by all the instruments.'

The reviewer complained of Beethoven being rude to the audience:

> 'The public and Herr van Beethoven, who conducted, were not satisfied with each other on this evening; the public thought the Symphony too heavy, too long, and himself too discourteous, because he did not nod his head in recognition of the applause which came from a portion of the audience ... Beethoven found that the applause was not strong enough.'

In response to the criticism that his Symphony was too long, it is alleged Beethoven riposted: 'If I [Beethoven's italics] write a symphony an hour long it will be found short enough!' He did, however, concede that on account of the length of the Symphony it should be played near the beginning of a concert before the audience had tired.[16]

SUBSEQUENT PERFORMANCES

1807

The *Eroica* Symphony was performed on a number of occasions in 1807. These provided music critics with further opportunities to hear the work and to come to terms with its daring departures from the symphonic genre that had preceded it – including Beethoven's own First and Second Symphonies. In its issue of 28 January, the correspondent of the Allgemeine musikalische Zeitung reported on a performance of the *Eroica* Symphony that had taken place on 3 January. The event was described as being 'noteworthy through the performance of the newest Beethoven Symphony'. The correspondent provided readers with a summary account of the work's four movements:

> 'The first movement is impressive and full of power and sublimity. The working out is true and comprehensible; the reinforcement of the bass lines with the wind instruments, particularly the horns, heightens the effect ... The funeral march is new and bears the character of noble melancholy. As long as it is, even in relation to the other movements, we are still glad to linger in the emotion it arouses. The blending of harmonies is extremely pure and correct ... The Scherzo-Menuetto is a piece full of lively, restless motion, against which the sustained tones of the three horns in the Trio contrast extremely well.
>
> 'The finale has much value ... however, it cannot escape very well from the charge of great bizarrerie ... for example, no composer before Beethoven has dared to begin a piece in E-flat major in such a way that the instruments begin al unisono on the leading note, and then continue with progressions that belong to the scale of G minor ... The theme that follows immediately afterward ... comes out, for the sake of novelty, a

little too empty. Are all these peculiarities necessary: per festeggiar il Sovvenire d'un grand Uomo — as Herr Beethoven describes on the title page?'[17]

In the following issue of the AmZ of 18 February, the music correspondent further informed the journal's readers of 'the uniqueness and the rich content of the [the *Eroica* Symphony]' that he deemed required serious examination, particularly with regard to its 'technical aspects'. He then subjects the score to an extended, movement-by-movement critique accompanied by musical illustrations. As such, this text is amongst the first of its kind — arguably the first — to submit the *Eroica* Symphony to such a detailed, musicological analysis. The following extracts are offered to convey a flavour — but no more — of this pioneering and perceptive text:

> '[The] allegro closes powerfully and splendidly and now follows a grand funeral march, in C minor in two-four time, which the reviewer would like to declare without hesitation to be Beethoven's triumph, at least [with] regard to invention and design ... The entire piece is solemn and deeply moving: the minore nobly plaintive and gloomy, and the majore soothing and lovely, where flute, oboe, and bassoon — to speak with Luther — seem to be leading "a heavenly dance of tones and sweet melodies". [The editors to the translation suggest the quotation from Luther is derived from Luther and Music as given in Paul Nettl, Philadelphia, 1948, pp. 15–16] ... If the entire funeral music is to come off properly, then every voice in the orchestra must enter into the idea itself with skill and

the best intentions, at least so that, for example, the short notes are performed ostentatiously and solemnly, the sustained ones are given their full value and make an impression ... Even for the most practised orchestra this will only be possible if the movement is played through several times and all the players adjust precisely to one another ... The Scherzo in three-four time that follows is a sort of companion piece to the one in Beethoven's Second Symphony, only a great deal stronger, more piquant, loftier, and also much longer ... The reviewer would gladly cite some of the thoroughly original details in which it abounds, if he did not have to think about saving space ... The theme of the finale, allegro molto, has already been arranged once by Beethoven for the keyboard [*Eroica* Variations, Op. 35], and, apparently, he has diligently taken it up again in order to develop it more richly and grandly. It deserved this distinction. Except for a few variation themes of Haydn, the reviewer can think of none that is so well laid out, and used afterwards with such economy ... Incidentally, this finale is certainly once again very long, contrived, very contrived; indeed, several of its merits lie somewhere hidden. They presuppose a great deal if they are to be discovered and enjoyed ... Much here is shrill and strange, but the reviewer is very far from criticizing this outright. Is this not also the case with any extremely rich painterly or poetic composition?'[18]

Two months later, in its 29 April edition, the AmZ reviewer discussed the *Eroica* Symphony once more. This was in response to a performance that had taken place a few weeks previously in Leipzig. From this account we learn:

> 'The orchestra had voluntarily gathered for extra rehearsals without recompense, except for the honour and special enjoyment of the work itself. At these rehearsals the Symphony was available in score, so that even the slightest triviality would not escape observation, and overall the players would penetrate the meaning and purpose of the composer with greater certainty. [This was unusual for the time insofar as it was still the custom for orchestral parts only to be available, the music being directed by the first violinist] And so this most difficult of all symphonies ... was performed not only with the greatest accuracy and precision, but also everywhere with congruence and consistency, with grace, neatness and delicacy, and with an accommodation of the specially combined instruments to each other. In short, it was performed just as anyone could wish who had studied the score, even the ingenious composer himself.'[19]

The Journal Des Luxus und der Moden was a German fashion magazine that appeared under this title from 1787 to 1812 and under other titles until 1827. It was published monthly and reached around 25,000 readers. In 1807, the Journal's music correspondent reported on a number of symphonies he had heard that included discerning remarks about the *Eroica* Symphony:

> 'Among the new productions in this genre we heard: a symphony by [Adelbert] Gyrowetz in D

major, of brilliant effect; two by Friedrich Schneider in Leipzig that showed a lot of talent and fire; and finally, especially, Beethoven's [original italics] new, great heroic Symphony, the biggest, most original most artful, and at the same time, most interesting of all symphonies, a production that will remain an eternal monument of the eminent genius, the rich imagination, the deep feeling, and the educated art of its author. One could not present it [the Symphony] as a high ideal of this genre, without being unfair to Mozart's and Haydn's excellent symphonies and without forgetting that even this ingenious and great work of art would not exist in its present form if these earlier magnificent symphonies — including Beethoven's earlier ones — had not preceded it.'[20]

In 1807 the Berlin journal Morgenblatt für die gebildete Stände included an appreciation of the *Eroica* Symphony by the Berlin music critic Heinrich Herman. He described the E minor episode from the first movement in florid, literary terms:

'But how sweetly then the soul recovers again in the first decrescendo, where the bass speaks such comforting pizzicato in the soft minor mode. Through this we feel called forth in the following passage into an almost Shakespearian world of magic! In these extremes, and in the frequent exchanges of fearful, violent, percussive rebukes with the most ingratiating flowers of melody, lies a great part of Beethoven's humour.'

Thomas Sipe, from whom we have just quoted, remarks that the word humour had an aesthetic connotation, at the period in question, and that Herman's style of writing prefigures that of the later Romantic approach to music criticism.[21] Also of interest is that Beethoven's music was now being placed on a level worthy of comparison with the work of Shakespeare. This established a precedent that other music critics and musicologists would adopt in the years to follow.

To close our survey of 1807, worthy of mention of the support for Beethoven's symphonic music was that shown by the Gewandhaus Orchestra; it became a staunch supporter of Beethoven's orchestral music. The Gewandhaus Orchestra had performed Beethoven's First Symphony in 1801 with that of his Second Symphony following in 1804 and the *Eroica* three years later. In 1809, the Pastoral Symphony was heard and in the same year the C minor Symphony was given from manuscript parts. The Gewandhaus Orchestra featured the Choral Symphony in its 1826 concert season. Ten years later, the standing of the Gewandhaus Orchestra was raised by the appointment of Felix Mendelsohn as the Orchestra's Music Director — Gewandhauskapellmeister — an appointment he held until his untimely death in 1847.

For the 1807 concert season in Leipzig, the secretary to the Gewandhaus Orchestra, Friedrich Rochlitz, prepared the audience for a performance of the *Eroica* Symphony by issuing a short interpretive programme note. It read: 'Fiery, magnificent, Allegro/sublime, solemn Funeral March/imperious, Scherzando/grand, Finale, partially in strict style.' Writing, for once, from the perspective of the performer, Rochlitz wrote:

'You burn like fire ... you are frightened and

uneasy! You play well, and still – you hardly know what and how you are playing! You have to contain yourself with all your might so as not to tear into the instrument, or to rush the tempo and carry the others with you. Everything has to come out right, be it ever so terribly difficult!'[22]

1808

Sebastian Mayer was an accomplished singer who could claim Mozart as his brother-in-law. Mayer helped in the preparations for the première of Fidelio on 20 November 1805 and created the role of the villain Pizarro. Later, he was among the small group who met the following month to persuade Beethoven to make certain cuts to his score – that proved to be no easy undertaking. Mayer sang the role of Pizarro in the revised version of the opera that was given the following year on 29 March 1806. It is a measure of Beethoven's respect for Mayer's singing that, when a concert was given on 11 April 1808 for his benefit, he allowed the *Eroica* Symphony to be performed.[23]

1809

During the French occupation of Vienna in 1809, many of Vienna's theatres closed, as a consequence of which actors were without work. In response, a charity was established to support them and their families and Beethoven was called upon to contribute to the this by giving a performance of one his works. He supported philanthropic causes on several occasions – for example the fund for The Widows and Orphans – and subsequently received the freedom of the city for his charitable works. Sometime in September 1809, Beethoven contributed to the support of the actors in straitened circumstances by conducting his *Eroica* Symphony. Thayer remarks:

> 'Was this selected in the expectation that Napoleon would be present, to do him homage? If so, it failed of its aim. The day before, Napoleon journeyed from Schönbrunn [his headquarters] to Krems and Mölk. Or was it [with] bitter sarcasm that Beethoven chose it?'[24]

Beethoven's personal life was touched at this time by two particular events. His personal physician Dr. Johann Schmidt, on whose council he had so much relied, died on 19 February and his former teacher Joseph Haydn, whom he had come to respect and admire, passed away on 31 May — thereby leaving Beethoven as Vienna's pre-eminent living composer. On 14 October, Austria concluded a peace treaty with France. With the signing of an armistice things gradually started to improve somewhat in Vienna, such that on 2 November Beethoven felt disposed to write to Breitkopf & Härtel:

> 'We are enjoying a little peace after violent destruction, after suffering every hardship that one could conceivably endure. I worked for a few weeks in succession, but it seemed to me more for death than for immortality ...'.[25]

1810

Carl Maria von Weber is recognised as one of the most significant composers of the Romantic era and for being a crucial figure in the development of German opera. However, even such a progressively-minded composer as Weber found Beethoven's music too innovative for his taste. We learn this indirectly from Anton Schindler who relates:

> 'Among the papers left at the death of the music publisher Hans Georg Nägeli, there was a letter

to him from [the 24 year old] Carl Maria von Weber, written from Mannheim on 21 May 1810; it was later published in 1853.'

Weber had taken offence at the suggestion that in his newly composed String Quartet there were traces of the influence of Beethoven. Weber was not amused and responded:

'[Though] this might strike many as flattering, it is not at all pleasing to me. First of all, I detest everything that bears the stamp of imitation, and secondly, my views differ so radically from Beethoven's that I do not think I could ever stand on common ground with him. The fiery, indeed almost incredible, inventiveness of which he is possessed is accompanied by such confusion in the organization of his ideas that only his early compositions appeal to me, while the later ones seem to me nothing but utter chaos, an incomprehensible striving for novelty, from which there shines forth an occasional lightening-like bolt of genius, showing how great he might be if he would only rein in his extraordinary fantasy.'[26]

1812

In his biography of the composer Beethoven as I knew Him, Anton Schindler remarks on the reception of Beethoven's symphonies in England – to which we make further reference later in our account. He states:

'As early as 1812 the first six symphonies of Beethoven were taken into the repertoire of the Philharmonic Society in London, and all of them enjoyed an equally enthusiastic reception.

As for the Pastoral, it is noteworthy that this symphony aroused less offence in England than anywhere else, and after a few performances it was fully appreciated. It is not surprising that there were some who criticized the Third, Fourth, Fifth, and Six Symphonies, and valued only the first two, when we consider the time, for as late as the 1850s Oulibicheff recognised only the First Symphony as worthy of praise. In his biography of Mozart, he calls this Symphony "admirable" for the reason that he finds in it Mozart's style.'[27]

Alexander Oulibicheff published a three-volume study of Mozart, Nouvelle biographie de Mozart (Dresden, 1843), and later, Beethoven, ses critiques et ses glossateurs (Leipzig and Paris, 1857).

In its 3 June 1812 issue of the Allgemeine musikalische Zeitung, the journal's correspondent reflected on the Winter Season's musical productions that had taken place in Mannheim. In his discussion of Beethoven's Fourth Symphony — that had just received its first public performance in Mannheim — the correspondent made passing reference to the *Eroica* Symphony:

> '[The] *Eroica* — a work that in genius, fire, and effect can be compared only to the C minor Symphony, and in clarity only to the First in C major but that in difficulty of execution can be compared to none.'[28]

1815

For circumstances relating to 1815, and the *Eroica* Symphony, we draw once more on Schindler's account:

'The occupation of Paris by the Allied Powers in 1815 brought to the French capital a Prussian commissariat officer by the name of Paris who gave the next impetus in the direction of Beethoven's instrumental music. An ardent music-lover, and a performer himself, this officer made the acquaintance of a number of [French] musicians, including [the violinist-composer [Chrétien] Urhan and [the harpist Franz Anton] Stockhausen.'

These two shared lodgings, and at the Prussian officer's recommendation Stockhausen ordered a copy of the *Eroica* Symphony.

Schindler comments:

'Urhan took it to [François Antoine] Habeneck, who by then was conductor of the students' concerts at the [Paris] Conservatoire. It was a long time before he decided to rehearse the new work [new to the Conservatoire – see later]. At the end of the first movement everyone burst out laughing. After the second it was the same thing, and it took no little persuasion to induce the orchestra to play through the remaining movements. Thus, Beethoven's music seemed to be condemned to death as far as Paris audiences were concerned; and since Habeneck himself had lost heart, and may have had too little insight into the matter, all further attempts were abandoned. Time had to wait for a more cultured society, or for another foreign impulse before renewed efforts could be dared.'[29]

1818

Vinzenz Hauschka was a civil servant with whom Beethoven appears to have established a friendly relationship, addressing him in his letters with the familiar 'Du' and 'My dear Hauschka'.[30] He settled in Vienna in 1793 where he was employed in the government's finance department. More significantly, in the context of music-making, Hauschka was soon recognised as an outstanding amateur musician, popularly recognised as 'one of our most brilliant cellists' He became a founder member of the Gesellschaft der Musikfreunde and conducted several of its concerts. In February 1817, these included a performance of the then very popular Seventh Symphony and on 3 May the following year Hauschka conducted the first movement of the *Eroica* Symphony.[31]

1819–1820

The Vienna concert season of 1819–20 was significant for the introduction of a new series of concerts promoted under the title of Concerts Spirituels. These were styled on a concert series, of the same name, that had been founded in Paris some years earlier. The aim of both series was to offer public concerts whose programmes combined sacred choral and instrumental music. The Vienna concerts owed their inception to Franz Xaver Gebauer, an organist-composer, choirmaster, music director of the city's Augustinian Church, and a committee member of the Gesellschaft der Musikfreunde. A notice in the Allgemeine musikalische Zeitung announced:

> 'On 1 October 1819, a new concert series was started, soon to be known as the Concerts Spirituels ... Herr Gebauer makes the proposal to form a special society of a moderate number to bring

to performance only symphonies and choruses excluding all virtuoso music [pure display music] and bravura singing.'

The 'moderate number' refers to the performers who were all amateurs and who played largely from sight. In the eighteen concerts of the first season, 1819–20, Beethoven's first four symphonies were performed together with the Pastoral Symphony.[32] Since the players were performing from sight, it is not surprising the music correspondent of the Allgemeine musikalische Zeitung, commenting on the performance at the 9 April concert, felt obliged to report to Beethoven: 'I forgot to tell you that the dilettantes scraped through your symphony [unspecified] yesterday.'[33] Beethoven responded by writing to Gebauer, sometime in April 1820, requesting tickets to judge the performances himself – insofar as his hearing would permit. He appears, though, to have made up his mind in advance referring to them as Winkelmusik – a pejorative term suggesting 'incompetence' and as 'hole-and-corner musical performances'.[34]

Of more elevated standing were the performances of Beethoven's symphonies presented by the Gesellschaft der Musikfreunde. The Society was formally established in 1814, with the Archduke Rudolph – Beethoven's (only) composition pupil – as its Protector (Patron). The driving force behind its foundation was Joseph Sonnleithner who served as its unpaid Secretary. Beethoven's music was frequently performed at the Society's concerts. The first movement of the *Eroica* was tried out on 3 May 1818 and received its full performance on 20 February 1820.

Although somewhat outside the scope of our discussion, in 1820 there occurred something of sensation in Vienna's music circles. The circumstance relates to Marie Leopoldine Pachler (née Koschak), described as 'one of the finest women pianists of the day'. She was a youthful Beethoven enthusiast from Graz who, when only eight-years old (!), gave a performance of the B flat Concerto on 4 April. More than this, Leopoldine was possessed of exceptional beauty. Such was her pulchritude, Anselm Hüttenbrenner was disposed to describe her as 'the most beautiful girl ... the most beautiful woman in Graz ... the daughter of heaven'.[35]

1822

Having reached the year 1822, we pause for a moment in our discussion of the early reception of the *Eroica* Symphony and make reference to accounts of two meetings with Beethoven at this time. From these we learn of his appearance and his domestic circumstances:

Gioacchino Rossini was in Vienna around April 1822 and has left a pen-portrait of Beethoven; he himself was then being lionised through the popularity of his Il Barbiere di Seviglia. Rossini was familiar with some of the composer's string quartets, that he regarded 'with admiration', and, likewise, 'a number of his piano compositions'. Notwithstanding, he describes how he could barely master his emotions as he mounted the stairs to Beethoven's lodgings. He continues:

> 'When the door opened, I found myself in a sort of attic, terribly disordered and dirty ... The portraits of Beethoven, which we know, reproduce fairly well his physiognomy. But what no etcher's needle could not express was the indefinable sadness spread over his features — while from under heavy eyebrows his eyes shone as from out of caverns and, though small, seemed to pierce one.'

*

When Rossini took leave of Beethoven, he encouraged his young contemporary 'to compose 'some more Barbers'.[36]

Rossini's description of Beethoven accords with the impression of him left by the English statesman Sir John Russell. In the years 1820–22, he travelled extensively in Europe and published an account of his journeys in A Tour in Germany and Some of the Southern Provinces of the Austrian Empire. In this he makes reference to Beethoven's appearance:

> 'The carelessness of his dress gives him a savage appearance; his features are marked and prominent; his eyes expressive; his hair, which looks as if it had not been touched by comb or scissors for some years, falls over his broad brow in a disorderly mass, being comparable only to the serpents on Medusa's head.'

Russell heard the composer perform on the piano, prompting him to comment: 'It required no little tact to induce him to play, so great is his dislike of anything like a pressing request.' When he was finally persuaded to perform Russell comments:

> 'Left to himself, Beethoven sat down at the piano. At first, he struck a few short chords ... but soon he forgot his surroundings, and for about half an hour lost himself in an improvisation, the style of which was exceedingly varied, and especially distinguished by sudden transitions ... he revelled rather in bold stormy moods than in soft and gentle ones.'[37]

1824

The German music theorist and musicologist Adolf Bernhard Marx is remembered today for his pioneering biography Ludwig van Beethoven: Leben und Schaffen (Berlin, 1859). He was also the founder of the Berliner Allgemeine musikalische Zeitung — sister journal to Leipzig's contemporary Journal the Allgemeine musikalische Zeitung.

In the 12 May 1824 issue of the Berliner AmZ, Marx wrote an extensive article titled 'A few words on the symphony and Beethoven's achievements in this field'. Marx first remarked on 'the numerous performances of Beethoven's symphonies in Berlin' — testimony to their having been assimilated into the symphony-concert repertoire. He acknowledged Beethoven's debt to his predecessors, notably, Haydn and Mozart of which he states:

> 'In the areas of the sonata and symphony, Beethoven began at Mozart's level, and his first outpourings can be called lyrical, even though the feeling in them was expressed more definitely and more intimately. Even if many a moment shone forth more freshly and brightly than in the more gentle Mozart and echoed the Haydn school, and even if a greater, more deeply-founded unity became manifest in Beethoven's compositions.'

In his discussion of the progress of the symphony, Marx reflected on developments in its construction:

> 'Its novelty was expressed, as it were, in various directions (keys) and configurations (fragments and so forth) until it assumed its most appropriate position ... in the principal key. To this more richly developed section was added ... a conclud-

ing section, representing the principal idea. Above all, however, the minuet — usually under the name scherzo — was elevated to an essential part of the entire piece.'

Marx concluded by positioning Beethoven's early symphonic writing within this framework:

'To this period belong Beethoven's Symphonies in C major [No. 1, Op, 21] and D major [No.2, Op. 36]. The first can be called Mozartian without hesitation; the second is written in a similar spirit, but is expanded more and therefor goes beyond Mozartian symphonies in size.'[38]

Marx's views, regarding the *Eroica* Symphony, are included in the closing part of our account.

1825

Towards the end of Beethoven's, life the *Eroica* Symphony was well-established in the concert repertoire. Such was its standing that, in the 19 January 1825 issue of the Allgemeine musikalische Zeitung, verses appeared in celebration of it:

'Allegro
Rock against rock the heroes stand fighting!
Shield to shield and knee pressing knee,
And helmet to helmet, and bush crowding bush,
Strength struggles with counter-strength midst the
 menace of death.

'March funebre
Dreadful fall of the earthly sublime!
Here a procession approaches, pain delays it expressively,

And melancholy, barely checking the tears,
Restraints the hero's word, with which the spirit has fled!

'Scherzo
Flourish now, you heirs of that great name,
In child's play to the songs of the shawm [c.f. oboe]
And joyful fanfares of the hunting horn!

'Finale
Then rush forth, like eagles in flight,
And hasten to tournaments and serious games,
In gratitude to the most beauteous ladies — often winning!'[39]

These are fitting, celebratory lines with which to close this part of our account.

TRANSCRIPTIONS

Transcriptions of Beethoven's symphonies, and indeed other of his compositions, provided the means whereby pianists, and various instrumental ensembles, could experience and enjoy the music without having recourse to the resources of a full orchestra. This had particular significance for the musically-inclined residing in remote communities not having the benefit of a resident orchestra or seldom visited by one.

Beethoven himself remained aloof — although with noteworthy exceptions — from making transcriptions of his own works from one instrumental medium to another. We learn of this from a circumstance in 1802 when he was prevailed upon to arrange his Piano Sonata Op. 14, No. 1 for string quartet. This was despite his misgivings over such an undertaking, as he made clear in a letter to the music publisher Breitkopf and Härtel of Leipzig. He wrote:

> 'The unnatural mania, now so prevalent, for transferring even pianoforte compositions to stringed instruments, instruments which in all respects are utterly different from one another, should really be checked.'

Beethoven was of the opinion: 'Only Mozart could arrange for other instruments the works he composed for the pianoforte; and Haydn could do this too'.[40]

Despite his reservations, Beethoven undertook a number of transcriptions of his chamber and orchestral works for the piano, or collaborated with others in their creation – notably his pupil Carl Czerny; these include the Seventh Symphony and his celebrated four-hand arrangement of the Grosse Fugue – completed on his deathbed.[41] With Beethoven's supervision, Czerny prepared a piano reduction of the second version of Fidelio, adapted the score of the Eighth Symphony for two pianos, and the Overture to Die Weihe des Hauses – also for four hands at two pianos. After Beethoven's death, he made piano-duet arrangements of all Nine Symphonies that were published by Anton Diabelli & Co. between 1827 and 1829.

In time, Czerny's piano transcriptions were eclipsed by the more grandiose transcriptions of Franz Liszt. He made piano transcriptions of all Beethoven's nine symphonies that preoccupied him over a period of almost thirty years. The pianos available to Liszt had a more extended octave-range and greater sonority than those of Czerny's day. Such instruments – precursors of the modern-day concert grand – doubtless served to embolden Liszt in his keyboard figuration.

By 1837, Liszt had completed transcriptions of the Fifth,

Sixth, and Seventh Symphonies. In 1839, Heinrich Adam heard Liszt play his arrangements of the last three movements of the Pastoral Symphony. Although not a musician himself — he was a painter of landscapes and architectural subjects — he wrote in the Allgemeine Theaterzeitung:

> 'Only an artist like Liszt, who, in addition to a limitless veneration of Beethoven, possess the rare gift of understanding the great German composer; only such an artist was able, and could venture, to undertake so hazardous an undertaking'.[42]

In 1843, Liszt arranged the third movement of the *Eroica* Symphony that was later published in 1850. It was not until 1863 that Beethoven's former publisher, Breitkopf & Härtel, suggested to Liszt that he should transcribe the complete set of Beethoven symphonies. He applied himself to the task with the diligence of a disciple following in the steps of his master. He noted down the names of the orchestral instruments, for the pianist to imitate, and added pedal marks and fingerings for the benefit of amateurs and sight readers. The full set of transcriptions was finally published in 1865, bearing a dedication to Hans von Bülow — himself a pianist possessed of formidable powers. Musicologist Alan Walker is of the opinion Liszt's Beethoven Symphony transcriptions 'are arguably the greatest work of transcription ever completed in the history of music'.[43]

As the nineteenth century progressed, other composers transcribed the *Eroica* Symphony for the piano. These included two-piano, four-hand arrangements by:

> August Everard Müller, published in 1807 — only a year after publication of the *Eroica* Symphony;
> Wilhelm Meve, published in 1890 by the pianist-

publisher Henry Litolff;
Otto Singer, published by Peters, c. 1900; and
an arrangement, of unknown date by Ferdinand Lukas Schubert, published by Breitkopf and Härtel.

Arrangements for two pianos and eight-hands were made by August Horn, published by Breitkopf and Härtel and Theodor Kirchner, published by Peters, both of unknown date.

Piano-quartet arrangements (piano, violin, viola, cello) appeared shorty after publication of the *Eroica* Symphony. The earliest of these appeared, anonymously, by the Bureau des Arts et d'Industrie in 1807. Perhaps the most celebrated of the piano-quartet arrangers was Johann Nepomuk Hummel, a pupil of Mozart, Salieri, Clementi, and Haydn (!) and a friend of Beethoven. Hummel eventually made piano-quartet arrangements of all of Beethoven's nine symphonies. He also made a quartet arrangement of the *Eroica* Symphony for piano, flute, violin and cello. A piano-quartet arrangement by Beethoven's pupil Ferdinand Ries had to wait until 1870 for its eventual publication by Simrock.

Other arrangements of the *Eroica* Symphony, for various combinations of instruments, were brought out by a number of publishers. These may be considered as continuing the long-established tradition, in Germany, of tafelmusik ('table-music'). This was a term used to describe music played to entertain guests at banquets — what today we call 'background music'. Adaptations of melodies from Mozart's operas, for example, were very popular. In 1818, Friedrich Hoffmeister of Leipzig published an arrangement of the *Eroica* Symphony by Carl Friedrich Ebers, for violins, violas, flutes, clarinets, horns and cello or double bass.

EARLY RECEPTION IN FRANCE

Beethoven's symphonies began to find acceptance in France. In Paris, students of the Conservatoire commenced a series of concerts — Concerts Français — that they modestly called Exercises Publics. Notwithstanding their modest status, they were assisted by François-Antoine Habeneck who from 1804 served as their lauréat, initially as violinist-leader and from 1806 as conductor. The following year the students' orchestra gave the first performance in Paris of Beethoven's First Symphony. The Second Symphony and the *Eroica* followed in 1811. Such was the precision of the students' playing that the correspondent of a contemporary issue of The Quarterly Music Magazine enthused: 'The Exercises of its [the Conservatoire's] pupils are the most brilliant concert's in Paris.'

Music-making in Paris was placed on a more secure footing with the establishment, in 1828, of the Orchestre de la Société des Concerts du Conservatoire. It gave its first concert in March of that year in which Habeneck conducted a programme including music by Beethoven, Cherubini, and Rossini.[44]

In his Mémoires, Hector Berlioz remarks on Habeneck's achievements in the promotion of Beethoven's music in France:

> 'The Société des Concerts du Conservatoire had just been formed under the active and dedicated direction of Habeneck ... [His] good intentions, indeed his talent deserve recognition, and justice requires that to him alone should belong the glory and credit for popularising Beethoven's works in Paris. He had to work hard to succeed in creating the fine institution which is now famous in the

whole civilised world. He had to communicate his enthusiasm to numerous musicians whose indifference would turn to hostility when they were faced with the prospect of numerous rehearsals and hard work that brought no material gain. This was necessary if they were to achieve a high standard of execution in works which at the time were known only for their eccentric difficulties in performance.'[45]

We learn something of the impression early performances of Beethoven's symphonies made in France from the records of the Italian composer and violinist Giuseppe Cambini. In 1811, when living in Paris, he heard the composer's first two symphonies and expressed his opinion of them in Alexis de Garaudé's Journal, Les Tablettes de Polymnie, a music periodical the had a circulation among the fashionable of Paris. Cambini wrote:

'The composer Beethoven, often bizarre and baroque, sometimes sparkles with extraordinary beauties. Now he takes the majestic flight of the eagle; then he creeps along grotesque paths. After penetrating the soul with a sweet melancholy, he soon tears it by a mass of barbaric chords. He seems to harbour doves and crocodiles at the same time.'

Writing later of the *Eroica* Symphony, Cambini was generous, appraising the composition as 'the most beautiful work Beethoven has composed ... except for some Germanisms, a bit harsh, into which force of habit thrust him.' Additionally, he considered the composition to be 'wisely arranged and correct, though full of vehemence'.[46] Germanisms, at the period in question, was taken to mean music 'marred by ugly proportions'.

Antoine Elwart is largely forgotten today but in his lifetime was recognised for being a composer and musicologist of standing. He secured the coveted Grand prix de Rome and in 1837 was appointed assistant professor at the Paris Conservatoire. From his student days at the Conservatoire, he recalled the events of St. Cecilia's Day, 22 November, 1826:

> 'Habeneck invited a number of his colleagues to lunch: most of them belonged to the Opéra Orchestra, and they were asked to bring their instruments with them. Several accepted, and on their arrival Habeneck put before them the parts of Beethoven's *Eroica* Symphony. This work was practiced, and so intently that it was not until 4 o'clock that the guests were able to sit down to the meal provided by Madame Habeneck ... At first, the Symphony merely astonished the select group of instrumentalists, but after some further meetings had been held, astonishment gave way to intense admiration.'[47]

In his scholarly study Beethoven in France, Leo Schrade states:

> 'Not until Habeneck founded the Société des Concerts du Conservatoire in [5 February] 1828 did his [orchestral] music finally triumph in France. Indeed, these concerts, with programmes more or less exclusively devoted to Beethoven's compositions, filled some glorious pages in the history of the Conservatoire.'

Schrade writes of the tide turning in favour of Beethoven when his compositions 'took foremost place in the musical repertory'. He identifies 'two men of letters' who took up the pen in defence of Habeneck's enterprise. These were, François-Henri-Joseph Blaze, known as Castil-Blaze, and Hector Berlioz. In 1827 Castil-Blaze wrote:

> 'The symphonies of Beethoven present a union of all musical potentialities, the severe harmony without effort with the charms of melody. The phrases of song, conceived together with the sentiment of varied harmonies which receive those phrases, accept without repugnance all the embellishments that a wise hand puts upon them.'

Writing in 1828, in his role as music critic for the Journal des débats, Castil-Blaze enthused:

> 'Those, who have not attended former concerts, cannot imagine the astounding superiority of the orchestra which has just now executed the *Eroica* of Beethoven; it is rapturous, a prodigy.'

Of Berlioz, Schrade enthuses:

> 'Berlioz ... romantic enthusiasm created the poetic image of Beethoven in France. Berlioz observed keenly the true state of musical affairs and knew that the coming of Beethoven into France was equivalent to a final combat between Italian and German music on French ground.'[48]

By 1828, Beethoven's music had made a great impact on

the youthful Hector Berlioz. This was despite the very considerable difference between the musical language he himself was fashioning and that of his hero — his own Symphonie Fantastique was only two years distant. Berlioz particularly admired Beethoven's slow movements — notably that of the Seventh Symphony — and disposed him to liken Beethoven to an eagle soaring aloft. Writing to his father on 20 December 1828, he exclaimed: 'This is no longer music but a new art.'[49]

Berlioz regarded himself as one of Beethoven's champions in France, against those of the old school who remained hostile to the composer's new-sounding music. He relates, for example, his attempt to win over his own teacher Jean-François Le Sueur following a performance of the Fifth Symphony at the Conservatoire. To his regret, though initially shaken by the experience, Lesueur remained aloof (Berlioz's Memoirs, chapter 20).

In his study of Berlioz, Michel Austin observes:

> 'Berlioz's distinctive contribution to the promotion of Beethoven came initially not through performances directed by himself but through his critical writings. As early as 1829, he published a biography of Beethoven in three instalments of composers he particularly admired (Critique Musicale, 1, pp. 47–61) ... After his return from Italy [Berlioz had been awarded the Grand prix de Rome] in 1832, he started to write a series of detailed studies prompted by the regular performances at the Conservatoire; these were published in a number of journals especially the Journal des débats and the Revue et gazette musicale de Paris.'[50]

On March 1828, the first concert of the Société des Concerts took place in Paris in the large hall of the Conservatoire — just a year after Beethoven's death. The orchestra that performed at the concerts of the Société contained many of the best of the younger instrumentalists of Paris. They had studied together and shared the same esprit de corps and youthful enthusiasm. Six regular concerts were given each music season with the addition of one-or-two others to mark special occasions. Beethoven's *Eroica* Symphony was included in the first concert that, as we have seen, had been studied in 1826 by Habeneck's youthful followers. According to the records, 'by general consensus the same Symphony was repeated at the second concert'.

An analysis of the early concert programmes of the Société reveals that between 1828 and 1837, Beethoven led the way with 68 performances of his symphonies, followed by Haydn, with 7, and Mozart with just 5. It should be remarked that only a few of Mozart's symphonies were then available in printed score. Between 1838 and 1847, Beethoven's symphonies again featured prominently in the concerts of the Société. Beethoven still held sway with 90 performances, Haydn having 23 and Mozart 15. By now the symphonies of Mendelssohn had also begun to feature in the concerts of the Société, receiving five performances. By 1859, the number of performances of Beethoven's symphonies played by the Société were as follows:

No.1 13	No.4 24	No.7 52
No.2 26	No.5 53	No.8 14
No.3 28	No.6 51	No.9 19

In due course Habeneck's contemporaries considered the orchestra of the Société des Concerts to be one of the finest, if not the finest, of the day. Even Richard Wagner, not naturally disposed to flattery, remarked:

> 'I received a good lesson at Paris in 1839, when I heard the orchestra of the Conservatoire rehearse the enigmatical Ninth Symphony. The scales fell from my eyes: I came to understand the value of correct execution ... .'[51]

Reference to Richard Wagner leads our discussion to the year 1860 when he travelled to Paris to meet with Gioachino Rossini. Wagner, an ardent admirer of Beethoven, was aware that Rossini had met Beethoven and was eager to learn, first-hand, what the Italian could tell him of the encounter. Rossini was then long into his retirement as a composer for the lyric theatre. Edmond Michotte, a wealthy Belgian amateur composer-pianist, claimed to have been present at the meeting between Rossini and Wagner and later (1906) published an account of his recollections of what took place under the title La Visite de R. Wagner À Rossini — subsequently published in translation as Richard Wagner's visit to Rossini.

It requires an act of trust to believe all that Michotte has to say, but, writing of his recollections (Preface to the translation) Herbert Weinstock remarks: 'Michotte's dignified and completely honourable character, finds no doubt possible that the Belgian was a reliable, truth-telling witness.' In that spirit, we relate the following extracts from Rossini's reminisces.

Rossini told Wagner how he had first heard the string quartets by Beethoven performed when he was in Milan and of his admiration for them. He stated he was also familiar with some of the composer's piano compositions. But, he told Wagner, it was hearing a performance of the *Eroica*

Symphony that resolved Rossini to see Beethoven in person: 'That music bowled me over. I had only one thought: to meet that great genius, to see him, even if only once.'[52] (For the account of Rossini's meeting with Beethoven, see our opening remarks.)

EARLY RECEPTION IN ENGLAND

THE PHILHARMONIC
(LATER, ROYAL PHILHARMONIC) SOCIETY

The early reception of Beethoven's orchestral music in England is closely associated with the foundation years of The Philharmonic Society. The Society was founded in London in 1813. Its stated aims were 'to promote the performance, in the most perfect manner possible, of the best and most approved instrumental music, and 'to encourage an appreciation by the public in the art of music'. The founding Directors were enterprising insofar as they resolved to promote 'that species of music which called forth the efforts and displayed the genius of the greatest masters'. These included contemporary composers such as Beethoven, Cherubini, and Carl Maria von Weber. Beethoven's pupil Ferdinand Ries was elected a Director of the Society and was active in the promotion of his former teacher's symphonies. Perhaps Ries's most significant contribution, in this context, was the role he played in 1822 in encouraging the Philharmonic Society to commission Beethoven's Choral Symphony.

The following is a record of the number of occasions the Philharmonic Society performed Beethoven's symphonies from the period of its inception to the close of the nineteenth century: Symphony No. 1, (19); Symphony No. 2, (39); Symphony No. 3, (52); Symphony No. 4, (54); Symphony

No. 5; (77); Symphony No. 6; (69); Symphony No. 7, (65); Symphony No. 8, (47); Symphony No. 9, (73).

The Society gave its first concert in the Argyll Rooms, Regent Street, London on Monday 8 March 1813. The impresario Johann Salomon was the Leader and Muzio Clementi directed at the piano. A Beethoven symphony was performed but was not identified in the records. At the second concert, on Monday 15 March, another Beethoven symphony was performed, also not identified. At the fourth concert, on 3 May, the British-African violinist George Polgreen Bridgetower took part in a performance of a Beethoven string quartet; Bridgetower is remembered today as the intended dedicatee of the Kreutzer Violin Sonata. In this opening season of concerts, J. B. Cramer and Charles Neate — the latter an associate of Beethoven and a founder-member of the Society — performed at the pianoforte. On 21 June another Beethoven symphony was performed.

The *Eroica* Symphony made its first appearance at a concert of the Philharmonic Society on Monday 28 February 1814. However, this was not the first English performance. The Symphony had been premiered on 26 March 1807 at the Covent Garden Theatre — and, remarkably, overseas in Boston on 17 April 1810 by the newly founded Boston Philharmonic Society. The 1815 Philharmonic music season was significant insofar as the Society purchased from Beethoven, for the considerable sum of £200, the performing rights for three Overtures. These were, incorporating Beethoven's sub-titles: King Stephen — 'To Hungary's first benefactor'; The Ruins of Athens, and Overture in C — The Consecration of the House — 'Written for the opening of the Josephstädter Theater'. The Society performed the Fifth Symphony for the first time in England on Monday 29 April 1816. The notes accompanying the programme enthused:

'It is scarcely necessary to enlarge upon this important production, for it is so well known, and likely to become even more so as the Symphony in which Beethoven revealed himself and his own rugged strength, having discarded the formalism which restricted his earlier works.'

Regarding its construction, the Society's music correspondent noted: 'It is orchestrally interesting as first employing trombones and double-bassoon in a symphony.' The pianist-composer Cipriani Potter received a mention in the Society's notices for 1816. He was acquainted with Beethoven who once remarked to Ries: 'Potter visited me several times; he seems to be a good man and has a talent for composition.'

The 1817 music season was noteworthy for the Society's first performance of the Seventh Symphony on 26 May, with the Pastoral Symphony having been presented earlier at a concert on 24 March. Of related interest is that the Directors of the Society, through the offices of Ferdinand Ries, invited Beethoven to compose and direct two symphonies for the sum of three-hundred guineas. His response was to request four-hundred and fifty guineas that the Directors declined; the outcome was Beethoven did not complete the commission nor did he undertake a planned visit to England. The 1821 season was noteworthy for the performance of no fewer than six Beethoven symphonies, namely, Nos. 1, 2, 4, 5, 6, and 7.

In the second decade of the Society's programmes, it became usual for six or seven Beethoven symphonies to be performed each year. 1825 was memorable in the history of the Society for realizing, on 21 March, the first performance in England of the Choral Symphony. It was described as a 'New Grand Characteristic Sinfonia with Vocal Finale ... (composed expressly for the Society).' On the Title Page of the MS copy of the score that Beethoven sent to the

Society, he inscribed the words 'Geschrieben für die Philharmonische Gesellschaft, London'.

In 1827, the Directors were informed by Ignaz Moscheles that Beethoven was ill and was in need of financial assistance. The Society undertook to give a concert for his benefit and to send him the sum of one hundred pounds. In one of his final letters, Beethoven wrote to Ignaz Moscheles on 18 March 1827 requesting him to thank the Philharmonic Society for their generous gift:

> 'May Heaven soon restore me to health, and I will then prove to the generous English how much I appreciate the sympathy which they have shown for my condition.'[53]

He undertook to write a new symphony for the Society — that he described as 'already sketched in outline'; his death on 26 March precluded its completion.

1829 was a significant year in the annals of the Society since it heralded the appearance of Felix Mendelsohn in its concert programmes for the first time. He would in due course exert a considerable influence on English musical taste and become a favourite of Queen Victoria and Prince Albert.

The 1844 season was memorable insofar as the thirteen-year old boy-violinist Joseph Joachim performed Beethoven's Violin Concerto — from memory, then something of an innovation — and also supplied his own cadenzas. Beethoven's Overture Leonora No.1 was performed for the first time disposing the Society's music correspondent to enthuse: 'Its large proportions and grand style almost gave it the importance of a symphony.' During his stay in London, in 1856, Richard Wagner conducted the Philharmonic Society Orchestra and complimented it for being a 'strong esprit de corps' possessed of 'superb tone' and 'the finest instruments'. He complained, though, of the length of the programmes that typically did not finish until after 11.00 p.m. In 1873, the eminent interpreter of Beethoven Hans von Bülow made his debut on 28 April with a performance of Beethoven's Emperor Piano Concerto and would earn fame later in his capacity as an orchestral conductor – for both of which endeavours he received the Philharmonic Society's coveted Beethoven Gold Medal.

In 1885, the Society appointed Sir Arthur Sullivan as its resident conductor, a position he held for the next three years; his failing health deprived him of remaining in office for longer than he wished. The Philharmonic Society's Centenary Year of 1912–13 provided the opportunity for a reflection of its achievements. The contributor to the records enthused:

> 'If the reader has the patience to wade through the pages of this long history, a history unique in the annals of musical institutions of this kind ... he will see what efforts were made to keep pace with all the changes in musical progress; what numbers of works, since acknowledged everywhere as masterpieces, first made their appeal to English audiences at the Philharmonic Concerts , and what crowds of singers and players, since acclaimed great, first sang and played there.'[54]

THE CRYSTAL PALACE

Shortly after its construction to house the Great Exhibition of 1851, the Chrystal Palace, London became a venue for music making. In 1855 the German-born August Manns was invited to conduct the summer season at the Crystal Palace after which he became Director of Music, the management of which was then under the direction of (Sir) George Grove. It was hearing Manns conduct Beethoven's Overture The Consecration of the House, Op. 124 that disposed Grove to remark of the composer's works: 'I like them very much, and would like to give a great deal to have such music done in the Crystal Palace.

Regarding the orchestra, Manns had to start from scratch, as had the pioneers of the Philharmonic Concerts in London and those of the Hallé Concerts in Manchester. He soon augmented a nucleus of players to provide the basis for a functioning orchestra. In the concert season 1856–57, Manns could command a force of some forty-five players comprising twenty-four strings, eight wind (flutes, clarinets and bassoons), twelve brass (horns, trumpets and trombones) with side drum and kettledrums. By 1866, the strings had been augmented to thirty violins, ten violas, and sixteen cellos and basses to give a compliment of seventy-six players. The Crystal Palace Orchestra, as it was called, started to be compared in size and standing with the London Philharmonic and the Leipzig Gewandhaus. It was with these resources that Londoners at the Chrystal Palace heard a pioneering performance of the *Eroica* Symphony on 9 March 1859.

They had to wait until 1895 for a repeat performance, but Beethovenians would not have been disappointed. The programme for 14 December 1895 was an all-Beethoven event — to commemorate the 125th Anniversary of his Birth. It comprised: Overture, Prometheus; First Symphony, slow movement; Emperor Piano Concerto; Grand Scena 'Ah! Perfidio'; *Eroica* Symphony; two Beethoven songs; and to close the Overture Egmont, No. 3. August Manns conducted the proceedings that did not conclude until about 11.00 pm!

Of related interest is that Grove provided background

material for the audiences attending the Crystal Palace concerts. These took the form of programme notes that were an innovation for the time. For expansive compositions, such as the *Eroica* and Choral Symphonies, these notes could extend to upwards of twenty pages, with several musical illustrations per page. These subsequently formed the basis for Groves celebrated Dictionary of Music and Musicians.[55]

As the nineteenth century progressed, and gave way to the twentieth, the *Eroica* Symphony, alongside that of Beethoven's other symphonies, entered the repertoire of an ever-growing number of orchestras. We consider the 'later reception' of the *Eroica* Symphony in the following, and concluding, part of our discussion.

[1] Elliot Forbes editor, Thayer's Life of Beethoven, 1967 pp. 328—30.
[2] Franz Wegeler, Remembering Beethoven: The Biographical Notes of Franz Wegeler and Ferdinand Ries, 1988.
[3] Elliot Forbes editor, Thayer's Life of Beethoven, 1967 p. 350. For a similar account see: Oscar George Theodore Sonneck, 1927, p. 54. In his study Ludwig van Beethoven, Carl Dahlhaus reproduces the page from the score of the *Eroica* Symphony at the moment of the dissonant horn entry, four bars before the recapitulation. See: Carl Dahlhaus, 1991, Illustration 9.
[4] Martin Cooper, 1965, 11.
[5] Elliot Forbes editor, Thayer's Life of Beethoven, 1967, pp. 350—51. See also: Peter Clive, 2000, pp. 216—17.
[6] Thayer, ibid. Peter Clive (see above) remarks: 'Walther Brauneis, former Secretary to the Vienna Beethoven Society, believes Beethoven may even have originally had Louis Ferdinand in mind as the original dedicatee of the *Eroica* Symphony, although this opinion is not widely shared.' p. 217.
[7] Elliot Forbes editor, Thayer's Life of Beethoven, 1967 pp. 374—75.
[8] H. C. Robbins Landon, 1977, p. 333.
[9] As suggested, for example, by the German musicologist Peter Schleuning (cited by Thomas Sipe, 1998, p. 28) and Peter Clive, 2000, p. 213.
[10] Wayne M. Senner, Robin Wallace and William Meredith editors, 1999, Vol. 1, pp. 167—68.
[11] Theodore Albrecht, translator and editor, 1996, Vol. 1, Letter No. 98, pp. 158—60.
[12] Elliot Forbes editor, Thayer's Life of Beethoven, 1967, p. 350.
[13] Ibid.
[14] Anton Felix Schindler edited by Donald W. MacArdle and translated by

Constance S. Jolly from the German edition of 1860, 1966, p. 151.
15 As quoted in: Jacques Barzun, 1977, p. 158.
16 Elliot Forbes editor, Thayer's Life of Beethoven, 1967, pp, 375–76. See also: H. C. Robbins Landon, 1970, p. 92.
17 Wayne M. Senner, Robin Wallace and William Meredith, editors, 1999, Vol.2, p. 19.
18 Ibid, pp. 24–36.
19 Ibid, pp. 82–83.
20 Quoted in: Alfred Peter Brown, 2002, p. 475.
21 Thomas Sipe, 1998, p. 31.
22 Scott G Burnham and Michael P. Steinberg editors, 2000, pp. 12–13.
23 With acknowledgment to Peter Clive, 2000, pp. 230–31.
24 Elliot Forbes editor, Thayer' Llife of Beethoven, 1967, pp. 470–71.
25 Emily Anderson, editor and translator, 1961, Vol. 1, Letter No. 228, pp. 245–47.
26 Anton Felix Schindler edited by Donald W. MacArdle and translated by Constance S. Jolly from the German edition of 1860, 1966, p. 479.
27 Ibid. p. 504.
28 Wayne M. Senner, Robin Wallace and William Meredith editors. The Critical Reception of Beethoven's Compositions by his German Contemporaries. 1999, Vol.1, p. 57.
29 See ref. 26, pp. 502–3.
30 See, for example, Emily Anderson, editor and translator, 1961, Vol. 1, Letter No. 716, pp. 639–70.
31 Peter Clive, 2000, pp. 153–54.
32 The second season (1820–21) consisted of ten concerts which included the Symphonies in C minor, Op. 67, A major, Op. 92, and F major, Op. 93. In 1821–22 the *Eroica* appeared once more with Symphonies One, Two and Six and in 1825 it received a further performance alongside Symphonies Five and Six. With acknowledgement to David Wyn Jones, 2006, p. 188.
33 Elliot Forbes editor, Thayer's Life of Beethoven, 1967 pp. 770–71.
34 Emily Anderson editor and translator, 1961, Vol. 2, Letter No. 1066, p. 935.
35 Elliot Forbes editor, Thayer's Life of Beethoven, 1967 p. 771, H. C. Robbins Landon, 1992, p. 185.
36 Quoted in: Oscar George Theodore Sonneck, 1927, pp. 116–20. See also: Edmond Michotte, Souvenirs personnels: La Visite de R. Wagner à Rossini ('Richard Wagner's visit to Rossini'), 1860: and, An evening at Rossini's in Beau-Sejour (Passy), 1858, republished 1982.
37 Derived from Ludwig Nohl, 1880, pp. 200–1. See also: Oscar George Theodore Sonneck, 1927, pp. 114–16 and Peter Clive, 2001, pp. 298–99.
38 Wayne M. Senner, Robin Wallace and William Meredith, editors, 1999, Vol. 1, p. 59 and p. 64.
39 Ibid, Vol.2, p. 19, pp. 24–36 and p. 82–83.
40 Emily Anderson, editor and translator, 1961, Vol. 1, Letter No. 59, pp. 74-5.
41 The score of this was considered lost but came to light in an American seminary in recent times. Beethoven only made the transcription because he was dissatisfied by the efforts of others to whom he had first entrusted the assignment.

material for the audiences attending the Crystal Palace concerts. These took the form of programme notes that were an innovation for the time. For expansive compositions, such as the *Eroica* and Choral Symphonies, these notes could extend to upwards of twenty pages, with several musical illustrations per page. These subsequently formed the basis for Groves celebrated Dictionary of Music and Musicians.[55]

As the nineteenth century progressed, and gave way to the twentieth, the *Eroica* Symphony, alongside that of Beethoven's other symphonies, entered the repertoire of an ever-growing number of orchestras. We consider the 'later reception' of the *Eroica* Symphony in the following, and concluding, part of our discussion.

[1] Elliot Forbes editor, Thayer's Life of Beethoven, 1967 pp. 328—30.
[2] Franz Wegeler, Remembering Beethoven: The Biographical Notes of Franz Wegeler and Ferdinand Ries, 1988.
[3] Elliot Forbes editor, Thayer's Life of Beethoven, 1967 p. 350. For a similar account see: Oscar George Theodore Sonneck, 1927, p. 54. In his study Ludwig van Beethoven, Carl Dahlhaus reproduces the page from the score of the *Eroica* Symphony at the moment of the dissonant horn entry, four bars before the recapitulation. See: Carl Dahlhaus, 1991, Illustration 9.
[4] Martin Cooper, 1965, 11.
[5] Elliot Forbes editor, Thayer's Life of Beethoven, 1967, pp. 350—51. See also: Peter Clive, 2000, pp. 216—17.
[6] Thayer, ibid. Peter Clive (see above) remarks: 'Walther Brauneis, former Secretary to the Vienna Beethoven Society, believes Beethoven may even have originally had Louis Ferdinand in mind as the original dedicatee of the *Eroica* Symphony, although this opinion is not widely shared.' p. 217.
[7] Elliot Forbes editor, Thayer's Life of Beethoven, 1967 pp. 374—75.
[8] H. C. Robbins Landon, 1977, p. 333.
[9] As suggested, for example, by the German musicologist Peter Schleuning (cited by Thomas Sipe, 1998, p. 28) and Peter Clive, 2000, p. 213.
[10] Wayne M. Senner, Robin Wallace and William Meredith editors, 1999, Vol. 1, pp. 167—68.
[11] Theodore Albrecht, translator and editor, 1996, Vol. 1, Letter No. 98, pp. 158—60.
[12] Elliot Forbes editor, Thayer's Life of Beethoven, 1967, p. 350.
[13] Ibid.
[14] Anton Felix Schindler edited by Donald W. MacArdle and translated by

Constance S. Jolly from the German edition of 1860, 1966, p. 151.
15 As quoted in: Jacques Barzun, 1977, p. 158.
16 Elliot Forbes editor, Thayer's Life of Beethoven, 1967, pp. 375—76. See also: H. C. Robbins Landon, 1970, p. 92.
17 Wayne M. Senner, Robin Wallace and William Meredith, editors, 1999, Vol.2, p. 19.
18 Ibid, pp. 24—36.
19 Ibid, pp. 82—83.
20 Quoted in: Alfred Peter Brown, 2002, p. 475.
21 Thomas Sipe, 1998, p. 31.
22 Scott G Burnham and Michael P. Steinberg editors, 2000, pp. 12—13.
23 With acknowledgment to Peter Clive, 2000, pp. 230—31.
24 Elliot Forbes editor, Thayer' Llife of Beethoven, 1967, pp. 470—71.
25 Emily Anderson, editor and translator, 1961, Vol. 1, Letter No. 228, pp. 245—47.
26 Anton Felix Schindler edited by Donald W. MacArdle and translated by Constance S. Jolly from the German edition of 1860, 1966, p. 479.
27 Ibid. p. 504.
28 Wayne M. Senner, Robin Wallace and William Meredith editors. The Critical Reception of Beethoven's Compositions by his German Contemporaries. 1999, Vol.1, p. 57.
29 See ref. 26, pp. 502—3.
30 See, for example, Emily Anderson, editor and translator, 1961, Vol. 1, Letter No. 716, pp. 639—70.
31 Peter Clive, 2000, pp. 153—54.
32 The second season (1820—21) consisted of ten concerts which included the Symphonies in C minor, Op. 67, A major, Op. 92, and F major, Op. 93. In 1821—22 the *Eroica* appeared once more with Symphonies One, Two and Six and in 1825 it received a further performance alongside Symphonies Five and Six. With acknowledgement to David Wyn Jones, 2006, p. 188.
33 Elliot Forbes editor, Thayer's Life of Beethoven, 1967 pp. 770—71.
34 Emily Anderson editor and translator, 1961, Vol. 2, Letter No. 1066, p. 935.
35 Elliot Forbes editor, Thayer's Life of Beethoven, 1967 p. 771, H. C. Robbins Landon, 1992, p. 185.
36 Quoted in: Oscar George Theodore Sonneck, 1927, pp. 116—20. See also: Edmond Michotte, Souvenirs personnels: La Visite de R. Wagner à Rossini ('Richard Wagner's visit to Rossini'), 1860: and, An evening at Rossini's in Beau-Sejour (Passy), 1858, republished 1982.
37 Derived from Ludwig Nohl, 1880, pp. 200—1. See also: Oscar George Theodore Sonneck, 1927, pp. 114—16 and Peter Clive, 2001, pp. 298—99.
38 Wayne M. Senner, Robin Wallace and William Meredith, editors, 1999, Vol. 1, p. 59 and p. 64.
39 Ibid, Vol.2, p. 19, pp. 24—36 and p. 82—83.
40 Emily Anderson, editor and translator, 1961, Vol. 1, Letter No. 59, pp. 74-5.
41 The score of this was considered lost but came to light in an American seminary in recent times. Beethoven only made the transcription because he was dissatisfied by the efforts of others to whom he had first entrusted the assignment.

42 Quoted by Peter Clive, 2001, pp. 210–11.
43 Alan Walker, Reflections on Liszt, 2005.
44 Adam von Ahnen Carse, 1948, p. 90.
45 Mémoires de Hector Berlioz, 1865, English translation David Cairns, 1912 and 2002 The Memoirs of Hector Berlioz, Chapter 10.
46 Leo Schrade, 1942, p. 3.
47 As related in: Adam von Ahnen, 1948.
48 Leo Schrade, 1942, p. 27.
49 The Hector Berlioz website: Berlioz, Predecessors and Contemporaries: Berlioz and Beethoven.
50 Michel Austin, translator, Berlioz, Predecessors and Contemporaries, The Hector Berlioz website. Originally published in: Hector Berlioz, The art of music and other essays (A travers chants).
51 Adam von Ahnen Carse, 1948, pp. 92–95. The statistical information, preceding the quotation, is also derived from this source.
52 Edmond Michotte, Richard Wagner's visit to Rossini (Paris 1860): and, An Evening at Rossini's in Beau-Sejour (Passy), 1858, English translation, 1982, pp. 40–4, p. 49 and p. 52. See also: Ferruccio Bonavia, Musicians on Music, 1956, pp. 215–6 and p. 235.
53 Emily Anderson editor and translator, 1961, Vol. 3, letter No. 1566, pp. 1343–44.
54 Pamela J. Willetts, Beethoven and England: An Account of Sources in the British Museum. London: British Museum, 1970.
55 Michael Musgrave, The Musical Life of the Crystal Palace, 1995, pp. 68–69, 75 and 114.

LATER RECEPTION: MUSICOLOGY

We close our discussion of the *Eroica* Symphony by tracing its reception, following on from the period of the work's creation and subsequent reception by the composer's contemporaries. Our text is presented in the form of an anthology of writings derived from the works of musicologists and others who have reflected on the musicological significance of Beethoven's Third Symphony. The writings selected for inclusion derive from a diverse genre of critical assessments of the *Eroica* Symphony as expressed in works published in the nineteenth and twentieth centuries.

The selected authors are presented in alphabetical order. Some of these have been introduced previously, in the opening part of our study, and are identified by an asterisk. Those writers not previously cited are introduced with brief remarks to place their quoted words in context.

THEODOR W. ADORNO

The German philosopher, sociologist and composer Theodor W. Adorno spent many years compiling notes for a projected study of Beethoven. His work remained in this form at the time of his death but was edited and collated by the writer and philosopher Rolf Tiedemann, being published in English translation (Edmund Jephcott) as *Beethoven: The philosophy of music, Fragments and texts* (1998). Adorno worked on his projected Beethoven text through the years 1938–56. Despite this long period of gestation, his work did not progress beyond a great accumulation of diverse texts – 'fragments' – arbitrarily arranged in his files. In his reworking of this material, Tiedemann recast Adorno's texts into 370 numbered sub-texts to which he appended scholarly commentaries. Thereby, he sought 'to organize the material as Adorno himself might have done, had he written the projected book' (*Preface*). From the great body of material, thus co-ordinated by Tiedemann, we have selected the following citations:

> 'Among the most astonishing features of Beethoven's work is that nothing is ever typecast, fixed, repeated, each work being a unique conception from a very early stage. Even the prototypical *Eroica*, the model *par excellence*, is never repeated ... Each work is a cosmos, each one the whole – and for that very reason different.' p. 66.

> *FIRST MOVEMENT:*
> 'The first movement of the *Eroica*, Beethoven's most "Classical" symphony, is in a certain sense the most Romantic ... [The] first movement of the *Eroica* ... is really *the* Beethoven piece, the

purest embodiment of principle; the most careful composition, the absolute peak to which all the earlier works lead up ... Four bars before the *pianissimo* entry is the critical passage, the caesura of the movement, a dragging or falling which is only retrospectively revoked. *Everything* depends on the understanding of such bars ... Little in Beethoven is as close to Schubert as the development, for example the *Scherzo* of the C major Symphony and probably that of the String Quintet [D. 956].'

SECOND MOVEMENT:
'The truly magnificent aspect of the slow movement of the *Eroica* is that the recapitulation is drawn fully into the momentum of the development.'

THIRD MOVEMENT:
'The most characteristic feature of the *Scherzo* of the *Eroica* seems to me to lie in the first six bars, before the entry — emphasised by the doubling of the oboe — of the main theme ... The six bars are not an "introduction". The movement "begins with them" ... Nor are they a mere tonal design against the background of which the theme stands out — that would be Romantic, quite un-Beethovenian; the character is too rudimentary and melodic for that.'

FOURTH MOVEMENT:
'[In] the finale of the *Eroica* ... [Beethoven] sought the characteristic synthesis because, in the deeper formal sense, he needed a contrast to the

first movement; but, at the same time, he wanted to produce something no less committed than that movement.'

Theodor W. Adorno, *Beethoven: The Philosophy of Music, Fragments and Texts*. Cambridge: Polity Press, 1998, p. 66, p.101, and pp. 104–05.

TERRY BARFOOT*

In his contribution to the BBC's celebration of Beethoven's music in June 2005, Terry Barfoot introduced listeners to the *Eroica* Symphony with a form of programme note from which we cite the following:

'The first movement is constructed on a huge scale, with a Coda long enough to count as a second development section. Two abrupt fortissimo chords provide the shortest of orchestral introductions, and the mobile principal theme is heard immediately. Its treatment is wide-ranging, yet the flow of inspiration is taut and continuous ... The succeeding slow movement is equally demanding in its concentration. The outer sections are intense and heavily funereal in mood, but the central part is more mobile and brings a balance and contrast. Throughout this movement the instrumental colours emphasise the solemnity, for the vast and slow-moving principal theme is wholly serious, a characteristic confirmed by its treatment in the development.

'The *Scherzo* occupies a different world from that of the eighteenth-century minuet. The tempo is an unequivocal *Allegro vivace*, and the movement opens with a quiet staccato-rhythmic activity in the strings, who are soon joined by the woodwinds. The full orchestra bursts in to insist upon a lively conclusion, while the central Trio ... is notable for the imaginative writing for the horns.

'The joyful finale is built upon a theme which Beethoven had used in several compositions, the best known of them [being] the score for the Ballet *The Creatures of Prometheus*. A fragmented outline eventually leads to a full presentation and a free-ranging series of variations in which imaginative textures play a full part. Fugato, imitation and counterpoint are all prominently featured, until an extensive Coda moves the Symphony to its blazing climax.'

Terry Barfoot, *Symphony No. 3, Op. 55 (Eroica): Notes to the BBC Radio Three Beethoven,* Monday 6 and Friday 10 June 2005, www.bbc.co.uk/radio3/Beethoven

PAUL BEKKER*

In his pioneering English-language study *Beethoven*, the American-based, German music critic gives his interpretation of the *Eroica* Symphony:

FIRST MOVEMENT:

'At the opening of the movement, Beethoven portrays a conflict within the soul of his hero between impetuous forceful activity and pensive resignation. The active side of his nature triumphs. A little before this time, when

Beethoven's ear-trouble threatened to cripple his creative work, he wrote to [his friend] Wegeler, "I will take Fate by the throat." The *Eroica* is perhaps the artistic echo of that resolve. The two opposing tendencies are perceptible throughout the movement, crossing each other, pressing upon each other, coming to grips, the resolve to heroic action conquering in the end ... The vital power of Beethoven's *poetic idea* is shown in the unfolding germ of an entire movement out of a germ, existing as it were in the title, in the organic connection between the themes in the unbroken development of the content. A grand and logical sequence, not only of emotion but of thought, is preserved throughout ... So definite a plan of the whole work could only spring from a clear consciousness of aim, and the possession of an unusually wide outlook gave the thoughts of the musician the spiritual horizon of the poet.'

SECOND MOVEMENT:

'The *Marche funebre* was an interesting symphonic innovation which Beethoven had already introduced in the *adagio* of [Piano Sonata] Op. 26. Yet there are great differences between the two pieces. The first, in A flat minor, is a true march, portraying a mournful and stately funeral train with roll of muffled drums and blare of trumpets. The Sonata represents a very striking picture, the Symphony a poem inspired by that picture. It is no history of the life of a man, seen from the perspective of the bier, like Wagner's

Götterdämmerung, but it gives the emotions of a spectator who watches the long train as it approaches from afar and fades again into the distance.

'Beside the modelling of the themes, the marvellous art with which the musical ideas are developed, and the steady power with which the tone-poem is carried on to the last note, colourism plays a noble part in the novel effect here attained.'

THIRD MOVEMENT:

'The minuet of the Third Symphony threatens at first to be ... conventional. The chains of rhythm are, however, soon loosened, and an elusive motive for the strings appears and develops into a restless and rapid theme. A phantasmal dance of tones is interspersed with broad harmonic passages strongly accentuated. A Trio follows, opening with a cheerful passage for the horns suggesting a hunting theme, but plaintive string harmonies bring back the mysterious mood of the movement and lead on to a wild and stirring Coda.

'It was, however, a mistake to introduce this movement after the Dead March, thus interrupting the even development of the whole work towards its climax ... It may seem impertinent to correct Beethoven, but if we could make up our minds to perform the *Eroica Scherzo* before the Dead March, we should be giving it its proper place, a place which Beethoven did not dare to assign to it at that time, having offered his contemporaries enough innovation for one occasion.'

FOURTH MOVEMENT:

'The inner meaning of the work carries on uninterruptedly from the Dead March to the finale ... The theme which appears in the *Eroica* finale had been used in the finale of [the Ballet] *Prometheus*, in a collection of *contredanses* for the pianoforte, and again as the subject of the Pianoforte Variations, Op. 35 ... The stimulus afforded by Napoleon was exhausted in the first movement; the person of the hero is changed in the Dead March, and there was no reason why it should not be changed once more and be celebrated as bringer of freedom and knowledge in the finale under the symbol of *Prometheus*.

'In his former treatment of the same idea, Beethoven had been limited by his own inability at that time to see all the implications of his wide subject or to treat it exhaustively. Under the inspiration of the idea of a heroic symphony, he now approached his task armed with far greater powers ... The result was a finale, inferior perhaps, in intensity of thought and emotional depth to the two preceding main movements, yet technically triumphant and affording a magnificent crown to the whole work.'

Paul Bekker, *Beethoven.* London: J. M. Dent & Sons, 1925, pp. 153–64.

LUCIANO BERIO*

David Osmond-Smith was an authority on post-war Italian music, in particular that of Luciano Berio who was his longtime friend and collaborator. In an interview with the composer, sometime in the 1980s, he asked him: '[Are] you sure that Beethoven would conduct his symphonies better than [Herbert von] Karajan?' Berio responded:

> 'That was an epoch in which the conductor had a different function and a different relation with his musicians. Indeed, it was at precisely that time, at the beginning of the last century, that the figure of the orchestral conductor began to define itself. But conditions were so different then, from every point of view, that comparisons are impossible. Just think that Beethoven conducted the Third and Fourth Symphonies with an orchestra of about 30 musicians! ... The performances of a modern orchestra with 90 players are almost transcriptions when compared with the conditions that prevailed then: not that there's anything wrong with that — on the contrary.'

Berio then recalled his own experience of conducting Beethoven with an orchestra of reduced numbers:

> 'Several years ago, when I was working on the television programme *C'è musica e musica*, I allowed myself the satisfaction of recording part of the Third Symphony with the same number of players that Beethoven used (29). I was afraid that the different quality and power of the sound from woodwind and brass would alter the orchestral equilibrium, especially in the *fortissimi*. But it didn't. It was an unforgettable experience to hear the *Eroica* as transparent and well-defined

as chamber music. Extremely dilated and explosive chamber music naturally.'

David Osmond-Smith editor and translator, *Luciano Berio: Two Interviews with Rossana Dalmonte and Bálint András Varga.* New York; London: Boyars, 1985, p. 132.

HECTOR BERLIOZ*

In 1827 the Belgian musicologist François Joseph Fétis, then professor of counterpoint at the Paris Conservatoire, founded the *Revue Musicale* — the first French-language journal dedicated entirely to the discussion and evaluation of classical music. The *Revue Musicale* was later combined with Maurice Schlesinger's rival publication the *Gazette Musicale de Paris*; Maurice and his father Adolph had published a number of Beethoven's compositions. The resulting *La Revue et Gazette Musicale de Paris* provided an outlet for musical writings and criticism from the period of its inception in 1834 until 1880. One of its earliest, and most respected, contributors was Hector Berlioz. He contributed an article on the *Eroica* Symphony in the journal's edition of 9 April 1837. Of its four movements he writes:

FIRST MOVEMENT:

'The first movement is in three-quarter time; its tempo is more-or-less that of a waltz. Yet what could be more serious and dramatic than this *Allegro*? The vigorous theme that forms its foundation is not presented in its entirety at the start, contrary to custom, the composer begins by giving us only a partial glimpse of his melodic idea; only after some introductory measures is it displayed to full effect.

'The rhythm is extraordinarily remarkable both for its frequent syncopations and for the way that duple meter is thrown by the stressing of weak beats, on top of the meter [measure 128]. When rough dissonances are added to these conflicting rhythms — as we hear in the middle of the development section, where the violins play a high F against E natural as the fifth of the A-minor triad [measures 276–79] one can barely restrain a shudder at this spectacle of uncontrollable fury. Here is the voice of despair almost of rage ... It is impossible to describe or even suggest the myriad aspects of the theme.

SECOND MOVEMENT:
'The highly tragic funeral march is like a translation into music of Virgil's beautiful lines on the funeral procession of young Pallas [*Aeneid* XI, verses 78–79 and 89–90]':

"Many trophies from the battle of Laurentis are borne.
And spoils of war are brought in a long line.
Then the warhorse, Aethon, stripped of his trappings,
Follows weeping, great tears rolling down his face."

THIRD MOVEMENT:
'The third movement has the customary title, *Scherzo*, the Italian word for play or homage. At first sight it is none too clear why music of this kind should be included in this epic work. It must be heard to be understood. It has indeed the rhythm and tempo of a scherzo, and sure enough, these are games, but they are funeral games repeatedly darkened by thoughts of

mourning, in short, games such as those with which the warriors of the *Iliad* celebrated their leaders at the graveside. Here, even in the most playful orchestral developments, Beethoven keeps a dark and solemn tone and the deep sadness fitting the subject.'

FOURTH MOVEMENT:

'The finale, though greatly varied, is based entirely on a very simple fugue theme. In addition to a thousand ingenious details, the composer superimposes on it two other themes, one of them very beautiful. It is not readily seen from the shape of the line that this melody is, so to speak, mined from another. For its expressive quality is by contrast much more touching and incomparably more graceful than the original, which rather resembles a harmonic baseline and indeed serves as such very well ... The hero calls forth many tears. After these final lamentations, the poet abandons the elegiac mood and strikes up an enraptured hymn to glory. Though somewhat terse, it is a brilliant peroration, a worthy crown to a musical monument.'

Elizabeth Csicserry-Ronay translator and editor, *Hector Berlioz: The Art of Music and other Essays: (À Travers Chants)*. Bloomington: Indiana University Press, 1994 pp. 13–15. For an alternative translation see: Michel Austin translator, *Berlioz, Predecessors and contemporaries, The Hector Berlioz website.*

JOSEPH BRAUNSTEIN

Joseph Braunstein was an American musicologist, teacher and Senior Programme annotator for the Chamber Music Society of the Lincoln Center. Over his long career — he attained the great age of 104 — Braunstein wrote more than 500 programme notes for the Chamber Orchestra *Musica Aeterna* that he had co-founded. His collected writings were published in three volumes, in the second volume of which he discussed the Second Symphony within the wider context of Beethoven's symphonies, including the *Eroica*:

> 'Viewed in the context of Beethoven's entire symphonic work, and also in that of his stylistic development, the Second Symphony occupies a particular position: it stands between two worlds. Beethoven's First Symphony symbolises, with Mozart's and Haydn's last symphonies, the peak of the eighteenth-century type and the nineteenth-century symphony as created in the Third (*Eroica*, 1804). The step Beethoven made from the Second to the Third Symphony was paralleled half a century later by Richard Wagner in the evolution from *Lohengrin* to *Rheingold*. Although Beethoven's Second Symphony shows new traits, it is basically oriented in the concept of the eighteenth century ... If the Symphony, viewed as a whole, kept to the Haydn-Mozart tradition, it went beyond the eighteenth-century technique in the orchestral treatment. The alternation between wind and string instruments sometimes applied from measure-to-measure and the distribution of one melody among several instruments anticipate the technique used in the *Eroica*. It may have confused the musicians

around 1804 and later on. As Berlioz records, even in the 1820s incredible cuts were inflicted on the score of the Second Symphony to make it performable in Paris. This was not necessary in Vienna. There, the Symphony soon won the favour of the public and critics, who implored Beethoven, after the first public reading of the Third Symphony (*Eroica*), "to give us works that resemble the First and Second Symphonies ... that will always place Beethoven among the first-rate instrumental composers".'

Joseph Braunstein, *Musica Aeterna, Program Notes for 1961–1971*. New York: *Musica Æterna*, 1972, pp. 31–32.

ALFRED PETER BROWN*

The American musicologist Alfred Peter Brown submitted the *Eroica* Symphony to a detailed musicological scrutiny, incorporating extensive musical quotations. From his extended text we cite the following:

FIRST MOVEMENT:

'The massive scale of the *Eroica* is immediately evident [illustration]. The first movement extends to 691 measures; if the expository repeat is observed, which was seemingly Beethoven's final intent, the dimensions increase by an additional 155 bars. The size of the movement has often been a rationale for not repeating the exposition, but its numerous ideas demand a rehearing. The first movement is twice the length of Symphony No. 1/1, Op. 21 and nearly a third longer than No. 2/1, Op. 26 ... The opening movement is the first of Beethoven's symphonies to commence without a slow introduction; but like its predecessors, it bows to tradition by opening with the hammer-strokes of the Italian overture ... This double-call to attention identifies neither a tonality nor a meter, but it establishes an important motif whose significance will become apparent ... The exposition takes a rather different tack from that of the previous symphonies; rather than a few concentrated ideas, Beethoven presents a large number of contrasting themes. Each has an unusually strong profile, so that they are almost all identifiable through their rhythm [illustration] ... The horn entry has been one of the most misunderstood moments in all orchestral music from its first rehearsal, when Beethoven almost boxed the ears of his friend [Ferdinand] Ries, who accused the horn player of being unable to count. Apparently, many conductors "corrected" this passage during the nineteenth century ... In this first movement, Beethoven mustered all the resources at his disposal to present a large and thoroughly coherent statement.'

SECOND MOVEMENT:

'Beethoven had toyed with the idea of the *march funebre* long before the slow movement of Op. 55; the Piano Sonata Op. 26 contains a *march funebre sulla morte d'un Eroe* (funeral march) and the fifth variation of Op. 34 [Piano Variations in F major] has been characterised as a *Trauermarsch* (funeral march) ... Nevertheless, it has been forcefully argued that the materials of the *Eroica marcia* are derived from post-French revolutionary models by [François-Joseph] Gossec, [Ignaz] Pleyel, and A. P. Martini, as an idea congruent with the original Bonaparte topic and Beethoven's intent on dedicating the work to the First Consul. But there is no evidence of Beethoven's knowing any of these French funeral marches from *c.* 1800. It would make more sense to search for a funeral-march tradition in Vienna.

'Modern performances of this movement often fail because they render it as more of a symphonic poem than a march, for which the primary requirements are a steady pace and a tempo that is a deliberate but comfortable walk. Whatever qualifications conductors following late-nineteenth century tradition have about Beethoven's own tempos, a speed of any slower than the composer's own marking (quaver = 80) violates the designated genre of the piece itself.'

THIRD MOVEMENT:

'Within the narrative implied by the *Allegro con brio* and the *marcia funebre*, the Scherzo can only be regarded as a post-mortem recall of the hero. [illustration] Such an interpretation is underlined by the ambiguities present in the Scherzo proper and the hunting scene of the Trio, with its dissonant macabre touches in the horns.'

FOURTH MOVEMENT:

'Since the theme of the finale in both meaning and content is the wellspring for the entire symphony, it provides not only an appropriate but also a powerful concluding chapter to Beethoven's essay on the heroic. In this movement Beethoven composes a hybrid of variation and sonata forms framed by an introduction and Coda. [illustration]

'Beethoven created in the finale of the *Eroica* a kind of piece no one had yet imagined. The least dramatic of musical forms, the variation, was combined with the sonata idea to create a musical struggle between melody and bass. During its course, Beethoven surprises us with his deft transition to the central section and his seemingly effortless use of contrapuntal textures. The conclusion of this movement sets it apart from the *Prometheus* Finale and the end of Op. 35 [*Eroica* Variations] ... For the Symphony, Beethoven captures the heroic character at the end with a summary of its various facets and a mighty transformation of the *Prometheus* melody.'

Alfred Peter Brown, *The Symphonic Repertoire. Vol. 2, The First Golden Age of the Viennese Symphony: Haydn, Mozart, Beethoven, and Schubert.* Bloomington, Indiana: Indiana University Press, 2002, pp.460–76.

MICHAEL BROYLES*

The American musicologist Michael Broyles discusses Beethoven's style and genre in the early 1800s, making extensive (illustrated) reference to the *Eroica* Symphony:

FIRST MOVEMENT:
'The *Eroica* Symphony is so large, so complex

and so centrally rooted in music historiography that one of the chief problems when confronting it is to sort out its many dimensions ... [The] first movement, particularly, of the *Eroica* reflects Beethoven's continuing symphonic evolution whose direction had become manifest with the Second Symphony. In the Second Symphony, Beethoven had discovered the theoretical breadth inherent in the symphony style and the structural implications of the new tone. In the *Eroica* he pursued them to their Classical limits. The symphonic style of Classicism is not abandoned with the first movement of the *Eroica*, but no subsequent movement in all of Classicism will surpass this one as a Classical drama ... [illustrations] ...'.

'Because of its shear size and intensity, the *Eroica* constantly verges on structural disaster, appearing at any moment to spin apart, a victim of its own centrifugal momentum. Centrifugal tendencies are held in check, however, primarily upon an emphasis on meter and elemental tonal forces, the most important being the tonic triad. Whatever the changes in melodic shape, the resolution is primarily a reaffirmation of the rhythmic-harmonic framework projected at the very beginning. The newness of the *Eroica* is due to the boldness and scale of the departures. But the success of the movement depends upon those elements — melodic simplicity, tonal clarity, metric drive, and phrase continuity — that were at the very core of the Classical symphonic style.'

SECOND MOVEMENT:

'The slow movement of the *Eroica* differs from the slow movement of the Second Symphony in much the same way that the other movements of the two symphonies do — in size and intensity. The specific moods are clearly different, but in the prevalence of poetic mood and the use of orchestral sonority to maintain them, the two works share common ground. In that sense the Second Symphony is closer to the *Eroica* than to the First Symphony.'

FOURTH MOVEMENT:

Broyles proceeds directly to a discussion of the final movement, remarking:

'The problem of the finale was inherited from the early eighteenth century and had at its root changing concepts of unity ... With the *Eroica* the question of the function and balance of the finale in relation to the rest of the work takes a unique and highly significant turn. The finale is still an independent movement; it is not explicitly linked with earlier movements as the finales of Symphonies Five, Six, and Nine are, either through direct connection, recall of material, or both, and it is not organically linked to earlier movements, because Beethoven still considered each movement an organic entity in itself ...'.

'In the finale, Beethoven faced the problem of composing a movement which would be derived from the same tonal forces as the first movement, which would balance the first movement and use similar thematic shape, but which would not duplicate or imitate it. He responded with a structure that has stubbornly resisted easy identification. What precisely is the form of the finale? There is no question that Beethoven avoids the *traditional* sonata-form movement for something different, but how different? Most writers have attempted to interpret it within a framework of theme and variations, but with reservations. Some have found sonata-form elements. Is it a theme and variations, is it an unusual sonata form, is it a hybrid, or is it an entirely unique structure?'

Michael Broyles, *Beethoven: The Emergence and Evolution of Beethoven's Heroic Style.* New York: Excelsior Music Publishing Co., 1987, pp. 59–94.

NEVILLE CARDUS

The English writer and music critic Sir Neville Cardus was widely read in his contributions to *The Manchester Guardian* — on both cricket and music. He counted several distinguished musicians amongst his personal friends, including Sir Thomas Beecham whose musicianship he greatly admired. This is discernible from the review Cardus reported of a performance of the *Eroica* Symphony that Beecham gave with the London Philharmonic Orchestra on the autumn of 1933:

> 'Sir Thomas Beecham leaves us with little to do but praise. It may be that occasionally we do not agree with his interpretations, but what of that? It is not the business of genius to agree with us. He places his stamp of his own style on everything

with the glow of his own personality. He creates the standards and laws by which we must judge him ... Yet it is a mistake to persist with the old notion that Sir Thomas is mereley a tasteful and cultivated conductor His interpretation of the *Eroica* Symphony on Saturday was big and noble — it was, in fact, the most possessed piece of conducting I have experienced since [Arthur] Nikisch; it made the Symphony sound the greatest symphony written by anybody; it made the heart throb and the mind to thrill with delight at the invention, the marvellous mutations, of the music; it made us love Beethoven and bow the head in gratitude that we have the blessed fortune to become acquainted with the genius of the man.

'Sir Thomas gave the first performance pace, and he pointed the rhythm in a way which with other conductors might have diminished the stature; but Sir Thomas has his own intensity, which ran through the transitions like a current of electricity, so that the great wheel of the first movement never stopped ... The second movement was grave and eloquent and never pretentious; the Scherzo was perhaps more a dance than the spirit of the grotesque calls for. But the fourth movement crowned the interpretation. I have known no other conductor give to this movement the unfolding grandeur of variation-from which we could feel in every outward course of the music on Saturday. The emotion, the heart of the work, was there, beating stupendous, but, rarer still, the musical art was there — the transforming force and shapes of music's most wonderful device, which is variation-form. This is Sir Thomas's way with

Beethoven — to shut his mind to all the accumulated weight of extraneous, non-musical significances which have been dumped upon Beethoven by his metaphysical commentators.'

Donald Wright editor, *Cardus on Music: A Centenary Collection*. London: Hamish Hamilton, 1988, pp. 266–68. Originally published in *The Manchester Guardian*, 30 October 1933. See also: Neville Cardus, *Talking of music*. London: Collins, 1957.

ELIOT CARTER

The American writer and musicologist Allen Edwards interviewed the modernist American composer Eliot Carter. Their conversation turned to the question of structure in music, prompting Edwards to ask: '[In] what way do you feel ... very large-scale rhythmic processes can or should be consciously perceived ...?' Carter responded:

> 'Well, it seemed very obvious to me that in older music the "periodic effect" of multiples of two and three beats was used with great power, and could also be modified with enormous effect. For instance, Beethoven began to use larger rhythmic periods as actual architectonic elements — such as the repeated chords at the beginning of the *Eroica* Symphony and at the end of movements. These chords at the ends of movements give the impression that the music has been emptied of everything but the "marking time" of big periods of grandly epic scale.'

Allen Edwards, *Flawed Words and Stubborn Sounds: A*

Conversation with Elliott Carter. New York: Norton & Company, 1971, p. 111.

ANNE-LOUISE COLDICOTT
The author and musicologist Anne-Louise Coldicott writes about the changing attitude to the interpretation of Beethoven's orchestral music:

> 'Wilhelm Furtwängler (1886–1954) was one of the last of the Romantic school of conductors. In his recordings he showed himself capable of imposing overall unity on the works by bringing to them a great breadth which did not lose sight of clarity through precision of detail. But the somewhat improvisatory quality of his interpretations led to criticisms of too much freedom. Otto Klemperer (1855–1973) is recognised as one of the most authoritative interpreters of Beethoven. Beginning his career when it was still commonplace to 'retouch', he resisted this practice except for some doubling of woodwind and horns to achieve a better balance, a practice now common where large string sections are used. In later years he became notorious for exceptionally slow tempi, but previously he achieved heroic dimensions and great power, resulting from his tremendous architectural grasp of a work. The Karajan performances of the 1960s have a special place for the new standards of orchestral playing he demanded of the Berlin Philharmonic Orchestra and the energy, brilliance and commitment he brought to performances.'

Anne-Louise Coldicott, *Performance Styles Since Beethoven's Day* in: Barry Cooper, *The Beethoven Compendium: A Guide to Beethoven's Life and Music.* London: Thames and Hudson, 1991, pp. 300–01. See also the entry for Gustave Mahler.

BARRY COOPER*

Barry Cooper discusses the originality to be found in the *Eroica* Symphony. Of the first movement he comments:

'Beethoven had been trying out increasingly remote keys as the tonal goals of his developments in the preceding years, and E minor afer E-flat major [the key of the *Eroica* Symphony] was his furthest yet ... What is so astonishing here, however, is the complete contrast of character that Beethoven achieves through a combination of remote keys, unusual instrumentation, and the change of register, coupled with an extraordinarily prolonged build-up to this point.

'Throughout the movement ... the proportions between the sections are unusual, even though the sonata-form structure is regular in outline, Beethoven's sketches show much effort to obtain proportions that satisfied him ...'.

'The rest of the movement contains many more surprises, including the famous premature entry of the second horn just before the recapitulation, a sudden excursion to F major shortly afterwards (with the dissonant C sharp used as a pivot note in the modulation), and an extremely long coda to resolve earlier instabilities and bring the disparate ideas into an overall unity. The extraordinary level of ingenuity and originality in the movement has generated an enormous amount of literature, yet much still remains to be said about its composition and structure.'

Of the other movements, Cooper observes:

'The second movement is a funeral march in C major ... It seems odd to have a funeral march so early in a heroic symphony, especially when the hero Napoleon was still alive and overrunning half of Europe. Thus, the Symphony is clearly not a portrait of Napoleon or anyone else. Beethoven perceived true heroes as immortal, and indeed had a strong interest in the concept of immortality ... To represent immortality in the Symphony, he therefore placed the funeral march second, after a lifelong struggle and ultimate triumph in the first movement; this enabled the third movement apparently to symbolize resurrection (though it is simply headed "Scherzo"), and the fourth to represent the hero taking his place among the immortals.'

Barry Cooper, *Beethoven, The Master Musicians Series*. Oxford: Oxford University Press, 2000, pp. 130–31.

LOUISE ELVIRA CUYLER*

The American musicologist Louise Elvira Cuyler discusses the structure and character of the *Eroica* Symphony:

FIRST MOVEMENT:
'Our present-day surfeit with the voluptuous

sounds of late Romantic music, not to mention the cerebral inventions of the serialists, makes difficult a candid assessment of such direct, eloquent music as Beethoven's *Eroica*. The essential quality of the work derives from nobility of idea and an unfettered plan for dispersal of materials within the confines of a traditional design. That critic who called the Symphony "a wild fantasia" sensed this freedom and, although he may not have understood the music, he was basically right about it. The bold, generous quality of the Symphony is apparent in its opening statement [illustration]. Two E-flat major triads in a full orchestral tutti dispense impatiently with the traditional introduction. Then the *Eroica* motto is revealed in simple grandeur, but truncated summarily with the chromatic note C sharp ... Then a sizable portion explores the potential of the *Eroica* motto in the kind of germinating section Beethoven had learned to structure so successfully. The heroic scope of the first movement is indicated by its total length of 691 measures, as compared with 327 measures for the *Allegro con brio* portion of the Second Symphony.'

SECOND MOVEMENT:

'The pathos of the second movement, inscribed *Marcia funebre*, undoubtedly helped endear the entire symphony to the Romantic generations that followed Beethoven. In a sense this was Beethoven's own encounter with the *Sturm und Drang*, even though it was a quarter of a century delayed ... [The] *Marcia funebre*, which takes the place of the traditional slow movement, is cast in the type of large ternary design used routinely for a Menuetto-Scherzo: the middle portion (in C major), indicated *Maggiore* ('Major') is in lieu of the usual Trio. We might call that a March, even one with lugubrious overtones, may be regarded as a dance-form. Hence the choice of design is not unsuitable.'

THIRD MOVEMENT:

'The Scherzo resembles the parallel movement of the Second Symphony, but exceeds it in the extended and varied *da capo* portion, which includes a brief *alla breve* insert (measures 381–84). The design is a routine scherzo with Trio, in which the horns are conspicuous, especially in the Trio.'

FOURTH MOVEMENT:

'The basic materials for this imposing and daring set of variations are derived from Beethoven's music for *Prometheus*. They must have pleased the composer especially, since he used them in two other contexts in a *kontretanz* (country dance) and again in the Piano Variations, Op. 35. The *Prometheus* excerpt yields two fine linear subjects, the first is its robust bass part, the second is the melodic upper part. [illustration].'

Cuyler concludes her text by subjecting the seven variations and fugue of the final movement to individual scrutiny.

Louise Elvira Cuyler, *The Symphony*. New York: Harcourt Brace Jovanovich, 1973, pp. 59–65.

SAMUEL BASIL DEANE*

The Irish musicologist and academic Samuel Basil Deane, considers the construction of the *Eroica* Symphony in relation to its precursors:

FIRST MOVEMENT:
'To see how Beethoven's thematic technique has developed we may compare the opening of the movement with the corresponding passages in the earlier symphonies. In the First Symphony the first theme leads to a tutti statement of a new theme. In the Second Symphony the tutti begins as a restatement of the first theme, and then moves in a new direction. In the *Eroica* the opening theme occurs three times as the full tutti (this fanfare-like climax, at bar 37, in which all the wind proclaim the opening figure, lends support to Schmitz's view that the theme is a form of military signal). So Beethoven has at once expanded his form and made it more thematically coherent.' [Eugen Schmitz was a German musicologist and music critic]

'The premature entry of the second horn, ... an early inspiration of Beethoven's, is psychologically entirely plausible in its context. The recapitulation is followed by a Coda of enormous dimensions. In it Beethoven continues to "develop" his material. But the effect is one of stabilization, and some events of the development are now absorbed into the home tonality and transformed in significance.'

SECOND MOVEMENT:

Deane positions the funeral march within the wider context of Beethoven's interest in the genre and beyond to possible sources of influence:

> 'The march as a category interested Beethoven throughout his life, from the early Variations on a March by Dressler of 1782 to the *Alla marcia* in the A-minor String Quartet, Op. 132, of 1825 ... Of the fifty or so marches, or march sections, only three are specifically labelled march: The *Marcia funebre sulla morte d'un eroe* in the Piano Sonata in A flat, Op. 26, of 1800; the *Marcia funebre* of the *Eroica*; and the *Trauermarsch* for *Lenore Prohaska* of 1815. Ernst Bücken [German musicologist] suggested that the funeral march in C minor from the Opera *Giulio Sabino* (1781) by Giuseppe Sarti may have been a model for Beethoven. But a more likely, if still hypothetical, precursor is Sarti's pupil Cherubini. A taste for funeral marches developed in France during the Revolution, and one example which became widely known was the slow march which begins the *Hymne funebre sur la morte du Général* Hoche by Cherubini, written in 1797. Cherubini's march is an extended composition in D minor in which the solemn phrases are expressed by short drum rolls. The melodic line, although naïve in its rhythmic monotony, has some points of contact with Beethoven's theme.' [illustration]

THIRD MOVEMENT:

'The Scherzo ... apparently so spontaneous in rush of energy, reached its final form after much alteration. The constant factors throughout the creative process were the melodic phrase beginning in the seventh bar, and the thematic use of the three horns. In the final version the melody provides much of the thematic material, appearing as it does in a variety of keys; and the Trio is dominated by the horn group.'

FOURTH MOVEMENT:

'It seems unlikely that Beethoven, in his choice of material for the finale, was indifferent to its earlier associations. He had used the theme on three previous occasions, an occurrence remarkable in itself; a contradanse, as the theme for a set of Piano Variations, Op. 35, and as part of the final dance in his Ballet *The Creatures of Prometheus*, Op. 43. The official playbill described Prometheus as "an exalted spirit, who found the men of his time in a condition of ignorance, and who refined them through science and art and brought them civilized customs". Such a figure, closer to the divinely inspired artist than to the politician or general, embodied for Beethoven, as for many of his idealistic contemporaries, the highest of heroic action. As he had, in the second movement, transformed the funeral march into a full-scale symphonic form, so here he creates an entirely new type of variation movement, one in which the maximum amount of freedom is achieved in relation to the original material consistent with coherence, so that the form might be described a variation fantasy. The widely varying sections — fugato, march, slow movement, as well as more directly related material — are welded together in a continuous whole. In the final *presto* the horns which have set their stamp on the whole work, burst into a blaze of exaltation.'

Samuel Basil Deane, *The Symphonies and Overtures* in: Denis Arnold and Nigel Fortune editors, *The Beethoven Companion*. London: Faber and Faber, 1973, pp. 288—93.

ANATAL DORÁTI

The African-born British cellist Alexander Kok recalls the occasion when the Hungarian-born composer and conductor Anatal Doráti was appointed as the new Permanent Conductor of the BBC Symphony Orchestra — of which Kok was then the principal cellist. Dorati announced he wanted everyone to get to know each other by playing through the *Eroica* Symphony. Kok relates:

'He gave the first down beat. The orchestra responded. Then came the second down beat for the second bar. Finally, on the third down beat, the cellos are supposed to set off on the exposition of a work that is surely Beethoven's finest symphony. Dorati stopped the orchestra. Looking in my direction, and without attempting to disguise his displeasure, he barked, "Play on my beat!"

'The orchestra started again from the beginning. Again, he stopped. This time he is really angry. A profusion of remarks about lack of attention to rhythmic discipline was directed at me and we had to start again. I was at a loss to understand why the cellos were being singled out when quite obviously *all* the players in the orchestra had come in late.'

Kok explains:

'For some reason the third bar is usually played slightly behind the pulse beat; it had become a tradition. Perhaps Doráti was right. Perhaps we had got into the habit of taking too much time to get back to the heel of the bow after the first two chords.'

Kok was later to discover that Doráti was deaf in his right ear, the side of the rostrum occupied by the cellos. This meant he heard the upper frequencies (notably the violins to his left) ahead of the lower-frequency instruments to his right. Happily, Kok concludes: '[Somehow] we survived the first encounter.'

Alexander Kok, *A Voice in the Dark: The Philharmonia Years*. Ampleforth: Emerson Edition, 2002, pp. 330–33.

PHILIP G. DOWNS*

In his essay 'Beethoven's "New Way" and the *Eroica* Symphony', the American musicologist Philip G. Downs subjected the first movement to detailed musicological scrutiny. The following extracts are offered by way of conveying a flavour of his authoritative text:

'The [first] movement opens with the well-known chords of E-flat major. Whether one calls them introduction or not is immaterial, since from the First Symphony, Beethoven has shown that the introduction can be given a function far removed from the relatively detached architectural idea that Mozart and Haydn's introductions most frequently represent. The onus rests with the listener to assess the chords in the light of what the music tells him, and what he knows of Beethoven's artistic goals.

'It is worth remembering that Beethoven once thought of opening the Symphony with chords similar to those dominants which open the First Symphony, but the idea was abandoned ... The two chords have a function which extends beyond themselves insofar as the rhythm is concerned, and insofar as the drama is concerned they act as portents of things to come ... The first sounds give a pulse, the next sounds divide the pulse into a rhythm, and the next sounds move to modify the rhythm ... The division of the development into four sections has long been noticed, and commentators have remarked that the first two sections form a thesis and antithesis while the last two form the synthesis ... Formally, the recapitulation is perfect and serious in intent: dramatically it is equivalent to the tolerant looking-back on former weaknesses. As if to show the reality of the situation, the French horn now takes its melody, which it so desperately wanted to take at the start of the recapitulation. The famous horn anticipation can now be seen as a stroke of humour in which the formality of the recapitulation of the old version of the theme forces the new version to give way to it, and the new version has the strength to stand back and wait its due place ... The Coda provides Beethoven with an opportunity for fulfilling the sonata principle of recapitulation; therefore, its function in this symphony is virtually entirely formal ... [For] some listeners the final measures, from 677 to the end, can be the most important. Every point which has had a bearing on Beethoven's method of musical dramatization has been emphasized by the composer, has been made to stand out from its surroundings by one means or another ... No music has ever stated an argument in purely musical terms and simultaneously in extra-musical terms so clearly as the *Eroica*.'

Philip G. Downs, *Beethoven's "New Way" and the Eroica* in: Paul Henry Lang, *The Creative World of Beethoven*. New York: W. W. Norton 1971, pp. 86–101.

ALFRED EINSTEIN*

The German-American musicologist Alfred Einstein was a contributor for a period to the London *Daily Telegraph*. In the issue for 23 June 1934, he wrote an article titled '*Rest and Unrest: Music's Changing Function in a Changing World*'. He opened his text with reference to Beethoven and the *Eroica* Symphony:

'Beethoven expressed a strange wish when he gave his *Eroica* to the world, or rather, one that has come to appear strange to us. He wished the work to be placed at the beginning and not the end of the concert programme. He considered his symphony too long, too difficult and exhausting to be performed at the end of the evening when the audience might not be alert, attentive and understanding.

'Nowhere today is there a conductor who respects Beethoven's wish. No doubt the present-day conductor would plead that the *Eroica* long ago ceased to be a difficult work, and that in dimensions and pretensions it has been outdone by dozens of symphonies.

'And he would be right; modern conductors are always right. There is no contradicting them. But an interesting point remains — why is it that modern conductors always put the *Eroica* at the end of the programme? The reason is that, in spite of its one-hundred and thirty-years of age, the *Eroica*, though it may have been surpassed in dimensions and pretensions, has never been surpassed in effect. The conductor wants his audience to disperse with minds freshly stamped with the most powerful impression of the whole concert. And no matter how jaded and drooping the audience, it cannot help responding to the *Eroica's* whip and spur — most certainly not when the theme of the Finale is shouted out by eight horns as I can remember having heard it once.

'The aim of the conductor of the twentieth century — and of the latter half of the nineteenth — is effectiveness, excitement, intoxication, where Beethoven wanted understanding, or better, elevation through understanding. The difference is profound.'

Catherine Dower, *Alfred Einstein on Music: Selected Music Criticisms*. New York: Greenwood Press, 1991, pp. 168–69.

In his study of Mozart's later music for mechanical instruments, Einstein considers its influence on the youthful Beethoven and, *inter alia*, the *Eroica* Symphony. In Mozart's time there was a vogue for mechanical clocks that had organs built into them. Towards the end of his life, Mozart was commissioned to write music for these elaborate mechanisms of which his *Fantasia* in F Minor K. 608 is the most celebrated. Beethoven had a copy of the piece and made his own version of the fugue section. He thereby became one of many composers, and performers, who endowed the work with a life of its own separate from its original form and purpose. Einstein remarks:

> 'The whole piece is an unceasing and mighty flow of melody, alive in every detail, and although arrangements have been made of it — for the contradiction between its garb and its contents was felt long ago — the only appropriate one would be for a large orchestra. The function of the polyphony is a grandiose objectivity of expression, a monumental form of mourning that seeks to avoid the slightest trace of sentimentality. It is understandable that the composer of the *Marcia funebre* in the *Eroica* Symphony should have made a copy of the work; and many points of contact between Mozart and Beethoven may be found in it.'

Alfred Einstein, *Mozart: His Character, his Work*. London: Cassell and Company Ltd., 1946, pp. 269–70.

EDWARD ELGAR

The thought of embodying the concept of heroism in a symphony, somewhat after the manner of Beethoven in the *Eroica*, appears to have stirred the imagination of Edward Elgar. He was apparently seized by the exploits and personal courage of Major-General Charles Gordon — 'Gordon of Khartoum' — that had earned the admiration of the Empire-minded British public. Elgar revealed his enthusiasm for the subject in a letter he wrote in 1898 to his friend August Jaeger — Gordon had died a much-romanticised death in 1858. Elgar wrote: 'Now, as to Gordon: the thing possesses me, but I can't write it down yet.' Jaeger, perhaps with the intention of stirring Elgar into action, sent a note to *The Musical Times* averring:

> 'Mr. Edward Elgar has several interesting works "on the stocks". Chief among them is the new symphony for the Worcester Festival, which is to bear the title 'Gordon'. As in the case of Beethoven's No. 3, Mr. Elgar has selected a great hero for his theme, though of a very different type from that of the *Eroica*. The extraordinary career of General Gordon — his military achievements, his unbounded energy, his self-sacrifice, his resolution, his deep religious fervour — offers to a composer of Mr. Elgar's temperament a magnificent subject, and affords full scope for the exercise of his genius; moreover, it is a subject that appeals to the sympathies of all true-hearted Englishmen.'

The 'Gordon Symphony' of course never appeared but some consider the 'heroic' idea is to be found in much of Elgar's noble and expansive orchestral writing.

Percy M. Young editor, *Letters to Nimrod: Edward Elgar to August Jaeger, 1897–1908*. London: Dennis Dobson, 1965, p. 25 and p. 356.

BRIAN FERNEYHOUGH

The British composer Brian Ferneyhough is recognised for being a central figure in what has been described as the 'New Complexity' movement of contemporary music. In an interview with Ferneyhough, the American composer and writer on music James Boros discussed complexity in music remarking:

> 'Is there really a difference between simple and complex music? ... I mean: simple music might not be just simple; when its great music, Beethoven for example, those simple notes are able to evoke something more, and be very significant, capable of astonishing?'

This proposition prompted Ferneyhough to respond:

> 'You think Beethoven simple? I spent many hours, once, working out what happened in the first four measures of the *Eroica*, and I still wasn't at the end of it.'

Boros persisted: 'No, but the first impression is of graspability and clarity, not of complexity.' Ferneyhough offered the rejoinder:

> 'Well, on that level it is indeed rather clear, but that's only because we find ourselves at some distance, both in time and social perception, from

it. Perhaps the public of the day found such gestures as the First Symphony [of Beethoven] beginning on the dominant chord incomprehensible and provocative.'

James Boros and Richard Toop editors, *Brian Ferneyhough: Collected Writings*. Amsterdam: Harwood Academic, 1995, pp. 230–31.

WILHELM FURTWÄNGLER

For more than thirty years the German conductor Wilhelm Furtwängler kept a notebook in which, diary-fashion, he preserved his thoughts on a variety of subjects. From an entry in his notebook for 1939 he observed:

'*Eroica*! Exaggeration of the [composer's] earlier style, sometime almost abstract (first movement). For all its greatness a unique work, i.e. a work of transition. Even the Fourth [Symphony] is freer and, consequently, greater. A sign that any style, even the most natural, can rigidify, indeed rigidifies immediately upon ceasing to be a completely natural expression. And it is always only this for one moment. The differences between Beethoven's early and middle styles, particularly in the transition periods, are not so tangible as that which we now call Beethoven's style. There is no "development" of harmony or rhythm, but only of the soul, which makes use of the musical space to a higher degree than before. The soul expresses itself more freely, that is the whole thing.'

Michael Tanner editor, *Notebooks, 1924–1954: Wilhelm Furtwängler*. London: Quartet Books, 1989, p. 97.

HANS GAL*

In his survey of *The Golden Age of Vienna*, the Austrian-British composer and author Hans Gal has trenchant things to say about the *astute* reception of the *Eroica* Symphony:

> 'No sensible listener will ever find anything puzzling in the second half of this Symphony, as far as a general approach is concerned. After the second movement, his capacity for emotional tension is utterly exhausted. The bustling gaiety of the Scherzo, the splendour and affirmative optimism of the finale, are the healthiest possible restoratives. He will take the music for what it is: an incomparably exciting, grand work of art, in which the idea implied in the title remains just a general background. All attempts on the part of well-meaning commentators to explain the second half of the Symphony as a consistent continuation of the poetic idea are bound to result in abstruse nonsense, such as, for example, the suggestion that we regard the Scherzo as a memory of a hunting party from happy bygone times and the finale as a panorama of Homeric funeral games, as described in the *Iliad*.
>
> 'If any super-logical listener wants the heroic business properly finished, I would refer him to a more recent '*Eroica*' by Richard Strauss, called *Eine Heldenleben*, where everything proceeds according to plan and in right order, up to a nice powerful death in old age and a solemn salvo

and drum-roll at the graveside. But it was not Beethoven's intention to write a biography; he wrote music. The undeniable fact that in exceptional cases, for instance in the *Pastoral* Symphony, he followed a sort of extra-musical idea must not mislead us into assuming that this was his invariable practice. If there really were any inconsistency in the idea of his great heroic epic, there would be a very simple explanation ... [For] all we know, the title may have occurred to the composer only after having finished his work, or at a very advanced stage of it. But besides this, the fact remains that for any sane listener the question never presents itself. For him, the second half of the Symphony is not only in no way contradictory to the first, but its most convincing continuation and no less *heroic*, if one understands this term in a higher and purer sense than the crude, material one of battle, death and funeral.'

Hans Gal, *The Golden Age of Vienna*, London: Max Parrish & Co. Limited, 1948, pp. 52–53.

STEWART GORDON

Stewart Gordon is an American musician and Professor of Keyboard Studies at the University of Southern California. In his *A History of Keyboard Literature* he discusses the concept in music of movement through time:

'The forces shaping the movement of a work by Beethoven or Mozart are ... immediately audible. The dissonance in the seventh bar of the *Eroica* audibly implies the modulation to F minor that Beethoven only makes when he repeats the passage hundreds of bars later ... The material of the great classical composers is directional — we can hear the opening of the *Eroica* moving towards something, even if we cannot name it, and its arrival, presented as a surprise, is also a logical satisfying of a dynamic tonal impulse, the resolution of a tension.'

Stewart Gordon, *A History of Keyboard Literature: Music for the Piano and its Forerunners.* Schirmer Books: New York: London: Prentice Hall International, 1996, pp. 32–33.

GEORGE GROVE*

In 1896 Sir George Grove published *Beethoven and his Nine Symphonies*; by then he was well qualified to do so. Following a successful career as a civil engineer, he turned his gifts to musical administration. He was appointed Secretary at the Chrystal Palace, where he established an orchestra with the assistance of the conductor August Manns. Among the composers Grove introduced to the public was Franz Schubert, much of whose music was unknown in England. After nearly twenty years of service at the Crystal Palace, Grove resigned the Secretaryship and joined the staff of the publishers Macmillan and Co.. Of his scholarly writings, *The Musical Times* wrote: 'His masterly biographies of Beethoven, Mendelssohn, and Schubert are models of biographical literature ...'. They eventually formed the basis of *Grove's Dictionary of Music and Musicians.* Writing of the *Eroica* Symphony Grove states:

FIRST MOVEMENT:
'The first subject of the opening *Allegro con Brio*, the animating soul of the whole movement, is ushered in by two great chords of E flat from the orchestra, in which all the force of the entire piece seems to be concentrated: [illustration] Beethoven's sketches show that these chords were originally discords, as is the case in the First Symphony: [illustration] The main theme itself, given by the cellos alone, is but four bars long; the exquisite completion by the fiddles ... is added merely for the occasion, and does not occur again ... How broad and gay, and how beautiful and dignified! ... Surly no one ever made such openings as the openings to these symphonies ... How pregnant are these great themes! How everlasting, not only in the never-ending delight which the hearing of them gives, but in the long chain of followers to which they give birth! ... '[The] way they are expressed and connected; the sunlight and cloud, the alternate fury and tenderness, the nobility, the beauty, the obstinacy, the human character! Certainly, nothing like it was ever done in music before, and very little like it has been done in the ninety years since 1808.'

At this point, Grove quotes from Wordsworth's *The Prelude*:

> "Bliss was it in that dawn to be alive,
> But to be young was very Heaven!"

SECOND MOVEMENT:
'The second movement, very slow, *Adagio assai*,

is in the form of a funeral march, and bears the title of *Marcia funebre* — the very title itself an important innovation on established practice. And a March it is, worthy to accompany the obsequies of a hero of the noblest mould, such a one as Napoleon to his admirers in 1808: [illustration] ... In this noble and expressive passage of fugal music, we might be assisting at the actual funeral of the hero, with all that is good and great in the nation looking on as he was lowered into his tomb; and the motto might well be Tennyson's words on Wellington — "In the vast cathedral leave him / God accept him, Christ receive him".'

THIRD MOVEMENT:

'This is the earliest of those great movements which Beethoven was the first to give to the world, which are perhaps the most *Beethovenish* of all his compositions, and in which the tragedy and comedy of life are so startlingly combined ... For the *Scherzo*, we return to the key of E flat; and it is impossible to imagine a more complete relief than it presents to the March. It begins *Allegro vivace, sempre pianissimo e staccato*, and after a prelude of six bars in the strings, the oboe and first violins join in this most fresh and lively tune: [illustration] ... The Trio, or alternative to the *Scherzo*, is mainly in the hands of the horns, the other instruments being chiefly occupied in interludes between the strains of those most interesting and most human members of the orchestra. And surely, if ever horns talked like flesh and blood, and in their own human accents, they do here:' [illustration]

The close of the third movement affected Grove deeply:

'What is it makes these late few notes so touching, so almost awful? There is in them a feeling of infinitude or eternity as is conveyed by no other passage in Beethoven's music. To the [present] writer the notes speak the lofty, mystical, yearning tone of Wordsworth's beautiful lines:'

"Our destiny, our being's heart and home,
Is with infinitude, and only there;
With hope it is, hope that can never die,
Effort, and expectation, and desire.
And something evermore absent to be."

FOURTH MOVEMENT:

'The finale has often been a puzzle. Some have thought it trivial, some laboured, others that its intention was to divert the audience after the too great stain of the earlier movements ... No one who hears the finale through, and allows it to produce its own proper and intended *effect* upon him, need be in doubt as to its meaning, or hesitate to recognise in it characteristics as *heroic* as those of any other portion of the work, though clothed in different forms. The art and skill employed throughout it are extraordinary. But Beethoven never used these powers for mere display, He must have written it because he had something to say about his hero he had not in the other three movements.' [Grove elaborates this part of his text with several musical illustrations]

George Grove, *Beethoven and his Nine Symphonies*. London: Novello, Ewer, 1896, pp. 57–80.

DONALD J. GROUT AND CLAUDE V. PALISCA*
The American-born musicologist Donald J. Grout and the Italian-born Claudia V. Palisca consider the grandeur and evolving construction of the first movement of the *Eroica* Symphony:

> '[The] Third Symphony stands as an immortal expression in music of the ideal of heroic greatness. It was a revolutionary work, of such unprecedented length and complexity that audiences at first found it difficult to grasp. It begins, after two introductory chords, with one of the simplest imaginable themes on the notes of the B-flat major triad, but an unexpected C sharp at this point gives rise to endless variations and development in the course of the movement ... Most remarkable, however, in this movement, as in all of Beethoven's, is neither the formal pattern nor the abundance of ideas, but the way all the material is propelled constantly along one theme seeming to unfold in a steady dynamic growth which mounts one climax to the next, driving with a sense of utter inevitability to the end.'

As with other writers, the authors consider the putative influence of solemn French orchestral music, of the period, on Beethoven's scoring in the second movement:

'It is the funeral march more than anything else in the Symphony that links it with France and the Republican experiment there. Certain traits that [François Joseph] Gossec's *March lugubre* have in common with Beethoven's march suggest the latter's dependence on the conventions of the genre: dotted rhythms, muffled drum rolls, which Beethoven imitated in the string basses, melody interrupted by sobs, minor mode in the main march, major Trio, half step melodic motion in the minor sections, unison effects, and the prominence given to the winds.' [Gossec and Beethoven illustrations follow]

The author's detect other French influences on Beethoven's writing:

'The Maggiore middle section or Trio of Beethoven's march seems to take its inspiration from another French source, namely, the hymns and cantatas sung in praise of Republican ideals and heroes, such as Ignaz Pleyel's *Hymne à la liberté* (1791) or Gossec's *Aux manes de la Grande* ('To the Shades of the Grande') ... Although Beethoven may have had Napoleon specifically in mind, the funeral march addresses itself generally to the subject of heroism, sacrifice, and mourning.'

Donald Jay Grout and Claude V. Palisca, editors: *A History of Western Music*, London: J. M. Dent, 1988, pp. 637–39.

BERNARD HAITINK

Reflecting on aspects of his career, the Dutch conductor Bernard Haitink makes reference to the *Eroica* Symphony in the context of the challenges of performing and recording Beethoven's symphonies. He begins with some generalizations:

> 'Beethoven is so varied; each symphony is different and that is a mark of genius of the man. Number Six is a unique achievement, and then the changes between Seven, Eight and Nine are incredible. In a way it is superhuman to ask one man to do all nine symphonies equally well. They encompass so many different worlds that one conductor will do number Five brilliantly while another will do a very poetic performance of the *Pastoral*, but that is not to say that the same person can do them all. I think we are all frightened of them. You cannot pretend in Beethoven.
>
> 'When you remember all those conductors who have recorded the symphonies, you wonder what you can add to that whole heap of knowledge and experience. As a young man you think you should try some unusual interpretation, but of course that is quite wrong. One has to come to a realization of the works through maturing and growing. Confidence is perhaps the greatest asset one gains with years.
>
> 'I think I have changed my overall approach because I am, I hope, more mature and more experienced, and I think that they could all gain from that, both technically and musically ...'.
>
> 'As far as the detail is concerned, I take most

of the repeats, except the first movement of the *Eroica*. If you do that one I feel you lose the intensity of the development. Nor do I repeat the exposition in the finale of the Fifth Symphony. I do not think I have the sheer physical energy for that, though I know Carlos Klieber makes it; so did Klemperer on his records. But I do not have the stamina to hold the concentration twice over.'

Simon Mundy, *Bernard Haitink: A Working Life*. London: Robson Books, 1987, pp. 118–19.

HALLÉ ORCHESTRA: CHARLES HALLÉ AND HANS RICHTER

In June 1851, at the age of sixteen, the German-born Carl (Charles) Hallé went to Darmstadt to study harmony and counterpoint. He analysed Beethoven's symphonies and heard the *Eroica* for the first time. Recalling this experience years later he enthused:

'I remember up to the present day the deep impression which Beethoven's *Eroica* Symphony made upon me, especially the marvellous Funeral March. Sitting in a dark corner of the half-lighted theatre ... I was rapt in wonderment and trembling all over. There is in particular a long A flat for the oboe, about thirty-four bars before the close of the march, for which I always waited with perfect awe, and which made my flesh creep. The rehearsals of this one Symphony were continued a full month, by the end of which I knew it by heart, not having missed a single one. During that month it was the all-absorbing topic of conversation amongst musicians, and the rehearsals, far from being shunned by the members of the orchestra, as is so often the case, were expected with impatience.'

Such was Hallé's enthusiasm for the Funeral March of the *Eroica* Symphony that he requested it to be played at his own funeral which took place in 1895.

Hallé, C. E. *Life and Letters of Sir Charles Hallé: Being an Autobiography (1819–1860) with Correspondence and Diaries.* London: Smith, Elder & Co., 1896, p. 29. See also: Michael Kennedy, *Hallé Tradition: A Century of Music.* Manchester: Manchester University Press, 1960, p. 8.

For many years, in England, Hallé was known and celebrated as a pianist; he was, for example, the first pianist in England to perform the complete series of Beethoven's piano sonatas. In 1853 Hallé moved to Manchester to direct what were known as *Manchester's Gentlemans' Concerts.* In due course Hallé enhanced their standing in the form of the *Hallé Orchestra Concert Series*, performed under his baton. From 1899 until 1909, the Hallé was directed by the Austrian-Hungarian conductor Hans Richter. We learn something of Richter's work with the Hallé Orchestra, and of its musical standing, from the account of a performance of the *Eroica* Symphony directed by the Belgian violinist-conductor Eugène Ysaÿe:

'Ysaÿe and the *Eroica*, these were the features of last night's concert in Bradford ... Both reached the highest possible level of interpretation. Beethoven's great work can hardly have been often played with equal perfection, even under so great a Beethoven interpreter as Dr. Richter, and the Hallé Band showed very strikingly the advance it has made in finish and refinement. There was plenty to be done in this direction when Sir Charles Hallé died and much was accomplished by Mr. Cowan during his tenure of the conductorship. [Sir Frederic Hymen Cowen conducted the Hallé for three years before Richter — he was knighted in 1911] Dr. Richter has gone still further and has now effected some changes in the personnel of the Band, the fruits of which are gradually making themselves felt as the newcomers are finding their feet. Certainly, no more finished playing could be desired than was heard in the *Eroica*; the Funeral March was notable, not only for the dignity and deep feeling with which Richter always invests it, but for refinement of phrasing especially noticeable in the strings, though a word must be given to the very expressive playing of the first oboe. Perfection and delicacy were again a remarkable feature in the Scherzo, while throughout there was the closest possible attention to detail and the balance between the different sections of the orchestra was maintained with quite exceptional care and success; altogether it was a very notable performance.'

Originally published in *The Yorkshire Post* of 10 November 1900 and reproduced in: Christopher Fifield, *True Artist and True Friend: A Biography of Hans Richter*. Oxford: Clarendon Press, 1993, p. 149.

HAMILTON HARTY

In 1927 *The Musical Times* invited the Irish composer, conductor, and pianist. Sir Herbert Hamilton Harty to contribute to its *Special Issue,* published to commemorate Beethoven's Death Centenary. He did so in an article titled *Beethoven's Orchestra: A Conductor's Reflections.* He makes the following general remarks concerning Beethoven's orchestration:

> 'Beethoven's general habit and manner in orchestration is fully exemplified in his symphonies, and it is not necessary to go further afield, even if, in other works, he makes use of some instrument which does not appear in his scores. If we take the nine symphonies and regard them from a merely technical point of view, they reveal, to an impartial eye, that the strings are always used with the greatest fullness and resource, the bassoons and drums with a special originality. And the flutes, oboes, clarinets, horns, trumpets, and trombones in a way we might expect (and that we get) from any well-equipped typical musician of those days. There are obscurities and miscalculations in certain places, some of which appear to be due to the impatience and brusqueness which were part of the composer's character, others which are undoubtedly the result of simple errors in questions of balance. Instances of both will occur to the minds of those familiar with the scores.'

Harty next considered the detrimental changes he considered some orchestral instruments had undergone since Beethoven's time:

'[Nowadays] we use a very much larger body of strings than was the general custom in Beethoven's lifetime [and] there is no doubt that many of the wind instruments have undergone, since then, a considerable change and have gained in ease of manipulation at the expense of beauty of tone. The flute, for instance, must have frequently possessed a much sweeter and more characteristic tone before it was furnished with the ingenious mechanism in use today, and there is no doubt that the horn has also suffered in this respect by the addition of valves, and the trumpet, probably for the same reason. The oboe and bassoon, on the other hand, were rougher and coarser in quality, and the timpani less accurate and shallower in tone. It is likely that the trombone is the only wind instrument which has not altered in timbre, for there has been no change in its mechanism. Keeping these considerations in mind, it is interesting to imagine how Beethoven's symphonies may have sounded to his audiences, and, at the same time, it may give some justification for the readjustments it is felt necessary to make in modern performances.'

Harty concluded his essay:

'It is worthwhile to consider whether over-caution is in the best interest of these bold and unconventional masterpieces, or whether, in reality, it does not cripple freedom and candour of interpretation. What Beethoven would have said to our modern methods of preforming his works it is impossible to tell. Wagner was not above taking the advice of Richter, nor Brahms or a Joachim, and, on the whole, it seems probable that Beethoven, great autocrat as he was, would not have rejected without consideration any suggestions made to him by a qualified craftsman who revered his music, and who disclaimed any wish or intention to interfere with essentials ... In the end, this is all that anyone entitled to the name of a good musician has ever proposed, or ever will propose in connection with the music of Beethoven – "To amend the letter so that the spirit may shine forth more brightly".'

Hamilton Harty, *Beethoven's Orchestra: A Conductor's Reflections* in: *Beethoven:* London, Special Number, *Music & Letters*, 1927, pp. 172–77.

HANS WERNER HENZE

The German composer Hans Werner Henze describes the time in 1981 when he conducted a number of concerts in America with the Chicago Symphony Orchestra. These included performances of the *Eroica* Symphony, of which he writes:

'I had already conducted the *Eroica* in the Rhineland and in Edinburgh and had developed a very real affinity with a musical language that throws light on both present and future with staggering clarity. At each reacquaintance with the piece, I had to immerse myself in the score and re-examine its every detail to fathom its secrets and see how I could best impart to my audience the multiple meanings inherent in symphonic writing of this order.'

Henze, Hans Werner, *Bohemian Fifths: An Autobiography*.
London: Faber and Faber, 1998, pp. 391–92.

ANTHONY HOPKINS

The pianist, broadcaster, conductor and author Anthony Hopkins — not be confused with his celebrated namesake Sir Anthony Hopkins — endeared himself in the late 1950s to many radio listeners, the present writer included, when he discussed classical music in his BBC Third Programme broadcasts *Talking About Music*. In these he explored a particular piece of music with what has been described as 'a judicious mix of analysis and vivid metaphor', nothing less than 'a listener's *Baedeker*'. In his capacity as author, Hopkins preserved many of his thoughts about music in book-form — suitably adapted. From one of these texts he has the following to say about the *Eroica* Symphony:

> *FIRST MOVEMENT:*
> 'After two massive chords of E-flat major proclaiming the home key, the most significant theme of the first movement appears in the edifice. Its confirmation of the key is undermined by a disturbing alien note (C sharp) that immediately spreads a feeling of unease to the violins. The almost pastoral mood of the opening is deceptive, as though a sculptor were caressing the stone before the first hammer blow which will hew it into shape ... The opening is particularly rich in material; the mood changes frequently and yet there is a convincing unity to the conception. Ideas that should be mentioned include an

elegant "conversation" between oboe, clarinet, flute and violins, based on a three-note phrase, a leisurely rising tune played by clarinets, a strange rhythmic and athletic passage for strings, and a contrastingly gentle theme in the woodwind that begins with no less than nine repetitions of the same note ...'.

'A major structural feature of the movement is the extension of the Coda, normally something of a formality. Beethoven launches into it with two strange side-slips in harmony that must have seemed like a musical earthquake to listeners in 1805 ... Only real familiarity can bring a full appreciation of the magnificent architecture of this movement in which order and unity are imposed from within rather than by the application of academic rules.'

SECOND MOVEMENT:

'The second movement is a funeral march suitable for a mythical hero. Note the avoidance of the use of drums, the double-basses supplying a sound that is comparable to the rumble of muffled drums which is musically more interesting. The immense span of the phrases coupled with the very slow tempo means that the movement is very long, but for those who are prepared to adjust themselves to its measured tread there are ample rewards. Periodically the feeling of grief is softened by episodes in major keys like warming rays of sun on a grey afternoon.'

THIRD MOVEMENT:
'The Scherzo which follows could hardly be more different, bustling along without a care in the world, its rhythmic vitality unflagging. Excitedly the strings set the rhythm ticking; after six bars of quiet staccato chords, the oboe offers us a cheerful little tune with seven repetitions of the same note ... In due course we arrive at the central Trio, a term that is more apt than usual since it is mostly scored for three horns, one more than he uses in any other symphony except the Ninth where there are four ... The whole Scherzo is roughly twice the size of any comparable movement by Haydn, not that direct comparison can be made, so unique is its conception.'

FOURTH MOVEMENT:
'The theme of the finale must have been an especial favourite of Beethoven's since he used it in several other compositions including the ballet-music for *Prometheus*. The opening torrent of notes suggests high drama but there are rather different things in store. The strings pluck out a curiously fragmentary little tune punctuated by sudden three-note outbursts from wind brass and timpani. There are two possible interpretations of this enigmatic passage. It seems, in the *Prometheus* ballet, the hero breathed life into the statues that then took their first faltering steps. One can imagine such a scene to this music but, in the absence of any such programmatic explanation, it is more likely that Beethoven is once again playing a joke on his audience ...

> 'Perhaps the biggest surprise in a movement that is full of surprises comes near the end when there is a fundamental change of tempo. A choir of woodwind initiates a slow variation on the main theme. Gradually, the orchestra seems to take on the semblance of a great cathedral organ with the main theme transferred to the pedals while the organist improvises an elaborate Prelude above. Then, with a sudden memory of the opening flourish, we are whipped into a final Presto in which the horns present a hunting version of the main theme.'

Anthony Hopkins, *The Concertgoer's Companion*. London: J.M. Dent & Sons Ltd., 1984, pp. 66–67.

GORDON JACOB*

The English composer and educator Gordon Jacob contributed a musicological outline of the *Eroica* Symphony in his introduction to the Penguin Books miniature score of the composition:

FIRST MOVEMENT:

'The germ of the first movement is contained in bars 3–6 in the cello part. The violins continue and complete the melody at bar 14. The theme is identical in its first four bars with one to be found in an early work of Mozart's, the Overture to *Bastien et Bastienne*. This was of course a quite unconscious crib; the theme had no doubt lain dormant in Beethoven's mind for years after, perhaps hearing Mozart's little opera when he was a boy ... Out of this simple arpeggio theme Beethoven constructs one of his mightiest movements. It is interesting to note how many of Beethoven's first subjects are founded on common-chord arpeggios, sometimes interspersed with passing notes, but plain enough to hear. Random examples of this can be quoted from his First, Second, Fourth, and Ninth Symphonies, his Piano Sonatas Op. 2, No.1, Op. 10, No. 1, Op. 22, Op. 57, and the last movement of his Violin Concerto and the end of the Fifth Piano Concerto (*Emperor*).

'The horn entry at bar 394, which suggests the juxtaposition of tonic and dominant harmonies, caused a disproportionate amount of fuss and even some tampering with the score by scandalized pedants who wondered what on earth music was coming to. The recapitulation follows the main outlines of the exposition without being a mere repetition of it ... [The Coda] is of most unusual length and shows Beethoven's unending fertility of invention in its fresh treatment of now familiar ideas.'

SECOND MOVEMENT:

'The second movement (funeral march) is Beethoven at his most impressive and tragic. The independent double-bass part is most daring and original, and adds greatly to the sombre effect. There are two principal themes in the main section of the march, that heard at the opening and the E-flat major subject at bar 17. These with their subsidiary ideas occupy the composer until the change of key to C major, which brings both an atmosphere of resignation and, in its loud insistence on the major chord, expresses perhaps, the hero's defiance of death and assurance of immortality.'

THIRD MOVEMENT:

'The Scherzo, with its light-footed rhythm and delicate scoring, forms a splendid contrast to the dark colours and tense emotion of the funeral march, but the heroic element returns in the Trio with its fanfare-like passages for the three horns. No doubt this passage was responsible for Beethoven's decision to use three horns, a most unusual number, throughout the work.'

FOURTH MOVEMENT:

'The finale is in variation form ... The theme and its base were taken by Beethoven from his *Prometheus* ballet music. He also used it in his Piano Variations, Op. 35. The bass is used as a fugue subject in C minor later on (bar 117) ... At bar 211, a G minor section begins. It is wild and unconstrained in mood but is tied to earth by the bass of the original theme ... There is much conceptual ingenuity here, and a big climax is built up. A slow variation of great beauty begins at bar 349, and also works up to a climax at which the theme itself appears in the bass (bar 381). From bar 408 onwards we seem to feel the influence of the funeral march, but this is roughly dispelled by the *Presto* Coda (bar 431) which brings the Symphony to a triumphant conclusion.'

Gordon Jacob, Introduction to: *Beethoven, Symphony No. 3 in E flat, Op. 55,* London, Penguin Books, 1954, pp. 13–15.

OTTO JAHN

Otto Jahn is remembered for his pioneering biography of Mozart. In this he was among the first musicologists to recognize the kinship between the melody with which the youthful Mozart opened the Overture to his opera *Bastien und Bastienne* and that which heralds the start of Beethoven's *Eroica* Symphony. Placing the melody, in question, in context Jahn remarks:

> 'Mozart has given his music a strictly pastoral character, indicated wherever possible by its outward form. The orchestral introduction (*Intrada*) an *Allegro* (3—4) of about seventy bars, begins with a pastoral theme [the *Eroica* theme] interrupted by quick passages for oboes and horns, plainly intended to express a disturbance of the peaceful shepherd's life; this passes into a tender pianissimo, prefiguring *Basteinne's* song. Holmes remarks that the subject reminds one of Beethoven's *Sinfonia Eroica*, and still more so as the Overture proceeds; but no one, it is to be hoped, would think of an actual reminiscence.'
> [Jahn's reference is to the English musicologist Edward Holmes who published a *Thematic Index of Mozart's Piano-works.*]

Otto Jahn *Life of Mozart.* London: Novello, Ewer & Co., 1882, pp. 91—92.

WILLIAM KINDERMAN

In his Beethoven book-chapter: *The Heroic Style, 1805—06*, the American pianist and musicologist William Kinderman discusses the *Eroica* Symphony:

FIRST MOVEMENT:

'The immense scope of Beethoven's first movement is reflected in his open, continuously evolving treatment of the basic thematic material. Elements of dramatic tension are exposed from the outset [illustration] ... Beethoven's most striking formal innovation in the opening *Allegro con brio* is his expansion of the development section and Coda. With its 245 bars the development dwarfs the exposition, whereas the Coda approaches the length of the recapitulation. The climax of the development is generated by an intense rhythmic process involving accented, syncopated dissonances; so unrelenting is this rhythmic fragmentation and compression that the thematic material is virtually dissolved into nothing at about that point when the recapitulation would normally by expected ... The sense of scale is vastly expanded: in a long series of registrally enhanced motivic syncopated chords, with a dissonant collision of the A minor and F major triads marking the peak of intensification ...

'The Coda is expanded to almost the length of the exposition and recapitulation. Here, the "new" theme from the development is resolved to the tonic key of E-flat major. Thus, the Coda serves to recapitulate those musical passages that did not appear in the exposition or recapitulation ... Another reminder of the vast scale of this *Allegro con brio* comes in the emphatic chords, which correspond to the two great E flat chords at the beginning of the work ... their echo in Beethoven's final cadence also serves to cast unifying threads over this immense symphonic structure.'

SECOND MOVEMENT:

'Beethoven was particularly drawn to the genre of the *Marcia funebre* during the transitional period that gave rise to his "new path"; other examples, besides the slow movement of the *Eroica*, include the C minor variation in Op. 34 and the funeral march 'on the death of a hero' in *the* A flat Piano Sonata, Op. 26 from 1801. The Sonata 'with the funeral march' was one of the most popular of all Beethoven's works in the nineteenth century. Its *Marcia funebre* was performed during Beethoven's own funeral procession in Vienna in 1827, it is the only movement in his sonatas that he arranged for orchestra. It thus takes on unusual interest not just for its orchestral rhetoric but for the part it played in the evolution of Beethoven's posthumous reputation as artistic hero, a mythic role still very present today.'

THIRD MOVEMENT:

'The subtle opening of the Scherzo — which begins *pianissimo* and in the dominant instead of the tonic — is presumably connected with the symbolic *rebirth* of Prometheus, as [Constantin] Floros has suggested [*Beethoven Eroica und Prometheus*] A more obvious heroic note is sounded in the Trio, with its soloistic use of three horns — a special feature in the orchestration of the Symphony. The musical character here is animated, even joyous, making a convincing psychological transition to the comedy and high spirits of the finale.'

FOURTH MOVEMENT:
'In the finale, the association with Prometheus becomes explicit through the use of the theme from the ballet. As in the Op. 35 Variations, Beethoven first develops just the bass of the theme — with its grotesque humour of expressive silences — before joining to the upper-line melody ... The variations that follow in the *Eroica* finale are resourcefully blended with fugato passages, an *alla marcia* section, and an extended *andante* featuring wind solos to create a unique formal deign. As Lewis Lockwood has observed, "The *Eroica* finale emerges as the generating movement for the whole work and as the most fully original symphonic finale that Beethoven or anyone one else had written up to that time".' [Lewis Lockwood, *Beethoven Essays*, 1984]

William Kinderman, *Beethoven*, Oxford: Oxford University Press, 1997, pp.90–95.

OTTO KLEMPERER
The German born orchestral conductor Otto Klemperer contributed an essay to accompany his 1961 complete recordings of Beethoven's symphonies. This was later published in 1964 as his *Minor Recollections*. He writes how he had often conducted cycles of the Beethoven symphonies in such concert venues as Los Angels (1933), Milan (1935), Strasbourg (1936), Budapest (1947), Amster-

dam (1949), London (1957 and 1959), and Vienna (1960). As a consequence, he declared: 'The result was that, as time went by, I found myself wearing a sort of dog-collar marked "Beethoven Specialist".' He protested: 'I am neither a Beethoven specialist nor a "modern conductor". My aim has always been to conduct competently in all musical styles.'

Of Beethoven's symphonies he states:

> 'Beethoven was a revolutionary, and nothing could be more erroneous than to imagine that the great revolutionary arrived on the German scene like some well-behaved and docile lapdog. His symphonies are four-handed affairs, to say the least. Few people are familiar with Beethoven's metronome markings, though they sometimes appear to be very fast and provide only a rough indication of the tempo at which his music should be played.'

He adds:

> 'Most people think of Beethoven as a melancholy, tragic, gloomy character, but this is a crude distinction. He was, particularly in his youthful years, a happy-natured, cheerful person. The language of the First and Second Symphonies is unmistakable, and even the Fourth conveys a mood of exaltation ... It was not until the Sixth Symphony that the clouds began to gather. His hearing deteriorated progressively, but he put up a stout fight: "I shall seize Fate by the throat. It will never humble me".'

Martin Anderson editor, *Klemperer on Music: Shavings from a Musician's Workbench*. London: Toccata Press, 1986, pp. 97–99.

NIKOLAI RIMSKY-KORSAKOV (V.V. YASTREBTSEV)

The Russian composer Rimsky-Korsakov was a member of the so-called *Mighty Handful* of the New Russian School of composers who were prominent in the late nineteenth century; others in the group included Balakirev, Borodin and Mussorgsky. Rimsky's friend and associate V.V. Yastrebtsev was in regular contact with him during the last years of his life and kept a record, in diary form, of his meetings with the composer and his circle of friends. An entry for 19 January 1897 reveals Rimsky's estimation of Beethoven:

> 'You can't imagine how I envy Beethoven that he could say to his friend Stephan Breuning, a few hours before he died, "I did have talent, didn't I." These days, I'm coming more and more to love the classics: Bach, Beethoven, Haydn, and the others, whose music is still so fresh and full of life ... You may not believe this but Beethoven had such inexhaustible resources when it came to form and modulation that, in this regard, alongside of him all other composers are pygmies.'

Later, in December 1897, Yastrebtsev attended a concert given by the Russian Musical Society. The orchestra was conducted by Vasily Safonov, a respected teacher and Director of the Moscow Conservatory. His interpretation of the of *Eroica* Symphony did not meet with Yastrebtsev's approval:

> 'The programme of the third concert of the Russian Musical Society consisted of Beethoven's *Eroica* Symphony [and] Tchaikovsky's B-flat minor Piano Concerto ... The soloist in the Tchaikovsky Concerto, Osip Gabrilovich, scored a tremendous success ... As for Safonov, tonight he impressed me as a very mediocre conductor. His conducting of Beethoven's [*Eroica*] Symphony ... was extremely course and banal. On the whole I am becoming disenchanted with our native conductors.'

V.V. Yastrebtsev, edited and translated by Florence Jonas, *Reminiscences of Rimsky-Korsakov*, New York: Columbia University Press, 1985, p. 32, pp. 173—4, and p. 193.

ERNEST MARKHAM LEE*

Ernest Markham Lee introduces his assessment of the *Eroica* Symphony with the following prefatory remarks:

> 'The music, commenced in 1803, shows us a Beethoven moving away from the comparatively plain road of Haydn and Mozart; he had struck out a new path for himself. This, he has been treading with caution and somewhat tentatively; now he marches along boldly and confidently, sure of himself and of his own strength. We have only to note the very considerable length of the subjects in the opening allegro, and the soulful dignity of the Funeral March, to see that

Beethoven ... had turned his back on the models of his youth, and was manfully striking out and forcing a way for his extraordinary individuality.'

FIRST MOVEMENT:

'Those who know Mozart's delightful little opera *Bastien et Bastienne*, will find themselves strangely familiar with the introductory melody of its Overture. It is this theme, in all its simplicity, and yet with its wondrous possibilities, which Beethoven has, consciously or otherwise, adopted as the keystone to the opening allegro [illustration] This apparently simple meandering up and down the tonic chord becomes in his hands a thing of intense beauty and of extraordinary complexity. We have only to listen to the music as it progresses to discover what a mine of wealth Beethoven can extract from it ...' .

'The development is on a large scale, and is noticeable for the fact that it makes use of fresh material besides amply dealing with what has gone before ... As the orchestra is hushed to a pianissimo, the ear is led to expect the return of the first subject, this being tentatively announced in humorously premature fashion by the horn, at once followed by a cadence and the cellos as at the opening ... [The] coda, with all its wealth of material, is important as creating almost a new epoch in the history of form, so lengthy and majestic is it. New devices in the shape of tripping and delicate figures for the strings decorate the oft-heard themes, and constructive ingenuity is carried to a high pitch; the whole Coda forms a magnificent peroration.'

SECOND MOVEMENT:

'Of the *Marcia funebre*, Beethoven spoke in later days, for, when told of Napoleon's death, he said he had composed the music for that occasion seventeen years before; otherwise he made little reference to the original dedication of the Symphony. It is a noble and solemn march, based upon a truly elegiac idea, first heard in the violins and then repeated by the oboe [illustration] Its second strain, in the major, is one of greater hope, but the song of mourning returns, rhythmically accompanied by reiterated notes of sombre character. The middle section of the movement brings us to a suggestion of resignation, of comfort and relief ... The joy, however, is soon turned once more into sorrow, and the minor key is resumed with the main theme of the march, now broken up by the introduction of a considerable *fugato*, and by a lengthy episode founded upon a triplet basis ... With sad, almost despondent note, the end is reached.'

THIRD MOVEMENT:

'With the Scherzo ... comes an irresistible and abounding vivacity. Beethoven is here in his most original mood, and at the date of the production of the Symphony its music must have been a revelation to musicians. Where, before this time, could have been heard anything like this pattering *pianissimo* string figure with which the Scherzo begins? [illustration] The motive, full of delicate surprises, lends itself to most effective treatment, and the busy bustle of it is gaiety continued. The whole atmosphere is charged with gaiety and a delightful *abandon*. The same mood prevails in the Trio, a section which largely concerns itself with a subject for three horns — a new orchestral feature here first employed by Beethoven. [illustration] There is brightness and geniality through both this and the recapitulation of the Scherzo, and the necessary relief from the tension of the Funeral March is well attained.'

FOURTH MOVEMENT:

'The finale is constructed upon what was, at the time of its origination, a comparatively new plan for a symphonic movement — an air with variations. A vigorous passage for the strings preludes this air — really a bass to a theme to be introduced later. The first few variations correspond, both in theme and treatment, with a set of earlier variations for the pianoforte [illustration] ... The variations which follow take many forms, the natural sequence to which is a beautiful *poco andante* — by many considered the gem of the finale — upon an idea at once expressive and of noble mould. [illustration] Its continuation is decorated with graceful *arpeggi* for the clarinet and is somewhat prolonged, a beautiful bridge-passage leading to the brief final *presto*, where, with a brilliant series of passages, the Symphony, noble and heroic in character from first bar to last, comes to a glorious conclusion.'

Ernest Markham Lee, *The Story of the Symphony*. London: Scott Publishing Co., 1916, pp. 52–59.

LEWIS H. LOCKWOOD*

Lewis H. Lockwood positions the expanded scale of the first movement of the *Eroica* Symphony in the context of other of Beethoven's contemporaneous works that possess similarly expansive movements:

> 'In certain early works, Beethoven had written first movements of great length, by contemporary standards, even some in the less frequent 3/4. Among these are the first movements of the E-flat major Piano Quintet, Op. 16, which runs to 395 bars, and the still longer opening *Allegro* of the G minor Cello Sonata, Op. 5, No. 2 (not including the slow introductions). These are still short of the immense 691 of the *Eroica*, but of course neither movement possesses the rich profusion of ideas, the complexity, or the capacity for integration that is found here.'

Lewis Lockwood, *'Eroica', Perspectives and Design* in: Alan Tyson editor, *Beethoven Studies 3*. Cambridge: Cambridge University Press, 1982, pp. 85–86.

GUSTAV MAHLER

Gustav Mahler's high regard for Beethoven can be judged from remarks he once shared in conversation with a friend:

> 'In order to understand and appreciate Beethoven fully, we should not only accept him

for what he means to us today, but must realize what a tremendous revolutionary advance he represents in comparison with his forerunners. Only when we understand what a difference there is between Mozart's G minor Symphony and the Ninth can we properly evaluate Beethoven's achievement. Of geniuses like Beethoven, of such sublime and most universal kind, there are only two or three among millions. Among poets and composers of more recent times we can, perhaps, name but three: Shakespeare, Beethoven, and Wagner.'

Knud Martner editor, *Selected Letters of Gustav Mahler*, London; Boston: Faber and Faber, 1979, p.147.

Once, when in the company of several friends, Mahler played through a piano-reduction of the *Eroica* Symphony. Arriving at the final movement, he sang the *Prometheus* theme, imitating the errant manner in which he considered bad conductors of the day performed it; this was sometime in 1897. Mahler exclaimed:

'They mistake this for the theme [*Prometheus* theme, illustrated] and consequently take it far too quickly, instead of realizing its true meaning. Beethoven is trying it out meditatively — then playfully — he is learning to walk — he gets into his stride gradually. That's why the latter part of it — like an answer — should follow rather more quickly. Above this foundation, which serves as accompaniment throughout the whole piece, the themes sing out in all their fullness — and must by no means be rushed through casually.'

Mahler's interlocutor concludes his recollection:

> 'Mahler then gave us a shattering performance of the second movement. It was as if the funeral march precession of the hero were passing step by step before us in all its impressiveness and tragedy.'

Mahler's contemporaries have left accounts of his own conducting. On 6 November 1898, he gave the first of a series on concerts with the Vienna Philharmonic Orchestra. One of his friends enthusiastically recalled:

> 'Yesterday was a great occasion; Mahler's first Philharmonic Concert. For his programme he had chosen the *Coriolan* Overture, Mozart's G minor Symphony, and the *Eroica*, and performed them for the Viennese more divinely than they can ever have dreamed possible.'

It appears, though, Mahler was depressed by the occasion. Although some critics admired his interpretations, others had found fault with various details of the *Eroica*. Mahler was able to derive some consolation, however, from an enthusiastic *feuillton* written about him by none other than Eduard Hanslick, the eminent music critic and aesthetician.

In 1902, Mahler visited Russia where he gave three concerts in St Petersburg. At the first of these he once more conducted a performance of the *Eroica* Symphony. A review of the concert appeared in the St, Petersburg Journal *Vedomosti* that was later reprinted in the *Neues Wiener* Journal. On the rostrum, Mahler was depicted as appearing:

> '[An] austere, bespectacled little man who resembles a clergyman ... All his strength seems to be concentrated in his piercing, irresistible eyes, which hypnotize the musicians. His gestures are extremely simple ... He does not, like some other famous conductors, distract the musicians' attention with eccentric gestures. He sometimes leaves the orchestra completely to itself before then marking, with sudden and extreme determination, some characteristic point.'

Regarding Mahler's interpretation of the *Eroica*, the critic in question considered it to be inferior to that of the Austrian-Hungarian Hans Richter that he judged to be 'more balanced and less nervous'. Somewhat in contradiction to the foregoing, another report of the concert in the same Russian Journal commented:

> '[The] public gave Mahler only a moderately enthusiastic reception when he made his entrance, but he immediately proved himself as an *eminent* conductor and was warmly applauded after the *Eroica*.'

Apparently two members of the audience – who must have been musically well-informed – were overheard exchanging opinions, in French, to the effect: 'Mahler's tempi [in the *Eroica*] are not at all what we are accustomed to, but it's beautiful, and new, like that.'

Our final recollections of Mahler, the conductor, relate to five years later (1907) when he was on concert tour in Italy. One critic stated that under his baton the Roman Orchestra [not identified] had become 'a vigorous and perfectly balanced organism' from which emanated 'its innate power, and, where necessary, its vigour and energy'. He enthused: 'We have never heard more sustained *pianos* and *fortes*, or more extraordinary string sonorities.' The Italian music critic Nicola d'Atri noted Mahler's interpretation of the *Eroica* Symphony had caused some surprise, despite its effectiveness, on the grounds that Mahler seemed to be saying: 'This is the way I feel Beethoven, I have made him come alive for you, and now you can go and discuss traditions and everything else among yourselves.' D'Atri closed his account with some generalisations and rhetorical questions:

> 'The essential thing is that the artist's feeling is pure. Does Mahler go too far? Is he too excessive at times? Perhaps he is, but in fact Beethoven in his works revealed to us that he was a *monster of excess* with regard to sentiment and sensibility... '.

The music critics of other Italian newspapers were more generously disposed to Mahler's orchestral interpretation. *La Capitale* considered: 'Gustav Mahler is in truth everything an artist should be: an artist by temperament, by nature and by culture.' The *Avanti* newspaper believed Mahler knew how to 'extract surprising and unforgettable effects from the most secret recesses of the orchestra, with renewed vigour.' And *Il Populo Romano* thought Mahler was

> 'a musician of rare skill, who conducted in a clear, even obvious, energetic and assured manner, who dominated the orchestra and elicited striking effects and shadings'.

Natalie Bauer-Lechner, *Recollections of Gustav Mahler.*

London: Faber Music, 1980, p. 34, p. 112, p. 120, pp. 491–92, and p. 632.

For some, Mahler's interpretations of Beethoven's orchestral music, did, in Nicola d'Atri's words, 'go too far'. Accounts of him conducting Beethoven report, for example, with the *Eroica* Symphony he interposed a sustained pause between the opening chords and the start of the main theme. He took liberties with other of the composer's symphonies. In the Fifth Symphony, he underlined the 'fate motif' by the addition of tympani, and in the finale he doubled the bassoons with horns. The Ninth Symphony was not sacrosanct to Mahler. In his 1895 and 1901 performance he doubled the wind, added trombones and re-distributed the orchestra to achieve added dramatic effect. Although one critic condemned Mahler's interpretations as 'a transcription of Beethoven', the response from audiences 'was rapturous'.

Anne-Louise Coldicott, *Performance Styles Since Beethoven's Day* in: Barry Cooper, *The Beethoven Compendium: A Guide to Beethoven's Life and Music.* London: Thames and Hudson, 1991, pp. 300–01. See also, the entry for Anne-Louise Coldicott.

ADOLF BERNHARD MARX*

The German musicologist Adolf Bernhard Marx recognised Beethoven for having begun a new epoch in music, music that he considered approached a form of tone painting. He was a founder member of the *Berliner Allgemeine musikalische Zeitung*, to which he contributed articles about Beethoven and his music which he more fully expounded in his *Ludwig van Beethoven: Leben und Schaffen*, Berlin (1859). He also contributed to the *Berliner's* sister Journal, the Leipzig-based

Allgemeine musikalische Zeitung. In the 12 May 1824 issue of the *AmZ,* Marx contributed a reflective article titled, *A few words on the symphony and Beethoven's achievements in the field.* From this we cite the following:

> 'In the areas of the sonata and the symphony, Beethoven began at Mozart's level, and his first outpourings can be called lyrical, even though the feeling in them was expressed more definitely and more intimately. Even if many a moment shone forth more freshly and brightly than in the more gentle Mozart and echoed the Haydn school, and even if a greater, more deeply-founded unity became manifest in Beethoven's compositions.'

Marx devoted part of his article to the first two movements of the *Eroica* Symphony, the text of which he accompanied with musical illustrations. At the time of his writing (1824) the work was well-established in the repertoire, disposing Marx to open his account:

> 'There is no need for reference in the title to know that a hero is being celebrated here. Right away the first movement, with its bold principal idea, so accessible to the brass instruments, [illustration] which is passed on to all the parts and right away in the beginning victoriously counters a ferocious conflict of the entire orchestra [illustration] with the sound of trumpets and horns, which, after an even harder struggle, is extended overwhelmingly [illustration] and still further through fifteen measures, where, countering the incessant pressures of the basses, it resounds turbulently [illustration] from all parts

like the encouraging calls of comrades-in-arms, and in the end is celebrated by the joyful flight of the violins. This entire movement shows the successful image of heroic life, and also the painful lament of such loss.'

Of the second movement Marx writes:

'The *Adagio*, entitled *Funeral March*, is too grand for it to accompany us to the gravesite of a single individual. After having heard the war song of the first *Allegro*, who doesn't visualize in this *Adagio* the picture of a bloody battlefield, who doesn't understand the dark thoughts that here must press upon the victor too [illustration] and who isn't invigorated by the soft voices of that seek to console, in the change to C major, until the heroically bold cry rises above mourning and solace as if reminding us of immortality.'

Wayne M. Senner, Robin Wallace and William Meredith, editors, *The Critical Reception of Beethoven's Compositions by his German Contemporaries*, Lincoln: University of Nebraska Press, in association with the American Beethoven Society and the Ira F. Brilliant Center for Beethoven Studies, San José State University, 1999, Vol.2, p. 19, and pp. 59–77. See also the entry for *Allgemeine musikalische Zeitung*.

DENIS MATTHEWS*

In his discussion of the *Eroica* Symphony, Denis Matthews first speculates on the origins of the opening bars:

FIRST MOVEMENT:

'The sketches suggest that Beethoven planned a "shock" beginning with a pair of irregularly spaced dominant-seventh chords, though perhaps as the sequel to another slow introduction. These were filled in to clarify the rhythm but were eventually replaced by two simple but arresting E flat ones, providing the firmest possible launching pad for the tonal adventures to come. In the end it is striking how subsidiary or transitional ideas were seized upon to produce paragraphs of colossal cumulative power ...

'It became clear [to Beethoven] that sonata form on such an epic scale demanded a coda of unusual proportions, with room enough to recall the "new theme" before carrying the first subject home as a triumphant round in the most fundamental form. Such a peroration to a first movement had no symphonic precedent, though the ending of Mozart's *Jupiter* Symphony had pointed the way to Beethoven's climactic codas.

'The marking *con brio* is a key to the first movement's character, and it should go without saying that the comfortable "moderation" or *non troppo* sometimes heard can only remove or undermine its elemental drive.'

SECOND MOVEMENT:

'The Funeral March ... benefits from the broadest tempo compatible with sustained intensity of line. Some naïve observers queried Beethoven's placing of the march second, as though to kill off his hero early in the proceedings; but a symphony is not a biography, and to borrow his later remarks on the *Pastoral* Symphony, he was expressing feelings rather than depicting events. Viewed objectively, the march is a very slow movement on a large scale and in rondo form, but the scoring of the theme for low-lying strings, with rumbling basses suggesting muffled drums, sets a tragic mood from the start, enhanced by a counter-statement to the most plaintive register of a solo oboe. The themes' afterthoughts are spacious, thus delaying the first episode, which brings the tender consolation of C minor but produces triumphant cadences of a military nature ... Structurally and emotionally, the *Eroica* stands ahead of its time as a landmark in musical expression.'

THIRD MOVEMENT:

'It was ... imaginative to follow the grief-laden ending of the Funeral March with a rapid Scherzo that runs half its course in a subdued *pianissimo* and to pick out its salient melodic features with oboe or flute in keys other than the tonic, B flat or F major, saving the home-key statement (E flat) for the sudden and long-delayed *ff*. The addition of a third horn enabled the Trio to live up to its name for once, and the E flat fanfares inevitably recall the theme of the first movement ...'.

FOURTH MOVEMENT:

'For the finale, Beethoven took as his text the *Prometheus* theme and its bass that had already produced the Piano Variations and Fugue, Op. 35. The *Eroica* inherited some of its procedures and added others, and it is far too facile to describe the finale's unique form as an amalgam of variation and fugue. Its sequence of events may be summed up as: (a) a downward rush of strings obliterating the E flat key of the Scherzo in order to emphasize it afresh, and beginning as though in G minor; (b) variations on the bass of the theme eventually yielding the theme itself; (c) a fugato on the bass; (d) a return of the theme in D major with varied repeats and leading to; (e) a current episode in which a march in dotted rhythm is superimposed on part of the original bass and in G minor ... Its most sublime moment surely comes after the climax of the second fugal section when the wind offer the *Prometheus* theme *poco andante* and in a new and richer harmonisation; and this elevated manner, far removed from its origins in the ballet and as a contredanse, epitomises the grander and deeper emotions of the Symphony as a whole.'

Denis Matthews, *Beethoven*, (*Master Musicians*). London: J. M. Dent, 1985, pp. 155–57.

WILFRID MELLERS*

The English musicologist and composer Wilfrid Mellers subjects the *Eroica* Symphony to musicological analysis:

FIRST MOVEMENT:

'The first movement opens with two hammer blows of Fate, on the whole orchestra. Then the first theme enters, in the bass. It is not a melody, but an arpeggio of challenge; and it ends, not in triumph, but in conflict, for the bass-line lands up on an ambiguous C sharp which might be D flat [illustration] ... Then there is a transitional theme built on leaping ninths, another version of the arpeggio narrative ... The development is on a vast scale, modulating through two cycles of fifths: an upward followed by a downward cycle. Fugato — contrapuntal writing which is freely fugal in character — adds to the excitement; and the climax comes in a tremendous expansion of the hemiola rhythm [a cross rhythm of 3–2 against the basic 3–4] in which the whole orchestra builds upon a progressively accumulating dissonance. [illustration] Here, the orchestra is used like a gigantic percussion instrument ... [The] horns re-enter with the arpeggio motive; only too soon, so that they clash with the harmony of the strings! (Even as progressive a musician as the young Wagner used to *correct* it in performance) ... Beethoven expands the recapitulation into a Coda which is nearly as long as the exposition ... Conflict becomes triumphant apotheosis.'

SECOND AND THIRD MOVEMENTS:
'Both the slow movement and the [following] Scherzo are built on themes which have hidden affinities with the challenging arpeggio motive. In the *Marcia funebre* Beethoven deals, in the relatively static form of a rondo, with the hero's death; in the dynamic Scherzo with his resurgence. He was not thinking of a literal birth and death; he meant that for him,

life was the process of *Becoming* [italics added], so that being alive was a series of spiritual deaths and rebirths.'

FOURTH MOVEMENT:
'The goal of the work ... proves to be the last movement, which is built on the *monastic* principle of the chaconne; variations on a bass which remains constant ... It is significant that the theme had first been used by Beethoven in the ballet *Prometheus*, and again in the *Eroica* Variations, Op. 35.

'Now, Prometheus challenged the gods and, with the gift of fire, offered man the potentiality to control his own destiny. The Hero about whom Beethoven wrote his Symphony is not, of course, the God-King of eighteenth-century aristocracy, but the man of strife who is the architect of a new world. Napoleon seemed the man; though Beethoven contemptuously tore up his dedication when Napoleon proved to be only the architect of a new tyranny. In any case, the real Hero of the Symphony is Beethoven himself, as Prometheus; and the battle he fought is not Napoleon's, but the more terrible one he fought alone at Heiligenstadt.'

Wilfrid Howard Mellers, *The Sonata Principle (from c. 1750)*, London: Rockliff, 1957, pp. 62–64.

FELIX MENDELSSOHN
In his *A Portrait of Mendelssohn*, musicologist Clive Brown draws on contemporary accounts of the composer's style of

conducting. The following description of Mendelssohn conducting a performance of the *Eroica* Symphony, during one of his many visits to England, suggests his interpretation of the work was quite elastic:

> 'That Mendelssohn's conducting was not without nuances of tempo, albeit subtle ones, is suggested by a significant number of references in reviews and recollections ... [One such source] occurs in a notice of Mendelssohn's performance of the *Eroica* Symphony with the London Philharmonic in 1844: "He gave readings of various passages which had remained hidden among the complications of Beethoven's gigantic score. The boldness and vigour with which points were taken up — the effects produced by accelerating and retarding the time — and the delicate shades and gradations of tone — gave the whole composition quite a new character, and produced an extraordinary impression on the audience".'

Clive Brown, *A Portrait of Mendelssohn*, Yale University Press, 2003, p. 254.

YEHUDI MENUHIN*

In 1979, Yehudi Menuhin collaborated with the American television producer, Curtis W. Davis, in a series of programmes titled *The Music of Man*. Menuhin's TV narrative was later published in book-form from which we quote the following:

> 'To the uninitiated, Beethoven's axiomatic statements may seem misleadingly simple and self-

evident, until one interprets their symbolism. The most powerful element in the first movement of his Third Symphony (*Eroica*) is undoubtedly the two-bar unit, two great E-flat major chords, which rivet our attention and prompt the action. The passionate intensity is quickly revealed in the sixth bar as the melody drops to a C sharp against a breathless syncopated accompaniment in the violins. But it is the impalpable basic three-four beat (soon challenged by a two-four unit within it) as pronounced by the opening chords which, like the measured distance between waves, carries everything with it.

'Whether it is the solemnity of the epic funeral march, or the feverish drive of the Scherzo, Beethoven engulfs us in torrential purpose and direction, a single man's purpose, embodying, symbolizing a whole nation's raging energies, emotions, ideals and frustrations. Never before had mankind heard music with such single-minded drive. The more I think of Beethoven, the more he recalls for me the Hebrew prophet, some great figure of the Old Testament: unresigned, castigating, menacing, pleading and demanding.

'The *Eroica* was the longest symphony any composer had yet attempted; it took listeners on a voyage well beyond the safer waves of its predecessors. The E flat theme is like the chromosomes of a living cell, transmitting information for the reproduction of other cells, which gradually form themselves into and sustain the life of a unique entity unlike any other.'

Yehudi Menuhin and Curtis W. Davis, *The Music of Man*. London: Macdonald and Jane's, 1979, pp. 150–52.

GIACOMO MEYERBEER

The Jewish-born, German composer Giacomo Meyerbeer was celebrated during his lifetime as the most frequently performed opera composer, notably in France. The early success of his *Robert le diable* elevated him to the level of a superstar — to the chagrin of other composers, such as Hector Berlioz, who found their own works for the lyric theatre displaced. Meyerbeer kept a diary, and from his entry for 30 January 1831 we learn something of the performance, and standard, of orchestral music-making in Paris at this time:

> '[I went] to the Conservatoire, where the *Société des Concerts* are again giving a cycle of concerts, as they did last year ... They performed Beethoven's *Symphonia Eroica*, executed, as always, in an incomparable manner. This *Société des Concerts* is indisputably the most outstanding orchestra in Europe for the performance of Beethoven's symphonies — indeed, for any orchestral music. Each symphony is rehearsed with great care and many times, as opposed to the German practice of attempting the impossible by rehearsing a symphony only twice.'

Robert Ignatius Letellier editor and translator, *The Diaries of Giacomo Meyerbeer*. Madison: Fairleigh Dickinson University Press; London: Associated University Presses, Vol.1, 1999–2004, p. 404.

CHARLES MUNCH

In his *Autobiography* the Alsatian-French conductor and violinist Charles Munch advocated the benefits of a good memory:

> '[It] is one of the conductor's trumps. Studying, copying, orchestrating, sharpen the visual memory of the score-page. Every conductor should be naturally endowed with *la mémoire sonore* as well; the aural memory, the ability to remember sounds, to retain in the mind a sonorous image of the things heard as he might the visual image of things seen.'

Munch recalls the time when, for two years, he had charge of the teaching of conducting at the Paris Conservatory:

> 'Our first step in studying a symphonic movement was to analyse its construction, break down into phrases to see how it was put together. Take the opening of the *Eroica*, for example. The first two measures are two chords. Then there is a twelve-measure period that can bebroken down into three, four-measure phrases. You know a great deal about a piece of music when you know where every phrase starts and stops.'

After making a harmonic analysis of the structure of the music, Munch requested one of his students to play from the score at the piano while another stood up and conducted. He would urge this student to conduct 'simply' and above all 'clearly'. He did not permit conducting without a baton, concerning which Much believed:

'Unhappily this has become fashionable. It is a bad habit, in my opinion, that creates difficulties for the musicians. I am sure that anyone who has ever played in a professional orchestra will agree with me. I always consider the baton an extension of the body, magnifying every movement of arm and hand in space.'

Charles Munch, *I Am a Conductor*. New York: Oxford University Press, 1955, pp. 32–33.

RICHARD OSBORNE*

Richard Osborne reflects on the heroic character of the *Eroica* Symphony:

'The dangers of crediting the Symphony with the exploration of the fate of a particular hero are all too evident when it comes to explaining the work's continuing life after the funeral rites of the second movement, the *Marcia funebre*. "Funeral games around the grave of the warrior, such as those in the *Iliad* ", was Berlioz's somewhat lame exploration of the *Scherzo's* presence and mood. As this clearly will not do, it is better to approach the *Marcia funebre* as the exequies not of one hero but of any hero, and as an earnest of Beethoven's fascination with public ceremony and the rituals of power. Using some of the same key centres — C minor and E-flat major — that Mozart deploys in his Masonic Funeral Music, K. 477, Beethoven sublimates grief and at the same time creates a superb essay in the musical picturesque. This is a solemn cortège set against louring temples and crumbling classical pediments such as David or Delacroix might have painted. Later, such ideas will be distilled, abstracted almost, in the yet more impersonal grieving of the Seventh Symphony's A-minor *Allegretto*. The *Eroica* Symphony, though, requires more guile on Beethoven's part in getting from Funeral March to *Scherzo*. And how superbly he brings it off, the music-making its dancing entry *sempre pianissimo e staccato*, hushed and furtive in B flat; an opening as imaginative as the drum-troubled end is awesome.'

Richard Osborne, *Beethoven* in: Robert Layton editor, *A Guide to the Symphony*. Oxford: Oxford University Press, 1995, p. 89.

LEON B. PLANTINGA*

Leon Plantinga subjects the *Eroica* Symphony to musicological scrutiny:

FIRST MOVEMENT:

'The first movement of the *Eroica* Symphony begins with an enigmatic, seemingly fragmented exposition. Its harmonic direction, at least, is vaguely what we might expect. After unarguably establishing the key of E flat with two movements of the opening motive (mm, 3 and 15), Beethoven feints toward the dominant (mm. 18ff) only to establish the original key (m. 37) with another resounding assertion of the original melody ...

Two brusque *forte* tonic chords do duty for an introduction, followed by the triadic melody played in the bass range by the cellos. An unobtrusive G in the violins gradually becomes melody (m.10) but this melodic strand is virtually absorbed into the cadence that follows. If this opening thematic material seems curiously complete and without definition, it is followed by eight or nine other bits of his material that sound equally inconclusive ...

'[A] salient feature of [the] exposition is a determined disruption of meter ... The effect of the rhythmic displacement is hemiola, a metrical ambiguity in which a group of six beats (two measures here) is implicitly divided two ways: into two groups of three, and three groups of two ...

'Beethoven's development section makes extensive use of these cryptic melodic and rhythmic ideas in the exposition ... '.

Plantinga quotes from Hector Berlioz, *A Critical Study of Beethoven's Nine Symphonies*, Edwin Evans, 1958, p. 42:

'The rhythm is particularly remarkable by the frequency of syncopation and by combinations of duple measure, thrown, by accentuation of the week beat, into the triple bar. When, with this disjointed rhythm, rude dissonances come to present themselves in combination ... it is impossible to repress a sensation of fear at such a picture of ungovernable fury. It is the voice of despair, almost of rage.'

SECOND MOVEMENT:
'For the second movement, Beethoven writes another piece of unprecedented weight and proportions, in this case with a descriptive title *Marcia funebre*. Audiences of Beethoven's time would have had no trouble recognising the style of a movement such as this; it is plainly modelled after the grand dirges played at the funerals for heroes of the Revolution and Napoleonic wars. These marches, as well as the music for elaborate Republican *fêtes*, staged in Paris in the 1790s, were written by the leading French composers of the day such as François Joseph Gossec (1734–1829), Étienne-Nicolas Méhul (1763–1817), and Luigi Cherubini (1769–1842) [illustrations] ... Beethoven's movement goes far beyond its prototype; a secondary motive in E flat ... and a contrasting middle section in C minor, provide additional materials for a movement of intricate and imposing architectural design.'

THIRD AND FOURTH MOVEMENTS:
'After a lightening-swift Scherzo-Trio, featuring precarious solo roles for three horns and some very insistent hemiola effects, Beethoven begins his finale with an outraged fury in the strings, coming to a dead stop on a series of dominant chords ... A couple of leisurely variations of [the] bass line prolong the mysterification until the *real* melody at last enters (m. 75). Beethoven was apparently fond of this melody and bass; he had already used both as thematic material for his Piano Variations, Op. 35 of about a year previous and for several other pieces. [In a

footnote Plantinga adds: 'The funeral march in Beethoven's Piano Sonata Op. 26 is in a very similar style, and at some points bears a startling resemblance to Gossec's piece.'] A transformed and vastly expanded revision of the piano piece, this energetic movement, combining elements of theme-and-variations and rondo, makes a fittingly forceful conclusion to this unique Symphony.'

Leon Plantinga, *Romantic Music: A History of Musical Style in Nineteenth-Century Europe*. New York; London: Norton, 1984, pp. 38–43.

FRITZ REINER

The American-Hungarian conductor Fritz Reiner adopted a conducting technique that was defined by its precision and economy. Igor Stravinsky asserted the Chicago Symphony Orchestra, under Reiner, was 'the most precise and flexible orchestra in the world'. Reiner, however, seldom took liberties with the score:

'Reiner was, relatively speaking, a purist in keeping to the composer's wishes as given in a score. He thought conductors should always adhere faithfully to the score in the great classics; otherwise, it would be unclear where to draw the line with adaptations. Individuality of interpretation in this repertoire should observe certain limits. To try something startlingly original, with well-known scores, might be to misquote great art, and would be nothing short of criminal.'

Reiner was prepared to make occasional exceptions to his self-imposed strictures:

> 'One minor element of retouching that Reiner did observe ... was to allow the trumpets to complete the main theme at bars 655–62 of the first movement of the *Eroica* Symphony, a practice followed by many other modern conductors. In Beethoven's day the trumpets did not have all available notes on their instruments to play the theme in these bars, so the composer let them begin the passage and then allowed the woodwinds to finish it alone.'

On one occasion, Reiner — a conductor known, and feared by musicians, for his martinet-like independence of mind — was prepared to court controversy:

> 'In the 1930s he played Beethoven's *Eroica* with the Philadelphia Orchestra by reversing the order of the *Marcia funebre* and the Scherzo and Trio. Outlining his reasons for the alteration, Reiner argued that the funeral march was composed two years before the rest of the Symphony and had no mental connection with the other movements. Beethoven had changed the order of several compositions, including some of his later piano sonatas, the Ninth Symphony, and various chamber works. The proportions of the *Eroica* were better as a result of the change because two long movements of about fifteen minutes each, did not have to follow one another. There were other considerations. According to Reiner, the E-flat major of the finale sounded fresher after

the C minor of the funeral march, and, for psychological reasons, it did not seem reasonable to have all the rejoicing after a general apotheosis of the hero's life and deed of valour.'

Although Reiner's rearrangement may be regarded as testimony to him being prepared to depart, on occasions, from convention and to experiment with works in the classical repertoire, his changes to the *Eroica* so shocked many of his listeners that he did not try the experiment again!

Kenneth Morgan, *Fritz Reiner, Maestro and Martinet.* Urbana: University of Illinois Press, 2005, pp. 217–19.

ROMAIN ROLLAND*

Romain Rolland discusses the construction of the *Eroica* Symphony — styled in his characteristic word-imagery:

FIRST MOVEMENT:

'The great motive that dominates the Symphony [the opening theme] is a personality. What matters it to us whether it is a man or an idea, the obscure voice of instinct or the lucid will? It lives and it acts. Who can doubt its existence? Simple and upright it goes forward; from its first step it is marked with the seal of its destiny, that marches to its appointed end and knows no other. The soul into which this order has entered bends, at the fifth bar, under the burden. But this burden is its destiny, is a part of its essence; it accepts it with a sigh, and abandons itself to the stream ... This mighty motive gradually raises its head; it transforms itself into fragments, as if by that means to find a way through. But always it is met by the plaint that stays it and troubles its heart (bars 83 ff.)

'In the second section (the *Durchführung*) the soul's field of battle becomes co-extensive with the universe, and the fresco assumes colossal proportions ...

'On the boundless plain, the innumerable theme swells to an army corps. The flood mounts wave on wave; but here and there islets of elegy appear like clumps off trees in the middle of the torrent ...

'The Coda of the first movement of the *Eroica* is the Grand Army of the soul, that will not stop until it has trampled on the whole earth. After the spirit has for the last time evoked, in an imperious summing-up of isolated moments of the first two parts, the abrupt fall from the full tumult of the combat into the humming silence (bars 568—70) ...

'No more grief, no more regrets! Even the plaint and the elegy are drawn into the epic round; and the imperial cavalcade ends in a carousel, the dance of a jubilant people, set in motion by a hero's plot.'

SECOND MOVEMENT:
'In the *Adagio assai*, the hero is dead. Never has he been more truly alive; his spirit hovers above the coffin that is borne on the shoulders of humanity. A *Funeral March* ... The idea was a trite one in that epoch of heroic apotheoses! But how Beethoven has revived it by what he has put into it, the intimate accent, the soul laid

bare — his own genius! ... The major *dolce cantando* is, in my opinion, the modern poem that comes nearest to the elegiac choruses of Greek tragedy; it has the harmonious grace of Sophocles, his natural nobility, his perfection, his serene melancholy.'

THIRD MOVEMENT:

'His pen gives a leap. He writes *Presto*! ... Overboard with the minuet and its formal graces! The inspired rush of the Scherzo has been found!'

FOURTH MOVEMENT:

'The final movement of the Symphony cost him less time than the others, for he already had the theme he was to work upon ... '.

'Begun as a simple dance and brilliant contradanse in the Ballet *Prometheus* — taken up again as a contradanse at the end of 1801 — then in the Variations, Op. 35, it was still, at the time when the *Eroica* was being written, regarded by Beethoven as a motive for regular variations of the usual classical kind; no doubt when he began this salon work he had in view, as in *Prometheus*, a sort of final gallop. But as he proceeds to manipulate his theme, throwing all sorts of lights and shadows on it, he comes upon several of its hidden souls — the elegiac, the funeral, the heroic ... In the coda, the death of the hero is already announced; an ending on the ordinary lines is impossible! The finale is a fugue with a suggestion of combat about it; the germ of the Symphony is there. Having arrived at his goal, Beethoven returns on his steps; and now he recognises the true nature of the theme which he had been playing — those four mighty pillars! And the great builder sees the vast spaces he can cover with it. Then he takes it up again as the base for the last movement of the Symphony, in which the variations expand to epic proportions; the contrapuntal element weaves it into a cluster of colossal ogival mouldings.'

Romain Rolland, *Beethoven the Creator*. Garden City, New York: Garden City Publications, 1937, pp. 81–95.

STEPHEN RUMPH*

The American musicologist and academic Stephan Rumph positions Beethoven's choice of key for the *Eroica* Symphony in the context of other of his compositions:

'Throughout his career [Beethoven] reserved E flat for intimate, lyrical, and folk-like compositions. This appears most obviously in the later works with the *Lebewohl* Piano Sonata [Op. 81 a], the String Quartets, Opp. 74 and 127, and the Song *Cycle An der ferne Geliebte*. Beethoven's most prominent work in E flat, before the *Eroica*, is the popular Septet, Op. 20, the soul of Mozartian elegance. His choice of key for the Septet (and) probably for the *Eroica* as well) was dictated by the prominent role of concertante winds. Beethoven wrote a whole series of such E flat divertimenti during the 1790s: an Octet, Rondino, Quintet, and Sextet for wind band; a Sextet for String Quartet and two horns; and a Quintet for piano and winds. The French horn stands out in all these E flat works, not only in all the *divertimenti* (the Quintet, Hess 19, even has three horns [like the *Eroica*]), but also in the pianistic evocation of horn calls in the *Lebewohl* Piano Sonata and *An die ferne Geliebte* .... Among all of Beethoven's works in E flat, only the Fifth Piano Concerto (*The Emperor*) projects a genuinely militant, heroic character.'

The musically-minded reader will be aware that it was characteristic of composers such as Mozart and Haydn to score for *two* French horns only in their symphonic writing. Beethoven's use of *three* caused a stir to his contemporaries who considered it extravagant. Rumph expatiates on the importance of the French horn(s) in the *Eroica* Symphony:

'The French horn plays a particular role in the harmonic odyssey. The horns leap to the fore in the recapitulation of the first movement, both in the premature entry of the third player and in the continuation of the theme by the first. No less striking is the Trio of the Scherzo, where the horn section, expanded to a harmonically independent trio, shakes free of the orchestra entirely. In both the first and last movements, Beethoven entrusts the apotheistic final statement of his theme to the horns. The characteristic timbre of the horn, especially at climactic or pivotal moments in the form, enhances the sense of a quest after a lost natural unity "of man's arduous path to his true nature" in [Neala] Schleuning's words. Most eloquent, perhaps, is the premature reprise of the first movement. [Scott] Burnham unaccountably hears this horn solo as a "military horn call", symbolizing the character of the hero. Yet Beethoven everywhere else assigned military calls to trumpets, or at least trumpets doubled by horns, reserving horn calls for hunting or rustic representations (compare for instance the *Jagdlied* and *Kriegslied* from the *Ritterballett*). The murmuring solo in the *Eroica* reprise belongs to the same family of distant *ranz des vaches* in the *Pastoral* Symphony finale, the idyllic strains of the Eighth Symphony Trio, the opening lament of the *Lebewohl* Piano Sonata, Op. 81a, or the wayward *fourth* horn in the Ninth Symphony.'

Stephen C. Rumph, *Beethoven after Napoleon: Political Romanticism in the Late Works*, Berkeley; London: University of California Press, 2004, pp. 72–74.

MARION SCOTT*

Marion Scott's discussion of the *Eroica* Symphony is one of the most reflective passage in the whole of her *Beethoven* text. She asks, 'Who are the heroes celebrated?' She accepts most commentators agree Beethoven intended Napoleon to be celebrated, in the first and second movements, but recognizes Beethoven's close friends may have stirred thoughts of heroism in the composer's mind, with accounts of the heroic exploits of General Abercrombie. She further conjectures, in depicting Bonaparte could Beethoven unconsciously have portrayed himself? With regard to what we may describe as the intellectual underpinning of the *Eroica* Symphony, Scott states:

> 'I am disposed to believe that in the two opening movements Beethoven expressed everything that belonged to the glory, heroism and state of the hero in the material world ... For the last two movements – the parallel life – I think Beethoven removed everything into the ancient world which he looked upon as so much nobler than his own time – and took his music up on to its highest plane.'

Scott enlarges her discussion of the *Eroica* Symphony with an analysis of its individual movements.

FIRST MOVEMENT:

Scott admired what she refers to as the 'proportions' of the first movement:

> 'The first movement of the *Eroica* approaches a miracle. Beethoven lays out the exposition, development and recapitulation on a scale never before attempted, and then enlarges the Coda (which, with Haydn, had been a tiny tail on a movement) into a fourth section of importance equal with those preceding it and reflecting the development section, much as the recapitulation had reflected the exposition ... Beethoven's appreciation of the need for perspective in music and his power of producing it are amazing, and never more so than in the *Eroica* ... Beethoven [also] knew that in music melody is the thing most of the soul.'

SECOND MOVEMENT:
'The poet Coleridge once remarked it was like a funeral procession in deep purple. That conveys a true impression, and the C major section in the middle is like consolation from Heaven. Hitherto no composer had reached such an overwhelming intensity of emotion in a symphony.'

THIRD MOVEMENT:
At the period when Scott was writing her *Beethoven* – first edition 1934 – some musicologists were still debating the *legitimacy* of the *Scherzo* being accorded its location as the third movement. To this she responded:

> 'At first I inclined to think Beethoven had placed the Scherzo third, simply because that was its customary place. But when I examined his earlier works, I found one which disposed of this theory, for the very composition where he placed the Scherzo second was the Sonata in A-flat major, Op. 26, composed in 1801 – *which has the funeral march as its third movement.* [Scott's emphasis] What Beethoven did in 1801, he could certainly have done in 1803. The deduction is that his poetical plan for the *Eroica* required the movement to follow the order in which they now sound. I am therefore convinced he meant exactly what he did, and did not defer to any conventions.'

FOURTH MOVEMENT:
'For the finale Beethoven took his own *Prometheus* theme, and certainly identified himself with the that hero ... Beethoven here combines

sive layers of patterns, thus establishing the overall large-scale pattern.'

To illustrate his proposition, Sessions remarked:

Roger Sessions, *Questions about Music*. Cambridge, Massachusetts: Harvard University Press, 1970, pp. 87–88.

In conversation with the American musicologist Andrea Olmstead, Sessions had occasion to make reference to the opening of the first movement of the *Eroica* Symphony:

> 'The first four notes of the *Eroica* begin a little overture of an opera [*Bastien und Basteinne*] Mozart wrote when he was thirteen years old. People say that's a great theme, but what makes it great is what Beethoven did out of it.'

Andrea Olmstead, *Conversations with Roger Sessions*. Boston: Northeastern University Press, 1987, p. 61.

GEORGE BERNARD SHAW*

Writing on the occasion of Beethoven's death centenary, Shaw outlined what he considered the composer stood for:

> '[What] Beethoven did, and what made some of his greatest contemporaries give him up as a madman, with lucid intervals of clowning and bad taste, was that he used music altogether as a means of expressing moods, and completely threw over pattern-designing as an end in itself. It is true that he used the old patterns all his life

with dogged conservatism ... but he imposed on them an overwhelming charge of human energy and passion ... '.

Turning to the *Eroica* to further exemplify his feelings about Beethoven, he comments:

'The *Eroica* Symphony begins by a pattern (borrowed from an overture which Mozart wrote when he was a boy [*Bastien e Bastienne*]), followed by a couple more very pretty patterns; but they are tremendously energised, and in the middle of the movement the patterns are torn up savagely; and Beethoven, from the point of view of the mere pattern musician, goes raving mad, hurling out terrible chords in which all the notes of the scale are sounded simultaneously, just because he feels like that, and wants you to feel like it.

'And there you have the whole secret of Beethoven. He could design patterns with the best of them; he could write music whose beauty will last all your life; he could take the driest sticks of themes and work them up so interestingly that you find something new in them at the hundredth hearing; in short, you can say of him all that you can say of the greatest pattern-composers; but his diagnostic, the thing that marks him out from all the others, is his disturbing quality, his power of unsettling us and imposing his giant moods on us.'

Originally published in *The Radio Times*, 18 March 1927 and cited in: Dan H. Laurence editor, *Shaw's Music: The*

Complete Musical Criticism, London: Max Reinhardt, the Bodley Head, 1981, Vol. 3, p. 747.

ROBERT SIMPSON*

Robert Simpson discusses the first movement of the *Eroica* Symphony in the context of Romantic music's changing ideals:

> 'The romantic period created in many minds the assumption that expansion inescapably entailed the slowing-down of music; with Beethoven, expansion often meant filling a larger time-scale with more, not less, activity. The first movement of the *Eroica* is a ceaselessly mobile and concentrated a piece of high-pressure activity as has ever been generated; yet it is one of the longest first movements in existence. Vital energy could impel no greater athleticism than here, and the music never outruns its strength. This composition is *slower* than its precursors only because its great moments of tensions and relaxations are more widely spaced; in this sense its outlines are broader and it takes longer for the listener to absorb its processes. But the intervening stretches are packed with varied incident and action.'

Of the other three movements, Simpson remarks:

> 'In contrast to the first movement, the Funeral March shows the kind of bigness that comes from slowness; the main theme itself is vast, and when its figures are broken into for the purposes of development, their transformations are made even broader ... The inscrutability of the deeper

creative levels is illustrated in the early sketches of the Scherzo — they are marked *tempo di minuetto*; this at least suggests that the *prestissimo* performances we often hear are too fast — the tempo, though quick, should allow the quavers in bar 9, and wherever they occur, to be perfectly distinct. The second horn part in the Trio is impossible at some of the speeds often adopted, and to play the Trio at a slower pace than the Scherzo is a debased solution of the problem ... The finale, on a bass theme ... from *Prometheus*, anticipates that of the Ninth Symphony in being neither variations nor sonata, nor even rondo, using elements of all three for its organic growth into a purely individual structure. The variation elements are impelled to expand into development, and periodic incursions of comparatively regular variations have a rondo-like effect. The elation prompts the music to broaden its stride into a *poco andante*, and this inspired stroke has often been romantically misconstrued as a continuation of the funeral march into Heaven.'

Simpson closes by reflecting on the true nature of the hero who he believes lies at the heart of the *Eroica* Symphony:

'Beethoven's conception of a hero is not a romantic one; he is expressing the truth about human potential as he sensed it in himself. Napoleon is left far behind. The *andante* is no vision of Paradise — why, if it is, the powerful human stress, the intensely human doubt, even fear, that creeps across the music before the final *presto* breaks out like a last wave of heroic

> determination? ... [The] meaning of these last grand paragraphs is surely this, that the hero having experienced struggle, tragedy, joy, and awareness of power, surveys the past with a just and mounting sense of dignity ... Indomitably he faces the truth and the Symphony ends with a blaze of defiance. Beethoven is the objective realist even when, as here, he is undoubtedly painting a self-portrait.'

Robert Simpson, *Beethoven's Symphonies*. London: British Broadcasting Corporation, 1970, pp. 19–24.

ALEXANDER BRENT SMITH

To celebrate Beethoven's Death Centenary, the *Musical Times* issued a *Special Issue* in April 1927 devoted entirely to Beethoven and his music. Alexander Brent Smith was an organist, Director of Music at Lancing College – where Peter Pears was one of his pupils – and, in the role of musicologist, was an occasional contributor to *The Musical Times*. In his essay *His Infinite Variety* he has the following to say of Beethoven's powers of invention:

> 'For those who are influenced and impressed by statistics, it may be interesting to remember a few hard facts about the extent and variety of Beethoven's invention, such as, that each of his many piano sonatas, violin sonatas, cello sonatas, trios, quartets, concertos, and symphonies have, on average, four movements, and that each of the four movements has at least two subjects, that is, he wrote at least seven-hundred tunes each so full of character, and so independent of each other,

> that many musicians could easily locate each separate tune. And not only had Beethoven the power of creating individual melodies, but he had the additional power of creating subjects in pairs, or of providing each first subject with a suitable yet well-contrasted second subject. In this power of creating themes (subjects distinguished by heroic and manly qualities) and melodies (subjects distinguished by beauty grace and tenderness) other composers have not been so wholly successful as Beethoven.'

Directing his attention to Beethoven's harmony, Smith elucidates:

> 'A study of the variety of Beethoven's harmony is distinctly profitable, though perhaps the mention of the word *variety* in connection with nineteenth-century harmony may strike progressive minds as being slightly ridiculous. But variety of harmony does not mean the use or abuse of chromatic discords. Beethoven's discords may not be so harsh as those of some modern composers, but they are more effective because they are set against a background of simple, straight-forward harmony. Every chord of Beethoven makes its proper and intended effect. Consider that retiring second subject of the *Eroica* Symphony (first movement). There are two consecutive bars of the common chord of B-flat major; then one note is changed, but that semitone is worth the world "Quel semitone vale un mondo", as Geminiani said of a certain semitone in an overture by Handel. No: variety of Beethoven's harmony does not mean

the heaping of cacophonous Pelions on discordant Ossas, but upon the very real contrast between his two harmonic extremes.'

Alexander Brent Smith, *His Infinite Variety* in: *The Musical Times*, Vol. VIII, No. 2, April, 1927, pp. 202–5.

MAYNARD SOLOMON*

In his discussion of the *Eroica* Symphony, Maynard Solomon remarks:

> 'Innovative features of the *Eroica* (some anticipated by Haydn and Mozart) are often cited, including the use of a new theme in the development of the first movement, the employment of the winds for expressive rather than colouristic purposes, the introduction of a set of variations in the finale, of a funeral march in the slow movement, and of the use of three French horns for the first time in symphonic orchestration. More fundamentally, Beethoven's style is now informed with an organicity both of motion and structure which gives the Symphony its sense of unfolding continuity and wholeness within a constant interplay of moods.'

Maynard Solomon, *Beethoven*. New York: Schirmer, 1977, p. 197.

Later Solomon writes:

> 'We listen to Beethoven's *Eroica* Symphony differently than to his other symphonies because

of its extra-musical associations — its title, its subtitle, its funeral march, and its quotations from *The Creatures of Prometheus*. Beethoven has attempted to shape our responses, to direct them along avenues selected by himself. We listen to it differently, *nolens volens*, because of Ries's story about the rending of the inscription to Bonaparte. Now we will hear it differently because of what we have learned about Beethoven's intended journey to Paris as the proximate cause of the Symphony and of its original dedication, and about Beethoven's intention to use the piece as his musical passport to France. Listening to the *Eroica*, can we expel from our consciousness our knowledge of Beethoven's hero and rescue fantasies, his suicidal thoughts, his family romance, and his nobility pretence?'

Maynard Solomon, *Beethoven Essays*. Cambridge, Massachusetts; London: Harvard University Press, 1988, pp. 111–12.

WILLIAM PRESTON STEDMAN*

In his survey *The Symphony*, the American academic, musicologist and music administrator William Preston Stedman considers the construction of the *Eroica* Symphony:

FIRST MOVEMENT:

'The first movement is tightly constructed around several concise motives which lend themselves to frequent development even in the exposition. Counterpoint again becomes the primary treatment in the formal development section. In the heat of this development, a new theme is inserted (m 284) in a distant key (E minor: original key, E-flat major). The recapitulation progresses through the required material, cadences in the tonic key, and then moves abruptly into D-flat major for the start of the Coda (m 557). This immense appendage (134 mm long) almost equals the length of the exposition (147 mm). Much of the Coda is developmental; it even includes the tune from the development section (m 581).'

SECOND MOVEMENT:

'The second movement, a funeral march (*Adagio assai*), is a song-form with trio. It departs from this basic form in its return of an expanded song (normally a *da capo* in classical minuets); an elaborate fugal treatment occupies over a third of this returning section. A Coda, which starts with a deceptive resolution to A-flat major (tonic, C minor), actually starts in D-flat major, the Neopolitan key. The tonal area maintains dominance throughout the Coda.'

THIRD MOVEMENT:

'The third movement, a true Scherzo (*Allegro vivace*), is monothematic in the Scherzo section, with the second portion of the Scherzo being primarily developmental. The Trio features three horns in an ensemble display which has forever endeared the work to brass aficionados. The written-out *da capo* of the Scherzo is an exact repetition except for a single metric digression in which four measures of duple meter substitute for a syncopated passage in the original setting (mm 381–84).'

FOURTH MOVEMENT:

'The finale is a theme with ten variations. The theme itself adheres to the two-dimensional style noted also in the second movement of the Symphony No. 7. In both movements a rhythmic theme is established as the basic theme for the set of variations. In an early variation (third in the *Eroica*, first in the Seventh) a more lyric second theme appeared very much in the style of a countermelody. This lyric theme is then very much in the style of a countermelody. This lyric theme is then employed in each subsequent variation with some exceptions. The contrasts between the rhythmic theme and its more lyric countermelody is marked. The rhythmic theme of the *Eroica* resembles a ground and is introduced as a single-line, unison theme ... in the string pizzicato. The variations differ in length; some of the earlier ones are only a single statement of the theme without an extension. In the sixth variation, a new theme overlays the basic theme (mm 211–55). Variations 4 and 8 are both fugal. The ninth variation (*Poco andante*, m 348) is built primarily on the lyric countermelody introduced in the third variation. The tenth variation grows out of the ninth and very closely resembles it in style ... The writing for woodwind ensemble is particularly expressive and effective in this variation and stresses the composer's excellent appraisal of the technical possibilities of the clarinet.'

William Preston Stedman, *The Symphony.* Englewood Cliffs, New Jersey; London: Prentice-Hall, 1979, pp. 69–70.

MICHAEL P. STEINBERG*

The American scholar Michael P. Steinberg discusses the structure of the *Eroica* Symphony at length from which we cite the following:

> *FIRST MOVEMENT:*
> 'The *Eroica* begins with two forceful chords of E-flat major (but only forte, not *fortissimo*). They set key and tempo as well as giving us an idea of the character of the music. When the cellos start the *real music*, what they play is nothing more than an E flat chord tipped on its side, as it were — made horizontal and turned into a melody ... For a few moments everything proceeds calmly as the cello melody spreads through the orchestra and is beautifully expanded. But almost immediately, having already disturbed melodic regularity and harmony, Beethoven even more radically disturbs the rhythm with explosive off-beat accents that superimpose a two-beat pattern into the 3/4 measures.
>
> 'As we continue to listen, we sense another seeming contradiction: the music moves with exciting concentration and at high speed, yet it is amazingly filled with unhurried event ...

'The beginning of the development is hushed but hardly quiet. Harmonically, the music is in a state of unrest, and a growing density of counterpoint adds to our sense of agitation. Familiar ideas are so transformed as to seem like new themes. The dissident syncopations from the end of the exposition are picked up and heightened with harmonic clashes that still shock ...

'The Coda brings a last series of major surprises. In the first and last movements of the Second Symphony, Beethoven had discovered how to come close to the tail wag the dog. Here, not surprisingly, given the huge scale on which the music has unfolded, the Coda, only a few measures shorter than the exposition and the recapitulation, is to finally affirm the harmonic-centre and, so to speak, settle the music. The Coda here accomplishes this magnificently; it proffers so much action that we almost hear it as a second development.'

SECOND MOVEMENT:

'Next, in C minor, comes a Funeral March for the hero (whom we have probably forgotten in the musical excitement of the first movement). It begins in strings, *pianissimo* and *sotto voce*, but the instrumental colour most dominant in this movement is that of the oboe, a good instrument for mourning. Its first solo is accompanied by a symbolic drumming figure in the strings ...

'Eventually the music comes to rest in G minor, and there, again *sotto voce*, the violins attempt to start the first theme ...

'Persistent quick triplets agitate the air, and it is in this restless atmosphere that the last full statement of the opening theme is embedded ...

'At the end, over a final drumming in the cellos and basses, the woodwinds utter a last despairing cry.'

As a footnote to his remarks on the second movement, Steinberg makes reference to Hector Berlioz's discussion of the *Eroica* Symphony in his *À travers chant*. Of the celebrated *premature* horn entry, Berlioz called it 'ce caprice est une absurdité'.

THIRD MOVEMENT:

'The Scherzo has a mad coiled-spring energy, an impression that owes much to the prevalence of *piano* and *pianissimo*. The Trio is a virtuoso turn for the horn section. When the Scherzo itself returns, Beethoven introduces another of his violent metrical twists, cutting across the quick three-in-one gait with a series of slashing one-twos. The Coda, though brief, is powerful.'

FOURTH MOVEMENT:

'Facing a new challenge, Beethoven turned to old music; that is, he made for this finale a set of variations on a theme he had used three times before in a group of contradances in 1800–01, soon afterward in the finale of the Ballet *The Creatures of Prometheus*, and in 1802 in Fifteen Variations and Fugue for Piano, Op. 35 (often called the *Eroica* Variations). The bass of Beethoven's Contradance/Prometheus theme is simple, sturdy, easily grasped, remembered, and identified. It is also readily subject to transformation and decoration, though it has a sufficiently clear profile to keep it recognisable no matter what happens to it. [illustration] ...

'In the Symphony, Beethoven follows his own example, but since this is a work on a much larger scale than the Piano Variations, he provides a grander, more rhetorical introduction of *frame*. After the witty exploration of the possibilities of the base alone comes a powerful set of variations on the combined melody and bass ...

'Carefully, Beethoven dismantles this structure: the music is almost an echo of the *disintegration* of the Funeral March. Then, he resumes speed — returns in fact to a quasi-variation of the initial *frame* — to close, to fulfil his *heroic Symphony* in triumphantly affirmative noise.'

Michael P. Steinberg, *The Symphony: A Listener's Guide*, Oxford University Press; Reprint edition, 1998, pp. 14—19.

IGOR STRAVINSKY

Igor Stravinsky's reputation for being one of the most important composers of the 20th century has somewhat overshadowed his prowess as a pianist. As a child, he showed an aptitude for the piano and by the age of fifteen he had mastered Mendelssohn's Piano Concerto in G minor. In his student days he had lessons in orchestration with Rimsky-Korsakov. He was required to set passages of Beethoven sonatas and Schubert quartets, which his master then criticised and corrected. In his *Autobiography*, Stravinsky pays homage to Beethoven's piano music:

> 'I recognized in him [Beethoven] the indisputable monarch of the instrument. It is the instrument that inspires his thought and determines its substance. The relations of a composer to his sound-medium may be of two kinds. Some, for example, compose music *for* the piano; others compose *piano music*. Beethoven is clearly in the second category. In all his immense pianistic work, it is the "instrumental" side which is characteristic of him and makes him infinitely precious to me. It is the giant instrumentalist that predominates in him, and it is thanks to that quality that he cannot fail to reach any ear that is open to music.'

Igor Stravinsky, *An Autobiography*, London: Calder and Boyars, 1975, p. 116.

Reflecting more generally on Beethoven, Stravinsky summed up his feelings in relation to him:

> 'I did not hero-worship Beethoven, nor have I ever done so, and the nature of Beethoven's talent and work are more "human" and more comprehensible to me than are, say the talents and works of more "perfect" composers like Bach and Mozart; I think I know how Beethoven composed. I have little enough Beethoven in me, alas, but some people have found I have some.'

Igor Stravinsky and Robert Craft, *Memories and Commentaries*, London: Faber and Faber, 2002, p. 23, and p. 39.

Sometime in the early 1970s. the music critic of the *New York Review* interviewed Stravinsky and asked him for his views about the *Eroica* Symphony. In his *Autobiography* (see above) Stravinsky remarks:

> 'What does it matter whether the Third Symphony was inspired by the figure of Bonaparte the Republican or Napoleon the Emperor? It is only the music that matters.' (p. 117)

In his response to the music critic he was more fulsome:

> 'The first movement is usually so mangled by conductors' delayed beats and soggy retards that I seldom listen to much of it. The same can be said of the Funeral March, which conductors may come to praise but only succeed in burying. And, finally, the let-down movement – this *not* the fault of the performer – is all the worse for following the most marvellous Scherzo for orchestra ever composed.'

Igor Stravinsky, *Themes and Conclusions*. London: Faber and Faber, 1972, p. 168.

VIRGIL THOMSON

In his long life Virgil Thomson divided his gifts between composition, essay writing and music criticism – in the latter role for many years as music critic to the *New York Herald-Tribune*. In this capacity he was known for his uncompromising, feisty, and characteristically colloquial opinions. Of Beethoven he once wrote:

'[It] is hard to find much in Beethoven's life or music — beyond the legend of his having torn up the dedication of his "Heroic" Symphony to Napoleon [Symphony No. 3, the *Eroica*] when the defender of the French Revolution allowed himself to be crowned Emperor — to justify the adoration in which he has always been held by political liberals.'

In much the same spirit, Thomson once reviewed the *Eroica*, pronouncing its first movement to be a 'dud'! This so offended some of the readers — and fellow musicians — he felt obliged to recant his wayward judgement:

'I realize now that I should have explained myself more fully what I had on my mind, which was that that particular movement had always been more interesting to musicians, on account of its rich musical imagination and skilful writing, than to the listening public in general, which always seems to me to accept the movement passively and without great enthusiasm. Certainly, its direct expressive quality is less precise than that of the first movements of the Fifth, Sixth, and Eighth Symphonies, let us say.

'The second movement, though probably the finest funeral march in the world, presents such difficulties about tempo that not one conductor in twenty ever manages to keep it from sounding interminable. A beautiful work it is, yes, a very beautiful work, but far more often than not a well-known putter-to-sleep of audiences.

'I meant no slur on a great work by a great

composer in mentioning these facts ... Beethoven wrote some very great music. He also, like everybody else, wrote movements that are not up to his best.

'I sometimes differ with my musical colleagues about musical values, but I assure you I do not hold any controversial opinions about Beethoven. I do not think there is much possible controversy about Beethoven's musical works.'

Tim Page, and Vanessa Weeks editors, *Selected Letters of Virgil Thomson*, New York: Summit Books, 1988, pp. 156–57 and pp.186–67. Thomson's *apology* dates from 27 December 1940.

ARTURO TOSCANINI

Interpretations of Beethoven's music on record are outside our terms of reference, but we make an exception here and cite the impressions left by the Italian conductor Arturo Toscanini of his interpretation of the *Eroica* Symphony. Writing of Toscanini, Peter Gutman states:

'Toscanini believed that no performer had the right to deflect attention from the composer ... [His] aim was to let the music speak for itself and to add only those inflections necessary to elicit the structure, balance and image which the composer had written into the piece ... His overall aim was clarity in which each instrument was audible, even in the most densely scored passages.'

Peter Gutman, *Toscanini, The Recorded Legend*, Classical Notes, website text, 2003)

*

Before rehearsing the *Eroica* Symphony, Toscanini was given to mounting the rostrum and, about to embark on the first movement, say to the expectant players: 'To some it is Napoleon, to some it is Alexander the Great, to some it is philosophical struggle, to me it is *Allegro con brio!*' (Joseph Horowitz, *Understanding Toscanini.* London: Faber and Faber, 1987, p. 102)

Toscanini recorded the *Eroica* Symphony on shellac discs in the early 78 rpm format and was in demand by several recording companies. His earliest studio recording dates from 1938 and was soon followed by others in 1939, 1945, 1949, and 1953. A recording was also made from a live broadcast in 1949 with Toscanini and the NBC Symphony Orchestra. This was issued later in the UK on the HMV label. The jazz enthusiast, turned musicologist, Splke Hughes has made a bar-by-bar study of this recording with a view to gaining insights into Toscanini's interpretation of the *Eroica* Symphony. From this we quote the following:

> 'In a Beethoven series, [Toscanini] ... would play the *Eroica* after the Fourth Symphony for what one must regard as reasons of dramatic logic. But when he included the *Eroica* in an ordinary mixed concert programme, he still always ended with it. [Beethoven had advised it should be performed at the start of a programme].'

Directing his attention to the individual movements, Hughes expounds:

FIRST MOVEMENT:
'The tempo itself was roughly quarter note = 160, which is not nearly so unreasonable as the tempo

optimistically recommended by the editor of my full score, who hopes for something approaching 180 ... But, as one soon learned by experience, whatever the tempo adopted by Toscanini there was always time for the display of tenderness in the music ... In accordance with Beethoven's own custom, Toscanini did not make the repeat of the exposition but continued with the development section. This part of the movement always showed Toscanini at his greatest and most inimitable, electrifying the orchestral texture so that neither a single detail of the figures developed by the woodwind or strings was lost, nor — any of the tremendous dramatic intensity of the music sacrificed either ...

'The recapitulation presented no noticeable surprises; everything was as before so far as detail was concerned, but in a peculiar way, which was not achieved by any change of tempo of forcing of dynamics, as the music grew in intensity and urgency. Toscanini's control and command of the sheer physical potentialities of an orchestra were amazing, of course, and as this movement of the *Eroica* neared its end one was constantly aware of his masterly sense of timing, which always held something in reserve so that the climax could never be mistaken for the real thing.'

SECOND MOVEMENT:

'To talk of tension in connection with Toscanini's performances is not to suggest that lyrical warmth was absent when it was called for ... [In] this particular *Eroica* there was no disregard of the phrases marked "dolce" in the first movement in spite of the general hurly-burly of an *Allegro* with lots of *brio*. So, in this slow movement there were passages of quite beautiful *cantilena* super-imposed, as it were, on the unceasing rhythm of what is, after all, a funeral march. It was the funeral-march element of this movement that Toscanini stressed most strongly. He took it at a comfortable eighth note = 69, or thereabouts, and maintained that as the basic speed throughout ...

'While Toscanini maintained the steady march rhythm of the slow movement, there were one or two other instances of rubato to be heard besides the emphatic but unindicated *ritenuto* ...

'In the last moments of the Coda it was Beethoven, by his disjointing of the theme, rather than Toscanini, who created the effect of the march slowing down until it finally stops. Toscanini did in fact, take these bars at a slightly slower tempo, but he underplayed them in such a way that the final emotional impact of the movement acquired an added poignancy. The melancholy closing chords in the wind sounded indeed what Verdi often called "come un lamento".'

THIRD MOVEMENT:

'[Toscanini's] mastery of "matching dynamics" was never more apparent than in this Scherzo which abounds in phrases thrown about from one part of the orchestra to another, changing the colour but not the volume of sound. What Toscanini did not do, on the other hand, was to add dynamic flourishes where none was shown in the score ...

'Toscanini's tempo for the Trio of this Scherzo seems to exasperate many people, some of whom go so far as to insist that "everyone else slows down for it". It is just simply not true to say this, of course. Weingartner's recorded performance of the *Eroica* with the Vienna Philharmonic, for instance, shows quite clearly that the conductor carried straight on with the tempo without hesitation.

'Like Weingartner, Toscanini did not agree with "everyone else" and took the Trio at the tempo marked — or rather, *not* marked by the composer, since it is obvious that it is to be played at the same speed as the rest of the Scherzo.'

FOURTH MOVEMENT:

'If ever there was proof that the exception proves the rule it was surely provided by this finale as Toscanini recorded it. So far as tempo is concerned it was, to say the least, an elastic performance. There are frequent variations of speed to be noted which are by no means indicated in the score — instances of rubato, of slowing up, of whole sequences being played faster before returning to the basic quarter note = 132 ... But listened to all in one piece, as it were, one is barely conscious of any of this. It is only on examination, on checking closely with the score one discovers that Toscanini — *the human metronome* — permitted himself a great deal of latitude one way and another.'

Spike Hughes, *The Toscanini Legacy: A Critical Study of Arturo Toscanini's Performances of Beethoven, Verdi, and other Composers.* London: Putnam, 1959, pp. 39–47.

DONALD FRANCIS TOVEY*

Writing of selected aspects of the construction and form of the *Eroica* Symphony, Donald Francis Tovey observes:

> *FIRST MOVEMENT:*
> 'The passage that follows the return of the main theme in the first movement of Beethoven's *Eroica* Symphony is one of the supreme dramatic strokes in music. The hard-won tonic of E flat gives way first to F major then to the opposite extreme, a third lower, D flat. Another third down brings us safely to our own dominant chord.'

> *SECOND MOVEMENT:*
> 'The *Eroica* Symphony, though inspired by Beethoven's short-lived belief in Napoleon as the liberator of mankind, is not programme music at all. The Funeral March represents heroic death and a mourning world, but not the obsequies of a biographical subject ...'.

> *FOURTH MOVEMENT:*

Writing of Beethoven's adoption of the variation-form in his piano sonatas, Tovey adds:

> 'Beethoven also found other applications of the variation forms. Thus, the finale of the *Eroica* Symphony has not only the theme but many

other ideas in common with the brilliant set of Variations and Fugue for pianoforte on a theme from *Prometheus*, Op. 35; and the Fantasia for pianoforte, chorus and orchestra, and the Choral Finale of the Ninth Symphony, are sets of melodic variations with freely-developed connecting links and episodes.'

Donald Francis Tovey, *The Forms of Music: Musical Articles from The Encyclopaedia Britannica.* London: Oxford University Press, 1944.

Tovey gave further expression to his response to the *Eroica* Symphony in the first of his *Essays in Musical Analysis*:

ALLEGRO CON BRIO:
'After two strong introductory chords the violincellos state the principal theme. It is simply the notes of a common chord swinging backwards and forwards in a quietly energetic rhythm. Then the violins enter with a palpitating high note, the harmony becomes clouded, soon however to resolve in sunshine. Whatever you miss in the *Eroica* Symphony remember this cloud: it leads eventually to one of the most astonishing and subtle dramatic strokes in all music.'

Marcia Funebre:
'The great length of the funeral march results mainly from the size of its principal theme. This is a broad melody in two portions, each of which is given out by the strings and repeated ... by the wind. This takes time; and in addition there is a series of afterthoughts which brings the main

theme to a close on a scale almost large enough for a complete movement. Yet Beethoven's purpose is to work out the whole in rondo form; that is to say, a form in which the main theme recurs like a choral refrain alternating with at least two contrasted episodes. It is obvious that such a purpose can here be carried out only by a miracle of concentration and terseness, and this funeral march broadens in its flow as it develops.'

SCHERZO:

'This *Scherzo* is the first in which Beethoven fully attained Haydn's desire to replace the minuet by something on a scale comparable to the rest of the Symphony. Its characteristics are unmistakable, and we need only to mention the long, subdued whispering with its three horns, whose classical imperfections of technique Beethoven has exploited to poetic ends, which the perfectly equipped modern player has to rediscover by careful research, and the mysterious Coda with its menacing drums.'

FINALE:

'The finale is in a form which was unique when it appeared, and has remained unique ever since. This has given rise to a widespread notion that it is formless or incoherent. It is neither; and its life, which is its form, does not depend upon a label. The best way to understand it is not to think of the important earlier pianoforte *Variations and Fugue on a theme from Prometheus*, on which its material is based, but simply to identify its material under three headings, a Bass, a Tune, and a Fugue ... [The] Bass is solemnly given by the strings, pizzicato, and echoed by the wind ... [The] Tune comes sailing over it in full radiance and we think no more of the Bass, though it faithfully performs its duty as such ... So far Beethoven's design has been exactly that of his *Introduzione col basso del tema* in the *Prometheus* Variations; but now, instead of making variations, he leads in a few argumentative steps to a new key and then proceeds to the Fugue ...The Fugue, which is here throughout in the main key, now comes to a grand climax ending with an anticipatory pause. Then, like the opening of the gates of Paradise, the Tune enters slowly (*poco andante*) in a glorious double variation ...

'After all this climax all is Coda, and one of the most profound codas Beethoven ever wrote ... [It] melts into a mood we have not found before in the whole Symphony. It is a mood of that mysterious and true humour that is not far from tears ... [Just] upon the close of his *Heroic Symphony*, Beethoven holds us for the last time in suspense, until the orchestra blazes out in a larger version of the fiery introduction and brings the work to its triumphant end.'

Donald Francis Tovey, *Essays in Musical Analysis*. London: Oxford University Press, H. Milford, Vol.1, 1935, pp. 30–34.

RICHARD WAGNER*

Richard Wagner's prose works extend to seven voluminous tomes, with one further volume added posthumously. In Volume 3 he devotes an extensive text to the *Eroica* Symphony. In this he first establishes how he considers heroism in the composition should be regarded:

> 'In the first place, the designation *heroic* is to be taken in its widest sense, and in nowise to be conceived as relating merely to a military hero. If we broadly connote by *hero* the [German] *held* the whole, the full-fledged *man*, in whom are present all the purely human feelings — of love, of grief, of force — in their highest fill and strength, then we shall rightly grasp the subject which the artist lets appeal to us in the speaking accents of his tone work.'

In a characteristically fulsome paragraph, Wagner elaborates:

> 'The artistic space of this work is filled with all the varied, intercrossing feelings of a strong, a consummate individuality, to which nothing human is a stranger, but which includes within itself all [that is] truly HUMAN, [Wagner's capitalization] and utters it in such a fashion that — after frankly manifesting every noble passion — it reaches a final rounding of its nature, wherein the most feeling softness is wedded with the most energetic force. The heroic tenderness of this artwork is the progress toward that rounding off.'

In effusive prose, pregnant with imagery, Wagner outlines

the *psyche* that he finds prevailing throughout the composition:

FIRST MOVEMENT:

'The First Movement embraces, as in a glowing furnace, all the emotions of a richly-gifted nature in the heyday of unresting youth. Weal and woe, life and lack, awareness and sadness, living and longing, riot and revel, defiance, and an ungovernable sense of Self, make place for one another so directly, and interlace so closely that, however much we made each feeling with our own, we can single none of them from out the rest, but our whole interest is given merely to this one, this human being who shows himself brimful of every feeling. Yet all these feelings spring from one main faculty — and that is *Force*. This Force, immeasurably enhanced by each emotional impression and driven to vent its overfill, is the mainspring of the tone-piece: it clinches — towards the middle of the Movement — to the violence of the destroyer, and in its braggart strength we think we see a Wrecker of the World before us, a Titan wrestling with the Gods.'

SECOND MOVEMENT:

'This shattering Force, that filled us half with ecstasy and half with horror, was rushing toward a tragic-crises, whose serious import is set before our Feeling in the Second Movement. The tone-poet clothes its proclamation in the musical apparel of a funeral march. Emotion tamed by deep grief, moving sorrow, tells us its tale in stirring tones: an earnest, manly sadness goes from lamentation to thrills of softness, to memories, to tears of love, to searchings of the heart, to cries of transport. Out of grief there springs new Force, that fills us with a warmth sublime: instinctively we seek again this force's fountain-head in Grief; we give ourselves to it, sighing we swoon away; but here we rouse ourselves once more to fullest Force: we will not succumb, but endure. We battle no more against mourning, but bear it now ourselves on the mighty billows of man's outrageous heart. To whom were it possible to paint in words the endless play of quite unspeakable emotions, passing from Grief to highest Exaltation, and themes again to softest Melancholy, till they mount at last to endless Recollection? The Tone-poet alone could do it in this wondrous piece.'

THIRD MOVEMENT:
'Force robbed of its destructive arrogance — by the chastening of its own deep sorrow — the Third Movement shows in all its buoyant gaiety. Its wild unruliness has shaped itself to fresh, to blithe activity; we have before us now the loveable glad man, who paces hale and hearty through the fields of Nature, looks laughingly across the meadows, and winds his merry hunting-horn from woodland heights; and what he feels amid it all, the master tells us in the vigorous, healthy tints of tone-painting; he gives it lastly to the horns themselves to say — those horns which musically express the radiant, frolicsome, yet tender-hearted exultation of

man. In this Third Movement, the tone-poet shows us the man-of-feeling from the side directly opposite to that from which he showed him in its immediate predecessor: there, the deeply, stoutly suffering — here, the gladly, blithely doing-man.'

FOURTH MOVEMENT:
'These two sides the master now combines in the Fourth Movement, to show us finally the man entire, harmoniously at one with self, in those emotions where the memory of Sorrow becomes itself the shaping-force of noble Deeds. This closing section is the harvest, the lucid counterpart and commentary of the First. Just as there we saw all human feeling in infinitely varied utterance, now permeating one another, now each in haste repelling each: so here this manifold variety unites to one harmonious close, embracing all these feelings in itself and taking on a grateful plasticity of shape. This shape the master binds at first within one simple theme, which sets itself before us in sure distinctness, and yet is capable of infinite development, from gentlest delicacy to grandest strength. Around this theme, which we may regard as the firm-set Manly individuality, there wind and cling all tender and softer feelings, from the very onset of the movement, evolving to a proclamation of the purely Womanly element; and to the manlike principle theme — striking sturdily through all the tonepiece — this Womanly at last reveals itself in evermore intense, more many-sided sympathy, as the overwhelming power of Love ...

'Here it is, that once again this heart recalls the memory of its life-pang: high swells the breast filled by Love — that breast which harbours woe within its weal; for woe and weal, as purely-human Feeling, are one thing and the same ...

'Once more the heart-strings quiver, and tears of pure Humanity well forth; yet from out the very quick of sadness there bursts the jubilant cry of Force — that Force which lately wed itself to Love and nerved wherewith *the whole, the total Man* [Wagner's italics] now shouts to us the avowal of his Godhood.'

William Ashton Ellis, *Richard Wagner's Prose Works: Vol. 3, The Theatre*. Edited and translated by William Ashton Ellis. London: Kegan Paul, Trench, Trübner, 1907, pp. 223–24.

FELIX WEINGARTNER

The Austrian conductor, composer and pianist Felix Weingartner is remembered today for his interpretations of Beethoven's symphonies; he was the first conductor to make commercial recordings of all nine symphonies. Whilst they are still recognized for being pioneering, many consider his interpretations to be subjective by today's performance-standards on the basis, for example, of tempo fluctuations that are inconsistent with the printed score.

In his *Autobiography*, Weingartner recalls the period when he was studying composition with the Austro-Bohemian composer Wilhelm Mayer. Weingartner recalls the impression made on him of studying Beethoven's symphonies with his teacher and of how becoming acquainted with the *Eroica* Symphony determined his future destiny as a musician:

'The deep impression which Beethoven's Fourth Symphony, particularly the introductory movement, had made on me ... induced my music-master to go through all the symphonies, beginning with the first, in the form of duets which he played with me. I still remember the breathless expectation which the chromatically rising bass at the end of the first movement of the Second Symphony induced in me, and the bold subject of the finale, which burst on me with the force of an electric shock. The *Eroica* was, however, the climax of the series. My master had already told me of its connection with Napoleon, and this had had the effect of enhancing my anticipation. When we had finished playing the first movement, Dr. Mayer exclaimed: "You are much too excited my boy — that's enough for today." Deep in thought I went home: on my evening walk with my mother ... I was incapable of speech, though my mother implored me to tell her what was the matter. At last ... I told my mother of the greatest decision of which I was capable, that I had chosen my profession, that I was a musician and would remain one and that nothing in the world would induce me to change my mind.'

Weingartner further relates how his mother insisted, first he should complete his schooling — apparently Weingartner preferred Greek to Latin. The rest, as the saying goes, 'is history'.

Felix Weingartner, *Buffets and Rewards: A Musician's Reminiscences*. London: Hutchinson & Co., 1937, pp. 38–39.

RALPH VAUGHAN WILLIAMS

In 1954 Vaughan Williams visited the United States, having been invited to lecture at Cornell University and to conduct occasional concerts. At the latter, such was his fame, he received an enthusiastic welcome from large audiences. In one of his Cornell lectures he discussed form and content in music, stating:

> 'These two words are often taken to mean separate and opposite parts of an artistic structure. We talk about the form of a sonata being good and its content being poor; but is not the content poor because the form is bad? And so we go on, *ad infinitum*. It is the content which settles the form of any organic structure.'

Following these generalisations, Williams made reference to the *Eroica* Symphony:

> 'What, after all, is good content? Is it not a matter of suitability to its purpose? The opening theme of the *Eroica* Symphony is just an arpeggio, and nor original at that, but what a wonderful foundation for a great [first] movement!'

Ralph Vaughan Williams, *The Making of Music*. Ithaca, New York: Cornell University Press, 1955, p. 1.

CONRAD WILSON*

In his selection of *20 Crucial Works* of Beethoven, the Scottish musicologist and music critic Conrad Wilson includes the *Eroica* Symphony. Of this he writes:

FIRST MOVEMENT:

'[How] heroic is the *Eroica*? Or, for that matter, how Napoleonic is it? Not until a year after it was completed, in 1805, did the work receive its first performance in Vienna's Theater an der Wien, the setting for several Beethoven premiers. Beethoven was by then 35 years old, and his Symphony was the biggest ever written up to that time, with a first movement as long as an entire work by one of his predecessors. That it was no ordinary symphony was clear from the start. Nor was the heroic vigour of the opening movement, reaching a climax of dissonant, disruptive violence in the central development section, in any way in doubt. The sheer scale of this innovatory movement, with its unstoppable momentum and unprecedentedly extended Coda, was heroic.'

SECOND MOVEMENT:

'But for whom was the funeral march intended? The music, complete with sonorous oration, is hugely atmospheric and at times thunderously graphic. Napoleon was very much alive when it was written, though Beethoven may have been making the point that all heroes die in the end. He had already composed one heroic funeral march as the slow movement of his Piano Sonata, Op. 27, No. 1, written in the *Eroica* key of E-flat major — and here was its even grander descendant.'

THIRD MOVEMENT:

'After this substantial diversion, the quicksilver Scherzo, complete with the whirling Trio section for three horns and its slashing cross-rhythms during the Scherzo's repeat, retrieves something of the ferocious exuberance of the opening movement.'

FOURTH MOVEMENT:

'Dramatic tension is sustained in the finale, traditionally the lightest movement of a symphony, but not on this occasion. The spitfire opening-outburst leads to the bare bones of a theme which, when flashed out, becomes identifiable as one which Beethoven had previously employed in several works. Particularly apposite among these had been his *Prometheus* Ballet, whose subject was the civilising of art to uplift mankind. Here, then, was the final universal theme of the *Eroica*, delivered, as a set of variations filled with vitality, pungent humour and final grandeur.'

Conrad Wilson, *Notes on Beethoven: 20 Crucial Works*. Edinburgh: Saint Andrew Press, 2003, pp. 33–35.

BIBLIOGRAPHY

The author has individually consulted all the publications listed in this bibliography and can confirm that each makes reference, in some way or other, to Beethoven and his works. It will be evident from their titles which of these are publications devoted exclusively to the composer. Others that make only passing reference to Beethoven and his compositions, nevertheless unfailingly bear testimony to his genius and humanity. The diversity of the titles listed testifies to the centrality of Beethoven to western culture and beyond; the mere survey of these should be of itself a rewarding experience for a lover of so-called classical music. The entries are confined to book publications, reflecting the scope of the author's researches. The cut-off date for this was 2007; no works after this date are listed, notwithstanding the author is mindful that Beethoven musicology, and related publication, continue to be a major field of endeavour.

Abraham, Gerald. *Beethoven's second-period quartets*. London: Oxford University Press: Humphrey Milford, 1944.

Abraham, Gerald. *Essays on Russian and East European music*. Oxford: Clarendon Press: New York: Oxford University Press, 1985.

Abraham, Gerald, Editor. *The age of Beethoven, 1790-1830*. London: Oxford University Press, 1982.

Abraham, Gerald. *The tradition of Western music*. London: Oxford University Press, 1974.

Abse, Dannie and Joan. *The Music lover's literary companion*. London: Robson Books, 1988.

Adorno, Theodor W., Translator. *Alban Berg: master of the smallest link*. Cambridge: Cambridge University Press, 1991.

Adorno, Theodor W. *Beethoven: the philosophy of music; fragments and texts*. Cambridge: Polity Press, 1998.

Albrecht, Daniel, Editor. *Modernism and music: an anthology of sources*. Chicago; London: University of Chicago Press, 2004.

Albrecht, Theodore, Translator and Editor. *Letters to Beethoven and other correspondence*. Lincoln, New England: University of Nebraska Press, 3 vols., 1996.

Allsobrook, David Ian. *Liszt: my travelling circus life*. London: Macmillan, 1991.

Anderson, Christopher, Editor and Translator. *Selected writings of Max Reger*. New York; London: Routledge, 2006.

Anderson, Emily, Editor and Translator. *The letters of Beethoven*. London: Macmillan, 3 vols.,1961.

Anderson, Martin, Editor. *Klemperer on music: shavings from a musician's workbench*. London: Toccata Press, 1986.

Antheil, George. *Bad boy of music*. London; New York: Hurst & Blackett Ltd., 1945.

Appleby, David P. *Heitor Villa-Lobos: a bio-bibliography*. New York: Greenwood Press, 1988.

Aprahamian, Felix, Editor. *Essays on music: an anthology from The Listener*. London, Cassell, 1967.

Armero, Gonzalo and Jorge de Persia. *Manuel de Falla : his life & works*. London: Omnibus Press, 1999.

Arnold, Ben, Editor. *The Liszt companion*. Westport, Connecticut; London: Greenwood Press, 2002.

Arnold, Denis and Nigel Fortune, Editors. *The Beethoven companion*. London: Faber and Faber, 1973.

Ashbrook, William. *Donizetti*. London: Cassell, 1965.

Auner, Joseph Henry. *A Schoenberg reader: documents of a life*. New Haven Connecticut; London: Yale University Press, 2003.

Avins, Styra, Editor. *Johannes Brahms: life and letters*. Oxford: Oxford University Press, 1997.

Azoury, Pierre H. *Chopin through his contemporaries: friends, lovers, and rivals*. Westport, Connecticut: Greenwood Press, 1999.

Badura-Skoda, Paul. *Carl Czerny: On the Proper Performance of all Beethoven's Works for the Piano*. Universal Edition: A. G. Wien, 1970.

Bailey, Cyril. *Hugh Percy Allen*. London: Oxford University Press, 1948.

Bailey, Kathryn. *The life of Webern*. Cambridge: Cambridge University Press, 1998.

Barenboim, Daniel. *A life in music*. London: Weidenfeld & Nicolson, 1991.

Barlow, Michael. *Whom the gods love: the life and music of George Butterworth*. London: Toccata Press, 1997.

Barrett-Ayres, Reginald. *Joseph Haydn and the string quartet*. New York: Schirmer Books, 1974.

Bartos, Frantisek. *Bedrich Smetana: Letters and reminiscences*. Prague: Artia, 1953.

Barzun, Jacques. *Pleasures of music: an anthology of writing about music and musicians*. London: Cassell, 1977.

Bauer-Lechner, Natalie. *Recollections of Gustav Mahler*. London: Faber Music, 1980.

Bazhanov, N. Nikolai. *Rakhmaninov*. Moscow: Raduga, 1983.

Beaumont, Antony, Editor. *Ferruccio Busoni: Selected letters*. London: Faber and Faber, 1987.

Beaumont, Antony, Editor. *Gustav Mahler, letters to his wife*. London: Faber and Faber, 2004.

Beecham, Thomas. *A mingled chime: an autobiography*. New York: Da Capo Press, 1976.

Bekker, Paul. *Beethoven*. London: J. M. Dent & Sons, 1925.

Bellasis, Edward. *Cherubini: memorials illustrative of his life*. London: Burns and Oates, 1874.

Bennett, James R. Sterndale. *The life of William Sterndale Bennett*. Cambridge: University Press, 1907.

Benser, Caroline Cepin. *Egon Wellesz (1885–1974): chronicle of twentieth-century musician*. New York: P. Lang, 1985.

Berlioz, Hector. *Evenings in the orchestra*. Harmondsworth: Penguin Books, 1963.

Berlioz, Hector. *The musical madhouse (Les grotesques de la musique)*. Rochester, New York: University of Rochester Press, 2003.

Bernard, Jonathan W., Editor. *Elliott Carter: collected essays and lectures, 1937-1995*. Rochester, New York; Woodbridge: University of Rochester Press, 1998.

Bernstein, Leonard. *The joy of music*. New York: Simon and Schuster, 1959.

Bertensson, Sergei. *Sergei Rachmaninoff: a lifetime in music*. London: G. Allen & Unwin, 1965.

Biancolli, Louis. *The Flagstad manuscript*. New York: Putnam, 1952.

Bickley, Nora, Editor. *Letters from and to Joseph Joachim*. London: Macmillan, 1914.

Bie, Oskar. *A history of the pianoforte and pianoforte players*. New York: Da Capo Press, 1966.

Blaukopf, Herta. *Mahler's unknown letters*. London: Gollancz, 1986.

Blaukopf, Kurt and Herta. *Mahler: his life, work and world*. London: Thames and Hudson, 1991.

Bliss, Arthur. *As I remember*. London: Thames Publishing, 1989.

Block, Adrienne Fried. *Amy Beach, passionate Victorian: the life and work of an American composer, 1867–1944*. New York: Oxford University Press, 1998.

Bloch, Ernst. *Essays on the philosophy of music*. Cambridge: Cambridge University Press, 1985.

Blocker, Robert. *The Robert Shaw reader*. New Haven; London: Yale University Press, 2004.

Blom, Eric. *A musical postbag*. London: J. M. Dent, 1945.

Blom, Eric. *Beethoven's pianoforte sonatas discussed*. London: J. M. Dent, 1938.

Blom, Eric. *Classics major and minor: with some other musical ruminations*. London: J. M. Dent, 1958.

Blum, David. *The art of quartet playing: the Guarneri Quartet in conversation with David Blum*. London: Gollancz, 1986.

Blume, Friedrich. *Classic and Romantic music: a comprehensive survey*. London: Faber and Faber, 1972.

Boden, Anthony. *The Parrys of the Golden Vale: background to genius*. London: Thames Publishing, 1998.

Bonavia, Ferruccio. *Musicians on music*. London: Routledge & Kegan Paul, 1956.

Bonds, Mark Evan *After Beethoven: imperatives of originality in the symphony*. Cambridge, Massachusetts; London: Harvard University Press, 1996.

Bonis, Ferenc, Editor. *The selected writings of Zoltán Kodály*. London; New York: Boosey & Hawkes, 1974.

Bookspan, Martin. *André Previn: a biography*. London: Hamilton, 1981.

Boros, James and Richard Toop, Editors. *Brian Ferneyhough: Collected writings*. Amsterdam: Harwood Academic, 1995.

Boulez, Pierre. *Stocktakings from an apprenticeship*. Oxford: Clarendon Press, 1991.

Boult, Adrian. *Boult on music: words from a lifetime's communication*. London: Toccata Press, 1983.

Boult, Adrian. *My own trumpet*. London, Hamish Hamilton, 1973.

Boult, Adrian with Jerrold Northrop Moore. *Music and friends: seven decades of letters to Adrian Boult from Elgar, Vaughan Williams, Holst, Bruno Walter, Yehudi Menuhin and other friends*. London: Hamish Hamilton, 1979.

Bovet, Marie Anne de. *Charles Gounod: his life and his works*. London: S. Low, Marston, Searle & Rivington, Ltd., 1891.

Bowen, Catherine Drinker. *Beloved friend: the story of Tchaikowsky and Nadejda von Meck*. London: Hutchinson & Co., 1937.

Bowen, Meiron, Editor. *Gerhard on music: selected writings*. Brookfield, Vermont: Ashgate, 2000.

Bowen, Meirion. *Michael Tippett*. London: Robson Books, 1982.

Bowen, Meiron, Editor. *Music of the angels: essays and sketchbooks of Michael Tippett*. London: Eulenburg, 1980.

Bowen, Meiron, Editor. *Tippett on music*. Oxford: Clarendon Press, 1995.

Bowers, Faubion. *Scriabin: a biography*. Mineola: Dover; London: Constable, 1996.

Boyden, Matthew. *Richard Strauss*. London: Weidenfeld & Nicolson, 1999.

Bozarth, George S., Editor. *Brahms

studies: analytical and historical perspectives; papers delivered at the International Brahms Conference, Washington, DC, 5-8 May 1983. Oxford: Clarendon Press, 1990.

Brand, Juliane, Christopher Hailey and Donald Harris, Editors. *The Berg-Schoenberg correspondence: selected letters.* Basingstoke: Macmillan, 1987.

Brandenbugh, Sieghard, Editor. *Haydn, Mozart, & Beethoven: studies in the music of the classical period: essays in honor of Alan Tyson.* Oxford: Clarendon Press, 1998.

Braunstein, Joseph. *Musica Æterna, program notes for 1961–1971.* New York: Musica Æterna, 1972.

Braunstein, Joseph. *Musica Æterna, program notes for 1971–1976.* New York: Musica Æterna, 1978.

Brendel, Alfred. *Alfred Brendel on music: collected essays.* Chicago, Illinois: A Cappella Books, 2001.

Brendel, Alfred. *The veil of order: Alfred Brendel in conversation with Martin Meyer.* London: Faber and Faber, 2002.

Breuning, Gerhard von. *Memories of Beethoven: from the house of the black-robed Spaniards.* Cambridge: Cambridge University Press, 1992.

Briscoe, James R., Editor. (Brief Description): *Debussy in performance.* New Haven: Yale University Press, 1999.

Brott, Alexander Betty Nygaard King. *Alexander Brott: my lives in music.* Oakville, Ontario; Niagara Falls, New York: Mosaic Press, 2005.

Brown, Alfred Peter. *The symphonic repertoire. Vol. 2, The first golden age of the Viennese symphony: Haydn, Mozart, Beethoven, and Schubert.* Bloomington, Indiana: Indiana University Press, 2002.

Brown, Maurice John Edwin. *Schubert: a critical biography.* London: Macmillan; New York: St. Martin's Press, 1958.

Broyles, Michael. *Beethoven: the emergence and evolution of Beethoven's heroic style.* New York: Excelsior Music Publishing Co., 1987.

Brubaker, Bruce and Jane Gottlieb, Editors. *Pianist, scholar, connoisseur: essays in honor of Jacob Lateiner.* Stuyvesant, N.Y., Pendragon Press, 2000.

Buch, Esteban. *Beethoven's Ninth: a political history.* Chicago; London: University of Chicago Press, 2003.

Burk, John N., Editor. *Letters of Richard Wagner: the Burrell collection.* London: Gollancz, 1951.

Burnham, Scott G. *Beethoven hero.* Princeton, New Jersey: Princeton University Press, 1995.

Burnham, Scott G and Michael P. Steinberg, Editors. *Beethoven and his world.* Princeton, New Jersey; Oxford: Princeton University Press, 2000.

Burton, William Westbrook, Editor. *Conversations about Bernstein.* New York; Oxford: Oxford University Press, 1995.

Busch, Fritz. *Pages from a musician's life.* London: Hogarth Press, 1953.

Busch, Hans, Editor. *Verdi's Aida: the history of an opera in letters and documents*. Minneapolis: University of Minnesota Press, 1978.

Busch, Hans, Editor. *Verdi's Falstaff in letters and contemporary reviews*. Bloomington: Indiana University Press, 1997.

Busch, Marie, Translator. *Memoirs of Eugenie Schumann*. London: W. Heinemann, 1927.

Bush, Alan Dudley. *In my eighth decade and other essays*. London: Kahn & Averill, 1980.

Busoni, Ferruccio. *Letters to his wife*. Translated by Rosamond Ley. New York: Da Capo Press, 1975.

Byron, Reginald. *Music, culture, & experience: selected papers of John Blacking*. Chicago: University of Chicago Press, 1995.

Cairns, David. *Responses: musical essays and reviews*. New York: Da Capo Press, 1980.

Cardus, Neville. *Talking of music*. London: Collins, 1957.

Carley, Lionel. *Delius: a life in letters*. London: Scolar Press in association with the Delius Trust, 1988.

Carley, Lionel. *Grieg and Delius: a chronicle of their friendship in letters*. London: Marion Boyars, 1993.

Carner, Mosco. *Major and minor*. London: Duckworth, 1980

Carner, Mosco. *Puccini: a critical biography*. London: Duckworth, 1958.

Carroll, Brendan G. *The last prodigy: a biography of Erich Wolfgang Korngold*. Portland, Oregon: Amadeus Press, 1997.

Carse, Adam von Ahn. *The life of Jullien: adventurer, showman-conductor and establisher of the Promenade Concerts in England, together with a history of those concerts up to 1895*. Cambridge England: Heffer, 1951.

Carse, Adam von Ahn. *The orchestra from Beethoven to Berlioz: a history of the orchestra in the first half of the 19th century, and of the development of orchestral baton-conducting*. Cambridge: W. Heffer, 1948.

Casals, Pablo. *Joys and sorrows: reflections by Pablo Casals as told to Albert E. Kahn*. London: Macdonald, 1970.

Casals, Pablo. *The memoirs of Pablo Casals as told to Thomas Dozier*. London: Life en Español, 1959.

Chappell, Paul. *Dr. S. S. Wesley, 1810–1876: portrait of a Victorian musician*. Great Wakering: Mayhew-McCrimmon, 1977.

Chasins, Abram. *Leopold Stokowski, a profile*. New York: Hawthorn Books, 1979.

Charlton, Davi, Editor and Martyn Clarke Translator. *E.T.A. Hoffmann's musical writings: Kreisleriana, The Poet and the Composer*. Cambridge: Cambridge University Press, 1989.

Chávez, Carlos. *Musical thought*. Cambridge: Harvard University Press, 1961.

Chesterman, Robert, Editor. *Conversations with conductors: Bruno Walter, Sir Adrian Boult, Leonard Bernstein, Ernest Ansermet, Otto Klemperer, Leopold Stokowski*. Totowa, New Jersey: Rowman and Littlefield, 1976.

Chissell, Joan. *Clara Schumann: a dedicated spirit; a study of her life and work*. London: Hamilton, 1983.

Chua, Daniel K. L. *The "Galitzin" quartets of Beethoven: Opp.127, 132, 130*. Princeton: Princeton University Press, 1995.

Citron, Marcia, Editor. *The letters of Fanny Hensel to Felix Mendelssohn*. Stuyvesant, New York: Pendragon Press, 1987.

Clark, Walter Aaron. *Enrique Granados: poet of the piano*. Oxford, England; New York, N.Y.: Oxford University Press, 2006.

Clark, Walter Aaron. *Isaac Albéniz: portrait of a romantic*. Oxford; New York: Oxford University Press, 1999.

Clive, Peter. *Beethoven and his world*. Oxford University Press, 2001.

Closson, Ernest. *History of the piano*. Translated by Delano Ames and edited by Robin Golding. London: Paul Elek, 1947.

Cockshoot, John V. *The fugue in Beethoven's piano music*. London: Routledge & Kegan Paul, 1959.

Coe, Richard N, Translator. *Life of Rossini by Stendhal*. London: Calder & Boyars, 1970.

Coleman, Alexander, Editor. *Diversions & animadversions: essays from The new criterion*. New Brunswick, New Jersey; London: Transaction Publishers, 2005.

Colerick, George. *From the Italian girl to Cabaret: musical humour, parody and burlesque*. London: Juventus, 1998.

Coleridge, A. D. *Life of Moscheles, with selections from his diaries and correspondence by his wife*. London: Hurst & Blackett, 1873.

Colles, Henry Cope. *Essays and lectures*. London: Humphrey Milford, Oxford University Press, 1945.

Cone, Edward T., Editor. *Roger Sessions on music: collected essays*. Princeton, New Jersey: Princeton University Press, 1979.

Cone, Edward T. *The composer's voice*. Berkeley; London: University of California Press, 1974.

Cook, Susan and Judy S. Tsou, Editors. *Cecilia reclaimed: feminist perspectives on gender and music*. Urbana: University of Illinois Press, 1994.

Cooper, Barry. *Beethoven*: The master musicians series. Oxford: Oxford University Press, 2000.

Cooper, Barry. *Beethoven and the creative process*. Oxford: Clarendon Press, 1990.

Cooper, Barry. *Beethoven's folksong settings: chronology, sources, style*. Cambridge: Cambridge University Press, 1991.

Cooper, Barry. *The Beethoven compendium: a guide to Beethoven's life and music*. London: Thames and Hudson, 1991.

Cooper, Martin. *Beethoven: the last decade, 1817–1827*. London: Oxford University Press, 1970.

Cooper, Martin. *Judgements of value: selected writings on music*. Oxford; New York: Oxford University Press, 1988.

Cooper, Martin. *Ideas and music*. London: Barrie and Rockliff, 1965.

Cooper, Victoria L. *The house of Novello: the practice and policy of a Victorian music publisher, 1829–1866*. Aldershot, Hants: Ashgate, 2003.

Coover, James. *Music at auction: Puttick and Simpson (of London), *1794–1971: being an annotated, chronological list of sales of musical materials*. Warren, Michigan: Harmonie Park Press, 1988.

Copland, Aaron. *Copland on music*. London: Deutsch, 1961.

Corredor, J. Ma. *Conversations with Casals*. London: Hutchinson, 1956.

Cott, Jonathan. *Stockhausen: conversations with the composer*. London: Picador, 1974.

Cottrell, Stephen. *Professional music making in London: ethnography and experience*. Aldershot: Ashgate, 2004.

Cowell, Henry. *Charles Ives and his music*. New York: Oxford University Press, 1955.

Cowling, Elizabeth. *The cello*. London: Batsford, 1983.

Crabbe, John. *Beethoven's empire of the mind*. Newbury: Lovell Baines, 1982.

Craft, Robert. *An improbable life: memoirs*. Nashville: Vanderbilt University Press, 2002.

Craft, Robert, Editor. *Stravinsky: selected correspondence*. London: Faber and Faber, 3 Vols. 1982–1985.

Craw, Howard Allen. *A biography and thematic catalog of the works of J. L. Dussek: 1760–1812*. Ann Arbor: Michigan, 1965.

Crawford, Richard, R. Allen Lott and Carol J. Oja, Editors. *A Celebration of American music: words and music in honor of H. Wiley Hitchcock*. Ann Arbor: University of Michigan Press, 1990.

Craxton, Harold and Tovey, Donald Francis. *Beethoven: Sonatas for Pianoforte*. London: The Associated Board, [1931].

Crichton, Ronald: Editor. *The memoirs of Ethel Smyth*. New York: Viking, 1987.

Crist, Stephen A. and Roberta M. Marvin, Editors. *Historical musicology: sources, methods, interpretations*. Rochester, New York: University of Rochester Press, 2004.

Crofton, Ian and Donald Fraser, Editors. *A dictionary of musical quotations*. London: Croom Helm, 1985.

Crompton, Louis, Editor. *Shaw, Bernard: The great composers: reviews and bombardments*. Berkeley; London: University of California Press, 1978.

Csicserry-Ronay, Elizabeth, Translator and Editor. *Hector Berlioz: The art of music and other essays: (A travers chants)*. Bloomington: Indiana University Press, 1994.

Curtiss, Mina Kirstein. *Bizet and his world*. London: Secker & Warburg, 1959.

Cuyler, Louise Elvira. *The symphony*. New York: Harcourt Brace Jovanovich, 1973.

Dahlhaus, Carl. *Ludwig van Beethoven: approaches to his music*. Oxford: Clarendon Press, 1991.

Dahlhaus, Carl. *Nineteenth-century music*. Translated by J. Bradford Robinson. Berkeley; London: University of California Press, 1989.

Daniels, Robin. *Conversations with Cardus*. London: Gollancz, 1976.

Daniels, Robin. Conversations with Menuhin. London: Macdonald General Books, 1979.

Day, James. *Vaughan Williams*. London: Dent, 1961.

Davies, Peter Maxwell. *Studies from two decades*. Selected and introduced by Stephen Pruslin. London: Boosey & Hawkes, 1979.

Dean, Winton. *Georges Bizet: his life and work*. London: J.M. Dent, 1965.

Deas, Stewart. *In defence of Hanslick*. London: Williams and Norgate, 1940.

Debussy, Claude. *Debussy on music*. London: Secker & Warburg, 1977.

Delbanco, Nicholas. *The Beaux Arts Trio*. London: Gollancz, 1985.

Demény, Janos, Editor. *Béla Bartók: letters*. London: Faber and Faber, 1971.

Dent, Edward Joseph. *Selected essays*. Edited by Hugh Taylor. Cambridge; New York: Cambridge University Press, 1979.

Deutsch, Otto Erich. *Mozart: a documentary biography*. London: Adam & Charles Black, 1965.

Deutsch, Otto Erich. *Schubert: a documentary biography*. London: J.M. Dent, 1946

Deutsch, Otto Erich. *Schubert: memoirs by his friends*. London: Adam & Charles Black, 1958.

Dibble, Jeremy. *C. Hubert H. Parry: his life and music*. Oxford: Clarendon Press, 1992.

Dibble, Jeremy. *Charles Villiers Stanford: man and musician*. Oxford: Oxford University Press, 2002.

Donakowski, Conrad L. *A muse for the masses: ritual and music in an age of democratic revolution, 1770-1870*. Chicago: University of Chicago Press, 1977.

Dower, Catherine. *Alfred Einstein on music: selected music criticisms*. New York: Greenwood Press, 1991.

Downs, Philip G. *Classical music: the era of Haydn, Mozart, and Beethoven*. New York: W.W. Norton, 1992.

Drabkin, William. *Beethoven: Missa Solemnis*. Cambridge: Cambridge University Press, 1991.

Dreyfus, Kay. *The farthest north of humanness: letters of Percy Grainger, 1901-1914*. South Melbourne; Basingstoke: Macmillan, 1985.

Dubal, David, Editor. *Remembering Horowitz: 125 pianists recall a legend*. New York: Schirmer Books, 1993.

Dubal, David. *The world of the concert pianist*. London: Victor Gollancz, 1985.

Dvorák, Otakar. *Antonín Dvorák, my father*. Spillville, Iowa: Czech Historical Research Center, 1993.

Dyson, George. *The progress of music*. London: Oxford University Press, Humphrey Milford, 1932.

Eastaugh, Kenneth. *Havergal Brian: the making of a composer*. London: Harrap, 1976.

Edwards, Allen. *Flawed words and stubborn sounds: a conversation with Elliott Carter*. New York: Norton & Company, 1971.

Edwards, Frederick George. *Musical haunts in London*. London: J. Curwen & Sons, 1895.

Ehrlich, Cyril. *First philharmonic: a history of the Royal Philharmonic Society*. Oxford: Clarendon Press, 1995.

Einstein, Alfred. *A short history of music*. London: Cassell and Company Ltd., 1948.

Einstein, Alfred. *Essays on music*. London: Faber and Faber, 1958.

Einstein, Alfred. *Mozart: his character, his work*. London: Cassell and Company Ltd., 1946.

Einstein, Alfred. *Music in the Romantic era*. London: J.M. Dent Ltd., 1947.

Ekman, Karl. *Jean Sibelius, his life and personality*. New York: Tudor Publishing. Co., 1945.

Elgar, Edward. *A future for English music: and other lectures*, Edited by Percy M. Young. London: Dobson, 1968.

Elkin, Robert. *Queen's Hall, 1893–1941*. London: Rider, 1944.

Ella, John. *Musical sketches, abroad and at home: with original music by Mozart, Czerny, Graun, etc., vocal cadenzas and other musical illustrations*. London: Ridgway, Vol. 1., 1869.

Ellis, William Ashton. *The family letters of Richard Wagner*. Edited and translated by William Ashton Ellis and enlarged with introduction and notes by John Deathridge. Basingstoke: Macmillan, 1991.

Ellis, William Ashton. *Richard Wagner's prose works: Vol. 1, The art-work of the future*. Edited and translated by William Ashton Ellis. London: Kegan Paul, Trench, Trübner, 1895.

Ellis, William Ashton. *Richard Wagner's prose works: Vol. 2, Opera and drama*. Edited and translated by William Ashton Ellis. London: Kegan Paul, Trench, Trübner, 1900.

Ellis, William Ashton. *Richard Wagner's prose works: Vol. 3, The theatre*. Edited and translated by William Ashton Ellis. London: Kegan Paul, Trench, Trübner, 1907.

Ellis, William Ashton. *Richard Wagner's prose works: Vol. 4, Art and politics*. Edited and translated by William Ashton Ellis. London: Kegan Paul, Trench, Trübner, 1895.

Ellis, William Ashton. *Richard Wagner's prose works: Vol. 5, Actors and singers*. Edited and translated by William Ashton Ellis. London: Kegan Paul, Trench, Trübner, 1896.

Ellis, William Ashton. *Richard Wagner's prose works: Vol. 6, Religion and art*. Edited and translated by William Ashton Ellis. London: Kegan Paul, Trench, Trübner, 1897.

Ellis, William Ashton. *Richard Wagner's prose works: Vol. 7, In Paris and Dresden*. Edited and translated by William Ashton Ellis. London: Kegan Paul, Trench, Trübner, 1898.

Ellis, William Ashton. *Richard Wagner's prose works: Vol. 8, Posthumous*. Edited and translated by William Ashton Ellis. London: Kegan Paul, Trench, Trübner, 1899.

Elterlein, Ernst von. *Beethoven's pianoforte sonatas: explained for the lovers of the musical art*. London: W. Reeves, 1898.

Engel, Carl. *Musical myths and facts*. London: Novello, Ewer & Co.; New York: J.L. Peters, 1876.

Eosze, László. *Zoltán Kodály: his life and work*. London: Collet's, 1962.

Etter, Brian K. *From classicism to modernism: Western musical culture and the metaphysics of order*. Aldershot: Ashgate, 2001.

Ewen, David. *From Bach to Stravinsky: the history of music by its foremost critics. New York, Greenwood Press, 1968.

Ewen, David. *Romain Rolland's Essays on music*. New York: Dover Publications, 1959.

Fay, Amy. *Music-study in Germany: from the home correspondence of Amy Fay*. New York: Dover Publications, 1965.

Fenby, Eric. *Delius as I knew him*. London: Quality Press, 1936.

Ferguson, Donald Nivison. *Masterworks of the orchestral repertoire: a guide for listeners*. Minneapolis: University of Minnesota Press, 1954.

Fétis, François-Joseph. *Curiosités historiques de la musique: complément nécessaire de la Musique mise à la portée de tout le monde*. Paris: Janet et Cotelle, 1830.

Fifield, Christopher. *Max Bruch: his life and works*. London: Gollancz, 1988.

Fifield, Christopher. *True artist and true friend: a biography of Hans Richter*. Oxford: Clarendon Press, 1993.

Finson, Jon and R. Larry Todd, Editors. *Mendelssohn and Schumann: essays on their music and its context*. Durham, N.C.: Duke University Press, 1984.

Fischer, Edwin. *Beethoven's pianoforte sonatas: a guide for students & amateurs*. London: Faber and Faber, 1959.

Fischer, Edwin. *Reflections on music*. London: Williams and Norgate, 1951.

Fischer, Hans Conrad and Erich Kock. *Ludwig van Beethoven: a study in text and pictures*. London: Macmillan; New York, St. Martin's Press, 1972.

Fischmann, Zdenka E. *Janáček-Newmarch correspondence*. 1st limited and numbered edition. Rockville, MD: Kabel Publishers, 1986.

Fitzlyon, April. *Maria Malibran: diva of the romantic age*. London: Souvenir Press, 1987.

FitzLyon, April. *The price of genius: a life of Pauline Viardot*. London: John Calder, 1964.

Forbes, Elliot, Editor. *Thayer's life of Beethoven*. Princeton, New Jersey: Princeton University Press, 1967.

Foreman, Lewis. *Bax: a composer and his times*. London: Scolar Press, 1983.

Foreman, Lewis, Editor. *Farewell, my youth, and other writings by Arnold Bax*. Aldershot: Scolar Press, 1992.

Foster, Myles Birket. *History of the Philharmonic Society of London, 1813–1912: a record of a hundred years' work in the cause of music*. London: Bodley Head, 1912.

Foulds, John. *Music today: its heritage from the past, and legacy to the future*. London: I. Nicholson and Watson, limited, 1934.

Frank, Mortimer H. *Arturo Toscanini: the NBC years*. Portland, Oregon: Amadeus Press, 2002.

Fraser, Andrew Alastair. *Essays on music*. London: Oxford University Press, H. Milford, 1930.

Frohlich, Martha. *Beethoven's Appassionata' sonata*. Oxford: Clarendon Press, 1991.

Gal, Hans. *The golden age of Vienna*. London: Max Parrish & Co. Limited, 1948.

Gal, Hans. *The musician's world:*

great composers in their letters. London: Thames and Hudson, 1965.

Galatopoulos, Stelios. *Bellini: life, times, music*. London: Sanctuary, 2002.

Garden, Edward and Nigel Gottrei, Editors. *'To my best friend': correspondence between Tchaikovsky and Nadezhda von Meck, 1876–1878*. Oxford: Clarendon Press, 1993.

Geck, Martin. Beethoven. London: Haus, 2003.

Gerig, Reginald. *Famous pianists & their technique*. Washington: R. B. Luce, 1974.

Gilliam, Bryan. *The life of Richard Strauss*. Cambridge: Cambridge University Press, 1999.

Gilliam, Bryan, Editor. *Richard Strauss and his world*. Princeton, New Jersey: Princeton University Press, 1992.

Gillies, Malcolm and Bruce Clunies Ross, Editors. *Grainger on music*. Oxford; New York: Oxford University Press, 1999.

Gillies, Malcolm and David Pear, Editors. *The all-round man: selected letters of Percy Grainger, 1914–1961*. Oxford: Clarendon Press, 1994.

Gillies, Malcolm, Editor. *The Bartók companion*. London: Faber and Faber, 1993.

Gillmor, Alan M. *Erik Satie*. Basingstoke: Macmillan Press, 1988.

Glehn, M. E. *Goethe and Mendelssohn : (1821–1831)*. London: Macmillan, 1874.

Glowacki, John, Editor. *Paul A. Pisk: Essays in his honor*. Austin, Texas: University of Texas, 1966

Gollancz, Victor. *Journey towards music: a memoir*. London: Victor Gollancz Ltd., 1964.

Good, Edwin Marshall. *Giraffes, black dragons, and other pianos: a technological history from Cristofori to the modern concert grand*. Stanford, California: Stanford University Press, 1982.

Gordon, David. *Musical visitors to Britain*. London: Routledge, 2005.

Gordon, Stewart. *A history of keyboard literature: music for the piano and its forerunners*. Schirmer Books: New York: London : Prentice Hall International, 1996.

Gorrell, Lorraine. *The nineteenth-century German lied*. Portland, Oregon: Amadeus Press, 1993.

Goss, Glenda D. *Jean Sibelius: the Hämeenlinna letters: scenes from a musical life, 1875–1895*. Esbo, Finland: Schildts, 1997.

Goss, Madeleine. *Bolero: the life of Maurice Ravel*. New York: Tudor, 1945.

Gotch, Rosamund Brunel, Editor. *Mendelssohn and his friends in Kensington: letters from Fanny and Sophy Horsley, written 1833–36*. London: Oxford University Press, 1938.

Gounod, Charles. *Charles Gounod; autobiographical reminiscences: with family letters and notes on music; from the French*. London: William Heinemann, 1896.

Grabs, Manfred, Editor. *Hanns Eisler: a rebel in music; selected writings*. Berlin: Seven Seas Publishers, 1978.

Grace, Harvey. *A musician at large*. London: Oxford University Press, H. Milford, 1928.

(La) Grange, Henry-Louis de. *Gustav Mahler*. Oxford: Oxford University Press, 1995.

Graves, Charles L. *Hubert Parry: his life and works*. London: Macmillan, 1926.

Graves, Charles L. *Post-Victorian music: with other studies and sketches*. London: Macmillan and Co., limited, 1911.

Graves, Charles L. *The life & letters of Sir George Grove, Hon. D.C.L. (Durham), Hon. LL.D. (Glasgow), formerly director of the Royal college of music*. London: Macmillan and Co., Ltd.; New York: The Macmillan Co., 1903.

Gray, Cecil. *Musical chairs, or, between two stools: being the life and memoirs of Cecil Gray*. London: Home & Van Thal, 1948.

Gregor-Dellin and Dietrich Mack, Editors. *Cosima Wagner's diaries.: Vol. 1, 1869 – 1877*. London: Collins, 1978-1980.

Griffiths, Paul. *Modern music: the avant-garde since 1945*. London: J. M. Dent & Sons Ltd., 1981.

Griffiths, Paul. *Olivier Messiaen and the music of time*. London: Faber and Faber, 1985.

Griffiths, Paul. *Peter Maxwell Davies*. London: Robson Books, 1988.

Griffiths, Paul. *The sea on fire: Jean Barraqué*. Rochester, New York: Woodbridge: University of Rochester Press, 2003.

Griffiths, Paul. *The string quartet*. London: Thames and Hudson, 1983.

Grout, Donald Jay and Claude V. Palisca, Editors. *A history of Western music*. London: J. M. Dent, 1988.

Grove, George. *Beethoven and his nine symphonies*. London: Novello, Ewer, 1896.

Grover, Ralph Scott. *Ernest Chausson: the man and his music*. London: The Athlone Press, 1980.

Grover, Ralph Scott. *The music of Edmund Rubbra*. Aldershot: Scolar Press, 1993.

Grun, Bernard. *Alban Berg: letters to his wife*. Edited and translated by Bernard Grun. London: Faber and Faber, 1971.

Gutman, David. *Prokofiev*. London: Omnibus Press, 1990.

Hadow, William Henry. *Collected essays*. London: H. Milford at the Oxford University Press, 1928.

Hadow, William Henry. *Beethoven's Op. 18 Quartets*. London: H. Milford at the Oxford University Press, 1926.

Haggin, Bernard H. *Music observed*. New York: Oxford University Press, 1964.

Hailey, Christopher. *Franz Schreker, 1878–1934: a cultural biography*. Cambridge: Cambridge University Press, 1993.

Hall, Michael. *Leaving home: a conducted tour of twentieth-century music with Simon Rattle*. London: Faber and Faber, 1996.

Hall, Patricia and Friedemann Sallis, Editors. (Brief Description): *A handbook to twentieth-century musical sketches*. Cambridge: Cambridge University Press, 2004.

Hallé, C. E. *Life and letters of Sir Charles Hallé: being an autobiography (1819–1860) with correspondence and diaries*. London: Smith, Elder & Co., 1896.

Halstead, Jill. *The woman composer: creativity and the gendered politics of musical composition.* Aldershot: Ashgate, 1997.

Hamburger, Michael, Editor and Translator. *Beethoven letters, journals, and conversations.* New York: Thames and Hudson, 1951.

Hammelmann, Hanns A. and Ewald Osers. *The correspondence between Richard Strauss and Hugo von Hofmannsthal.* London: Collins, 1961.

Hanson, Lawrence and Elisabeth Hanson. *Tchaikovsky: the man behind the music.* New York: Dodd, Mead & Co, 1967.

Harding, James. *Massenet.* London: J. M. Dent & Sons Ltd., 1970.

Harding, James. *Saint-Saëns and his circle.* London: Chapman & Hall, 1965.

Harding, Rosamond E. M. *Origins of musical time and expression.* London: Oxford University Press, 1938.

Harman, Alec with Anthony Milner and Wilfrid Mellers. *Man and his music: the story of musical experience in the West.* London: Barrie & Jenkins, 1988.

Harper, Nancy Lee. *Manuel de Falla: his life and music.* Lanham, Maryland; London: The Scarecrow Press, 2005.

Hartmann, Arthur. *'Claude Debussy as I knew him' and other writings of Arthur Hartmann.* Edited by Samuel Hsu, Sidney Grolnic, and Mark Peters. Rochester, New York; Woodbridge: University of Rochester Press, 2003.

Haugen, Einar and Camilla Cai. *Ole Bull: Norway's romantic musician and cosmopolitan patriot.* Madison: The University of Wisconsin Press, 1993.

Headington, Christopher. *The Bodley Head history of Western music.* London: The Bodley Head, 1974.

Heartz, Daniel. *Music in European capitals: the galant style, 1720–1780.* New York; London: W. W. Norton, 2003.

Hedley, Arthur, Editor. *Selected correspondence of Fryderyk Chopin: abridged from Fryderyk Chopin's correspondence.* London: Heinemann, 1962.

Heiles, Anne Mischakoff. *Mischa Mischakoff: journeys of a concertmaster.* Sterling Heights, Michigan: Harmonie Park Press, 2006.

Henderson, Sanya Shoilevska. *Alex North, film composer: a biography, with musical analyses of a Streetcar named desire, Spartacus, The misfits, Under the volcano, and Prizzi's honor.* Jefferson, N.C.; London: McFarland, 2003.

Henschel, George. *Personal recollections of Johannes Brahms: some of his letters to and pages from a journal kept by George Henschel.* Boston: R G. Badger, 1907.

Henze, Hans Werner. *Bohemian fifths: an autobiography.* London: Faber and Faber, 1998.

Henze, Hans Werner. *Music and politics: collected writings 1953–81.* London: Faber and Faber, 1982.

Herbert, May, Translator. *Early letters of Robert Schumann.* London: George Bell and Sons, 1888.

Heyman, Barbara B. *Samuel Barber:*

the composer and his music. New York: Oxford University Press, 1992.

Heyworth, Peter. *Otto Klemperer, his life and times.* Cambridge: Cambridge University Press, 2 Vols. 1983–1996.

Hildebrandt, Dieter. *Pianoforte: a social history of the piano.* London: Hutchinson, 1988.

Hill, Peter. *The Messiaen companion.* London: Faber and Faber, 1995.

Hill, Peter and Nigel Simeone. *Messiaen.* New Haven Connecticut; London: Yale University Press, 2005.

Hiller, Ferdinand. *Mendelssohn: Letters and recollections.* New York: Vienna House, 1972.

Hines, Robert Stephan. *The orchestral composer's point of view: essays on twentieth-century music by those who wrote it.* Norman: University of Oklahoma Press, 1970.

Ho, Allan B. *Shostakovich reconsidered.* London: Toccata Press, 1998.

Hodeir, André. *Since Debussy: a view of contemporary music.* New York: Da Capo Press, 1975.

Holmes, Edward. *The life of Mozart: including his correspondence.* London: Chapman and Hall, 1845.

Holmes, John L. *Composers on composers.* New York: Greenwood Press, 1990.

Hopkins, Anthony. *The concertgoer's companion.* London: J.M. Dent & Sons Ltd., 1984.

Hopkins, Anthony. *The seven concertos of Beethoven.* Aldershot: Scolar Press, 1996.

Holt, Richard. *Nicolas Medtner (1879–1951): a tribute to his art and personality.* London: D. Dobson, 1955.

Honegger, Arthur. *I am a composer.* London: Faber and Faber, 1966.

Hoover, Kathleen and John Cage. *Virgil Thomson: his life and music.* New York; London: T. Yoseloff, 1959.

Horgan, Paul. *Encounters with Stravinsky: a personal record.* London: The Bodley Head, 1972.

Horowitz, Joseph. *Conversations with Arrau.* London: Collins, 1982.

Horowitz, Joseph. Understanding Toscanini. London: Faber and Faber, 1987.

Horwood, Wally. *Adolphe Sax, 1814–1894: his life and legacy.* Bramley: Bramley Books, 1980.

Howie, Crawford. *Anton Bruckner: a documentary biography.* Lewiston, N.Y.; Lampeter: Edwin Mellen Press, 2002.

Hueffer, Francis. *Correspondence of Wagner and Liszt.* New York: Greenwood Press, 2 Vols.1969.

Hughes, Spike. *The Toscanini legacy: a critical study of Arturo Toscanini's performances of Beethoven, Verdi, and other composers.* London: Putnam, 1959.

Hullah, Annette. *Theodor Leschetizky.* London and New York: J. Land & Co., 1906.

Le Huray, Peter and James Day, Editors. *Music and aesthetics in the eighteenth and early-nineteenth centuries.* Cambridge: Cambridge University Press, 1988.

D'Indy, Vincent. *César Franck.* New York: Dover Publications, 1965.

Jacobs, Arthur. *Arthur Sullivan: A*

Victorian musician. Aldershot: Scolar Press, 1992.

Jahn, Otto. *Life of Mozart*. London: Novello, Ewer & Co., 1882.

Jefferson, Alan. *Sir Thomas Beecham: a centenary tribute*. London: World Records Ltd., 1979.

Jezic, Diane. *The musical migration and Ernst Toch*. Ames: Iowa State University Press, 1989.

Johnson, Douglas Porter, Editor. *The Beethoven sketchbooks: history, reconstruction, inventory.*

Oxford: Clarendon, 1985.

Johnson, Stephen. *Bruckner remembered*. London: Faber and Faber, 1998.

Jones, David, Wyn. *Beethoven: Pastoral symphony*. Cambridge: Cambridge University Press, 1995.

Jones, David Wyn. *The life of Beethoven*. Cambridge: Cambridge University Press, 1998.

Jones, David Wyn. *The symphony in Beethoven's Vienna*. Cambridge: Cambridge University Press, 2006.

Jones, J. Barrie, Editor. *Gabriel Fauré: a life in letters*. London: Batsford, 1989.

Jones, Peter Ward, Editor and Translator. *The Mendelssohns on honeymoon: the 1837 diary of Felix and Cécile Mendelssohn Bartholdy, together with letters to their families*. Oxford: Clarendon Press, 1997.

Jones, Timothy. *Beethoven, the Moonlight and other sonatas, Op. 27 and Op. 31*. Cambridge; New York, N.Y.: Cambridge University Press, 1999.

Kalischer, A. C., Editor. *Beethoven's letters: a critical edition*. London: J. M. Dent, 1909.

Kárpáti, János. *Bartók's chamber music*. Stuyvesant, New York: Pendragon Press, 1994.

Keefe, Simon P. *The Cambridge companion to the concerto*. Cambridge, New York, N.Y.: Cambridge University Press, 2005.

Keller, Hans. *The great Haydn quartets: their interpretation*. London: J. M. Dent, 1986.

Keller, Hans, Editor. *The memoirs of Carl Flesch*. New York: Macmillan, 1958.

Keller, Hans, and Christopher Wintle. *Beethoven's string quartets in F minor, Op. 95 and C minor, Op. 131: two studies*. Nottingham: Department of Music, University of Nottingham, 1995.

Kelly, Thomas Forrest. *First nights at the opera: five musical premiers*. New Haven: Yale University Press, 2004.

Kennedy, Michael. *Adrian Boult*. London: Hamish Hamilton, 1987.

Kennedy, Michael. *Barbirolli, conductor laureate: the authorised biography*. London: Hart-Davis, MacGibbon, 1973.

Kennedy, Michael, Editor. *The autobiography of Charles Hallé; with correspondence and diaries.*

London: Paul Elek, 1972.

Kennedy, Michael. *Hallé tradition: a century of music*. Manchester: Manchester University Press, 1960.

Kennedy, Michael. *The works of Ralph Vaughan Williams*. London: Oxford University Press, 1964.

Kemp, Ian. *Tippett: the composer and his music*. London; New York: Eulenburg Books, 1984.

Kerman, Joseph. *The Beethoven quartets.* London: Oxford University Press, 1967, c1966.

Kerman, Joseph. *Write all these down: essays on music.* Berkeley, California; London: University of California Press, 1994.

Kildea, Paul, Editor. *Britten on music.* Oxford: Oxford University Press, 2003.

Kinderman, William. *Beethoven.* Oxford: Oxford University Press, 1997.

Kinderman, William. *Beethoven's Diabelli variations.* Oxford: Clarendon Press; New York: Oxford University Press, 1987.

Kinderman, William, Editor. *The string quartets of Beethoven.* Urbana, Ilinois: University of Illinois Press, 2005.

King, Alec Hyatt. *Musical pursuits: selected essays.* London: British Library, 1987.

Kirby, F. E. *Music for piano: a short history.* Amadeus Press: Portland, 1995.

Kirkpatrick, John, Editor. *Charles E. Ives: Memos.* New York: W.W. Norton, 1972.

Knapp, Raymond. *Brahms and the challenge of the symphony.* Stuyvesant, N.Y.: Pendragon Press, c.1997.

Knight, Frida. *Cambridge music: from the Middle Ages to modern times.* Cambridge, England.: New York: Oleander Press, 1980.

Knight, Max, Translator. *A confidential matter: the letters of Richard Strauss and Stefan Zweig, 1931–1935.* Berkeley; London: University of California Press, 1977.

Kok, Alexander. *A voice in the dark: the philharmonia years.* Ampleforth: Emerson Edition, 2002.

Kopelson, Kevin. *Beethoven's kiss: pianism, perversion, and the mastery of desire.* Stanford, California: Stanford University Press, 1996.

Kostelanetz, Richard, Editor. *Aaron Copland: a reader; selected writings 1923–1972.* New York; London: Routledge, 2003.

Kostelanetz, Richard. *Conversing with Cage.* New York; London: Routledge, 2003.

Kostelanetz, Richard. *On innovative musicians.* New York: Limelight Editions, 1989.

Kostelanetz, Richard, Editor. *Virgil Thomson: a reader ; selected writings, 1924–1984.* New York; London: Routledge, 2002.

Kowalke, Kim H. *Kurt Weill in Europe.* Ann Arbor, Michigan: UMI Research Press, 1979.

Krehbiel, Henry Edward. *The pianoforte and its music.* New York: Cooper Square Publishers, 1971.

Kruseman, Philip, Editor. *Beethoven's own words.* London: Hinrichsen Edition, 1948.

Kurtz, Michael. *Stockhausen: a biography.* London: Faber and Faber, 1992.

Lam, Basil. *Beethoven string quartets.* Seattle: University of Washington Press, 1975.

Lambert, Constant. *Music ho!: a study of music in decline.* London: Faber and Faber, Ltd. 1934.

Landon, H. C. Robbins. *Beethoven: a documentary study.* London: Thames and Hudson, 1970.

Landon, H. C. Robbins. *Beethoven: his life, work and world.*

Landon, H. C. Robbins. *Essays on the Viennese classical style: Gluck, Haydn, Mozart, Beethoven.* London: Barrie & Rockliff The Cresset Press, 1970.

Landon, H. C. Robbins. *Haydn: chronicle and works/Haydn, the late years, 1801–1809.* Bloomington: Indiana University Press, 1977.

Landon, H. C. Robbins. *Haydn: his life and music.* London: Thames and Hudson, 1988.

Landon, H. C. Robbins. *Haydn in England, 1791–1795.* London: Thames and Hudson, 1976.

Landon, H. C. Robbins. *Haydn: the years of 'The creation', 1796–800.* London: Thames and Hudson, 1977.

Landon, H. C. Robbins. *Mozart: the golden years, 1781–1791.* New York: Schirmer Books, 1989.

Landon, H. C. Robbins. *1791, Mozart's last year.* London: Thames and Hudson, 1988.

Landon, H. C. Robbins *The collected correspondence and London notebooks of Joseph Haydn.* London: Barrie and Rockliff, 1959.

Landon, H. C. Robbins: Editor. *The Mozart companion. London: Faber, 1956.*

Landowska, Wanda. *Music of the past.* London: Geoffrey Bles, 1926.

Lang, Paul Henry. *Musicology and performance.* New Haven: Yale University Press, 1997.

Lang, Paul Henry. *The creative world of Beethoven.* New York: W. W. Norton 1971.

Laurence, Dan H., Editor. *Shaw's music: the complete musical criticism in three volumes.* London: Max Reinhardt, the Bodley Head, 1981.

Lawford-Hinrichsen, Irene. *Music publishing and patronage: C. F. Peters, 1800 to the Holocaust.* Kenton: Edition Press, 2000.

Layton, Robert, Editor. *A guide to the concerto.* Oxford: Oxford University Press, 1996.

Layton, Robert, Editor. *A guide to the symphony.* Oxford: Oxford University Press, 1995.

Lebrecht, Norman. *The maestro myth: great conductors in pursuit of power.* London: Simon & Schuster, 1991.

Lee, Ernest Markham. *The story of the symphony.* London: Scott Publishing Co., 1916.

Leibowitz, Herbert A., Editor. *Musical impressions: selections from Paul Rosenfeld's criticism.* London: G. Allen & Unwin, 1970.

Lenrow, Elbert, Editor and Translator. *The letters of Richard Wagner to Anton Pusinelli.* New York: Vienna House, 1972.

Leonard, Maurice. *Kathleen: the life of Kathleen Ferrier: 1912–1953.* London: Hutchinson, 1988.

Lesure, François and Roger Nichols, Editors. *Debussy, letters.* London: Faber and Faber, 1987.

Letellier, Robert Ignatius, Editor and Translator. *The diaries of Giacomo Meyerbeer.* Madison: Fairleigh Dickinson University Press; London: Associated University Presses, 4 Vols., 1999–2004.

Levas, Santeri. *Sibelius: a personal portrait.* London: J. M. Dent, 1972.

Levy, Alan Howard. *Edward MacDowell, an American master.* Lanham, Md. & London: Scarecrow Press, 1998.

Levy, David Benjamin. *Beethoven: the Ninth Symphony.* New Haven, Connecticut; London: Yale University Press, 2003.

Leyda, Jay and Sergi Bertensson. *The Musorgsky reader: a life of Modeste Petrovich Musorgsky in letters and documents.* New York: W.W. Norton, 1947.

Lewis, Thomas P., Editor. *Raymond Leppard on music: an anthology of critical and personal writings.* White Plains, N.Y.: Pro/Am Music Resources, 1993.

Liébert, Georges. *Nietzsche and music.* Chicago: University of Chicago Press, 2004.

Liszt, Franz. *An artist's journey: lettres d'un bachelier ès musique, 1835–1841.* Chicago: University of Chicago Press, 1989.

Litzmann, Berthold, Editor. *Clara Schumann: an artist's life, based on material found in diaries and letters.* London: Macmillan; Leipzig: Breitkopf & Härtel, 2 Vols. 1913.

Litzmann, Berthold, Editor. *Letters of Clara Schumann and Johannes Brahms, 1853–1896.* New York, Vienna House. 2 Vols. 1971.

Lloyd, Stephen. *William Walton: muse of fire.* Woodbridge, Suffolk: The Boydell Press, 2001.

Locke, Ralph P. and Cyrilla Barr, Editors. *Cultivating music in America: women patrons and activists since 1860.* Berkeley: University of California Press, 1997.

Lockspeiser, Edward. *Debussy: his life and mind.* London: Cassell. 2 Vols. 1962–1965.

Lockspeiser, Edward. *The literary clef: an anthology of letters and writings by French composers.* London: J. Calder. 1958.

Lockwood, Lewis, Editor. *Beethoven essays: studies in honor of Elliot Forbes.* Cambridge, Massachusetts: Harvard University Department of Music: Distributed by Harvard University Press, 1984.

Lockwood, Lewis and Mark Kroll, Editors. *The Beethoven violin sonatas: history, criticism, performance.* Urbana: University of Illinois Press, 2004.

Loft, Abram. *Violin and keyboard: the duo repertoire.* New York: Grossman Publishers. 2 Vols. 1973.

Longyear, Rey Morgan. *Nineteenth-century romanticism in music.* Englewood Cliffs: Prentice-Hall, 1969.

Lowe, C. Egerton. *Beethoven's pianoforte sonatas: hints on their rendering, form, etc., with appendices on definition of sonata, music forms, ornaments, pianoforte pedals, and how to discover keys.* London: Novello, 1929.

Macdonald, Hugh, Editor. *Berlioz: Selected letters.* London: Faber and Faber, 1995.

Macdonald, Malcolm, Editor. *Havergal Brian on music: selections from his journalism: Volume One, British music.* London: Toccata Press, 1986.

MacDonald, Malcolm. *Varèse: astronomer in sound.* London: Kahn & Averill, 2003.

MacDowell, Edward. *Critical and historical essays: lectures delivered at Columbia University.* Edited by W. J. Baltzell. London: Elkin; Boston: A.P. Schmidt, 1912.

MacFarren, Walter. Memories: an autobiography. London: Walter Scott Publishing Co.,1905.

Mackenzie, Alexander Campbell. *A musician's narrative.* London: Cassell and company, Ltd, 1927.

McCarthy, Margaret William, Editor. *More letters of Amy Fay: the American years, 1879–1916.* Detroit: Information Coordinators, 1986.

McClary, Susan. *Feminine endings: music, gender, and sexuality.* Minneapolis: University of Minnesota Press, 1991.

McClatchie, Stephen, Editor and Translator. *The Mahler family letters.* Oxford: Oxford University Press, 2006.

McVeigh, Simon. *Concert life in London from Mozart to Haydn.* Cambridge: Cambridge University Press, 1993.

Mahler, Alma. *Gustav Mahler: memories and letters.* Enlarged edition revised and edited and with and introduction by Donald Mitchell. London: John Murray, 1968.

Mai, François Martin. *Diagnosing genius: the life and death of Beethoven.* Montreal; London: McGill-Queen's University Press, 2007.

Del Mar, Norman. *Orchestral variations: confusion and error in the orchestral repertoire.* London: Eulenburg, 1981.

Del Mar, Norman. *Richard Strauss: a critical commentary on his life and works.* London: Barrie & Jenkins. 3 Vols. 1978.

(La) Mara [pseudonym]. *Letters of Franz Liszt.* London: H. Grevel & Co., 2 Vols. 1894.

Marek, George Richard. *Puccini.* London: Cassell & Co., 1952.

Marek, George Richard. *Toscanini.* London: Vision, 1976.

(De) Marliave, Joseph. *Beethoven's quartets.* New York: Dover Publications (reprint), 1961.

Martin, George Whitney. *Verdi: his music, life and times.* London: Macmillan, 1965.

Martner, Knud, Editor. *Selected letters of Gustav Mahler.* London; Boston: Faber and Faber, 1979.

Martyn, Barrie. *Nicolas Medtner: his life and music.* Aldershot: Scolar Press, 1995.

Martyn, Barrie. *Rachmaninoff: composer, pianist, conductor.* Aldershot: Scolar, 1990.

Massenet, Jules. *My recollections.* Westport, Connecticut: Greenwood Press.1970.

Matheopoulos, Helena. *Maestro: encounters with conductors of today.* London: Hutchinson,1982.

Matthews, Denis. *Beethoven.* London: J. M. Dent, 1985.

Matthews, Denis. *Beethoven piano sonatas.* London: British Broadcasting Corporation, 1967.

Matthews, Denis. *In pursuit of music.* London: Victor Gollancz Ltd., 1968.

Matthews, Denis. *Keyboard music.* Newton Abbot: London David & Charles, 1972.

Mellers, Wilfrid Howard. *Caliban reborn: renewal in twentieth-century music.* London: Victor Gollancz, 1967.

Mellers, Wilfrid Howard. *The sonata principle (from c. 1750).* London: Rockliff, 1957.

Mendelssohn Bartholdy. *Letters from Italy and Switzerland.* London: Longman, Green, Longman, and Roberts, 1862.

Mendelssohn Bartholdy, Paul. *Letters of Felix Mendelssohn Bartholdy, from 1833 to 1847.* London: Longman, Green, Longman, Roberts, & Green, 1864.

Menuhin, Yehudi and Curtis W. Davis. *The music of man.* London: Macdonald and Jane's, 1979.

Menuhin, Yehudi. *Theme and variations.* London: Heinemann Educational Books Ltd., 1972.

Menuhin, Yehudi. *Unfinished journey.* London: Macdonald and Jane's, 1977.

Messian, Olivier. *Music and color: conversations with Claude Samuel.* Portland, Oregon: Amadeus, 1994.

Miall, Anthony. *Musical bumps.* London: J.M. Dent & Sons Ltd, 1981.

Michotte, Edmond. *Richard Wagner's visit to Rossini (Paris 1860): and, An evening at Rossini's in Beau-Sejour (Passy), 1858.* Chicago; London: University of Chicago Press, 1982.

Mies, Paul. *Beethoven's sketches: an analysis of his style based on a study of his sketchbooks.*
New York: Johnson Reprint, 1969.

Milhaud, Darius. *My happy life.* London: Boyars, 1995.

Miller, Mina. *The Nielsen companion.* London: Faber and Faber, 1994.

Milsom, David. *Theory and practice in late nineteenth-century violin performance: an examination of style in performance, 1850–1900.* Aldershot: Ashgate, 2003.

Mitchell, Donald, Editor. *Letters from a life: the selected letters and diaries of Benjamin Britten 1913–1976.* London: Faber and Faber. 3 Vols., 1991.

Mitchell, Donald and Hans Keller, Editors. *Music survey: new series 1949–1952.* London: Faber Music in association with Faber & Faber, 1981.

Mitchell, Jon C. *A comprehensive biography of composer Gustav Holst, with correspondence and diary excerpts: including his American years.* Lewiston, New York: Edwin Mellen Press, 2001.

Moldenhauer, Hans. *Anton von Webern: a chronicle of his life and work.* London: Victor Gollancz, 1978.

Monrad-Johansen. Edvard Grieg. New York: Tudor Publishing Co., 1945.

Moore, Gerald. *Am I too loud?: memoirs of an accompanist.* London: Hamish Hamilton, 1962.

Moore, Gerald. *Farewell recital: further memoirs.* Harmondsworth: Penguin Books, 1979.

Moore, Gerald. *Furthermoore: interludes in an accompanist's life.* London: Hamish Hamilton, 1983.

Moore, Jerrold Northrop. *Edward Elgar: a creative life.* Oxford: Oxford University Press, 1984.

Moore, Jerrold Northrop. *Elgar, Edward. The windflower letters: correspondence with Alice Caroline Stuart Wortley and her family.* Oxford: Clarendon

Press; New York: Oxford University Press, 1989.

Moore, Jerrold Northrop. *Elgar, Edward. Edward Elgar: letters of a lifetime.* Oxford: Clarendon Press; New York: Oxford University Press, 1990.

Moore, Jerrold Northrop. *Elgar, Edward. Elgar and his publishers: letters of a creative life.* Oxford: Clarendon, 1987.

Moreux, Serge. *Béla Bartók.* London: Harvill Press, 1953.

Morgan, Kenneth. *Fritz Reiner, maestro and martinet.* Urbana: University of Illinois Press, 2005.

Cone, Edward T., Editor. *Music, a view from Delft: selected essays.* Chicago: University of Chicago Press, 1989.

Morgan, Robert P. *Twentieth-century music: a history of musical style in modern Europe and America.* New York: Norton, 1991.

Morgenstern, Sam., Editor. *Composers on music: an anthology of composers' writings.* London: Faber & Faber, 1956.

Morrow, Mary Sue. *Concert life in Haydn's Vienna: aspects of a developing musical and social institution.* Stuyvesant, New York: Pendragon Press, 1989.

Moscheles, Felix, Editor and Translator. *Letters from Felix Mendelssohn-Bartholdy to Ignaz and Charlotte Moscheles.* London: Trübner and Co., 1888.

Mudge, Richard B., Translator. *Glinka, Mikhail Ivanovich: Memoirs.* Norman: University of Oklahoma Press, 1963.

Munch, Charles. *I am a conductor.* New York: Oxford University Press, 1955.

Mundy, Simon. *Bernard Haitink: a working life.* London: Robson Books, 1987.

Musgrave, Michael. *The musical life of the Crystal Palace.* Cambridge: Cambridge University Press, 1995.

Music & Letters. *Beethoven: special number.* London: Music & Letters, 1927.

Musical Times. *Special Issue.* John A. Fuller-Maitland London: Vol. VIII, No. 2, 1927.

Myers, Rollo H., Editor. *Twentieth-century music.* London: Calder and Boyars, 1960.

National Gallery (Great Britain). *Music performed at the National Gallery concerts, 10th October 1939 to 10th April 1946.* London: Privately printed, 1948.

Nattiez, Jean-Jacques, Editor. *Orientations: collected writings — Pierre Boulez.* London: Faber and Faber, 1986.

Nauhaus, Gerd, Editor. *The marriage diaries of Robert & Clara Schumann.* London: Robson Books, 1994.

Nectoux, Jean Michel. *Gabriel Fauré: a musical life.* Translated by Roger Nichols. Cambridge: Cambridge University Press, 1991.

Nettl, Paul. *Beethoven handbook.* Westport, Connecticut: Greenwood Press, 1975.

Neumayr, Anton. *Music and medicine.* Bloomington, Illinois: Medi-Ed Press, 1994–1997

Newbould, Brian. *Schubert and the symphony: a new perspective.* Surbiton: Toccata Press, 1992.

Newlin, Dika. *Schoenberg remembered: diaries and recollections (1938–76).* New York: Pendragon Press, 1980.

Newman, Ernest. *From the world of music: essays from 'The Sunday Times'*. London: J. Calder, 1956.

Newman, Ernest. Hugo Wolf. New York: Dover Publications, 1966.

Newman, Ernest, Annotated and Translated. *Memoirs of Hector Berlioz from 1803 to 1865, comprising his travels in Germany, Italy, Russia, and England.* New York: Knopf, 1932.

Newman, Ernest. *More essays from the world of music: essays from the 'Sunday Times'.* London: John Calder, 1958.

Newman, Ernest. *Musical studies.* London; New York: John Lane, 1910.

Newman, Ernest. *Testament of music: essays and papers.* London: Putnam, 1962.

Newman, Richard. *Alma Rosé: Vienna to Auschwitz.* Portland, Oregon: Amadeus Press, 2000.

Newman, William S. *The sonata in the classic era.* Chapel Hill: University of North Carolina Press 1963.

Newman, William S. *The sonata in the Classic era.* New York; London: W.W. Norton, 1983.

Newmarch, Rosa Harriet. *Henry J. Wood.* London & New York: John Lane, 1904.

Nicholas, Jeremy. *Godowsky: the pianists' pianist; a biography of Leopold Godowsky.* Hexham: Appian Publications & Recordings, 1989.

Nichols, Roger. *Debussy remembered.* London: Faber and Faber, 1992.

Nichols, Roger. *Mendelssohn remembered.* London: Faber and Faber, 1997.

Nichols, Roger. *Ravel remembered.* London: Faber and Faber, 1987.

Niecks, Frederick. *Robert Schumann.* London: J. M. Dent, 1925.

Nielsen, Carl. *Living music.* Copenhagen, Wilhelm Hansen, 1968.

Nielsen, Carl. *My childhood.* Copenhagen, Wilhelm Hansen, 1972.

Nikolska, Irina. *Conversations with Witold Lutoslawski, (1987–92).* Stockholm: Melos, 1994.

Nohl, Ludwig. *Beethoven depicted by his contemporaries.* London: Reeves, 1880.

De Nora, Tia. *Beethoven and the construction of genius: musical politics in Vienna, 1792–1803.* Berkeley: University of California Press, 1997.

Norton, Spencer, Editor and Translator. *Music in my time: the memoirs of Alfredo Casella.* Norman: University of Oklahoma Press, 1955.

Nottebohm, Gustav. *Two Beethoven sketchbooks: a description with musical extracts.* London: Gollancz, 1979.

Oakeley, Edward Murray. *The life of Sir Herbert Stanley Oakeley.* London: George Allen, 1904.

Lucas, Brenda and Michael Kerr. *Virtuoso: the story of John Ogdon.* London: H. Hamilton, 1981.

Oliver, Michael, Editor. *Settling the score: a journey through the music of the twentieth century.* London: Faber and Faber, 1999.

Olleson, Philip. *Samuel Wesley: the man and his music.* Woodbridge: Boydell Press, 2003.

Olleson, Philip, Editor. *The letters of Samuel Wesley: professional* and social correspondence, *1797–1837*. Oxford; New York: Oxford University Press, 2001.

Olmstead, Andrea. *Conversations with Roger Sessions*. Boston: Northeastern University Press, 1987.

Orenstein, Arbie, Editor. *A Ravel reader: correspondence, articles, interviews*. New York: Columbia University Press, 1990.

Orenstein, Arbie. *Ravel: man and musician*. New York: Columbia University Press, 1975.

Orledge, Robert. *Charles Koechlin (1867–1950): his life and works*. New York: Harwood Academic Publishers, 1989.

Orledge, Robert. *Gabriel Fauré*. London: Eulenburg Books, 1979.

Orledge, Robert. *Satie remembered*. London: Faber and Faber, 1995.

Orledge, Robert. *Satie the composer*. Cambridge: Cambridge University Press, 1990.

Orlova, Alexandra. *Glinka's life in music: a chronicle*. Ann Arbor: UMI Research Press, 1988.

Orlova, Alexandra. *Musorgsky's days and works: a biography in documents*. Ann Arbor: UMI Research Press, 1983.

Orlova, Alexandra. *Tchaikovsky: a self-portrait*. Oxford: Oxford University Press, 1990.

Osborne, Charles, Editor and Translator. *Letters of Giuseppe Verdi*. London: Victor Gollancz, 1971.

Osmond-Smith David, Editor and Translator. *Luciano Berio: Two interviews with Rossana Dalmonte and Bálint András Varga*. New York; London: Boyars, 1985.

Ouellette, Fernand. *Edgard Varèse*. London: Calder & Boyars, 1973.

Paderewski, Ignacy Jan and Mary Lawton. *The Paderewski memoirs*. London: Collins, 1939.

Page, Tim: Editor. *The Glenn Gould reader*. London: Faber and Faber, 1987.

Page, Tim. *Music from the road: views and reviews, 1978–1992*. New York; Oxford: Oxford University Press, 1992.

Page, Tim and Vanessa Weeks, Editors. *Selected letters of Virgil Thomson*. New York: Summit Books, 1988.

Page, Tim. *Tim Page on music: views and reviews*. Portland, Oregon: Amadeus Press, 2002.

Palmer, Christopher. *Herbert Howells, (1892–1983): a celebration*. London: Thames, 1996.

Palmer, Christopher, Editor. *Sergei Prokofiev: Soviet diary 1927 and other writings*. London: Faber and Faber, 1991.

Palmer, Fiona M. *Domenico Dragonetti in England (1794–1846): the career of a double bass virtuoso*. Oxford: Clarendon, 1997.

Palmieri, Robert, Editor. *Encyclopedia of the piano*. New York: Garland, 1996.

Panufnik, Andrzej. *Composing myself*. London: Methuen, 1987.

Parsons, James, Editor. *The Cambridge companion to the Lied*. Cambridge: Cambridge University Press, 2004.

Paynter, John, Editor. *Between old worlds and new: occasional writings on music by Wilfrid Mellers*. London: Cygnus Arts, 1997.

Pestelli, Giorgio. *The age of Mozart and Beethoven*. Cambridge:

Cambridge University Press, 1984.
Peyser, Joan. *Bernstein: a biography: revised & updated.* New York: Billboard Books, 1998.
Phillips-Matz, Mary Jane. *Verdi: a biography.* Oxford: Oxford University Press, 1993.
Piggott, Patrick. *The life and music of John Field, 1782–1837: creator of the nocturne.* London: Faber and Faber, 1973.
Plantinga, Leon. *Beethoven's concertos: history, style, performance.* New York: Norton, 1999.
Plantinga, Leon. *Clementi: his life and music.* London: Oxford University Press, 1977.
Plantinga, Leon. *Romantic music: a history of musical style in nineteenth-century Europe.* New York; London: Norton, 1984.
Plaskin, Glenn. *Horowitz: a biography of Vladimir Horowitz.* London: Macdonald, 1983.
Pleasants, Henry, Editor and Translator. *Hanslick, Eduard: Music criticisms, 1846–99.* Baltimore: Penguin Books, 1963.
Pleasants, Henry, Editor and Translator. *Hanslick's music criticisms.* New York: Dover Publications, 1988.
Pleasants, Henry, Editor and Translator. *The music criticism of Hugo Wolf.* New York: Holmes & Meier Publishers, 1978.
Pleasants, Henry, Editor and Translator. *The musical journeys of Louis Spohr.* Norman: University of Oklahoma Press, 1961.
Pollack, Howard. *Aaron Copland: the life and work of an uncommon man.* New York: Henry Holt, 1999.
Poulenc, Francis. *My friends and myself.* London: Dennis Dobson, 1978.
Powell, Richard, Mrs. *Edward Elgar: memories of a variation.* Aldershot, Hants, England: Scolar Press; Brookfield, Vermont, USA: Ashgate Publishing. Co., 1994.
Poznansky, Alexander, Editor. *Tchaikovsky through others' eyes.* Bloomington: Indiana University Press, 1999.
Praeger, Ferdinand. *Wagner as I knew him.* London; New York: Longmans, Green, 1892.
Previn, Andre. *Anthony Hopkins. Music face to face.* London, Hamish Hamilton, 1971.
Prieberg, Fred K. *Trial of strength: Wilhelm Furtwängler and the Third Reich.* London: Quartet, 1991.
Procter-Gregg, Humphrey. *Beecham remembered.* London: Duckworth, 1976.
Prokofiev, Sergey. *Prokofiev by Prokofiev: a composer's memoir.* London: Macdonald and Jane's, 1979.
Rachmaninoff, Sergei. *Rachmaninoff's recollections told to Oskar von Riesemann.* London: George Allen & Unwin, 1934.
Radcliffe, Philip. *Beethoven's string quartets.* Cambridge: Cambridge University Press, 1978.
Radcliffe, Philip. *Piano Music in: The Age of Beethoven, The New Oxford History of Music, Vol. VIII.* Gerald Abraham, (Editor), 1988, p. 340.
Ratner, Leonard G. *Romantic music: sound and syntax.* New York: Schirmer Books, 1992.
Raynor, Henry. *A social history of music: from the middle ages to*

Beethoven. London: Barrie & Jenkins, 1972.

Rees, Brian. *Camille Saint-Saëns: a life*. London: Chatto & Windus, 1999.

Reich, Willi, Editor. *Anton Webern: The path to the new music*. London; Bryn Mawr: Theodore Presser in association with Universal Edition, 1963.

Reid, Charles. *John Barbirolli: a biography*. London, Hamish Hamilton, 1971.

Reid, Charles. *Malcolm Sargent: a biography*. London: Hamilton, 1968.

Rennert, Jonathan. *William Crotch (1775–1847): composer, artist, teacher*. Lavenham: Terence Dalton, 1975.

Rice, John A. *Antonio Salieri and Viennese Opera*. Chicago, Illinois: University of Chicago Press, 1998.

Rice, John A. *Empress Marie Therese and music at the Viennese court, 1792–1807*. Cambridge: Cambridge University Press, 2003.

Richards, Fiona. *The Music of John Ireland*. Aldershot: Ashgate, 2000.

Rigby, Charles. *Sir Charles Hallé: a portrait for today*. Manchester: Dolphin Press, 1952.

Ringer, Alexander, Editor. *The early Romantic era: between Revolutions; 1789 and 1848*. Basingstoke: Macmillan, 1990.

Roberts, John P.L. and Ghyslaine Guertin, Editors. *Glenn Gould: Selected letters*. Toronto; Oxford: Oxford University Press, 1992.

Robertson, Alec. *More than music*. London: Collins, 1961.

Robinson, Harlow, Editor and Translator. *Selected letters of Sergei Prokofiev*. Boston: Northeastern University Press, 1998.

Robinson, Harlow. *Sergei Prokofiev: a biography*. London: Hale, 1987.

Robinson, Paul A. *Ludwig van Beethoven, Fidelio*. Cambridge: Cambridge University Press, 1996.

Robinson, Suzanne, Editor. *Michael Tippett: music and literature*. Aldershot: Ashgate, 2002.

Rochberg, George. *The aesthetics of survival: a composer's view of twentieth-century music*. Ann Arbor, Michigan: University of Michigan Press, 2004.

Rodmell, Paul. *Charles Villiers Stanford*. Aldershot: Ashgate, 2002.

Roeder, Michael Thomas. *A history of the concerto*. Portland, Oregon: Amadeus Press, 1994.

Rohr, Deborah Adams. *The careers of British musicians, 1750–1850: a profession of artisans*. Cambridge: Cambridge University Press, 2001.

Rolland, Romain. *Goethe and Beethoven*. New York; London: Blom, 1968.

Rolland, Romain. *Beethoven and Handel*. London: Waverley Book Co., 1917.

Rolland, Romain. *Beethoven the creator*. Garden City, New York: Garden City Pub., 1937.

Roscow, Gregory, Editor. *Bliss on music: selected writings of Arthur Bliss, 1920–1975*. Oxford: Oxford University Press, 1991.

Rosen, Charles. *Beethoven's piano sonatas: a short companion*. New Haven, Connecticut:

Rosen, Charles. *Critical entertainments: music old and new.* Cambridge, Massachusetts; London: Harvard University Press, 2000.

Rosen, Charles. *The classical style: Haydn, Mozart, Beethoven.* London: Faber and Faber, 1976.

Rosen, Charles. *The romantic generation.* Cambridge, Massachusetts: Harvard University Press, 1995.

Rosenthal, Albi. *Obiter scripta: essays, lectures, articles, interviews and reviews on music, and other subjects.* Oxford: Offox Press; Lanham: Scarecrow Press, 2000.

Rostal, Max. *Beethoven: the sonatas for piano and violin; thoughts on their interpretation.* London: Toccata Press, 1985.

Rostropovich, Mstislav and Galina Vishnevskaya. *Russia, music, and liberty.* Portland, Oregan: Amadeus Press, 1995.

Rubinstein, Arthur. *My many years.* London: Jonathan Cape, 1980.

Rubinstein, Arthur. *My young years.* London: Jonathan Cape, 1973.

Rumph, Stephen C. *Beethoven after Napoleon: political romanticism in the late works.* Berkeley; London: University of California Press, 2004.

Rye, Matthew Rye. *Notes to the BBC Radio Three Beethoven Experience, Friday 10 June 2005,* www.bbc.co.uk/radio3/Beethoven.

Sachs, Harvey. *Toscanini.* London: Weidenfeld and Nicholson, 1978.

Sachs, Joel. *Kapellmeister Hummel in England and France.* Detroit: Information Coordinators, 1977.

Saffle, Michael, Editor. *Liszt and his world: proceedings of the International Liszt Conference held at Virginia Polytechnic Institute and State University, 20–23 May 1993.* Stuyvesant, New York: Pendragon Press, 1998.

Safránek, Milos. *Bohuslav Martinu, his life and works.* London: Allan Wingate, 1962.

Saint-Saëns, Camille. *Outspoken essays on music.* Westport, Connecticut: Greenwood Press, 1970.

Saussine, Renée de. *Paganini.* Westport, Connecticut: Greenwood Press, 1976.

Sayers, W. C. Berwick. *Samuel Coleridge-Taylor, musician: his life and letters.* London; New York: Cassell and Co., 1915.

Schaarwächter, Jürgen. *HB: aspects of Havergal Brian.* Aldershot: Ashgate, 1997.

Schafer, R. Murray. *E.T.A. Hoffmann and music.* Toronto: University of Toronto Press, 1975.

Schafer, R. Murray, Editor. *Ezra Pound and music: the complete criticism.* London: Faber and Faber, 1978.

Schat, Peter. *The tone clock.* Chur, Switzerland; Langhorne, Pa.: Harwood Academic Publishers, 1993.

Schenk, Erich. *Mozart and his times.* Edited and Translated by Richard and Clara Winstin. London: Secker & Warburg, 1960.

Schindler, Anton Felix. *Beethoven as I knew him.* Edited by Donald W. MacArdle and Translated by Constance S. Jolly from the

Schlosser, Johann. *Beethoven: the first biography, 1827.* Edited by Barry Cooper. Portland, Oregon: Amadeus Press, 1996.

Schnabel, Artur. *My life and music.* London: Longmans, 1961.

Schnittke, Alfred. *A Schnittke reader.* Bloomington: Indiana University Press, 2002.

Scholes, Percy Alfred. *Crotchets: a few short musical notes.* London: John Lane, 1924.

Schonberg, Harold C. *The great pianists.* London: Victor Gollancz, 1964.

Schrade, Leo. *Beethoven in France: the growth of an idea.* New Haven; London: Yale University Press, H. Milford, Oxford University Press, 1942.

Schrade, Leo. *Tragedy in the art of music.* Cambridge, Massachusetts: Harvard University Press, 1964.

Schuh, Willi. *Richard Strauss: a chronicle of the early years 1864–1898.* Cambridge: Cambridge University Press, 1982.

Schuh, Willi, Editor. *Richard Strauss: Recollections and reflections.* London; New York: Boosey & Hawkes, 1953.

Schuller, Gunther. *Musings: the musical worlds of Gunther Schuller.* New York: Oxford University Press, 1986.

Schumann, Robert. *Music and musicians: essays and criticisms.* London: William Reeves, 1877.

Schuttenhelm, Editor. *Selected letters of Michael Tippett.* London: Faber and Faber, 2005.

Schwartz, Elliott. *Music since 1945: issues, materials, and literature.* New York: Schirmer Books, 1993.

Scott, Marion M. *Beethoven: (The master musicians).* London: Dent, 1940.

Scott-Sutherland, Colin. *Arnold Bax.* London: J. M. Dent, 1973.

Searle, Muriel V. *John Ireland: the man and his music.* Tunbridge Wells: Midas Books, 1979.

Secrest, Meryle. *Leonard Bernstein: a life.* London: Bloomsbury, 1995.

Seeger, Charles. *Studies in musicology II, 1929–1979.* Edited by Anne M. Pescatello. Berkeley; London: University of California Press, 1994.

Selden-Goth, Gisela, Editor. *Felix Mendelssohn: letters.* London: Paul Elek Publishers Ltd, 1946.

Senner, Wayne M., Robin Wallace and William Meredith, Editors. *The critical reception of Beethoven's compositions by his German contemporaries.* Lincoln: University of Nebraska Press, in association with the American Beethoven Society and the Ira F. Brilliant Center for Beethoven Studies, San José State University, 1999.

Seroff, Victor I. *Rachmaninoff.* London: Cassell & Company, 1951.

Sessions, Roger. *Questions about music.* Cambridge, Massachusetts: Harvard University Press, 1970.

Sessions, Roger. *The musical experience of composer, performer, listener.* New York: Atheneum, 1966, 1950.

Seyfried, Ignaz von. *Louis van Beethoven's Studies in thorough-bass, counterpoint and the art of scientific composition.* Leipzig; New-York: Schuberth and Company, 1853.

Sharma, Bhesham R. *Music and culture in the age of mechanical reproduction.* New York: Peter Lang, 2000.

Shaw, Bernard. *How to become a musical critic.* London: R. Hart Davis, 1960.

Shaw, Bernard. *London music in 1888–89 as heard by Corno di Bassetto (later known as Bernard Shaw): with some further autobiographical particulars.* London: Constable and Company, 1937.

Shaw, Bernard. *Music in London, 1890–1894.* London: Constable and Company Limited, 3 Vols., 1932.

Shedlock, John South. *Beethoven's pianoforte sonatas: the origin and respective values of various readings.* London: Augener Ltd., 1918.

Shedlock, John South. *The pianoforte sonata: its origin and development.* London: Methuen, 1895.

Shepherd, Arthur. *The string quartets of Ludwig van Beethoven.* Cleveland: H. Carr, The Printing Press, 1935.

Sheppard, Leslie and Herbert R. Axelrod. *Paganini: containing a portfolio of drawings by Vido Polikarpus.* Neptune City, New Jersey: Paganiniana Publications, 1979.

Short, Michael. *Gustav Holst: the man and his music.* Oxford: Oxford University Press, 1990.

Shostakovich, Dmitry. *Dmitry Shostakovich: about himself and his times.* Moscow: Progress Publishers, 1981.

Simpson, John Palgrave. *Carl Maria von Weber: the life of an artist, from the German of his son Baron, Max Maria von Weber.* London: Chapman and Hall, 1865.

Simpson, Robert. *Beethoven symphonies.* London: British Broadcasting Corporation, 1970.

Sipe, Thomas. *Beethoven: Eroica symphony.* Cambridge: Cambridge University Press, 1998.

Sitwell, Sacheverell. *Mozart.* Edinburgh: Peter Davies Limited, 1932.

Skelton, Geoffrey. *Paul Hindemith: the man behind the music; a biography.* London: Victor Gollancz, 1975.

Smallman, Basil. *The piano trio: its history, technique, and repertoire.* Oxford: Clarendon Press; Oxford; New York: Oxford University Press, 1990.

Smidak, Emil. *Isaak-Ignaz Moscheles: the life of the composer and his encounters with Beethoven, Liszt, Chopin, and Mendelssohn.* Aldershot, Hampshire, England: Scolar Press; Brookfield, Vermont, USA: Gower Publishing Co., 1989.

Smith, Barry. *Peter Warlock: the life of Philip Heseltine.* Oxford: Oxford University Press, 1994.

Smith, Joan Allen. *Schoenberg and his circle: a Viennese portrait.* New York: Schirmer Books, London: Collier Macmillan, 1986.

Smith, Richard Langham, Editor. *Debussy on music: the critical writings of the great French composer Claude Debussy.* London: Secker & Warburg, 1977.

Smith, Ronald. *Alkan.* London: Kahn and Averill, 1976.

Snowman, Daniel. *The Amadeus Quartet: the men and the music.* London: Robson Books, 1981.

Solomon, Maynard. *Beethoven.* New York: Schirmer, 1977.

Solomon, Maynard. *Beethoven essays.* Cambridge, Massachusetts; London: Harvard University Press, 1988.

Solomon, Maynard. *Late Beethoven: music, thought, imagination.* Berkeley; London: University of California Press, 2003.

Solomon, Maynard. *Mozart: a life.* London: Hutchinson, 1995.

Sonneck, Oscar George Theodore. *Beethoven: impressions of contemporaries.* London: Oxford University Press, 1927.

Spalding, Albert. *Rise to follow: an autobiography.* London: Frederick Muller Ltd., 1946.

Spohr, Louis. *Louis Spohr's autobiography.* London: Longman, Green, Longman, Roberts, & Green, 1865.

Stafford, William. *Mozart myths: a critical reassessment.* Stanford, California: Stanford University Press, 1991.

Stanford, Charles Villiers. *Interludes: records and reflections.* London: John Murray, 1922.

Stanley, Glen, Editor. *The Cambridge companion to Beethoven.* Cambridge; New York: Cambridge University Press, 2000

Stedman, Preston. *The symphony.* Englewood Cliffs, New Jersey; London: Prentice-Hall, 1979.

Stedron, Bohumír, Editor and Translator. *Leos Janácek: letters and reminiscences.* Prague: Artia, 1955.

Stein, Erwin, Editor. *Arnold Schoenberg: letters.* London: Faber and Faber, 1964.

Stein, Erwin. *Orpheus in new guises.* London: Rockliff, 1953.

Stein, Jack Madison. *Poem and music in the German lied from Gluck to Hugo Wolf.* Cambridge, Massachusetts: Harvard University Press, 1971.

Stein, Leonard, Editor. *Style and idea: selected writings of Arnold Schoenberg.* London: Faber and Faber, 1975.

Steinberg, Michael P. *Listening to reason: culture, subjectivity, and nineteenth-century music.* Princeton, New Jersey: Princeton University Press, 2004.

Steinberg, Michael. *The concerto: a listener's guide.* New York: Oxford University Press, 1998.

Steinberg, Michael. *The symphony: a listener's guide.* Oxford; New York: Oxford University Press, 1995.

Sternfeld, Frederick William. *Goethe and music: a list of parodies and Goethe's relationship to music; a list of references.* New York: Da Capo Press, 1979.

Stivender, David. *Mascagni: an autobiography compiled, edited and translated from original sources.* New York: Pro/Am Music Resources; London: Kahn & Averill, 1988.

Stone, Else and Kurt Stone, Editors. *The writings of Elliott Carter: an American composer looks at modern music.* Bloomington: Indiana University Press, 1977.

Stowell, Robin. *Beethoven: violin concerto.* Cambridge: Cambridge University Press, 1998.

Stowell, Robin: Editor. *The Cambridge companion to the cello.*

Cambridge: Cambridge University Press, 1999.

Stowell, Robin: Editor. *The Cambridge companion to the string quartet.* Cambridge: Cambridge University Press, 2003.

Stratton, Stephen Samuel. *Mendelssohn.* London: J.M. Dent & Co.; New York: E.P. Dutton & Co., 1901.

Straus, Joseph N. *Remaking the past: musical modernism and the influence of the tonal tradition.* Cambridge, Massachusetts: Harvard University Press, 1990.

Stravinsky, Igor. *An autobiography.* London: Calder and Boyars, 1975.

Stravinsky, Igor. *Themes and conclusions.* London: Faber and Faber, 1972.

Stravinsky, Igor and Robert Craft. *Conversations with Igor Stravinsky.* London: Faber and Faber, 1959.

Stravinsky, Igor and Robert Craft. *Dialogues and a diary.* London: Faber and Faber 1968.

Stravinsky, Igor and Robert Craft. *Memories and commentaries.* London: Faber and Faber, 2002.

Strunk, Oliver. *Source readings in music history, 4: The Classic era.* London: Faber and Faber 1981.

Sullivan, Blair, Editor. *The echo of music: essays in honor of Marie Louise Göllner.* Warren, Michigan: Harmonie Park Press, 2004.

Sullivan, Jack, Editor. *Words on music: from Addison to Barzun.* Athens: Ohio University Press, 1990.

Symonette, Lys and Kim H. Kowalke, Editors and Translators. *Speak low (when you speak love): the letters of Kurt Weill and Lotte Lenya.* London: Hamish Hamilton, 1996.

Swalin, Benjamin F. *The violin concerto: a study in German romanticism.* New York, Da Capo Press, 1973.

Szigeti, Joseph. *With strings attached: reminiscences and reflections.* London: Cassell & Co. Ltd, 1949.

Tanner, Michael, Editor. *Notebooks, 1924–1954: Wilhelm Furtwängler.* London: Quartet Books, 1989.

Taylor, Robert, Editor. *Furtwängler on music: essays and addresses.* Aldershot: Scolar, 1991.

Taylor, Ronald. *Kurt Weill: composer in a divided world.* London: Simon & Schuster, 1991.

Tchaikovsky, Peter Ilich. *Letters to his family: an autobiography.* Translated by Galina von Meck. London: Dennis Dobson, 1981.

Tertis, Lionel. *My viola and I: a complete autobiography; with, 'Beauty of tone in string playing', and other essays.* London: Paul Elek, 1974.

Thayer, Alexander Wheelock. *Salieri: rival of Mozart.* Edited by Theodore Albrecht. Kansas City, Missouri: Philharmonia of Greater Kansas City, 1989.

Thomas, Michael Tilson. *Viva voce: conversations with Edward Seckerson.* London: Faber and Faber 1994.

Thomson, Andrew. *Vincent d'Indy and his world.* Oxford: Clarendon Press, 1996.

Thomson, Virgil. *The musical scene.* New York: Greenwood Press, 1968.

Thomson, Virgil. *Virgil Thomson.*

London: Weidenfeld & Nicolson, 1967.

Tillard, Françoise. *Fanny Mendelssohn.* Amadeus Press: Portland, 1996.

Tilmouth, Michael, Editor. *Donald Francis Tovey: The classics of music: talks, essays, and other writings previously uncollected.* Oxford: Oxford University Press, 2001

Tippett, Michael. *Moving into Aquarius.* London: Routledge and Kegan Paul, 1959.

Tippett, Michael. *Those twentieth century blues: an autobiography.* London: Hutchinson, 1991.

Todd, R. Larry, Editor. *Nineteenth-century piano music.* New York; London: Routledge, 2004.

Todd, R. Larry, Editor. *Schumann and his world.* Princeton: Princeton University Press, 1994.

Tommasini, Anthony. *Virgil Thomson: composer on the aisle.* New York: W.W. Norton, 1997.

Tortelier, Paul. *A self-portrait: in conversation with David Blum.* London: Heinemann, 1984.

Tovey, Donald Francis. *A Companion to Beethoven's Pianoforte Sonatas.* Revised by Barry Cooper. London: The Associated Board, [1931], 1998.

Tovey, Donald Francis. *Beethoven.* London: Oxford University Press, 1944.

Tovey, Donald Francis. *Essays and lectures on music.* London: Oxford University Press, 1949.

Tovey, Donald Francis. *Essays in musical analysis.* London: Oxford University Press, H. Milford, 7 Vols., 1935–41.

Tovey, Donald Francis. *The forms of music: musical articles from The Encyclopaedia Britannica.* London: Oxford University Press, 1944.

Toye, Francis. *Giuseppe Verdi: his life and works.* London: William Heinemann Ltd., 1931.

Truscott, Harold. *Beethoven's late string quartets.* London: Dobson, 1968.

Tyler, William R. *The letters of Franz Liszt to Olga von Meyendorff, 1871–1886, in the Mildred Bliss Collection at Dumbarton Oaks.* Translated by William R. Tyler. Washington: Dumbarton Oaks, Trustees for Harvard University; Cambridge, Massachusetts: distributed by Harvard University Press, 1979.

Tyrrell, John. *Janácek: years of a life. Vol. 1, (1854–1914) The lonely blackbird.* London: Faber and Faber, 2006.

Tyrrell, John, Editor and Translator. *My life with Janácek: the memoirs of Zdenka Janácková.* London: Faber and Faber, 1998.

Tyson, Alan, Editor. *Beethoven studies 2.* Cambridge: Cambridge University Press, 1977.

Tyson, Alan, Editor. *Beethoven studies 3.* Cambridge: Cambridge University Press, 1982.

Tyson, Alan. *Mozart: studies of the autograph scores.* Cambridge, Massachusetts; London: Harvard University Press, 1987.

Tyson, Alan. *The authentic English editions of Beethoven.* London: Faber and Faber, 1963.

Underwood, J. A., Editor. *Gabriel Fauré: his life through his letters.* London: Marion Boyars, 1984.

Vechten, Carl van, Editor. *Nikolay, Rimsky-Korsakov: My musical life*. London: Martin Secker & Warburg Ltd., 1942.

Vinton, John. *Essays after a dictionary: music and culture at the close of Western civilization*. Lewisburg: Bucknell University Press, 1977.

Volkov, Solomon, Editor. *Testimony: the memoirs of Dmitri Shostakovich*. London: Faber and Faber, 1981.

Volta, Ornella, Editor. *A mammal's notebook: collected writings of Erik Satie*. London: Atlas Press, 1996.

Wagner, Richard. Beethoven: *With [a] supplement from the philosophical works of A. Schopenhauer*. Translated by E. Dannreuther. London: Reeves, 1893.

Wagner, Richard. *My life*. London: Constable and Company Ltd., 1911.

Walden, Valerie. *One hundred years of violoncello: a history of technique and performance practice, 1740–1840*. Cambridge: Cambridge University Press, 1998.

Walker, Alan. *Franz Liszt. Volume 1, The virtuoso years: 1811–1847*. New York: Alfred A. Knopf, 1983.

Walker, Alan. *Franz Liszt. Volume 2, The Weimar years: 1848–1861*. London: Faber and Faber, 1989.

Walker, Alan. *Franz Liszt. Volume 3, The final years, 1861–1886*. London: Faber and Faber, 1997.

Walker, Bettina. *My musical experiences*. London: Richard Bentley and Son, 1890.

Walker, Ernest. *Free thought and the musician, and other essays*. London; New York: Oxford University Press, 1946.

Walker, Frank. *Hugo Wolf: a biography*. London: J. M. Dent, 1951.

Walker, Frank. *The man Verdi*. London: Dent, 1962.

Wallace, Grace, *[Lady Wallace]*. *Beethoven's letters (1790–1826): from the collection of Dr. Ludwig Nohl. Also his letters to the Archduke Rudolph, Cardinal-Archbishop of Olmutz, K.W., from the collection of Dr. Ludwig Ritter Von Koľchel*. London: Longmans, Green, 2 Vols., 1866.

Wallace, Robin. *Beethoven's critics: aesthetic dilemmas and resolutions during the composer's lifetime*. Cambridge; New York: Cambridge University Press, 1986.

Walter, Bruno. *Theme and variations: an autobiography*. London: H. Hamilton, 1948.

Warrack, John Hamilton. *Writings on music*. Cambridge: Cambridge University Press, 1981.

Wasielewski, Wilhelm Joseph von. *Life of Robert Schumann: with letters, 1833–1852*. London: William Reeves, 1878.

Watkins, Glenn. *Proof through the night: music and the Great War*. Berkeley: University of California Press, 2003.

Watkins, Glenn. *Pyramids at the Louvre: music, culture, and collage from Stravinsky to the postmodernists*. Cambridge, Massachusetts; London: Belknap Press of Harvard University Press, 1994.

Watkins, Glenn. *Soundings: music in the twentieth century*. New York: Schirmer Books London: Collier Macmillan, 1988.

Watson, Derek. *Liszt*. London: J. M. Dent, 1989.

Weaver, William, Editor. *The Verdi-Boito correspondence.* Chicago; London: University of Chicago Press, 1994.

Wegeler, Franz. *Remembering Beethoven: the biographical notes of Franz Wegeler and Ferdinand Ries.* London: Andre Deutsch, 1988.

Weingartner, Felix. *Buffets and rewards: a musician's reminiscences.* London: Hutchinson & Co., 1937.

Weinstock, Herbert. *Rossini: a biography.* New York: Limelight, 1987.

Weiss, Piero and Richard Taruskin. *Music in the Western World: a history in documents.* New York: Schirmer; London: Collier Macmillan, 1984.

Weissweiler, Eva *The complete correspondence of Clara and Robert Schumann.* New York: Peter Lang, 2 Vols., 1994.

Whittaker, William Gillies. *Collected essays.* London: Oxford University Press, 1940.

Whittall, Arnold. *Exploring twentieth-century music: tradition and innovation.* Cambridge; New York: Cambridge University Press, 2003.

Whittall, Arnold. *Music since the First World War.* London: J. M. Dent, 1977.

Whitton, Kenneth S. *Lieder: an introduction to German song.* London: Julia MacRae, 1984.

Wightman, Alistair, Editor. *Szymanowski on music: selected writings of Karol Szymanowski.* London: Toccata Press, 1999.

Wilhelm, Kurt. *Richard Strauss: an intimate portrait.* London: Thames and Hudson, 1999.

Will, Richard James. *The characteristic symphony in the age of Haydn and Beethoven.* Cambridge: Cambridge University Press, 2002.

Willetts, Pamela J. *Beethoven and England: an account of sources in the British Museum.* London: British Museum, 1970.

Williams, Adrian, Editor and Translator. *Liszt, Franz: Selected letters.* Oxford: Clarendon Press, 1998.

Williams, Adrian. *Portrait of Liszt: by himself and his contemporaries.* Oxford: Clarendon Press, 1990.

Williams, Ralph Vaughan. *Heirs and rebels: letters written to each other and occasional writings on music.* London; New York: Oxford University Press, 1959.

Williams, Ralph Vaughan. *Some thoughts on Beethoven's Choral symphony: with writings on other musical subjects.* London; Oxford University Press, 1953.

Williams, Ralph Vaughan. *The making of music.* Ithaca, New York: Cornell University Press, 1955.

Williams, Ursula Vaughan. *R.V.W.: a biography of Ralph Vaughan Williams.* London: Oxford University Press, 1964.

Wilson, Conrad. *Notes on Beethoven: 20 crucial works.* Edinburgh: Saint Andrew Press, 2003.

Wilson, Elizabeth. *Shostakovich: a life remembered.* Princeton, New Jersey: Princeton University Press, 1994.

Winter, Robert, Editor. *Beethoven, performers, and critics: the International Beethoven Congress, Detroit, 1977.* Detroit: Wayne State University Press, 1980.

Winter, Robert. *Compositional origins of Beethoven's opus 131.* Ann Arbor, Michigan: UMI Research Press, 1982.

Winter, Robert and Robert Martin, Editors. *The Beethoven quartet companion*. Berkeley: University of California Press, 1994.

Wolf, Eugene K. and Edward H. Roesner, Editors. *Studies in musical sources and style: essays in honor of Jan LaRue*. Madison, Wisconsin: A-R Editions, 1990.

Wolff, Christoph and Robert Riggs. *The string quartets of Haydn, Mozart and Beethoven: studies of the autograph manuscripts: a conference at Isham Memorial Library, March 15-17, 1979*. Cambridge, Massachusetts: Department of Music, Harvard University, 1980.

Wolff, Konrad. *Masters of the keyboard: individual style elements in the piano music of Bach, Haydn, Mozart, Beethoven, Schubert, Chopin, and Brahms*. Bloomington: Indiana University Press, 1990.

Wörner, Karl Heinrich. *Stockhausen: life and work*. London: Faber, 1973.

Wright, Donald, Editor. *Cardus on music: a centenary collection*. London: Hamish Hamilton, 1988.

Wyndham, Henry Saxe. *August Manns and the Saturday concerts: a memoir and a retrospect*. London and Felling-on-Tyne, New York, The Walter Scott Publishing Co., Ltd., 1909.

Yastrebtsev, V.V. Edited and Translated by Florence Jonas. *Reminiscences of Rimsky-Korsakov*. New York: Columbia University Press, 1985.

Yates, Peter. *Twentieth century music: its evolution from the end of the harmonic era into the present era of sound*. London: Allen & Unwin Ltd., 1968.

Young, Percy M. *Beethoven: a Victorian tribute based on the papers of Sir George Smart*. London: D. Dobson, 1976.

Young, Percy M. *George Grove, 1820-1900: a biography*. London: Macmillan, 1980.

Young, Percy M. *Letters of Edward Elgar and other writings*. London: Geoffrey Bles, 1956.

Young, Percy M., Editor. *Letters to Nimrod: Edward Elgar to August Jaeger, 1897-1908*. London: Dennis Dobson, 1965.

Young, Percy M. *The concert tradition: from the middle ages to the twentieth century*. London: Routledge and Kegan Paul, 1965.

Young, Rob, Editor. *(Brief Description): Undercurrents: the hidden wiring of modern music*. London; New York, N.Y.: Continuum, 2002.

Yourke, Electra Slonimsky, Editor. *Nicolas Slonimsky: writings on music*. New York, N.Y.; London: Routledge, 4 Vols. 2003-2005.

Slonimsky, Nicolas. *The great composers and their works*. Edited by Electra Slonimsky Yourke. New York: Schirmer Books, 2 Vols. 2000.

Ysaÿe, Antoine. *Ysaÿe: his life, work and influence*. London: W. Heinemann, 1947.

Zamoyski, Adam. *Paderewski*. London: Collins, 1982.

Zegers, Mirjam, Editor. *Louis Andriessen: The art of stealing time*. Todmorden: Arc Music, 2002.

Zemanova, Mirka, Editor. *Janáček's uncollected essays on music*. London: Marion Boyars, 1989.

INDEX

The order adopted for the listing of the individual entries in this index is chronological - according to the sequential unfolding of the events under discussion. Thereby, the reader is provided with both a guide to the contents discussed in the main text and a time-line of the principal events bearing on Beethoven's life and work.

HISTORICAL PERSPECTIVE
AN ANTHOLOGY PP.1-125
Allgemeine musikalische Zeitung
Sir John Barbirolli
Daniel Barenboim
Terry Barfoot
Paul Bekker
Luciano Berio
Hector Berlioz
Leonard Bernstein
Ernst Bloch
Alexander Brott
Alfred Peter Brown
Michael Broyles
Hans von Bülow
Pablo Casals
Barry Cooper / William Drabkin
Louise Elvira Cuyler
Samuel Basil Deane
Philip G. Downs
George Dyson
Alfred Einstein

Hans Conrad Fischer and Erich Kock
Hans Gal
Donald J. Grout and Claude v. Palisca
George Grove
Nikolaus Harnoncourt
Christopher Headington
Gordon Jacob
David Wyn Jones
H. C. Robbins Landon
Ernst Markham Lee
Lewis H. Lockwood
Nicholas Marston
Bohuslav Martinů
Adolf Bernhard Marx
Dennis Matthews
Wilfrid Mellers
Yehudi Menuhin
Paul Mies
Anton Neumayr
Ernest Newman
Margaret Notley
Richard Osborne
Hubert Parry
Leon B. Plantinga
Romain Rolland
Charles Rosen
Gioachino Rossini
Stephen Rumph
Camille Saint-Saëns
Clara Schuman
Marion Scott
George Bernard Shaw
Robert Simpson
Thomas Sipe
Maynard Solomon
William Preston Stedman
Michael P. Steinberg
Richard Strauss
Peter Tchaikovsky
Donald Francis Tovey
Richard Wagner
Anton Webern
Conrad Wilson

BEETHOVEN AND VIENNA: GESTATION OF THE *EROICA* SYMPHONY PP. 126-175
BEETHOVEN'S GROWING FAME PP. 127-129
Fame in France, England and Scotland
First and Second Symphonies recognised
Variations in E-flat major, Op. 35

PORTRAITS PP. 129-131
Joseph Mähler
Isidor Neugass

ANECDOTES: DESCRIPTIONS OF BEETHOVEN PP. 131-135
Ferdinand Ries
Josef August Röckel
Georg Joseph Vogler
Ignaz Pleyel
French army officers
Baron Louis Trémont

DEAFNESS HEILIGENSTADT PP. 135-142
Dr. Gerhard von Vering
Franz Gerhard Wegeler
Dr. Johann Schmidt
Sir Beerbohm Tree
René Fauchois
Napoleon Parker
Heiligenstadt, description of
Sébastien Érard, gift of piano
Heiligenstadt Testament
John Keats, quotation from
Anton Neumayr, medical opinions of
Jan Doležlálek, recollections of
Franz Grillparzer, recollections of
Maynard Solomon, views of
Barry Cooper, views of
Beethoven's resolve 'to make a fresh start'

RESIDENCES: BEETHOVEN AND VIENNA PP. 142-144
Theater an der Wien

Emmanuel Schikaneder
Vestus Feuer
Joseph Sonnleithner
Mölkerbastei

MUSIC MAKING IN VIENNA: CONCERT VENUES PP. 144-149
Redoutensaal
Kärntnertortheater
Augarten
Tonkünstler-Societät: The Society of Musicians
Liebhaber Concerte

BEETHOVEN'S ORCHESTRA PP. 149-156
Haydn-Mozart model
Donald Tovey, views of
Instruments, numbers of
Otto Biba, views of
Private orchestras
Sound and balance of
Clive Brown, views of
Ignaz Schuppanzig
Concertmeister: Franz Clement, Ignaz Schuppanzigh
Roger Norrington: authentic performance

BEETHOVEN AS CONDUCTOR PP. 156-159
Elector's Orchestra at Bonn
Ferdinand Ries, recollections of Beethoven conducting
Ignaz von Seyfried, recollections of
Louis Spohr, recollections of

BEETHOVEN AND HEROISM PP.159-168
Early Bonn influences
Utopian ideals
Beethoven the democrat
Joseph Cantata: death of a hero
Mythological Legend of Prometheus
Salvatore Viganò, Beethoven's collaboration with

Sir George Grove, views of
Horatio Nelson
Sir James Abercrombie
General Jean Baptiste Bernadotte: conjectured influence on *Eroica* Symphony
Anton Schindler, accounts of
Swedish Royal Academy of Arts and Sciences
BEETHOVEN AND NAPOLEON BONAPARTE PP. 168-175
Anton Schindler, account of
Ferdinand Ries, recollections of
Bonaparte's perceived ideals
Revolutionary Sonata, request for
Beethoven's changing outlook regarding Bonaparte
Beethoven's vacillation regarding dedication
Jérôme Bonaparte: Beethoven's offer of appointment
Archduke Rudolph, Prince Ferdinand Kinsky and Count Franz Joseph Lobkowitz: Beethoven's annuity
Carl Czerny, recollections of

CREATION ORIGINS PP. 180-219
BEETHOVEN'S COMPOSITIONAL PROCESS PP. 181-184
Working method: sketchbooks
Gustav Nottebohm
Alan Tyson, views of
Bonn precedents
Nicholas Cook, views of
Beethoven's autographs
Barry Cooper, compositional process
Paul Mies, views of

THE *EROICA* SKETCHES PP. 184-189
Wielhorsky Sketchbook
Landsberg 6, the *Eroica* Sketchbook
Romain Rolland, views of

AUTOGRAPH SCORE PP. 189-192
Ferdinand Ries, recollections of
Joseph Dessauer, purchase of score

Gesellschaft der Musikfreunde
Copyist's errors
Title modified

BEETHOVEN'S NEGOTIATIONS
    WITH PUBLISHERS PP. 192-
    206
  1803
    Gottfried Christoph Härtel
    Nikolaus Simrock
    Pirate editions, challenge of
    Ferdinand Ries recollections of
    Foreign tour, prospective plans
      for
  1804
    Anton Wranitsky, payments to
      orchestral players
    Prince Lobkowitz's orchestral
      rehearsals of *Eroica* Symphony
    Bonaparte Symphony, pro-
      jected name
    Request to publish in *score*
    Härtel negotiates with Muzio
      Clementi and William Freder-
      ick Collard
    Carl van Beethoven's negotia-
      tions
  1805
    Carl's further negotiations with
      Härtel
    Carl Möser, proposed transcrip-
      tion of *Eroica*
    Härtel breaks off negotiations
      with Beethoven
  1806
    Kunst- und Industrie-Comptoir,
      Bureau des arts et d'Industrie
      (Bureau d'arts et d'Industrie)
      — publication of *Eroica* Sym-
      phony
    Allgemeine musikalische Zei-
      tung, critical appraisal of
      Eroica — Herr von Rochlitz
  1807–1808, record of perform-
    ances of *Eroica*

DEDICATEE P. 207
Joseph Franz Maximilian Lobkowitz

TITLE PAGE PP. 207-208
Revised wording
Beethoven's concern over perform-
  ing time

BEETHOVEN'S TEMPO INDICA-
    TIONS PP.
Johann Nepomuk Maelzel's metro-
  nome
Wiener Vaterländische Blätter,
  Beethoven's enthusiasm for
  metronome
Allgemeine musikalische Zeitung,
  Beethoven's tempo indications
Sigmund Anton Steiner, letter to
Contemporary attitudes to
  Beethoven's orchestral tempi
Roger Norrington and Christopher
  Hogwood, views of
Jonathan Del Mar, study of
  Beethoven's scores
Nikolaus Harnoncourt, views of

PUBLICATION PP. 213-216
Early publication in parts and score
Gesellschaft der Musikfreunde, surviving score parts
Cianchettini & Sperati, score publication in England
1822, Nikolaus Simrock, full score
  publication
1862, Breitkopf & Härtel Beethoven
  complete edition (*Gesamtausgabe*)

RECEPTION HISTORY: PP. 220-268
FIRST PERFORMANCES PP. 221-321
  1803
    Theater-an-der-Wien
    Beethoven's first public appear-
      ance
    Der Freymüthige, reception of
      Symphonies One and Two

Beethoven works on *Eroica* Symphony

1804

Prince Lobkowitz, private performances

Ferdinand Ries, recollections of *Early* horn entry incident

Prince Louis Ferdinand of Prussia, response to *Eroica* Symphony

1805

Baron Andreas Fellner and Joseph Würth, support private performance of Op. 55

Allgemeine musikalische Zeitung, concert review

George August von Griesinger, recollections of

Hieronymous Payer, recollections of

7 April 1805, first public performance of Op. 55 at Theater an der Wien

Allgemeine musikalische Zeitung, concert review

Der Freimüthige, assessment of musical opinion of *Eroica* Symphony

SUBSEQUENT PERFORMANCES PP. 231-249

1807

Allgemeine musikalische Zeitung, Des Luxus und der Moden and *Morgenblatt für die gebildete Stände,* extended musicological evaluations of Op. 55

Gewandhaus Orchestra, supporter of Beethoven's orchestral music

Friedrich Rochlitz, programme notes for Op. 55

1808

Sebastian Mayer, benefit concert – Op. 55 performed

1809

Widows and Orphans concert, Op. 55 performed

Death of Dr. Johann Schmidt and Joseph Haydn

1810

Carl Maria von Weber, opinion of Beethoven's music

1812

Anton Schindler, recollections of

1815

Anton Schindler, further recollections of

Chrétien Urhan and Franz Anton Stockhausen, support for *Eroica* Symphony

François Antoine Habeneck, support for *Eroica* Symphony

1818

Vinzenz Hauschka conducts *Eroica* Symphony with Gesellschaft der Musikfreunde

1819–1820

Concerts Spirituels.

Franz Xaver Gebauer

Gesellschaft der Musikfreunde

1822

Gioacchino Rossini visits Beethoven

1824

Adolf Bernhard Marx, writes long article about *Eroica* Symphony in *Berliner Allgemeine musikalische Zeitung*

1825

Verses published in *Allgemeine musikalische Zeitung* in celebration of *Eroica* Symphony

TRANSCRIPTIONS PP. 249-252

Beethoven's opinions of transcriptions

Carl Czerny and Franz Liszt, piano transcriptions of *Eroica* Symphony

Ensemble transcriptions, August Everard Müller, Wilhelm Meve, Ferdinand Lukas Schubert, August Horn, Johann Nepomuk Hummel

EARLY RECEPTION IN FRANCE PP. 252-259
Concerts Français – Exercises Publics
Orchestre de la Société des Concerts du Conservatoire
Hector Berlioz, recollections of
Giuseppe Cambini recollections of in *Les Tablettes de Polymnie*
Antoine Elwart, recollections of
Castil-Blaze, recollections of
Hector Berlioz, recollections of
Société des Concerts, Paris concerts
Record of performances of Beethoven's symphonies
Richard Wagner meeting with Gioachino Rossini

EARLY RECEPTION IN ENGLAND PP. 259-265
Philharmonic Society, London
Foundation of
Record of Beethoven performances
Argyll Rooms, Regent Street
28 February 1814, *Eroica* Symphony first performed
Cipriani Potter, recollections of
1821: noteworthy performances of Beethoven symphonies Nos. 1, 2, 4, 5, 6, and 7
1825, first performance in England of *Choral* Symphony
1827, Society's financial support for Beethoven
1829, Beethoven symphonies directed by Felix Mendelsohn
1844, Joseph Joachim performed Beethoven's Violin Concerto – age thirteen
1885, Society appointed Sir Arthur Sullivan as resident conductor

The Crystal Palace
Sir George Grove, Beethoven pioneer
August Manns, role in creation of Crystal Palace Orchestra
Record of performances of Beethoven Symphonies

LATER RECEPTION MUSICOLOGY PP. 269-407
Theodor W. Adorno
Terry Barfoot
Paul Bekker
Luciano Berio
Hector Berlioz
Joseph Braunstein
Alfred Peter Brown
Michael Broyles
Neville Cardus
Eliot Carter
Anne-Louise Coldicott
Barry Cooper
Louise Elvira Cuyler
Samuel Basil Deane
Anatal Doráti
Philip G. Downs
Alfred Einstein
Edward Elgar
Brian Ferneyhough
Wilhelm Furtwängler
Hans Gal
Stewart Gordon
George Grove
Donald J. Grout and Claude V. Palisca
Bernard Haitink
Hallé Orchestra: Charles Hallé and Hans Richter
Hamilton Harty
Hans Werner Henze
Anthony Hopkins
Gordon Jacob
Otto Jahn
William Kinderman
Otto Klemperer
Nikolai Rimsky-Korsakov (V.V. Yastrebtsev)

Ernest Markham Lee
Lewis H. Lockwood
Gustav Mahler
Adolf Bernhard Marx
Denis Matthews
Wilfrid Mellers
Felix Mendelssohn
Yehudi Menuhin
Giacomo Meyerbeer
Charles Munch
Richard Osborne
Leon B. Plantinga
Fritz Reiner
Romain Rolland
Stephen Rumph
Marion Scott

Roger Sessions
George Bernard Shaw
Robert Simpson
Alexander Brent Smith
Maynard Solomon
William Preston Stedman
Michael P. Steinberg
Igor Stravinsky
Virgil Thomson
Arturo Toscanini
Donald Francis Tovey
Richard Wagner
Felix Weingartner
Ralph Vaughan Williams
Conrad Wilson

ABOUT THE AUTHOR

Terence M. Russell graduated with first class honours in architecture and was a nominee for the coveted Silver Medal of the Royal Institute of British Architects. He is a Fellow of the Royal Incorporation of Architects in Scotland (retired), was formerly Reader in the School of Arts, Culture and Environment at the University of Edinburgh, a Fellow of the British Higher Education Academy, and Senior Assessor to the Scottish Higher Education Funding Council. Alongside his professional work in the field of architecture – embracing practice, teaching and research – he has maintained a lifetime's interest in the music and musicology of Beethoven. He has an equal admiration for the work of Franz Schubert and was for many years an active member of the Schubert Institute, UK. His book writings in the field of architecture include the following:

The Built Environment: A Subject Index, Gregg Publishing (1989):
- Vol. 1: Town planning and urbanism, architecture, gardens and landscape design
- Vol. 2: Environmental technology, constructional engineering, building and materials
- Vol. 3: Decorative art and industrial design, international exhibitions and collections, recreational and performing arts
- Vol. 4: Public health, municipal services, community welfare

Architecture in the Encyclopédie of Diderot and D'Alemebert: The Letterpress Articles and Selected Engravings, Scolar Press (1993)

The Encyclopaedic Dictionary in the Eighteenth Century: Architecture, Arts and Crafts, Scolar Press (1997):
- Vol. 1: John Harris, Lexicon Technicum
- Vol. 2: Ephraim Chambers, Cyclopaedia
- Vol. 3: The Builder's Dictionary
- Vol. 4: Samuel Johnson, A Dictionary of the English Language
- Vol. 5: A Society of Gentlemen, Encyclopaedia Britannica

Gardens and Landscapes in the Encyclopédie of Diderot and D'Alemebert: The Letterpress Articles and Selected Engravings, 2 Vols., Ashgate (1999)

The Napoleonic Survey of Egypt: The Monuments and Customs of Egypt, 2 Vols., Ashgate (2001)

The Discovery of Egypt: Vivant Denon's Travels with Napoleon's Army, History Press (2005)

www.ingramcontent.com/pod-product-compliance
Lightning Source LLC
Chambersburg PA
CBHW011956090526
44590CB00023B/3743